Global Firms and Emerging
Markets in an Age of Anxiety

Global Firms and Emerging Markets in an Age of Anxiety

Edited by S. Benjamin Prasad and
Pervez N. Ghauri

PRAEGER

Westport, Connecticut
London

Library of Congress Cataloging-in-Publication Data

Global firms and emerging markets in an age of anxiety / edited by S. Benjamin Prasad
    and Pervez N. Ghauri.
    p. cm.
    Includes bibliographical references and index.
    ISBN 1–56720–421–X (alk. paper)
    1. International business enterprises—Management. 2. International business
enterprises—Cross-cultural studies. 3. Globalization. I. Prasad, Benjamin S., 1929– II.
Ghauri, Pervez N., 1948–
HD62.4.G5435 2004
338.8′8—dc22   2003062256

British Library Cataloguing in Publication Data is available.

Library of Congress Catalog Card Number: 2003062256
ISBN: 1–56720–421–X

First published in 2004

Praeger Publishers, 88 Post Road West, Westport, CT 06881
An imprint of Greenwood Publishing Group, Inc.
www.praeger.com

Printed in the United States of America

∞

The paper used in this book complies with the
Permanent Paper Standard issued by the National
Information Standards Organization (Z39.48–1984).

10   9   8   7   6   5   4   3   2   1

Contents

Illustrations

Tables

Figures

Preface

Multinationals, as most people would know, recognize, admire, fear, and criticize, have been variously characterized for more than three decades. In the 1970s, an American, a British, or a European company that had subsidiaries in two or more countries was called a multinational corporation. In the 1980s, considering the history of foreign investment, a variety of nonmanufacturing companies—such as banks, insurance companies, and trading companies—also came to be recognized as multinational companies. Different authors used different terms. For example, Frederick Donner, in 1967, wrote a book on multinationals with the title *Worldwide Industrial Enterprises*. Charles Kindleberger authored a book, titled *The International Corporation* (1970); Ananth Negandhi and S. Benjamin Prasad coauthored a volume called *The Frightening Angels: Multinationals in Developing Countries* (1975). The key point here is that the multinational phenomenon is not a contemporary development. At present, most companies can be regarded as global firms. During the past 25 years, many developing countries have followed the advice of the International Monetary Fund (IMF) to privatize, liberalize, and become a participant in the free-market economy. Many countries have dismantled their public-sector enterprises, and have opened up their economies to imports of goods, capital, and technology. As a result, the world is becoming more interconnected than before World War II, with the level of imports, exports, cross-border investments, and movement of managers and executives all increasing in noticeable proportions. In order to capture the essence of what was happening in the industrial and the service world—in, so to speak, the globalizing economy—many writers in the United States and the United Kingdom authored scores of books. A selected listing of 24 vintage books on multinationals can be found in Table 0.1. A complete reference of these books can be found in the bibliography.

These 24 books, along with other books, articles, and commentaries, not only described the nature and organization of the multinationals in the post–World War II era, but they also spoke implicitly of the problems of coordination, of relationships with host countries, and of the long-run impact of foreign commercial enterprises forging partnerships and alliances with domestic firms and state enterprises, to name a few.

The multinational corporate phenomenon can be seen either as an ancient institution (Moore and Lewis 1999) or as a post–World War II development. That is not to say that there were no multinational enterprises in the eighteenth or the nineteenth century. There were, but they were few in number, and they were financed not by common citizens, but by either the royalty, the

Table 0.1
Twenty-Four Books on Multinationals Identified as Unique Structural Forms of Organization 1964–1986

YEAR	AUTHOR(S)	DESCRIPTIVE TERMS USED IN THE BOOK TITLES*
1964	Kann	Multinational Empire
1965	Ogram	Multinational Corporation
1966	Steiner	Multinational Corporate Plan
1969	Penrose	International Firm
1969	Neufeld	Global Corporation
1970	Behrman	Multinational Corporation
1970	Brooke & Remmers	Multinational Enterprise
1970	Kindleberger	International Corporation
1970	Rolfe & Damm	Multinational Corporation
1970	Turner	Invisible Empires
1970	Wilkins	Multinational Enterprise
1972	Hays, Korth, & Roudiani	Multinational Firm
1972	Kolde	International Business Enterprise
1972	Stopford & Wells	Multinational Enterprise
1973	Robock & Simmonds	Multinational Enterprise
1973	Vaupel & Curhan	Multinational Enterprise
1974	Jackson	Multinational Corporation
1974	Phatak	Multinational Corporations
1975	Negandhi & Prasad	The Frightening Angels
1976	Buckley & Casson	Multinational Enterprise
1979	Heenan & Perlmutter	Multinational Corporation
1981	Rugman	Multinationals
1982	Caves	Multinational Enterprise
1986	Hornell & Vahlne	Multinationals

*Complete titles can be found in the Selected Bibliography.

literati, or the mercantile bankers. At any rate, one is at liberty to take a historical perspective of a multinational such as Ford, Nestle, or Unilever, or alternatively focus on the firms that have metamorphosed into multinationals in the period of 1975–2000. The perspective is in the beholder's eye, the researcher's interest, or the strategic intent of reading, thinking, and writing. We have found the historical perspective of multinationals to be a valuable one.

The current economic perspective of the multinational enterprise, or even the cross-cultural dimensions of firms, has a legitimate place and the inquiry is worthy of pursuit. Even though economics-based academic publications and their editors insist on robust studies of multinational enterprises (MNEs) grounded in theory, conducting business abroad has almost always remained more of an art than a science. One important aspect of this art has been interaction with the host nations and their governmental agencies. This aspect has taken on added dimensions since the September 11, 2001, tragedy. Subsequent to the tragedy, there have occurred numerous changes in the world economic, as well as political, arenas. In short, the landscape for the multinationals is, as we see it, completely different. There has been a rapid change in the relationships between guest firms and host nations, the multinationals and emerging nations in particular manifesting the dominant theme of anxiety. Multinationals' environmental uncertainty has gone up; in addition, anxiety levels have elevated. The hosts—emerging markets—are now unsure of the strategic implications of the decisions of multinationals. Attracting foreign direct investment (FDI) by means of creating a conducive host-country environment has been a standard approach for many years beginning in the early 1960s in the Republic of Ireland. We ponder whether that approach is now sufficient, in the post–9-11 era, to maintain an increasing inflow of precious capital from abroad.

In order to shed light on many of the underlying issues that have surfaced since 2001, we invited a cross section of scholars, who had shown a keen interest in the broad topics of interfirm cooperation, firm-host government relations, FDI, and the general well-being of relatively poorer nations. In order to narrow down the host country universe, we selected the emerging markets—some 25 nation-states. In response, we received 22 papers.

Among the 22 papers, 20 of them went through the blind-review process. Each was read by Ghauri, Prasad, and at least one external reviewer who had competence to critique and suggest concrete revisions. Fifteen of the papers were finally accepted after one or two revisions, and readers will find them as chapters dealing with a few key dimensions of managing either the internal efficiency or the external effectiveness of multinationals in the twenty-first century beset by post–9-11 anxiety. We identify external effectiveness as possessing the skills of networking, allying, and interfacing with a host of stakeholders or constituencies.

Many of the authors who contributed to this research compendium willingly did so, and we were pleased to note that many of their coauthors were of a younger generation who looked forward to pursuing their professional interests in the global economy. Others were mature scholars who had lived through the decades of the dollar devaluation, the preeminence of Japanese multinationals, the emergence of technology-driven competition, the unprecedented expansion of information technologies, the Y2K threat, the 9-11 tragedy, and the anxiety of threats and of conflicts.

Three groups of individuals deserve our gratitude and thanks. First and foremost are the contributors who were patient, responsive to our rewriting requests, and tolerant of minor criticisms. Some of the contributors, as readers will recognize, are senior researchers, and some are younger enthusiasts. To all of the contributors, we extend our heartfelt thanks.

The second group is the two editors at the Greenwood Publishing Group. We are grateful to both Eric Valentine, until recently editor of Quorum Books, the imprint that was consolidated with the Praeger Series. Praeger is now headed by editor Hilary Clagett who, during the past six months, has made numerous valuable suggestions, and the end result is the current title of this book: *Global Firms and Emerging Markets in the Age of Anxiety*. We believe that, at present, we are all living in an era of anxiety, but we hope the anxiety shall be ephemeral.

Finally, the third group comprises our faculty associates and the graduate/undergraduate students who were extremely helpful in the preparation of the manuscript. We would also like to thank Dr. Rose Prasad of the Finance Department, Management Departmental secretaries Marsha Dinkfield and Mary Jones, and student assistants—Amber, Alisha, Avinash, Gopal, Pratik, Satish—at Central Michigan University. We owe a debt of gratitude to some of our colleagues at UMIST, United Kingdom, including the staff of the international business unit and in particular Anna Zuyeva and Gillian Geraghty. Errors and omissions are those of the authors of the chapters.

February 27, 2003

S. Benjamin Prasad
York Research Center, New Jersey
Pervez N. Ghauri
UMIST, U.K.

PART I

Emerging Challenges

CHAPTER 1

On Multinationals after 1989

S. Benjamin Prasad

Since World War II, within the realm of industrial management and economics, the influence of international events has been significant. If one were to identify the basic factors leading to industrial development, then management is clearly an important dimension for economic growth. Management literature contains definitions of the term, management, as a process, a set of coordinated functions in a firm, a type and level of skill and ability, or a *cadre* of people. Most of these definitions are culture-oriented, and they are legitimately so. Yet, one ought not to take the culture route too far, because cultural explanations will have limits too.

When we, in the United States, consider *management and organization*, it is often in terms of the values and ends to which we are accustomed, and also, as the terms relate to the conduct of business enterprises as we see them in North America. The American economy has been an archetype of what is loosely known as the Western world. But since the 1980s, an Eastern influence has swept in—initially in terms of the soft skills that catapulted Japan to number one in the world in those skills, and later in the 1990s, in terms of the enterprise software that has been a boon to American business, to its cost effectiveness, and to its productivity.

International management is concerned with effectively managing a firm's resources abroad. Many multi-disciplinary approaches have been advanced toward this goal, as can be seen in Figure 1.1 (p. 8). The real challenges to global firms are in the emerging nations.

The industrial revolution began, not in the United States but in England, with the seminal observations made by Adam Smith in an English pin factory, on the beginning and growth of modern industrialism, conceptualizing the merits of specialization in the notion of division of labor. Industrialism, as most recognize, is a general organization of a society built largely on mechanized industry (or tertiary industries) rather than agriculture, craftsmanship, or commerce. It is different from mercantilism albeit the newly industrialized states often pursued mercantilist policies.

Commerce, from times immemorial, has been conducted on a small as well as on a large scale. Moore and Lewis (1999) identify some of the earliest trading companies and guild-like colonies established by the Phoenician merchants, the princes of their society. However, it is worth noting that in seventeenth century China, the Qing (Ching) dynastic emperors from the north (that is, the region of Manchuria) did not view the pursuits of the merchants in the southeast, as an accomplished modus vivendi (Spence 1990). The British rulers also "regarded merchants as a lesser breed in the hierarchy of imperial breed" (Keay 1991).

MULTINATIONALS AFTER 1989

Multinationals after 1989—the year in which the Berlin Wall came down—have undergone a variety of changes and have faced many new challenges. The best way to capture the essence of these changes is a two dimensional issue. First and foremost is for academics to learn how multinational firms—American or other parents—have weathered the storms of change. Some of the consumer multinationals, armed with global brands and appealing advertising, such as the Coca-Colas and the McDonalds were in the limelight at one time. Other consumer durable multinationals have either gone under, restructured, or have emerged as born-again multinationals. New market opportunities have accompanied new competitive challenges.

Even when cultural and social differences between the American and other firms are intentionally set aside to model the homogenized global firm, other differences remain. The most obvious is the difference in the currency values—various exchange regimes between the dollar and the other currencies have prevailed. However, since 1989 the free market maxim has caught on, currencies have floated rather than being pegged, and some of the developing countries have been transformed into global manufacturing platforms—even knowledge economies. The present volume highlights the fresh research contributions—post-September 11, 2001—included as chapters 2 through 15 in the following pages.

In the present research volume, several new topics have been addressed. Arbitrarily, we as editors have identified three important categories: part one deals with emerging challenges, part two highlights the changing contexts, and part three relates to the future prospects of global firms. Below is a chapter-by-chapter synopsis of the 14 research papers, excluding the present introductory chapter, and the final concluding perspective by Pervez N. Ghauri.

In part one, "Emerging Challenges," the ensuing four chapters focus on the challenges faced by the firms and the host nations. The theme of chapter 2 describes the difficulties that multinationals encounter in the emerging markets. Cuervo-Cazurra and Un analyze the sources of and potential solutions to the hurdles that multinational enterprises (MNEs) from industrialized nations encounter in the less developed countries. Despite being highly competitive and having large resource pools, these MNEs continue to encounter difficulties. The authors apply the resource-based theory, and the related knowledge-based view of the firm, to develop the internationalization literature pertaining to the problem. They explain that such difficulties arise from the countries' lack of advantageous resources, the presence of disadvantageous resources, and their lack of neutral complementary resources. They further discuss the characteristics of the firm, and the different types of difficulties they face, and analyze how such formidable challenges can be overcome by means of management and development of resources, particularly knowledge. One point of emphasis in the chapter is that managers of the MNEs must view the emerging markets not as difficult markets to be avoided, but as markets that require different sets of resources and knowledge that would contribute to the success of the firm and to profitable operations.

Heike Proff, in chapter 3, which explores the theme of industrial clustering, development and overcapacity, concentrates on export competition as a major challenge to the European automotive firms. In Proff's view, the developing countries are increasingly resorting to a developmental approach anchored on the basis of industrial clustering in order to enhance the value of networks through input-output linkages. Under this approach, investment promotion measures by the host country in selected core industries, such as automobiles, provide potential for economic rent—a matter of keen interest to the European automotive firms that are on the look out for such opportunities in their globalization efforts. However there are negatives. Overcapacity in the industrial networks tends to depress prices in the export market. How European automotive firms have coped with the issues arising from global overcapacity, including plans to reduce multi-market contacts, is a topic of current interest. The intriguing question remains: Do other industries go the same way as the auto firms?

Researchers López and Miozzo, in chapter 4, take a comparative approach to the recent developments in Latin America and Asia, in particular, East Asia. The role of the multinational corporations (or multinational enterprises) is seen as both the most important source of new technology and management know-how, and a significant contribution to the host country's technological modernization. On the other hand, host countries may be worse off thanks to the rent-extracting power of the multinationals—loss of control over national strategic sectors, displacement of indigenous firms resulting in the loss of jobs. López and Miozzo, in this context, focus on the successful development process in South Korea and Taiwan, and the less successful industrialization experiences of Argentina, Brazil, and Mexico.

In chapter 5, Lawton and McGuire address the recurring phenomenon and the perennial debate about the issue of subsidies to domestic firms by home governments. As such, the governance of the subsidy has been formulated under the auspices of the World Trade Organization (WTO). In spite of the uniformity sought in the international disciplines on subsidies, many nation-states continue to regard subsidies, in one form or another, as a vital and entirely legitimate form of government intervention in the economic affairs of a country. This perspective and practice is particularly true of the developing countries, which regard a subsidy as a necessary way of leveling the playing field. Indeed, they cite economic research studies on spillovers, externalities, and appropriability problems to buttress their argument. But how the WTO disciplines affected firms in the developing countries remains an unexplored question. Lawton and McGuire develop a case study of the commercial rivalry between two aircraft manufacturers—Canada's Bombardier and Brazil's Embraer—in order to demonstrate the growing importance of supranational regulation to corporate strategy and national industrial policy. The case is illustrative of the ways in which the WTO can have an impact on the policy context and strategy options of a multinational from Brazil. Of course, as many would easily recognize, the quagmire created by the very notion of subsidy makes it impractical, if not impossible, to contain hidden and indirect subsidies found in both the industrialized and the developing nations. It is the modern dilemma[1] of combining market freedom and national or supranational regulation.

Part two is titled "Changing Contexts." The six chapters that comprise part two address the evolving changes in the landscape itself. Chan, Hegarty, and Miller, in chapter 6, "Initial Trust of Joint Venture Partners in Emerging Nations," address the age-old issue of mutual trust as the cement that bonds partners and allies. The authors suggest that, as multinationals expand in ever-larger numbers into the emerging markets, both the academics and the executives need to develop a better understanding of trust. Recent studies have underscored the importance of the institutional environment in the emerging countries. The emphasis is particularly material since multinationals encounter institutional uncertainty, institutional distance, and uniquely embedded firms. A conceptual framework of initial trust that highlights both the institutional and the resource-based factors of significance in joint ventures are offered.

In chapter 7, Kandemir, Kim, and Cavusgil, in their chapter titled "Family Conglomerates: Key Features Relevant to Multinationals," recount that family enterprises, especially the family conglomerates, are the dominant players of the economic landscape in most of the emerging markets. To delve into the significance of the family conglomerates, the authors examined the origin, the expansion, and the role of 19 family conglomerates originating in 8 emerging markets. The 19 enterprises were selected according to a set of qualitative and quantitative parameters. The authors analyze these organizations through the stages of introduction, growth, and maturity. They further discuss two important and perhaps interrelated questions: What does the future hold for family conglomerates? How can Western multinationals collaborate with these domestic giants for the benefit of both sets of enterprises—family conglomerates and professionally managed American and European multinationals?

Collaboration takes various forms. How best to manage a joint venture enterprise is the theme, which Zhang and Li elaborate in chapter 8. In this chapter, *international joint venture control* (IJV), is examined in the form of an integrated approach to control or manage international joint ventures. The framework is built upon organization economics (or industrial organization) and the authors' comprehensive interview data on eight China-Japan ventures operating in China. The chapter addresses two important control issues: One, from the perspective of organization economics, what is the relationship between parent firms' task interdependencies with an international joint venture, and their levels of control over the IJVs; and, two, from an evolutionary perspective, how does the relationship between IJV control and performance evolve over time? In the light of these two issues, the authors develop propositions and bring forth the implications of the proposed framework.

That joint ventures have become the major component of a firm's global strategy has been accepted. Extant empirical studies point out that a proposed or announced joint venture tends to be favored by investors. In chapter 9, "An Analysis of Joint Venture Activities in Southeast Asia," Indro and Richards proceed to examine, employing logistic regression method, the nature of joint venture agreements in South East Asia. Specifically, they address the following two research questions: What factors determine the choice of joint ventures? How does membership of the host country in the World Trade Organization affect joint venture activities? The unit of analysis is the joint venture agreement. Their analysis finds scant support for transaction cost theory in regard to the impact of partner familiarity on the choice of activities pursued in joint ventures. Yet, when the cultural distance between partners is vast, the agreement tends to be more for joint marketing activities than for joint manufacturing functions. As could be expected, membership in the WTO of the partners is desired, for, such an affiliation is associated with a lower country risk score.

China, after being an ad hoc member finally achieved the status of a full member of the World Trade Organization in 2001. China has been the largest nation in demographic terms for many centuries. For example, China had a population of about 300 million at a time when the population in the United States was merely 60 million. Even though the Chinese empire comprised many regions and ethnicities, in the early nineteenth century, there evolved a Chinese way of life. In chapter 10, "National Culture in China and Multinationals' Performance," Li tests the effects of Chinese culture (modus vivendi, so to speak) on the performance of multinationals operating in China. He studied 85 multinational units operating in South China. Of these subsidiaries or affiliates, 38 were Japanese, 32 American, and the remaining 15 were European. His statistical analysis of these 85 firms confirms that national culture indeed has an impact on the human resource management practices of multinationals, but does not have any direct effect on the performance of the firm. Significantly, it was the firm's technological resources that mattered most in the economic performance of these multinationals in China.

In chapter 11, "Entering Emerging Markets: Ignorance and Discovery," Johanson and Johanson, present their findings based on detailed case studies of the entry into and operations of Swedish multinationals in three disparate nations—China, Russia, and Saudi Arabia—and offer some fresh hypotheses regarding the fundamental challenges of entering emerging markets. Their research is based on the assumption that the typical multinational entering emerging markets is ignorant about the nuances of those markets. While many other researchers contend that learning is a process that begins with discovery, here the authors focus on the role of discovery in experiential learning, a sine qua non for entry into foreign markets and launching operations. In essence, Johanson and Johanson theorize that discoveries constitute an important cause of change during the internationalization of the firm or the enterprise.

The third part of the book is titled "Prospects for Global Firms." The first paper in this section is chapter 12, "Strategies of Multinationals in Contemporary China," authored by Peter Enderwick. He starts out with the notion

Figure 1.1
Theoretical Streams Leading to MNE (Multinational Enterprise) Paradigms and International Corporate Management (Only the names of some exponents or the topical headings of theoretical interest are identified in the diagram.)

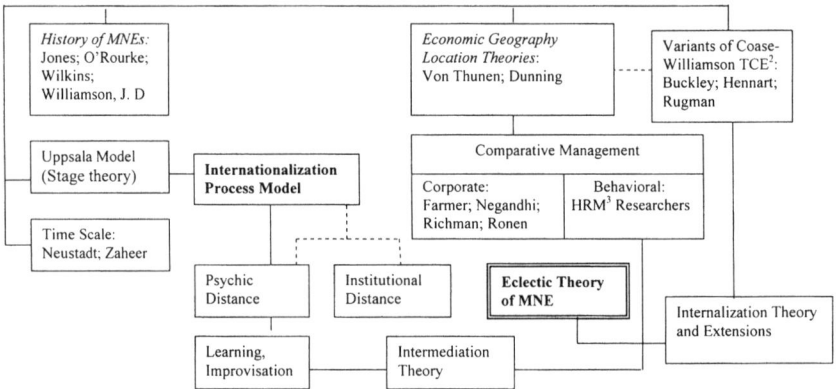

Notes: TCE = Transaction Cost Economics; HRM = Human Resource Management.
Source: Reproduced with the permission from York Research Center © 2002.

of the coexistence of market opportunities and competitive threats. In the minds of most managers and executives, China—being the largest country in the world—offers the most market opportunities to sell, to license, to produce, and to transact in other ways. In other words, of particular interest to multinationals from North America, Europe, and Japan are the two big emerging nations, namely India and China. The author's focus is on China, which, in his view, has followed a unique transitional path. China cannot remain a mere manufacturing platform. It has to go beyond that stage to be able to morph as a knowledge economy. But what effect will this development have on the strategy of multinationals? According to the author, MNE strategy in China will depend, in part, on the perceived level of risk and uncertainty. Uncertainties are from within and from without. Yet, China's role in the Pacific region will only increase given the Chinese government's preference for a multipolar world.

While China has been, in the last decade, in the forefront of exports, inward foreign direct investment (FDI), and foreign reserve accumulation, and it is now a member of WTO, there are other emerging markets in Asia, particularly East Asia. Yamin and Ghauri, in chapter 13, "Rethinking MNE-Emerging Market Relationships: Some Insights from East Asia," cogently argue for rethinking the government-firm relationship. Their aim is to contribute to the critical aspects of international business and the multinational enterprise. More specifically, the authors amplify the changing views regarding the positive and contributory role that policy intervention could have in maximizing the developmental impact of the presence of the multinational in emerging markets. In short, this means fostering not only the know-how, but also the know-why.

The know-why drive needs a context; it cannot happen in a vacuum—particularly the institutional vacuum. In chapter 14, "Institutions and Market Reforms: A Logical Guide for MNE Investments," Mudambi and Navarra examine the important topics of institutional and market reforms. Their focus is on electoral institutions. They apply the tools of economic theory in order to study the comparative politics of rent seeking in the context of economic reforms toward economic liberalization. Utilizing an index of economic freedom, and controlling for demographic and historical factors, the authors test data from 29 emerging nations. The main argument appears to be that multinational enterprises, in addition to considering the traditional variables about market potential, would benefit from knowledge of the rate institutional reforms in their target markets.

In chapter 15, "On Economic Liberalization in India," Rose Prasad blends her individual impressions with selected findings of research on economic liberalization. The central postulate of economic liberalization is said to be that when property rights are secured and when there is freedom for individuals to engage in economic transactions, the entire country will be better off. She briefly discusses the speed and scope of liberalization. Based upon published data, and confirmed by her own convictions based upon observations in India, she concludes that slow and gradual reforms are likely to have long-term payoffs for the majority of people in today's globalized markets, including those in the emerging nations.

The final chapter, chapter 16, "A Look Ahead: Multinational Enterprises and Emerging Markets," the author offers an optimistic perspective of global, or multinational, firms and the emerging markets. Ghauri contends that while the important changes in the pre-1990 era were in the realm of economics, the significant changes since the 1990s have been triggered by geopolitical events. The tragedy of September 11, 2001, has fostered inward looking and unilateral policies of the United States that has had an impact, though not always explicitly, on international trade and international investment decisions of the multinationals and host countries. This does not mean that the host countries have achieved greater bargaining clout; if anything, states Ghauri, a number of changes in the international environment have politically weakened the position of the host governments. Thus, the protectionist strategies induced by the shifting winds of geopolitics and international economics have had as much impact on the strategies of the multinationals, as they have had on the policies of the host countries. In short, as actors on the global economic stage, both the global (or multinational) firms and the governments should hasten to reduce the uncertainty by means of quick resolutions of impending issues.

In conclusion, as alluded to in the introduction to the volume (chapter 1), the multinationals of the 1980s have been transformed in many ways. As the primary agents of change that has ushered in the twentieth century globalization, their role in the progress of nations remains unquestioned. The political developments of the 1980s and the 1990s can only be regarded as geo-political events, for, the world since 1945 has grown more interdependent. It was only since September 2001 that political rifts have come to the surface. While there is uncertainty and risk (as there have been since times immemorial), the global economy—the context, the rules, the players, and the beneficiaries—is at present under the clouds of anxiety. Managing emerging economies or multinational firms, small and large, in the age of anxiety is a formidable challenge.

NOTE

1. In his article "Frail Orthodoxy," Martin Wolfe refers to the central bankers' private decisions to raise or lower interest rates. Comments on the article appear in Prasad 1998.

REFERENCES

Keay, John. 1991. *The Honourable Company: A History of the English East India Company*. London: HarperCollins.

Moore, Karl, and David A. Lewis. 1999. *Birth of the Multinational: 2000 Years of Ancient Business History, from Ashur to Augustus.* Copenhagen: Copenhagen Business School Press.

Prasad, Srinivas B. 1998. "The Modern Dilemma of Combining Marketing Freedom with Regulation." *Financial Times,* October 28.

Spence, Jonathan. 1990. *In Search of Modern China.* New York: Norton.

CHAPTER 2

The Bald Eagle Cannot Find Its Way in the Rain Forest

Alvaro Cuervo-Cazurra and C. Annique Un

INTRODUCTION

Developed country multinational enterprises (DCMNEs) are the dominant investors in the world (UNCTAD 2002), but they still face difficulties when they internationalize into less developed countries (LDCs) (Ghemawat 2001; Prahalad and Lieberthal 1998; Wells 1998). DCMNEs often view consumers in LDCs as less sophisticated, and firms from LDCs tend to have fewer resources and less developed technologies (Lall 1983; Wells 1983), thus being easier to outperform. However, extensive research focusing on the consequences of the difficulties in internationalization (e.g., Mezias 2002; Miller and Parkhe 2002; Zaheer 1995; Zaheer and Mosakowski 1997) indicates that foreign multinational enterprises (MNEs) actually achieve lower performance than their local competitors. For this reason, understanding the sources of and potential solutions to the difficulties of internationalization is crucial both for managers and for researchers, as the international expansion of firms from developed countries into developing countries is on the rise (Buckley 2002; Prahalad and Lieberthal 1998; Wells 1998).

In this paper we answer the following question: What are the sources of, and potential solutions to, the difficulties of developed country multinational enterprises entering less developed countries? To answer this question, we build on the resource-based theory of firm growth (Penrose 1959) and the related knowledge-based view (Conner and Prahalad 1996; Grant 1996; Kogut and Zander 1992, 1996; Spender 1996; Tsoukas 1996), which are increasingly being used in the field of international management (Kogut and Zander 1993; Madhok 1997; Tallman 1992). We argue that firms may face several related but separable potential difficulties arising from their lack of advantageous resources, the presence of disadvantageous resources, and a lack of neutral resources in the new operation. We also discuss how the characteristics of firms influence their specific difficulties, and then analyze potential solutions through the management and development of resources, particularly knowledge.

This chapter contributes to previous literature on the difficulties of internationalization by analyzing the sources of and potential solutions to these difficulties. It also examines the ways in which they vary with the characteristics of the firm, rather than focusing on their effects, which have been extensively researched, beginning with Hymer (1976). Hymer (1976) termed these difficulties "the cost of doing business abroad," a concept that was later used in other studies (Buckley and Casson 1976; Dunning 1977; Hennart 1982; Vernon 1977). This literature has recently seen a revival under the banner of "liability of foreignness" (Zaheer 1995; Zaheer and Mosakowski 1997) and researchers have tried to provide empirical support for the concept by analyzing its consequences. They indicate that, in comparison to domestic firms, foreign firms experience lower performance (Zaheer 1995), lower efficiency (Miller and Parkhe 2002), higher numbers of lawsuits (Mezias 2002), and lower survival rates (Zaheer and Mosakowski 1997), though the latter is under debate (Hennart, Roehl, and Zeng 2002; Mata and Portugal 2002).

This chapter is organized as follows. In section 2 we separate the sources of difficulties in internationalization into several distinct types by applying the resource-based theory of firm growth, discussing the special characteristics of DCMNEs entering and operating in LDCs. In section 3 we discuss how the characteristics of the DCMNEs influence the specific difficulties they will encounter in their internationalization into LDCs. In section 4 we provide some possible solutions to their difficulties that target the specific root causes of each of the types of difficulties. These solutions deal with different strategies for managing and developing resources. Finally, in section 5 we conclude with contributions to theory.

DIFFICULTIES IN INTERNATIONALIZATION OF DCMNEs IN LDCs

Taking the view that firms are bundles of resources, we analyze the sources of their difficulties in internationalizing from developed countries into less developed countries. The resource-based theory emerged as an explanation of the growth of the firm (Penrose 1959). Although it has recently been applied to the analysis of competitive advantage (Barney 1991; Peteraf 1993), the realm of the theory is broader (Rugman and Verbeke 2002), explaining firm behavior (Conner 1991), and the existence and limits of firms in relation to markets, especially in the related knowledge-based view of the firm (Conner and Prahalad 1996; Kogut and Zander 1992, 1996). Hence, in this paper we take a broader view of the resource-based theory in the analysis of the difficulties of DCMNEs in LDCs. To this end, we now briefly discuss the internationalization of firms from this theoretical basis, present the difficulties in the internationalization of MNEs, and then study the specific sources of difficulties that DCMNEs face when entering into and operating in LDCs.

Resource-Based Theory and Firms' Internationalization

Firms are bundles of resources (Penrose 1959), which are the tangible and intangible assets that are tied semipermanently to the firms (Wernerfelt 1984). These resources provide services used in the production process (Penrose 1959). Although some researchers define resources as those assets that provide the firm with an advantage and discuss the benefits of having such resources, such a definition runs the risk of becoming tautological (Priem and Butler 2001) and misses the fact that the advantage provided by the resources depends on the context in which they are applied. Therefore, we will follow the broader conceptualization of resources as firm-specific assets, and discuss how the advantage provided varies according to the country in which they are used.

We separate the resources of a firm into three types according to the advantage that they provide: (1) *advantageous*, or strategic resources (Amit and Schoemaker 1993), such as patented technology, which provide the firm with a competitive advantage if they have certain characteristics (Barney 1991; Peteraf 1993), and which have been the focus of most of the resource-based literature; (2) *disadvantageous* resources, which provide a competitive disadvantage (Leonard-Barton 1992), such as a negative image among clients; and (3) *neutral* resources, which are necessary for the operation of the firm, but not sufficient to provide an advantage (Montgomery 1995). One example of a neutral resource is access to external finance, which is necessary for operations but is easily imitable and therefore not a source of sustainable advantage. We need to take into account the full set of resources when analyzing the internationalization of the firm, rather than only those resources that provide an advantage, because the advantage provided by some resources will vary with time (Miller and Shamsie 1996), with the competitive environment (Amit and Schoemaker 1993), and with the institutional environment (Tallman 1992), as is discussed here.

The internationalization of the firm is based on its resource set and the search for increasing returns on investments, although such an international expansion strategy is complex (Hitt, Hoskisson, and Ireland 1994; Hitt, Hoskisson, and Kim 1997; Tallman and Li 1996). Resources that the firm possesses in excess or that are not consumable by use, such as knowledge, and that are perceived as advantageous in another context, induce the firm to expand (Penrose 1959). Applying this idea to the firm's internationalization, a firm takes this action to create additional value by *using existing resources*. This motive for international expansion has been discussed in the literature on internationalization not only from the point of view of the resource-based theory, but also in internalization (Buckley and Casson 1976; Dunning 1977) and transaction cost studies (Caves 1982; Hennart 1982; Rugman 1981; Teece 1986a). The literature assumes that firms have some kind of advantage in the home country that motivates them to enter foreign markets (Hymer 1976). However, the firm might also internationalize to create value by *developing new resources*, expanding abroad to obtain resources that are in better condition than those in the home country, such as natural resources, efficiency, or strategic assets or capabilities (Dunning 1993). Additionally, a firm might internationalize to defend value created by *protecting existing resources*, following competitors' (Knickerbocker 1973) or clients' international moves in order to avoid losing existing investments in resources in other locations. Regardless of the motive, in all cases the firm uses existing resources and transfers some of them to other locations.

Types and Sources of Difficulties in Firms' Internationalization

Figure 2.1 summarizes the research framework underlying the discussion. Difficulties in internationalization can be explained by postulating that firms develop resources and knowledge depending on the conditions of their competitive and institutional environments. The competitive environment induces firms to develop resources to compete against other firms present in the industry (Porter 1990; Van de Ven 1993), while the institutional environment induces firms to develop resources to operate within a set of institutions in the country (Oliver 1997). As a firm internationalizes, it transfers resources from existing operations to the new operation. While some of the transferred resources provide advantages (Hymer 1976; see Tallman and Yip 2001 for a review), which we will not discuss here, other resources that the firm transfers to its new operation may not provide an advantage, or may even reduce the advantage. Additionally, the new environment requires additional complementary resources to operate and compete there, resources that the firm does not yet have. Hence, we can separate the sources of difficulties in internationalization into three different types based on their relationship to the advantage provided by the resources. First, difficulties may arise because the resources transferred do not provide an advantage in the host country; we will term these difficulties *shortcomings*. Second, difficulties may arise because the resources transferred generate a disadvantage in the host country; we will term these difficulties *disadvantages*. Third, difficulties may arise because the firm lacks neutral complementary resources in the host country; we will term these difficulties *liabilities*. The first two types of difficulties arise from the transfer of resources, and the third from the need for resources. These claims build on previous work on the difficulties of internationalization (Cuervo-Cazurra,

Maloney, and Manrakhan 2002; Zaheer 1995) that we now integrate with the analysis of DCMNEs in LDCs (Prahalad and Lieberthal 1998; Wells 1998) to provide a comprehensive analysis of the difficulties of DCMNEs in LDCs.

Throughout the study we will assume that DCMNEs tend to be large companies with sufficient clout to access the external financing needed to obtain tangible resources. Thus, the challenge they face when operating in LDCs is more about managing their intangible resources, particularly knowledge. Even when they are not large, their presence in developed countries with advanced external sources of capital in the form of capital markets or banking systems allows them access to external finance on much better terms than those possible in developing countries (Booth et al. 2001). This easier access to external financing facilitates their acquisition of the tangible resources necessary to operate in LDCs. Thus, we will argue that the ultimate source of the difficulties that DCMNEs experience in LDCs is the management and development of a particular type of resource: knowledge. Knowledge is difficult to create (Leonard-Barton 1995; Nonaka and Takeuchi 1995; Von Krogh, Ichijo, and Nonaka, 2000) and even to transfer within the same firm, both in a single country (Szulanski 1996) and across countries (Kogut and Zander 1993; Zander and Kogut 1995). Here, we characterize LDCs as countries with lower average individual wealth, and institutions that are less developed and more unstable than in developed countries. These character-

Figure 2.1
Difficulties in the Internationalization of MNEs in the LDCs: A Research Framework

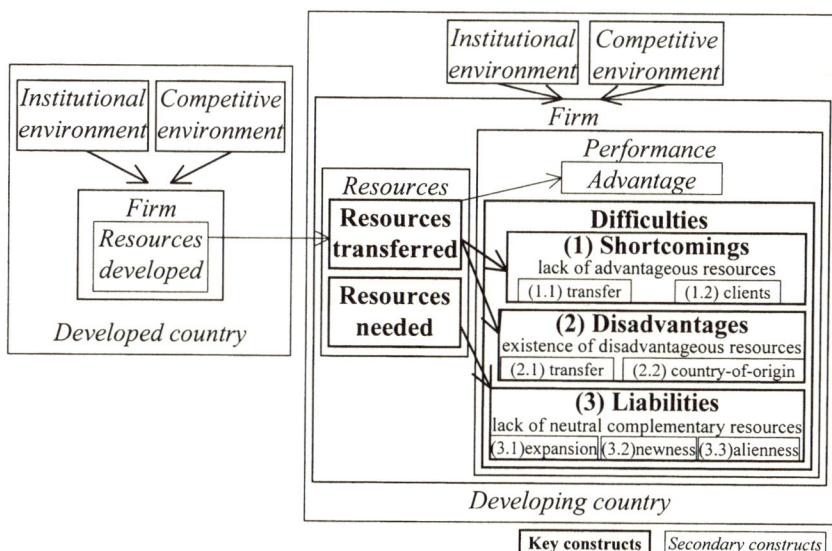

izations will play a role in the specific difficulties that DCMNEs are more likely to face when expanding into LDCs. Table 2.1 summarizes the claims that will be discussed throughout the chapter.

Shortcomings: Lack of Advantageous Resources

First, difficulties in internationalization may arise from the fact that resources that are advantageous in a developed country may not be in a developing country. We call these difficulties *shortcomings* and define them as the disadvantages experienced by firms that are unable to transfer the advantage associated with their resources to another country. These difficulties do not arise from the inability of the firm to transfer resources. Some resources may be difficult to transfer across borders because they have tacit components (Kogut and Zander 1993; Subramaniam and Venkatraman 2001) or because they are location-bound and cannot be moved across borders (Rugman and Verbeke 1992), including legal restrictions on their transfer (Hymer 1976; Zaheer 1995). In these cases, the firm cannot internationalize. However, even when the firm can transfer the resources, it may not be able to transfer their associated advantage. There are two possible reasons that the advantageous resources that the firm transfers might not create value in the new location, one related to the firm and the other to the clients. First, the products generated with the advantageous resources might not meet the basic needs of consumers in the LDCs. Second, consumers in LDCs may lack the complementary resources that are necessary if they are to obtain value from the products offered by the DCMNEs.

We call the first type the *shortcoming of transfer*, and define it as the disadvantage experienced by firms that do not create value for clients in another country because they do not serve their needs. It arises from the inability of the firm to obtain an advantage in the developing country from resources that are advantageous in its operations in developed countries because the products they offer do not cover the basic needs of the population in the LDC (Tallman 1992). In the case of DCMNEs in LDCs, the inability to serve the needs of clients in the host country does not arise from differences in culture (Hofstede 1984) or local taste (Bartlett and Ghoshal 1989) but because of fundamental differences in their level of wealth and education. For example, the marketing and technology knowledge that supports the offering of computer games popular among children in a developed country might not lead to an advantage among children in a less developed country who struggle to meet their basic needs, such as food and shelter.

We call the second type the *shortcoming of clients*, and define it as the disadvantage experienced by firms that do not create value for clients in another country because the clients do not have the necessary complementary resources to enable the creation of value. Even when the products generated with the advantageous resources meet the needs of consumers, they might not provide an advantage because consumers lack the complementary re-

Table 2.1
Summary of Arguments: Difficulties in the Internationalization of DCMNEs in the LDCs

Source	Types	Specific sources in the case of DCMNEs in LDCs	Firm is less likely to suffer it if:	Solutions targeted at solving the particular sources of difficulties
Lack of advantageous resources abroad	Shortcoming of transfer	Products created with resources of the firm do not cover needs of clients in LDCs	Products generated with advantageous resources are in the latter stages of the product life cycle	Focus on a different target market than the one at home but using the same advantageous resources
	Shortcoming of clients	Clients in LDCs need complementary resources to realize value of products created with firm resources	Products generated with advantageous resources are stand alone	Provide consumers with the complementary resources such as knowledge on how to use the product
Existence of disadvantageous resources abroad	Disadvantage of transfer	Firm transfers resources (capabilities) that reduce value created	Firm internationalizes through trade rather than foreign direct investment	Selective transfer of resources (capabilities) to LDC
	Disadvantage of foreignness	People in LDC dislike the country of origin	Country of origin and host country have good political relationships Countries have stable political systems	Hide the country of origin in marketing Use the region of origin rather than the country of origin Use a local company/brand to denote a local country of origin
Lack of neutral complementary resources	Liability of expansion	DCMNE does not have necessary knowledge to be able to manage different types of knowledge	Firm has experience of operating in several countries and has developed information technology (IT) and management systems to cope with additional knowledge Managers in headquarters are polycentric in their attitudes	Invest in IT to process different information Develop headquarter managers with a polycentric mentality, who have been exposed to different cultures or rotated in foreign assignments
	Liability of newness	DCMNE does not have necessary knowledge to be able to manage in a new competitive environment where potential clients are less wealthy or educated	Industry is global in nature Clients have been exposed to company offerings outside their country	Obtain (explicit) knowledge of competitive conditions by purchase from consultants Obtain (explicit and tacit) knowledge of competitive conditions by purchase or alliance with a domestic firm
	Liability of alienness	DCMNE does not have necessary knowledge to manage in a new institutional environment, especially when there is less protection of property rights, more regulations, or corruption	Company is from former colonial power of host country or from country with historical ties to host country	Use local managers exposed to developed MNEs or train expatriates in LDCs Incremental internationalization to develop knowledge and attitudes to cope with different assumptions

sources (Teece 1986b) necessary to make the resources advantageous (Tallman 1992). For example, the best fax machine might not be valuable if the potential customers do not have access to a phone line. This lack of complementary resources among clients in the LDC need not take the form of a tangible resource, as in the previous example, but could also be an intangible resource, such as a lack of knowledge of how to use the product. Again, the source of this difficulty may come from the lack of wealth or education of clients in LDCs that reduces their ability to obtain or develop the necessary complementary resources that would facilitate the creation of value from a firm's products. Thus, even when the DCMNE has advantageous resources at home that can be transferred to the LDC, either directly through products or indirectly through operations, the advantage conveyed by these resources cannot be achieved, because clients do not have the necessary complementary resources.

Although a firm might not be able to create value from the resources transferred because LDC clients do not have the complementary neutral resources, we should not interpret this as meaning that LDCs are not a good place to bring advanced technology (Prahalad and Lieberthal 1998). The developing country might leapfrog over older technologies and adopt new ones to catch up (Hobday 1994). An example of this is Indian villages that did not have fixed telephone lines but entered the telephone era using cellular phones, thus saving the cost of linking the villages and leapfrogging over the fixed-line stage that consumers in developed countries went through.

Disadvantages: Transfer of Resources that Become Disadvantageous

The second type of difficulty in internationalization originates from resources that DCMNEs have transferred to the new operation in the LDC, as in the previous case, but that reduce the firms' advantage in the host market. We call these types of difficulties *disadvantages*. As in the previous case, these can be separated into two types depending on whether the reduction of value is related to the firm or to the clients. The first type involves a transfer of resources to the host country that destroys value in the relationship between the firm and clients. The second type involves a transfer of resources that clients dislike and that reduce the value that the products create for them.

We call the first type of disadvantage the *disadvantage of transfer*. It is defined as the disadvantage experienced by firms bringing resources to the host country that reduces the value of their host operations. The resources that become disadvantageous would usually be intangible, that is, routines (Nelson and Winter 1982) or competencies (Prahalad and Hamel 1990) that are developed in one market and ingrained in the firm and the way it conducts its operations, but that become harmful when used in other countries. These resources are hard to drop or change, thus limiting the ability of the firm to reduce the disadvantage, although they can eventually be altered (Teece, Pisano, and

Shuen 1997), as is discussed later in this chapter. These difficulties are not strictly international, though. Resources developed in one area may create problems in another area or over time, such as when core capabilities become core rigidities that detract from the advantage of the firm (Leonard-Barton 1992). Even resources that are disadvantageous in the initial context may be carried over to the foreign operation. For example, firms that have a negative reputation for exploiting labor or polluting in their own country may see this disadvantage transferred across countries. In the case of DCMNEs in LDCs, transferred capabilities that reduce value for clients usually take the form of routines that are developed with the characteristics of the developed country in mind that are not appropriate in the less developed country but are nevertheless implemented. For example, when Bosch-Siemens bought the Turkish appliance manufacturer Profilo, it insisted on using contracts in their relationship with the distributors, which alienated them (Root and Quelch 1997).

The second type of disadvantage is what we term the *disadvantage of foreignness*. We define this as the disadvantage experienced by firms that are branded as foreign in a negative manner in another country. This resource, the country of origin, which is not an issue in the home country, becomes disadvantageous in the developing country. This disadvantage of foreignness is reflected in discrimination by governments (Buckley and Casson 1976; Hymer 1976; Vernon 1977) that know the nationality of the foreign firm. The host government might establish limitations on the operations of foreign firms in its country (Spar 2001; Stopford and Strange 1992). For example, government restrictions on Pepsi forced the company to use an indigenous brand name in India ("Lehar," meaning "wave") and subjected soft drink sales to a ceiling of 25 percent of the company's annual turnover (Sidhva 1993). Additionally, the country of origin (Bilkey and Nes 1982) has an effect on firms from the same country (Peterson and Jolibert 1995) and, although cases are rare, value may be reduced when people in the LDC dislike the country of origin of the DCMNE (Jaffe and Nebenzahl 2001). However, in the case of the citizens of the LDC, the discrimination depends on the perceived image of the country of origin of the firm (Bilkey and Nes 1982; Jaffe and Nebenzahl 2001). Although DCMNEs might face the disadvantage of foreignness in their operations in LDCs, this tends to be temporary, spurred by political events rather than by customers' general dislike for the country. Customers might even prefer the DCMNEs' products to those offered by domestic firms, as they perceive foreign firms as offering a better product (Jaffe and Nebenzahl 2001); that is, DCMNEs may even benefit from an advantage of foreignness. Hence, although it might be a problem for some firms, particularly in the case of political instability, DCMNEs are unlikely to face a disadvantage of foreignness in LDCs.

Liabilities: Lack of Neutral Complementary Resources

The third source of difficulties in internationalization may arise from the fact that the DCMNE requires neutral resources in order to operate in another country. As we argued earlier, not all resources are transferable across markets (Rugman and Verbeke 1992); this is particularly true of knowledge (Kogut and Zander 1993). Therefore, a firm might need to develop some resources to operate in the new country and complement the advantageous resources transferred. These complementary resources (Teece 1986b) are neutral in the sense that they are necessary to operate in the new market but insufficient to achieve an advantage in and of themselves. We will use the term *liabilities* to indicate those difficulties that originate from a lack of neutral resources in the firm. The firm might face difficulties obtaining such complementary resources, especially when the resources needed have thin markets or are difficult to trade (Wernerfelt 1984). However, these resources are key to the firm's success, especially in changing environments (Tripsas 1997). DCMNEs are large and tend to have access to external finance under better conditions than firms in developing countries, which gives them an advantage in obtaining the necessary neutral tangible resources in LDCs. However, they still face difficulties in obtaining knowledge (Eriksson et al. 1997; Johanson and Valhne 1977), which is difficult, especially in the case of tacit knowledge (Nonaka 1994; Nonaka and Takeuchi 1995). They also face difficulty integrating it into the firm, especially when there is no common knowledge (Grant 1996).

We can distinguish three types of liabilities that firms face in their internationalization according to the different types of neutral resources that they lack. In the particular case of DCMNEs in LDCs, different types of knowledge are the neutral resources that they are most likely to lack (Eriksson et al. 1997). The first is a lack of neutral complementary resources to operate at a larger scale, the second is a lack of neutral complementary resources to operate in a new competitive environment, and the third is a lack of neutral complementary resources to operate in a new institutional environment.

We term the first type the *liability of expansion*, and define it as the disadvantage experienced by firms new to a larger scale of operations. This liability emerges from the lack of neutral resources necessary to operate at a larger scale. The internationalization of the firm usually entails the expansion of scale of existing operations, which can create difficulties when the firm does not have the necessary resources to support the expansion. Firms tend to develop resources to operate within a determinate scale. As the firm refines its operations and learns, it releases resources that enable it to expand in scale (Penrose 1959). However, these same resources might establish a limit on the expansion of the firm at a certain point in time if there is not enough spare capacity to expand, especially in management, since increases in scale tend to be lumpy rather than incremental (Penrose 1959). The liability of expansion is not exclusive to internationalization, since companies face the liability of expansion even when they are not internationalizing; for example, this can occur when they move from being a local competitor to a regional or national one. DCMNEs in LDCs tend not to face the liability of expansion, particularly when they have already expanded into other countries and are managing diverse operations and different sets of information, meaning that they would have developed adequate managerial and information systems and structures to integrate increases in the scale of operations (Barkema and Vermeulen 1998). However, the DCMNE may still face a liability of expansion, albeit reduced, since it would still be necessary to incorporate information and knowledge that do not conform to existing standards in the developed countries. That is, the firm might face challenges not so much because of the quantity of information and knowledge that must be integrated from the operations in LDCs, but because of the differences in the nature and quality of the information and knowledge from the LDC that the firm must process. Managers in headquarters must have a different mindset in order to be able to understand the information coming from the developing country (Prahalad and Bettis 1986; Prahalad and Lieberthal 1998). This challenge of understanding different types of information can be traced back to managers' attitudes to foreign operations (Perlmutter 1969).

We term the second type of difficulty arising from the lack of neutral resources the *liability of newness*, and define it as the disadvantage experienced by firms new to a competitive environment. It arises from the fact that a firm lacks the neutral complementary resources necessary to operate in the new competitive environment. The internationalization of the firm entails operating in a different competitive environment, which can generate difficulties when the firm does not have the complementary resources necessary to do so. The DCMNE faces a situation similar to an entrepreneur starting a new company, or a domestic firm diversifying into a new business; in all these cases, the companies are lacking some of the neutral complementary resources needed to operate in the new competitive environment, such as a reputation among clients, established distribution channels, knowledge of the intricacies of selling in that market, or a lack of access to information networks that local firms have (Zaheer 1995). Nevertheless, the DCMNE might face a smaller problem, since it is likely that it is already operating in the industry in other locations, and will thus have some of the resources needed to compete, which the entrepreneur or diversifying domestic firm may not have. DCMNEs may have resources that provide them with a competitive advantage in existing operations, but as they move into other countries they need neutral resources, such as appropriate channels or a basic knowledge of the industry that enable them to operate effectively in the new competitive environment, but that are location bound (Hennart and Reddy 1997). For DCMNEs, the lack of neutral resources in the competitive environment manifests itself as a lack of knowledge of the needs of clients and the nature of competition in LDCs (Eriksson et al. 1997). Unlike the shortcomings of transfer that were discussed previously, in this case the advantageous resources of the DCMNE are still advantageous in the LDC, since the products generated are appreciated because they cover common needs; however, purchasing habits in LDCs are different. For example, firms used to selling a product in certain quantities to relatively wealthy developed-country consumers might find that they need to reduce the size of the package to what would be considered individual uses in developed countries, since potential clients in LDCs do not have enough disposable income to purchase normal sizes (Prahalad and Lieberthal 1998). Thus, the liability of newness of DCMNEs in LDCs originates in a lack of knowledge and understanding of the requirements to compete in an environment with different consumer demands, which are particularly influenced by lower average wealth and purchasing power rather than by a lack of demand for the products generated by the firm.

The third type of difficulty arising from the lack of neutral complementary resources is what we term the *liability of alienness*. We define it as the disadvantage experienced by firms new to an institutional environment. The liability of alienness arises from a lack of neutral complementary resources that are necessary to operate in the new institutional environment. The internationalizing firm might lack knowledge of the dimensions of the institutional environment, or of the set of norms and rules that influence human behavior (North 1990), such as language, cultural norms, the legal system, or religious customs. This may create problems for the firm when operating abroad. DCMNEs develop certain resources to deal with the particular conditions of the institutional environment from which they originate and operate (Oliver 1997). As they enter LDCs with different institutions, they lack these neutral resources, which domestic companies have obtained or developed in the process of creating and operating in their home market. For example, consider the case of a Western laundry detergent firm selling its product in a developing country. Its advertisements on the detergent box showed soiled clothes on the left, the detergent in the middle, and clean clothes on the right. What is wrong with this picture? The problem is that this advertisement was used in the Middle East, where people read from right to left. The result was that potential customers thought that the detergent could be used to dirty clothes (Ricks 1999). The liability of alienness for DCMNEs in LDCs tends to be the source of greatest difficulty and is often harder to tackle than other problems, primarily because it challenges assumptions that managers of DCMNEs take for granted about the characteristics of an institutional environment and how to operate within its parameters (Prahalad and Lieberthal 1998). The rules and norms of behavior differ dramatically between developed and developing countries, and problems are created by issues that managers might not be accustomed to even thinking about in developed countries, such as property rights protection or the degree to which there is corruption in a country (Calhoun 2002).

REDUCTIONS IN THE DIFFICULTIES OF INTERNATIONALIZATION: THE CHARACTERISTICS OF DCMNEs

The difficulties in internationalization that have been described are potential challenges that DCMNEs might face as they expand into LDCs. But the specific difficulties that will be experienced depend on the characteristics of a given firm's resource set. Thus, even if DCMNEs face similar competitive and institutional environments, the heterogeneity of their resource sets means that they will experience different types of difficulties in their internationalization. We now discuss the characteristics of DCMNEs and the different types of difficulties that they experience in LDCs. This discussion is structured in the same way as the previous one: first, we discuss the shortcomings, then the disadvantages, and finally the liabilities.

First, DCMNEs that enter LDCs will face less of a shortcoming of transfer when the products generated with the resources have universal use as a result of going through the product life cycle, being at the middle, or at the end of this cycle (Vernon 1966). In the case where a product generated by advantageous resources has gone through the product life cycle, it has become standardized and simple to use, although more technology may have been incorporated in the period since it was initially conceived (Vernon 1966). Examples of such products are watches, calculators, photographic equipment, or brown goods such as televisions and radios. The standardization of the products over time and the reduction in their price facilitate their adoption in both developed and developing countries, thus reducing the influence of differences in wealth or education in the adoption of the products. In this way, the resources that were created in developed countries to meet the needs of clients in those countries would also help companies meet the needs of clients in developing countries.

The firm faces less of a shortcoming of clients when products generated with the resources can stand alone, as in the case of canned food or liquids packed in Tetrapack containers that have a long shelf life and do not require cold storage, which may not be available in developing countries. When the products generated with the advantageous resources can stand alone, the firm will face less difficulty in transferring the advantage across countries, since clients can obtain the value without the need for further investments in other resources.

The firm will face less of a disadvantage of transfer when it internationalizes through trade rather than foreign direct investment. In this case, the resources of the firm are transferred indirectly through their embodiment in the firm's products, and are thus less subject to being location bound (Rugman and Verbeke 1992), in the sense that they were developed for the conditions of a particular country. Hence, the firm will reduce the overall transfer of resources to the LDC, and in the process, also reduce the transfer of resources that may become disadvantageous in the LDC.

In general, DCMNEs tend to face a reduced disadvantage of foreignness and even an advantage due to the country of origin when operating in LDCs. For example, foreign firms may have more legitimacy than domestic ones (Kostova and Zaheer 1999). Nevertheless, the firm may also face a disadvantage of foreignness because of political instability. For example, under unstable political conditions, LDC politicians might criticize foreigners, especially those from developed countries, as one way to attain and maintain power. These periods of disadvantage of foreignness are less likely to occur when relationships among governments are stable and peaceful, thus reducing the negative impact on MNEs (Spar 2001; Stopford and Strange 1992).

DCMNEs are less likely to face a liability of expansion when they have already accumulated experience operating in other countries, especially if those countries are LDCs. The establishment of new operations leads to an increase in the requirements of the managerial and information system to process higher amounts and different kinds of information. Although developments in information technology have reduced the cost of managing information and increased firms' capacity to integrate different types of information (Powell and Dent-Michallef 1997), the problem might not be the inability to process information, but rather that there is too much information to be processed (Hansen and Haas 2001). Companies that have already developed information systems to process large quantities of information will find it less of a challenge to expand into LDCs. Additionally, firms that are already operating in other LDCs, and whose headquarters thus already have experience integrating information that comes from diverse operations, would face fewer problems integrating new information that is different in nature (Barkema and Vermeulen 1998). The DCMNE will face less of a liability of expansion if the mindset of managers is polycentric rather than ethnocentric (Perlmutter 1969), a distinction that is reflected in the type of internationalization structure (Bartlett and Ghoshal 1989). Thus, in the particular case of the liability of expansion, internationalization into LDCs would be easier for European firms that have a polycentric attitude and are more accustomed to integrating different types of information. On the other hand, it would be more difficult for U.S. firms that have an ethnocentric attitude and prefer to apply one standard of information, the U.S. one, to foreign operations, regardless of differences among them (Bartlett and Ghoshal 1989).

DCMNEs might encounter a less serious liability of newness in LDCs if the industry in which they operate is global in nature, with less demand for local adaptation, or where the clients in the LDC have been exposed to the firm's products in other countries (Levitt 1983; Prahalad and Doz 1987). DCMNEs in global industries, where there is little need for products to be adapted to the requirements of local markets (Prahalad and Doz 1987), will find that they face less of a liability of expansion, especially if competition and clientele transcend the borders of the LDC. For example, the sale of commercial aircraft is done on a global scale and there is very little need to adapt to the characteristics of LDCs. Additionally, these companies face less of a liability of newness when clients have already been exposed to the products offered by a firm, even when the company has not served them in their country of origin. Exposure to the product can take different forms, such as international fairs and expositions, or contract bidding that is advertised on an international level in specialized industry magazines or international business newspapers. Even in the case of firms that serve final consumers, those that are concentrated in products targeted to the wealthy might find that customers in LDCs have been exposed to products offered by the firm in countries where the DCMNE already operates because these wealthy individuals have traveled there and know the company's products. That is, the firm has already created a reputation in the mind of LDC clients even when it does not operate in a LDC. For example, when introducing its cereals to the Indian market, the American breakfast cereal firm Kellogg targeted well-traveled, well-educated people in India who had been exposed to their products in their foreign travel (Bloomberg News Service 1995).

Finally, DCMNEs that come from developed countries with colonial or historical ties to the LDC will tend to face less of a liability of alienness. A firm will find that when there are connections to the countries in which it is already operating, the distance between the countries (Ghemawat 2001), and the liability of alienness, is reduced. Colonial or historical ties among countries lead to the development of common institutions, such as a legal system (La Porta et al. 1998). Although these institutions may have been put into place a long time previously, they change only slowly (North 1990). This allows DCMNEs that enter LDCs with colonial or historical connections to expand more easily, since assumptions about business relationships and behavior have a common origin.

In summary, although DCMNEs can potentially face several types of difficulties in their internationalization in LDCs, the characteristics of each individual firm will lead to a reduction in certain types of difficulties for that firm. In this way, the heterogeneity among firms in terms of their resource set is reflected in the heterogeneity of the difficulties that they face.

SOLVING DIFFICULTIES IN INTERNATIONALIZATION OF DCMNEs

We now propose potential solutions to the different difficulties faced by DCMNEs in LDCs, discussing each source of difficulty as well as solutions targeted to the root causes. As discussed previously, some firms may experience reduced difficulties when expanding into LDCs. However, even these firms need to find solutions to their difficulties. The solutions entail different actions depending on whether the challenge is a question of dealing with existing resources or of dealing with a lack of resources. In the first case, where the firm suffers from what we termed shortcomings or disadvantages, the

DCMNE needs to manage the existing resource set. In the second case, where the firm suffers from what we termed liabilities, the firm needs to develop new resources, primarily knowledge.

DCMNEs that face a shortcoming of transfer can focus on targeting a market segment that is different from the one it serves in the developed country, but that nevertheless has a similar need (Steenkamp and Hofstede 2002). For example, a fast food firm in a developed country may find that its original target market in the developing country is not wealthy enough to afford its products. However, it may find that individuals in these countries who are wealthier than the customers targeted at home might be a more appropriate market. In this case, the product offered by the firm is transformed from fast food, serving poor people, in the developed country into foreign food, serving wealthy people, in the developing country. Thus, although individuals in the LDC may not have the need for fast food, the company can make use of its advantageous resources to meet a different need—clean air-conditioned restaurants—while benefiting from its advantageous resources in the management of restaurants and their supply chain.

When the DCMNE encounters a shortcoming of clients, such as when clients in the LDC do not have the complementary resources necessary to obtain the value of advantageous resources, the company can resort to developing those complementary resources, especially in the case of lack of knowledge of the uses of a product. The DCMNE needs to invest in developing complementary resources among its clients so that they can use the product that the company generates utilizing its advantageous resources. For example, the firm may have to educate consumers on how the product is supposed to be used or taken.

In the case of DCMNEs facing a disadvantage of transfer, they can choose not to use some of their resources when expanding into LDCs in order to avoid reducing the value created in the host country. Whereas the firm might be inclined to use all the resources at its disposal in its expansion, especially when they are available in excess (Penrose 1959), some of these resources might reduce the value created, as was discussed previously in the section on the disadvantage of transfer. Thus, the firm might choose to not transfer the resources that create a disadvantage, but rather to develop new ones adapted to the conditions of the new environment (Prahalad and Doz 1987).

In the rare cases where DCMNEs face a disadvantage of foreignness, they can choose to market their products without identifying the country of origin (Jaffee and Nebenzahl 2001). The masking of a product's country of origin can either be done directly, by not indicating where the product has been manufactured, or it can be done indirectly, using the region of origin to denote the country of origin. For example, firms might use the label "Made in Europe" to mask the country of origin (Schweiger, Haubl, and Friederes 1995). Alternatively, the company can mask the country of origin by using a domestic brand that conveys the local image to the clients and capitalizes on their nationalistic sentiments. In any case, as indicated previously, DCMNEs are less likely to face a disadvantage of foreignness in LDCs because clients of these countries (still) tend to regard products created by firms in developed countries as superior to those made by their domestic companies.

The liability of expansion can be solved by investing in information technologies that allow additional information processing (Powell and Dent-Michallef 1997), and by ensuring that managers in headquarters have a polycentric mindset and are able to understand and integrate different information (Perlmutter 1969). As indicated previously, DCMNEs, especially large ones, are less likely to face a liability of expansion, especially in terms of their ability to process larger quantities of information coming from the expansion into LDCs. Nevertheless, the challenge they may face is that of managers with an inappropriate mindset who are unable to understand the information that is coming from the LDCs. This can be solved by hiring or training managers that have been exposed to different cultures through rotation in foreign assignments (Nohria and Ghoshal 1997). Such managers are able to understand that information coming from other countries can vary in quality and is thus more challenging to integrate within the existing information and managerial systems.

The liability of newness can be solved by obtaining the necessary resources, especially knowledge, of competitive conditions in the LDC through the purchase or alliance with domestic companies (Beamish 1987, 1999; Hennart and Reddy 1997; Hitt et al. 2000; Kogut and Singh 1988). A DCMNE that expands into the same industry in the LDC will already have the resources to operate in the industry, but will lack some resources to operate in the competitive environment of the LDC, especially knowledge. These resources can be thought of as assets that are complementary to the ones that the DCMNE transfers (Teece 1986b). There are several ways in which knowledge of the competitive conditions can be acquired. It can be obtained directly through purchase; that is, the hiring of international or local consultants in the LDC. This would constitute explicit knowledge that can be transferred to the firm, and in many cases, it would constitute general knowledge about the characteristics of the country; this knowledge would not be specific to the needs of the firm. The firm can also obtain both explicit and tacit knowledge of the competitive conditions by establishing an alliance with a domestic company or by purchasing a domestic company that possesses resources and knowledge that are specific to the firm's needs (Hennart and Reddy 1997; Kogut and Singh 1988). This solution can provide the firm not only with tacit knowledge of the competitive conditions, but also with additional resources that it might need to compete in the LDC. For example, it may acquire distribution systems, production facilities, or established brands and reputations on which it can capitalize, in combination with its own advantageous resources.

Finally, the liability of alienness can be solved through internal development, which is the most appropriate way to deal with this difficulty. The liability of alienness involves the transformation of the mindset of managers to deal with a different set of norms and rules of behavior in the developing country. Hence, the firm will need to hire managers with such abilities, that is, individuals with polycentric attitudes or local managers who understand the characteristics of the developing country but who have also worked in developed countries and are able to interact with headquarters (Nohria and Ghoshal 1997). In this case, however, the DCMNE will need to train them in the methods of operation of the firm (Erden 1988; Tahija 1993), which takes time. Another way of overcoming this disadvantage is for the firm to develop in its own managers the desired attitudes, using expatriate managers who will be able to understand both the operations of the DCMNE and the rules of behavior in the developing country (Matsuo 2000). Developing an understanding of institutions in the LDC results in an incremental internationalization process, which enables the firm to obtain tacit knowledge and change the attitudes of managers regarding LDCs (Johanson and Valhne 1977). This may be a more appropriate avenue than acquiring knowledge from consultants or through purchase of or alliance with a domestic firm, since it enables the DCMNE to alter the constraining mindset of managers that limits successful internationalization (Prahalad and Lieberthal 1998).

However, the DCMNE that solves its difficulties in internationalization over time will not necessarily achieve a competitive advantage and superior profitability in the LDC. At this point in time, the DCMNE's operation in the LDC will be on an equal footing with domestic firms, and it is equally likely to perform well or poorly. That is, it will achieve competitive parity as the playing field is leveled. A competitive advantage and superior profitability will be achieved only if the advantageous resources transferred from other operations or developed in the LDC operation provide it with an advantage over other competitors in the host country.

CONCLUSIONS

As the title of this paper suggests, DCMNEs, represented by the bald eagle native to North America, face problems when operating in LDCs, represented by the rain forest found in Africa, Central and South America, and Asia. Despite their larger and more developed resource pool, represented by the eagle being at the top of the food chain in North America, the DCMNEs face difficulties in internationalizing, which explains their lower performance compared to their local competitors (Zaheer 1995). We have applied the resource-based theory of the firm and its related knowledge-based approach to provide explanations for the sources of their difficulties. We propose three sources of difficulties in internationalization. First, advantageous resources at home are not necessarily advantageous abroad—we termed these difficulties *shortcoming of transfer* and *shortcoming of clients*. Second, the firm may transfer disadvantageous resources abroad—*disadvantage of transfer* and *disadvantage of foreignness.* Third, the firm may lack neutral complementary resources. We have termed these difficulties *liability of expansion*, *liability of newness*, and *liability of foreignness.*

In the particular case of DCMNEs entering LDCs, we argued that they are more likely to face shortcomings of transfer and clients, may face a disadvantage of transfer and liabilities of expansion and alienness, and are less likely to face a disadvantage of foreignness and liability of expansion. Our discussion contributes to the resource-based and knowledge-based approaches, extending them to include not only the use of resources and knowledge in the firm to achieve a competitive advantage, but also the ways in which a lack of resources and knowledge reduces the competitive advantage of a firm. Resources that the firm lacks in a new environment need to be integrated within the theoretical discussions of firm behavior and competitive advantage, highlighting the fact that the advantage provided by resources depends on the context. Additionally, the study complements the growing literature on the difficulties of internationalization and the consequences of such difficulties (Mezias 2002; Miller and Parkhe 2002; Zaheer 1995; Zaheer and Mosakowski 1997) by providing an explanation of the causes.

Although this paper is theoretical in tenor, the identification and understanding of the sources of difficulties of internationalization in less developed countries will assist managers of developed country MNEs in tackling these difficulties and achieve competitive parity in foreign markets. The separation of difficulties in internationalization into different types according to their source helps managers deal with them using the different solutions of resource management and development that have been discussed. Once the foreign operation achieves competitive parity, it can derive benefit from the advantageous resources transferred from other operations or developed in the host operation. Moreover, reducing the difficulties encountered by DCMNEs in LDCs will not only be beneficial to firms in the LDCs, but will also contribute to the development of the country (Stopford and Strange 1992). Managers of MNEs must view LDCs not as difficult markets to be avoided, but as markets that require different sets of resources and knowledge that can lead to successful and profitable international operations.

REFERENCES

Amit, R., and P.J.H. Schoemaker. 1993. "Strategic Assets and Organizational Rents." *Strategic Management Journal* 14: 33–46.

Barkema, H. G., and F. Vermeulen. 1998. "International Expansion through Start-Up or Acquisition: A Learning Perspective." *Academy of Management Journal* 41: 7–26.

Barney, J. 1991. "Firm Resources and Sustained Competitive Advantage." *Journal of Management* 17: 99–100.

Bartlett, C. A., and S. Ghoshal. 1989. *Managing across Borders: The Transnational Solution.* Boston: Harvard Business School Press.

Beamish, P. W. 1987. "Joint Ventures in LDCs: Partner Selection and Performance." *Management International Review* 27: 23–37.

———. 1999. "The Role of Alliances in International Entrepreneurship." *Research in Global Strategic Management* 7: 43–61.

Bilkey, W. J., and E. Nes. 1982. "Country-of-Origin Effects on Products Evaluations." *Journal of International Business Studies* 13 (1): 89–99.

Bloomberg News Service. 1995. "U.S. Brands Try for Foothold in Indian Markets." *The Plain Dealer,* 26 January, 8C.

Booth, L., V. Aivazian, A. Demirguc-Kunt, and V. Maksimovic. 2001. "Capital Structures in Developing Countries." *Journal of Finance* 56: 87–130

Buckley, P., and M. Casson. 1976. *The Future of the Multinational Corporation.* London: Macmillan.

Buckley, P. J. 2002. "Is the International Business Research Agenda Running Out of Steam?" *Journal of International Business Studies* 33: 10.

Calhoun, M. A. 2002. "Unpacking Liability of Foreignness: Identifying Culturally-Driven External and Internal Sources of Liability for the Foreign Subsidiary." *Journal of International Management.* Forthcoming.

Callick, R. 1999. "Protests Calm, but Relations Cool." *Australian Financial Review,* 12 May: 10.

Caves, R. 1982. *Multinational Enterprise and Economic Analysis.* Cambridge: Cambridge University Press.

Conner, K. R. 1991. "A Historical Comparison of Resource-Based Theory and Five Schools of Thought within Industrial Organization Economics: Do We Have a New Theory of the Firm?" *Journal of Management* 17: 121–54.

Conner, K. R., and C. K. Prahalad. 1996. "A Resource-Based Theory of the Firm: Knowledge Versus Opportunism." *Organization Science* 7: 477–501.

Cuervo-Cazurra, A., M. Maloney, and S. Manrakhan. 2002. *Difficulties in Internationalization: A Resource-Based Analysis.* Paper presented at the Academy of International Business annual meeting in Puerto Rico.

Dunning, J. 1977. "Trade, Location of Economic Activity, and the MNE: A Search for an Eclectic Approach." In *The International Allocation of Economic Activity,* edited by B. Ohlin, P. O. Hesselborn, and P. M. Wijkman. London: Macmillan.

Dunning, J. H. 1993. *Multinational Enterprises and the Global Economy.* New York: Addison-Wesley.

Erden, D. 1988. "Impact of Multinational Companies on Host Countries: Executive Training Programs." *Management International Review* 28: 39–47.

Eriksson, K., J. Johanson, A. Majkgard, and D. D. Sharma. 1997. "Experiential Knowledge and Cost in the Internationalization Process." *Journal of International Business Studies* 28: 337–60.

Ghemawat, P. 2001. "Distance Still Matters. The Hard Reality of Global Expansion." *Harvard Business Review* (September): 137–47.

Grant, R. M. 1966. "Toward a Knowledge-Based Theory of the Firm." *Strategic Management Journal* 17 (Special Issue): 109–22.

Hansen, M. T., and M. Haas. 2001. "Competing for Attention in Knowledge Markets: Electronic Document Dissemination in a Management Consulting Company." *Administrative Science Quarterly* 46: 1–28.

Hennart, J. F. 1982. *A Theory of Multinational Enterprise.* Ann Arbor: University of Michigan Press.

Hennart, J. F., and S. Reddy. 1997. "The Choice between Mergers/Acquisitions and Joint Ventures: The Case of Japanese Investors in the United States." *Strategic Management Journal* 18: 1–12.

Hennart, J. F., T. Roehl, and M. Zeng. 2002. "Do Exits Proxy a Liability of Foreignness? The Case of Japanese Exits from the United States." *Journal of International Management.* Forthcoming.

Hitt, M. A., M. T. Dacin, E. Levitas, J. Arregle, and A. Borza. 2000. "Partner Selection in Emerging and Developed Market Contexts: Resource-Based and Organizational Learning Perspectives." *Academy of Management Journal* 43: 449–67.

Hitt, M. A., R. E. Hoskisson, and R. D. Ireland. 1994. "A Mid-Range Theory of the Interactive Effects of International and Product Diversification on Innovation and Performance." *Journal of Management* 20: 297–326.

Hitt, M. A., R. E. Hoskisson, and H. Kim. 1997. "International Diversification: Effects on Innovation and Firm Performance in Product-Diversified Firms." *Academy of Management Journal* 40: 767–98.

Hobday, M. 1994. "Technological Learning in Singapore: A Test Case of Leapfrogging." *Journal of Development Studies* 30: 831–58.

Hofstede, G. 1984. *Culture's Consequences: International Differences in Work-Related Values.* Newbury Park, Calif.: Sage Publications.

Hymer, S. 1976. *The International Operations of National Firms: A Study of Direct Investment.* Cambridge, Mass.: M.I.T. Press.

Jaffe, E. D., and I. D. Nebenzahl. 2001. *National Image and Competitive Advantage: The Theory and Practice of Country-of-Origin Effect.* Copenhagen: Copenhagen Business School Press.

Johanson, J., and J. E. Valhne. 1977. "The Internationalization Process of the Firm: A Model of Knowledge Development and Increasing Foreign Market Commitments." *Journal of International Business Studies* 8: 23–32.

Johanson, J., and F. Wiedersheim-Paul. 1975. "The Internationalization of the Firm. Four Swedish Case Studies." *Journal of Management Studies* 12: 305–22.

Knickerbocker, F. 1973. *Oligopolistic Reaction and Multinational Enterprise.* Boston: Harvard Business School Press.

Kogut, B., and H. Singh. 1988. "The Effect of National Culture on the Choice of Entry Mode." *Journal of International Business Studies* 19: 411–32.

Kogut, B., and U. Zander. 1992. "Knowledge of the Firm, Combinative Capabilities, and the Replication of Technology." *Organization Science* 3: 383–97.

———. 1993. "Knowledge of the Firm and the Evolutionary Theory of the Multinational Corporation." *Journal of International Business Studies* 24: 625–45.

———. 1996. "What Do Firms Do? Coordination, Identity, and Learning." *Organization Science* 7: 502–18.

Kostova, T., and S. Zaheer. 1999. "Organizational Legitimacy under Conditions of Complexity: The Case of the Multinational Enterprise." *Academy of Management Review* 24: 64–81.

Lall, S. 1983. *The New Multinationals: The Spread of Third World Enterprises.* New York: Wiley and Sons.

La Porta, R., F. Lopez-de-Silanes, A. Shleifer, and R. W. Vishny. 1998. "Law and Finance." *Journal of Political Economy* 106: 1113–55.

Leonard-Barton, D. 1992. "Core Capabilities and Core Rigidities: A Paradox in Managing New Product Development." *Strategic Management Journal* 13: 111–26.
———. 1995. *Wellsprings of Knowledge.* Boston: Harvard Business School Press.
Levitt, T. 1983. "The Globalization of Markets." *Harvard Business Review* 61 (May/June): 92–102.
Madhok, A. 1997. "Cost, Value, and Foreign Market Entry Mode: The Transaction and the Firm." *Strategic Management Journal* 18: 39–61.
Mata, J., and P. Portugal. 2002. "The Survival of New Domestic and Foreign-Owned Firms." *Strategic Management Journal* 23: 323–43.
Matsuo, H. 2000. "Liabilities of Foreignness and the Uses of Expatriates in Japanese Multinational Corporations in the United States." *Sociological Inquiry* 70: 88–106.
Mezias, J. M. 2002. "Identifying Liabilities of Foreignness and Strategies to Minimize Their Effect: The Case of Labor Lawsuits Judgments in the United States." *Strategic Management Journal* 23: 229–44.
Miller, D., and J. Shamsie. 1996. "The Resource-Based View of the Firm in Two Environments: The Hollywood Film Studios from 1936 to 1965." *Academy of Management Journal* 39: 519–43.
Miller, S. R., and A. Parkhe. 2002. "Is There a Liability of Foreignness in Global Banking? An Empirical Test of Banks' X-Efficiency." *Strategic Management Journal* 23: 55–75.
Montgomery, C. A. 1995. "Of Diamonds and Rust: A New Look at Resources." In *Resource-Based and Evolutionary Theories of the Firm: Towards a Synthesis*, edited by C. A. Montgomery. Boston: Kluwer Academic Publishers.
Nelson, R. R., and S. G. Winter. 1982. *An Evolutionary Theory of Economic Change.* Cambridge, Mass.: Belknap/Harvard.
Nohria, N., and S. Ghoshal. 1997. *The Differentiated Network.* San Francisco: Jossey-Bass.
Nonaka, I. 1994. "A Dynamic Theory of Organizational Knowledge Creation." *Organization Science* 5: 14–37.
Nonaka, I., and H. Takeuchi. 1995. *The Knowledge-Creating Company. How Japanese Companies Create the Dynamics of Innovation.* New York: Oxford University Press.
North, D. C. 1990. *Institutions, Institutional Change, and Economic Performance.* New York: Cambridge University Press.
Oliver, C. 1997. "Sustainable Competitive Advantage: Combining Institutional and Resource-Based Perspectives." *Strategic Management Journal* 16: 145–79.
Penrose, E. 1959. *The Theory of the Growth of the Firm.* Oxford: Oxford University Press.
Perlmutter, H. 1969. "The Tortuous Evolution of the Multinational Corporation." *Columbia Journal of World Business* 4: 8–18.
Peteraf, M. A. 1993. "The Cornerstones of Competitive Advantage: A Resource-Based View." *Strategic Management Journal* 14: 179–91.
Peterson, R. A., and A. J. P. Jolibert. 1995. "A Meta-Analysis of Country-of-Origin Effects." *Journal of International Business Studies* 26: 883–900.
Porter, M. E. 1990. *The Competitive Advantage of Nations.* New York: The Free Press.
Powell, T. C., and A. Dent-Michallef. 1997. "Information Technology as Competitive

Advantage: The Role of Human, Business, and Technology Resources." *Strategic Management Journal* 18: 375–405.

Prahalad, C. K., and R. A. Bettis. 1986. "The Dominant Logic: A New Linkage between Diversity and Performance." *Strategic Management Journal* 7: 485–501.

Prahalad, C. K., and Y. L. Doz. 1987. *The Multinational Mission.* New York: The Free Press.

Prahalad, C. K., and G. Hamel. 1990. "The Core Competencies of the Corporation." *Harvard Business Review* 68 (May–June): 79–91.

Prahalad, C. K., and A. Hammond. 2002. "Serving the World's Poor, Profitably." *Harvard Business Review* 80 (September): 48–57.

Prahalad, C. K., and K. Lieberthal. 1998. "The End of Corporate Imperialism." *Harvard Business Review* 76 (April): 68–78.

Priem, R. L., and J. E. Butler. 2001. "Is the Resource-Based 'View' a Useful Perspective for Strategic Management Research?" *Academy of Management Review* 26: 22–40.

Ricks, D. A. 1999. *Blunders in International Business.* Malden, Mass.: Basil Blackwell Business.

Root, R., and R. Quelch. 1997. *Koc Holding: Arcelik White Goods.* Harvard Business School Case 9-598-033.

Rugman, A. M. 1981. *Inside the Multinationals: The Economics of Internal Markets.* New York: Columbia University Press.

Rugman, A. M., and A. Verbeke. 1992. "A Note on the Transnational Solution and the Transaction Cost Theory of Multinational Strategic Management." *Journal of International Business Studies* 23: 761–71.

———. 2002. "Edith Penrose's Contribution to the Resource-Based View of Strategic Management." *Strategic Management Journal* 23 (8): 769.

Schweiger, G., G. Haubl, and G. Friederes. 1995. "Consumers' Evaluations of Products Labeled 'Made in Europe.'" *Marketing and Research Today* 23 (1): 25–44.

Sidhva, S. 1993. "India Gets a Taste of the Great World Cola Battle." *Financial Times*, 31 July, 12.

Spar, D. L. 2001. "National Policies and Domestic Politics." In *The Oxford Handbook of International Business*, edited by A. M. Rugman and T. L. Brewer, 206–31. New York: Oxford University Press.

Spender, J. C. 1996. "Making Knowledge the Basis of a Dynamic Theory of the Firm." *Strategic Management Journal* 17: 45–62.

Steenkamp, J. B. E. M., and F. T. Hofstede. 2002. "International Market Segmentation: Issues and Perspectives." *International Journal of Research in Marketing*, 19 (3): 185–213.

Stopford, J., and S. Strange, with J. S. Henley. 1992. *Rival States, Rival Firms: Competition for World Market Shares.* New York: Cambridge University Press.

Stopford, J. M., and S. Strange. 1992. *Rival States, Rival Firms: Competition for World Market Shares.* New York: Cambridge University Press.

Subramaniam, M., and N. Venkatraman. 2001. "Determinants of Transnational New Product Development Capability: Testing the Influence of Transferring and Deploying Tacit Overseas Knowledge." *Strategic Management Journal* 22: 359–78.

Szulanski, G. 1996. "Exploring Internal Stickiness: Impediments to the Transfer of Best Practice within the Firm." *Strategic Management Journal* 17: 27–43.

Tahija, J. 1993. "Swapping Business Skills for Oil." *Harvard Business Review* 71: 64–73.

Tallman, S., and J. Li. 1996. "Effects of International Diversity and Product Diversity on the Performance of Multinational Firms." *Academy of Management Journal* 39 (1): 179–96.

Tallman, S. B. 1992. "A Strategic Management Perspective on Host Country Structure of Multinational Enterprises." *Journal of Management* 18 (3): 455–71.

Tallman, S. B., and G. S. Yip. 2001. "Strategy and the Multinational Enterprise." In *The Oxford Handbook of International Business*, edited by A. M. Rugman and T. L. Brewer, 317–48. New York: Oxford University Press.

Teece, D. 1986a. "Transaction Cost Economics and the Multinational Enterprise: An Assessment." *Journal of Economic Behavior and Organization* 7: 21–45.

———. 1986b. "Profiting from Technological Innovation: Implications for Integration, Collaboration, Licensing, and Public Policy." *Research Policy* 15: 295–305.

Teece, D., G. Pisano, and A. Shuen. 1997. "Dynamic Capabilities and Strategic Management." *Strategic Management Journal* 18: 509–33.

Tripsas, M. 1997. "Unraveling the Process of Creative Destruction: Complementary Assets and Incumbent Survival in the Typesetter Industry." *Strategic Management Journal* 18 (summer special issue): 119–42.

Tsoukas, H. 1996. "The Firm as a Distributed Knowledge System: A Constructionist Approach." *Strategic Management Journal* 17: 11–25.

UNCTAD. 2002. *World Investment Report 2002. Transnational Corporations and Export Competitiveness.* Geneva: United Nations Conference on Trade and Development.

Van de Ven, A. 1993. "The Development of an Infrastructure for Entrepreneurship." *Journal of Business Venturing* 8: 211–30.

Vernon, R. 1966. "International Investment and International Trade in the Product Life Cycle." *Quarterly Journal of Economics* 80: 190–207.

———. 1977. *Storm over the Multinationals: The Real Issues.* Boston: Harvard University Press.

Von Krogh, G., K. Ichijo, and I. Nonaka. 2000. *Enabling Knowledge Creation: How to Unlock the Mystery of Tacit Knowledge and Release the Power of Innovation.* Oxford: Oxford University Press.

Wells, L. T. 1983. *Third World Multinationals.* Cambridge, Mass.: M.I.T Press.

———. 1998. "Multinationals and the Developing Countries." *Journal of International Business Studies* 29: 101–15.

Wernerfelt, B. 1984. "A Resource-Based View of the Firm." *Strategic Management Journal* 5: 171–80.

Zaheer, S. 1995. "Overcoming the Liability of Foreignness." *Academy of Management Journal* 38: 341–63.

Zaheer, S., and E. Mosakowski. 1997. "The Dynamics of the Liability of Foreignness." *Strategic Management Journal* 18: 439–64.

Zander, U., and B. Kogut. 1995. "Knowledge and the Speed of the Transfer and Imitation of Organizational Capabilities: An Empirical Test." *Organization Science* 6: 76–91.

CHAPTER 3

Challenges for the European Auto Multinationals

Heike Proff

INTRODUCTION

More and more developing countries are turning to increased industrialization to improve the per capita income of their populations and to expand participation in world trade (Brada and Woo 1994; Hoen and van Leeuwen 1991).[1] By adopting an industrial cluster-based development approach, they hope to enhance value addition in a network with input-output linkages (DeBresson and Hu 1999; Holden 1996; Proff 1998). Massive investment incentives and protection mechanisms are expected to help build up large production capacities in a few industrial sectors, while local content requirements will ensure the establishment of important supplier industries. Given adequate protection and support, investments in these countries appear economically rational for both domestic producers and multinational corporations (MNCs) when viewed in isolation with regard to individual investment projects. However, such investment may not be rational for an MNC. On the contrary, the production capacity for standard products required to achieve international competitiveness will exceed the demand for such products in the host countries. Consequently, it becomes necessary to export large quantities of these products to world markets, thereby increasing global supply. Thus, export competition in world markets for standard goods is steadily rising even in developing countries (Muscatelli, Stevenson, and Montagna 1994, 44). In a situation in which global demand is growing slowly—such as in the 1970s when many countries in Eastern Asia, Latin America, and sub-Saharan Africa simultaneously promoted the cultivation of a few select agricultural export products (cash crops) thereby causing oversupply and a heavy global price recession—an expansion in the supply of manufactured goods in excess of global demand can negatively influence world market prices (Gandolfo 1998, 278). The result is overcapacity and export competition. Export competition is the growing competition in world markets to export certain goods; it results from developing countries' increased capacities to produce such goods, regardless of whether these production capacities have been set up by local manufacturers or by the subsidiaries of MNCs.[2]

The automotive industry is an example of an economically significant sector dealing with export competition. This holds true not only for the industrialized countries in Europe, but for other countries as well (Proff 2000). Due to the large number of possible linkages with a broad supplier industry and with distribution and marketing services, "clusters" of the industrialization endeavors of developing countries are formed. Evidence for these clusters can be found in Malaysia, Indonesia, and Thailand, which are neighboring East Asian countries and also members of the Asian Free Trade Agreement (AFTA) regional integration zone. At the same time, the European automotive industry, particularly, is characterized by expansive (i.e., distribution-oriented) foreign direct investment activities (Klodt and Maurer 1996, 11–14). The investment incentives offered by developing countries thus fulfill a strong demand for expansion opportunities in the European automotive industry.

As the growth in global demand for passenger cars has been quite average—increasing by just 7.1 percent from 33.9 million to 36.4 million vehicles between 1991 and 1998—an expansion in production capacities for the same automobile products in several developing countries has led to global overcapacities. In 1998 the figure was about 17.6 million vehicles (author's calculations based on press reports; see also Feige and Crooker 1999, 43). Korea alone had production capacities for over 3.4 million vehicles in 1998, 54 percent more than in 1991. Global overcapacity corresponds to 47 percent of worldwide production in this industrial sector. Figure 3.1a shows that the problem of overcapacity as regards passenger cars and commercial vehicles will persist, as capacity utilization on average for the years 1999 to 2005 is not expected to exceed 60 percent in Asia and the Pacific (including Japan), Eastern Europe, South America, and the Near East and Africa. Even in Western Europe only about 80 percent of production capacities will be fully utilized (AUTOFACTS Group, PricewaterhouseCoopers 2000). The case of European automobile manufacturers further demonstrates that underutilization or overcapacity is clearly higher for manufacturers adopting a cost leadership strategy in the low-volume segments (Fiat and Renault), in which there is a projected capacity utilization of approximately 55 percent to 65 percent. Capacity utilization of manufacturers adopting differentiation strategies, on the other hand, particularly those serving the upper market segments (DaimlerChrysler and BMW), is expected to be about 85 percent. The overcapacities of companies adopting a mixed strategy of minimal cost differentiation in a broad segment range (VW and PSA) lie somewhere in between with a projected 75 percent to 80 percent capacity utilization (Figure 3.1b).

The automotive industry (i.e., the road vehicle industry in Europe) is characterized both by high amounts of direct investment abroad and a high intensity of exports from Germany (Klodt and Maurer 1996, 16). Of course, one must take into consideration that the automotive sector requires much larger direct investments than, for example, the textile industry. Nevertheless, added foreign direct investments in developing countries and the resulting overcapacities and export competition appear to be of special relevance for the German and the European automotive industry (see Figure 3.2a).

It is clear from Figure 3.1b that the competitive strategy of the automobile manufacturers determines to what extent they are affected by overcapacity and export competition. While manufacturers using differentiation strategies in the upper segments are only indirectly affected by the general pressure on prices and can overcome this by product differentiation, it is the present cost leaders who face a much bigger threat. One can therefore expect that new production capacities in developing economies will lead to increased competition, especially in the low price segments, in which price pressure will increase the most (Brada and Woo 1994, 41). Similarly, in this segment the price premium achievable on the market (i.e., the price over and above that of a comparable, price-adjusted product with basic standard equipment— "value for money" [Proff 2000]),[3] also reduces the price maximum. The tendency toward falling price premiums affects all European automobile markets. This will be demonstrated on the basis of the largest market, Germany, as it is expected that the introduction of the Euro and the Internet will lead to a

Figure 3.1
Projected Capacity Utilization in the Automotive Industry Classified According to Region and European Manufacturers (Average figures for passenger cars and commercial vehicles for the years 1999 to 2005.)

1a Regional capacity utilization

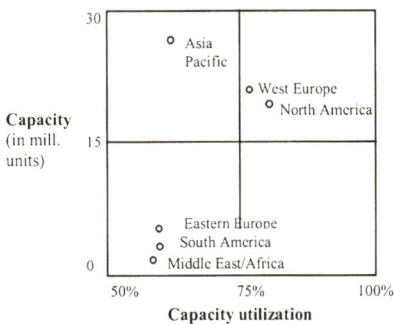

1b Capacity utilization for European manufacturers

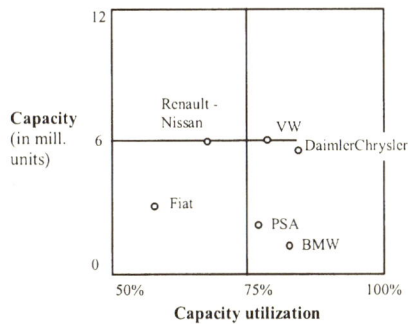

Figure 3.2
Export Intensity and Foreign Direct Investment of German Enterprises As Well As Falling Price Premiums in Germany

2a. Amount of FDI by German companies abroad and export intensity

Amount of German FDI abroad [1]

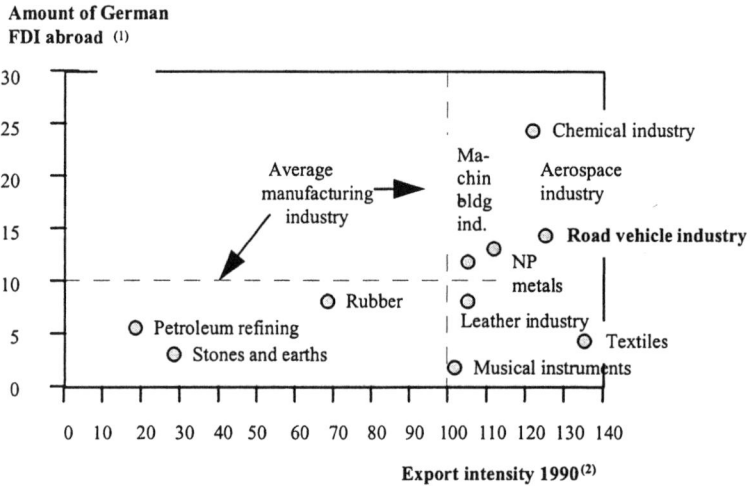

(1) As percentage of gross fixed capital 1994 at replacement costs
(2) Exports as percentage of gross value addition in respective prices (former federal territory)

2b. Trends in price premiums available on the German automobile market (1984-1996)

Segment [1] / Year	Entry-level class	Lower middle class	Traditional middle class	Upper middle class	Upper class
1984	27.0	20.8	18.2	18.7	32.8
1986	16.5	28.0	23.7	25.7	/ [2]
1988	7.9	15.6	10.5	10.9	/
1990	1.7	9.3	10.7	12.3	/
1992	5.3	6.9	9.3	24.0	/
1994	0.0	9.2	13.0	24.0	/
1996	2.4	3.8	13.8	25.9	33.4

(1) The luxury class comprising the S class, BMW 7 series and the A8 have not been considered Here because there is no comparable Asian product.
(2) In this year there was no comparable Asian product in the upper class.

⬇ Distinct tendency toward falling price premiums   ⬆⬆ Distinct trend reversal convergence in prices and therefore price premiums in Europe. A look at the 1996 announced price premiums for German passenger car manufacturers using differentiation strategies shows that, compared to Asian manufacturers, who usually offer basic standard equipment at no added price (premium) (see Figure 3.2b), the tendency toward falling price premiums has affected different market segments with varying intensity at different points of time since 1984.[4] While the first Asian competitors distinctly reduced the price premium available through differentiation in the entry level segment from 27 percent to 7 percent between 1984 and 1988, it is only since 1986 that this trend is visible in the middle class as well. German manufacturers in the middle-class segment have suffered continuously falling price premiums (from 28 percent to 3.8 percent) since 1986 (with the exception of 1994), while in the traditional and upper-middle-class segments they were able to stabilize and even consolidate price premiums after an initial crash. The upper-middle-class segment on the German market was thus able to shield the upper and luxury classes so well that there were no significant changes in this segment.

Figures 3.1 and 3.2 point to a negative multi-market impact that has largely been ignored in the theory of foreign direct investment and, consequently, in globalization strategies. During the "globalization wave" that began in the 1990s, several European automobile manufacturers set up production capacities in the growth markets outside the Triad countries (United States, European Union, and Japan). Their rational expectation was to obtain economic rents for individual projects in countries adopting an industrial cluster-based development strategy, as set out in the theory of foreign direct investment. What was not taken into account, however, was that overcapacities result when many MNCs simultaneously invest in a few industrial clusters of many developing countries. This leads to export pressure and to pressure on prices in world markets stemming from export competition.

This paper seeks to fill a twofold lacuna in research by

1. identifying reasons for overcapacities and export competition on global markets resulting from industrial clustering, using the automotive industry as an example; and

2. discussing the potential challenges that overcapacities and export competition pose, specifically for the European automotive industry. In addition, the arguments offered by the foreign direct investment and industrial organization theories need to be expanded to include industrial economic considerations regarding multi-market competition.

The paper concludes with a look at future developments.

OVERCAPACITIES AND EXPORT COMPETITION RESULTING FROM INDUSTRIAL CLUSTERING

This section first examines the structure of overcapacities in developing countries using the economics of the industry, in this case the automotive industry, as a basis. Subsequently, it examines the question of why the phenomenon of export competition was until now not considered within the theory of foreign direct investment.

Building up of Production Capacities for Select Standard Products in Developing Countries under an Industrial Cluster-Based Development Approach

Industrialization as a Means of Economic Development

Increasingly, developing countries are attempting to raise the per capita income of their populations, and consequently the welfare of all population groups, by adopting export-oriented industrialization strategies (Chow 1989; Jin 1995). In this paper, "development" is understood as structural change in an economy with simultaneously rising participation of the population in the formal economic system, growing industrialization, urbanization, and a change in trade structures and consumption habits (Sell 1993, 2). Five principal reasons are put forward for industrialization in developing countries (Proff 1995, 70):

1. The close correlation between economic growth and industrialization in the development process.
2. The tendency toward declining terms of trade for agricultural products.
3. The higher development potential of industry as opposed to agriculture, as income elasticity of domestic demand is higher for manufactured goods than for basic foodstuffs.
4. Industrialization creates positive employment effects.
5. Industry provides opportunities for import substitution.

As a development component, industrialization promotes the transition from a subsistence and barter economy to a market economy while simultaneously rationalizing all production processes. In Figure 3.3 the ideal development process in highly developed national economies is represented in relation to the share of the secondary sector in GDP (degree of industrialization) (Proff 1998; World Bank 2000). Even if one adopts a conservative approach in deriving inferences from this ideal development scenario, the figure illustrates that an increase in per capita income and consequently in economic development usually takes place as a result of an increase in the degree of industrialization.[5] A comparison of Burundi, Chile, and Korea confirms this development hypothesis. The Fourastié hypothesis of increasing tertiarization of the economic structure states that the degree of industrialization shows a reverse trend after a GDP share of about 45 percent, as evidenced by current World Bank data and as has already happened in countries such as the United States and Great Britain.

Figure 3.3
Industrialization As a Means of Economic Development

**Share of the secondary
sector in GDP** (in %)

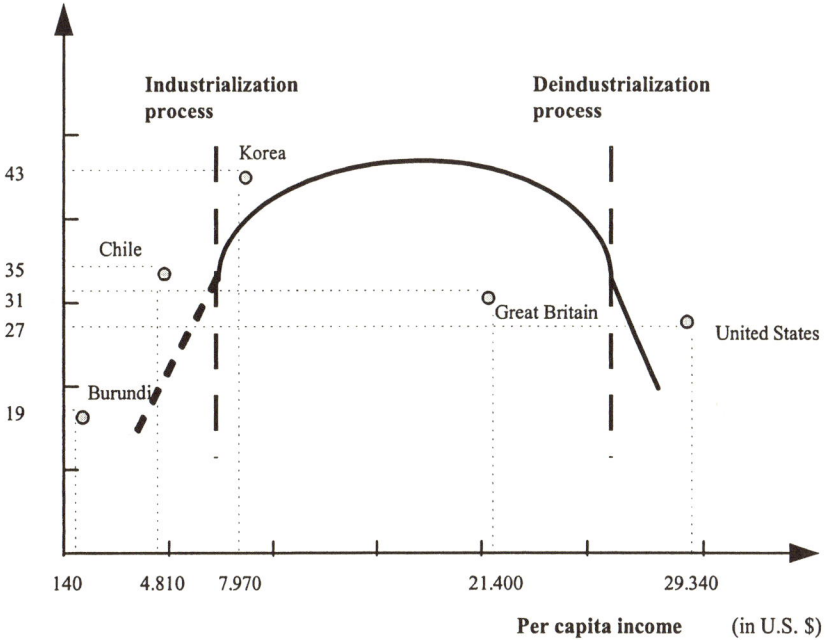

A successful development strategy, therefore, requires the creation of an industrial structure with production processes that are knowledge-, technology-, and capital-intensive rather than merely labor-intensive (Gundlach and Nunnenkamp 1996; Poapongsakorn and Fuller 1998). The objective must be the building up of competitive *pôles de croissance* (growth poles) or the creation of industrial clusters, as put forward by Perroux or Hirschman, that can spur growth in neighboring regions or upstream or downstream industrial sectors through positive trickle-down effects. Such industrial clusters forming the core of an industrialization strategy can, over time, develop into a diversified industrial network of linkages between users and suppliers. They achieve multiplier effects and create linkages that can be formalized using input-output tables (Armstrong and Taylor 1985; McGregor, Swales, and Ping Yin 1996).[6]

The Suitability of the Automotive Industry as a Cluster in Industrialization Strategies

The automotive industry is an industrial sector that creates multiplier effects and can contribute to the industrialization of a country. At the same time, it is often the industrial prestige and priority sector that is supposed to demonstrate the industrial maturity of a country. Many developing countries therefore attempt to develop the automotive industry into an industrial cluster as part of their industrialization strategy.[7]

Figure 3.4 shows the current linkages in the Malaysian automotive industry. The development of this industrial sector is being promoted as part of the cluster approach, and a further interlinking of passenger car and commercial vehicle production with the industry's most important suppliers is being targeted for the future (Ministry of Trade and Industry 1996).

Large-scale industrialization of automobile manufacturing is to be achieved through regulations regarding the extent of local value addition (local content requirements). A high degree of industrialization in a country (which includes the future production of components and aggregates such as cylinder heads or dynamos, a forging press unit, foundry, final assembly, and paint shop in Malaysia) clearly creates significantly greater multiplier effects than a low degree of industrialization (comprising merely final assembly and painting of imported kits in a country). Assembly units usually hire only a few hundred employees from the host country and do not require the establishment of a supplier industry.

Industrial Clustering and Rising Overcapacities

The newly established production capacities in developing countries are usually protected by very high duties. These high duties, however, will be difficult to maintain in the long term given the World Trade Organization's (WTO's) moves toward a reduction in global duty structures and the strong regional integration efforts by many developing countries. Thus the industrialization endeavors of developing countries and also the investment decisions of multinational corporations must, after a suitable transition period,

Figure 3.4
Current and Targeted Linkages in the Automotive Industry under the Malaysian "Cluster Approach"

Core industries	Passenger cars	Commercial vehicles	
Current	* Passenger cars	* Buses	
		* Trucks	
Future	* Cars incl. MPVs	* Different types of comm. vehicles	

Key suppliers	Engines	Electrical system	Accessories
Current	* Cooling systems	* Battery	* Radio
	* Engine controls	* Starter motor	* Air conditioning
Future	* Cylinder heads	* Dynamo	* Other
	* Motor blocks	* Wiring systems	equipment
	* Fuel system	* Instrument display	& accessories

strive for international competitiveness and an internationally competitive cost position. This distinguishes the current strategy from the import substitution strategies of many developing countries in the 1970s.

Industrial clusters in developing countries are initially protected by high duties because in most of these countries it would be cheaper to import a complete vehicle from an optimized production plant in an industrialized country than to assemble it from a kit; this is even truer for production with high value addition (see Figure 3.5). This is due to the fact that higher logistical costs and double investments in assembly units are incurred for low assembly volumes. When Singapore, for instance, decided in 1980 to do away with protective tariffs on completely knocked-down (CKD) kits, eight manufacturers in the country immediately shut down their assembly units and began importing vehicles.

A closer examination of manufacturing costs for automobile production in Malaysia shows that even if all components are imported (in extreme cases the local content is 0), the additional manufacturing costs of a small assembly unit are about 15 percent more than those of a streamlined production in an industrial country (see the base costs in Figure 3.5e).

Higher local value addition increases production costs because of the larger share of locally produced, technology-intensive intermediate products with a comparatively higher cost due to the low technological standard and low unit volumes in the country. While cost-efficient vehicle assembly is possible even from 100,000 units, the optimum production volume for engines is approximately 300,000 units, and for starter motors it is about 1.5 million units (see Figure 3.5b). Given a total requirement of just 100,000 vehicles in Malaysia and a maximum of 800,000 vehicles in the AFTA regional market (see Figure 3.5c), the optimum unit volumes are not achieved. Suppliers are thus constrained to go in for sub-optimal, low-volume, and hence more expensive production. Usually the parts that are sourced locally are just enough to make up the percentage of manufacturing costs needed to fulfill local content requirements. These parts may include components such as seats or tires (see Figures 3.5a and 3.5d), which frequently do not fall into the category of key suppliers (Figure 3.4) promoted under the industrialization strategy pursued by these countries. Malaysia and several other developing countries therefore specify local content requirements in the form of a points system in which the required local content is expressed as a minimum point value and different points are allocated to various intermediate products. Parts from key supplier industries with high technology content and correspondingly high linkage impacts (as shown in Figure 3.4) are given a much higher point value than items such as seats.

Assuming the production costs in industrial countries to be 100 percent, the production costs of highly technology-intensive intermediate products in sub-optimal volumes for a country like Malaysia are 135 percent for 15 percent local content and 155 percent for 25 percent local content. For a local

Figure 3.5
Industrial Clustering and the Need for Large-Scale Production Capacities

5a. Break-up of costs
for various components of a
  passenger car
  (in % of manufacturing costs for
  a middle class car)

Engine 15%

Transmission   Glass 2%
6.5
%   Body 14%

Braking   Seats 6%
system 3%
Plastic
parts 9%   Tires 2.5%
       Chassis parts 11.5%

5b. Optimum
  production volumes
  (in 1,000 units)

Vehicle assembly	100
Engines	300
Wiper motors	600
Starter	1.500

5c. Comparison with current
  market potential in the
  AFTA (in 1,000 units)

Vehicle assembly	800
Engines	800
Wiper motors	400
Starter	800

5d. Competence of local
  suppliers   (quality/costs)

Possible partial sourcing
in Malaysia (in the year 2000)

Shock absorbers
Exhaust unit
Wiring
Door paneling
Seats
Tires
Wiper unit
Heating/AC etc.

= approx. 40% local content

5e. Additional costs for automobile production in Malaysia depending on local content
  (assuming constant production volumes)

Manufacturing costs of automobile production
in Malaysia in comparison to an industrial country
country (industrial country = 100%)

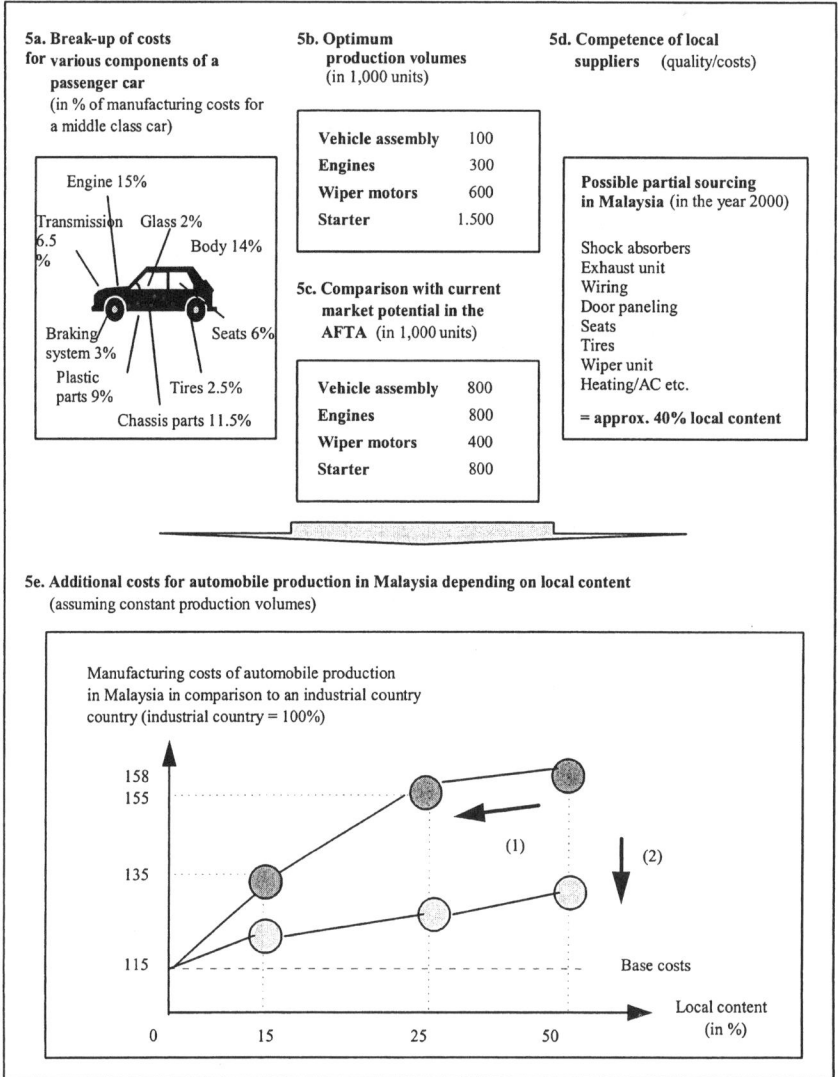

content of 50 percent, the costs are as high as 158 percent, assuming that production volumes remain constant (see Figure 3.5e).

One precondition for foreign direct investments in developing countries by MNCs, therefore, is an efficient supplier infrastructure, in which enterprises from the steel, chemical, textiles, glass, tire, and electrical sectors are present within the industrial cluster. On the other hand, an investment program offering adequate duty protection to offset high manufacturing costs is required for final assembly units and the supplier industry, which does not overcompensate for the multiplier effects.

Malaysia provides investors in the target industries with a package of tax and non-tax incentives. Cars assembled from CKD kits attract duties of 42 percent while duties of up to 222 percent are levied on imports of complete vehicles.

In a scenario comprising long-term lowering of global duty structures, direct investments in developing countries would no longer be competitive due to their high manufacturing costs. MNCs are then left with the option of either reducing local value addition, which the host countries would surely not permit (Alternative 1 in Figure 3.5e), or increasing production volumes (Alternative 2 in Figure 3.5e). If production volumes are increased, the minimum assembly costs of 15 percent for a small market as well as the higher production costs of increasing value addition for individual vehicles would become less significant due to cost regression effects for manufacturers and suppliers.

At the same time, the increased production volumes required to improve international competitiveness cannot be distributed on the domestic markets of developing countries. Though these markets show above-average growth rates, in absolute terms they are still very limited. An increase in production volume, therefore, leads to overcapacity, export competition, and a decline in the prices of standard products on global markets.

Overcapacity and price pressure are not just phenomena arising from competition between firms, such as the setting up of parallel capacities by Volkswagen and Fiat in many developing countries. Even internal competition between subsidiaries of the same concern at different locations resulting in duplicate capacities can intensify as a reaction to the industrialization attempts of many developing countries.

Explanations of Foreign Direct Investment Leading to a Skewed Assessment of Investment Incentives

In view of overcapacity, export competition, and pressure on prices, direct investments of standard products in developing countries are usually of limited rationality from the perspective of the overall corporation. However, viewed in terms of an individual investment project, they appear very rational. Foreign direct investments provide companies operating internationally with the opportunity to utilize profit opportunities existing in international markets (Broll and Gilroy 1989). Profit opportunities are as diverse as the definitions of direct investment in the theory of foreign direct investment (Macharzina 1982; Perlitz 2000; Welge and Holtbrügge 1998). As a rule, definitions are categorized according to the different reference planes or points of focus (direct investment and the theory of international trade, direct investment and the location theory, direct investment and the capital market theory, direct investment and the industrial organization theory, as well as direct investment and the theory of enterprise) (Bea 1995; Stein 1998). These theories essentially analyze segmentally and are monocausal in nature (Welge and Holtbrügge 1998, 79). The only attempt to integrate these theories has also been criticized as an "assortment of several variables not fitted into any framework" (Perlitz 2000, 129). Thus, so far no comprehensive theory of foreign direct investment has been postulated. Oesterle (1999), however, does not consider a comprehensive theory of foreign direct investment to be useful in the current context; although it would lead to greater formalization and a narrowing down in the scope of this field of research, it would then also lose relevance.

Despite the present lack of conclusiveness in the theory of foreign direct investment, discussions along the individual reference planes can be used to infer advantages for direct investments that would support MNCs in their investment decisions. Investment incentives in industrialization strategies are primarily considered under the foreign direct investment and industrial organization theory, as the restrictions on market entry due to duties, as in Malaysia, create market imperfections (Stein 1998, 48). Approaches based on the direct investment and industrial organization theory use this to explain the conduct of the oligopolistic automotive industry, which wishes to use foreign direct investment to realize its plans of worldwide expansion (Klodt and Maurer 1996, 7).

Industrial organization theory has come a long way since Hymer (1960) posited that "internal operations of national firms" was the reason for foreign direct investment instead of the international exchange of capital, as had been previously assumed. With this idea, he attempted to establish the theoretical foundations of foreign direct investment in industrial organization theory. This theory attempts to explain industrial market processes through the economic output of a firm within an industry, taking into account sector- and firm-specific determinants. Market performance can be derived from market conduct, and this conduct in turn from the market structure ("structure-conduct-performance" paradigm), in which market conduct is characterized by the market form, entry barriers, and demand (Stein 1998, 42–43).

The most significant among the various discussions on the foreign direct investment and the industrial organization theory is the monopolistic theory of foreign direct investment, as propounded by Hymer (1960 and 1977) and Kindleberger (1969), who justify direct investments in imperfect markets on the basis of monopolistic advantages that exist vis-à-vis domestic competitors despite market entry barriers. Such quasi-monopolistic profits result from advantages gained in home markets, such as the control over raw material sources. Stein (1998) has also emphasized the significance of the further theoretical developments of Johnson (1970) and Caves (1972) regarding monopolistic advantages arising from commercially exploitable knowledge and of Aliber (1970) regarding the advantages for firms from hard currency countries in international capital markets. In addition to these variations on the monopolistic theory of foreign direct investment, Knickerbocker (1973) and Graham (1978) developed the theory of oligopolistic parallel conduct within the framework of the industrial organization theory. This theory examines the bundling of direct investments in individual foreign markets, particularly as a reaction to investment decisions of competitors (from industrial countries), to prevent their comparative advantages from becoming too large ("follow-the-leader investments").[8]

An industrial cluster-based development approach with investment incentives in developing countries provides MNCs with the opportunity to exploit monopolistic advantages gained in their home market in the host country as well, or to initiate oligopolistic reactions to direct investments by competitors from industrial nations in these countries. Other motives, such as life cycle considerations, utilization of locational advantages, utilization of organizational learning processes, or the reduction of transaction and coordination costs in global production networks, may also influence direct investment decisions in these countries. However, they cannot be influenced by the initiatives of the host country and are therefore not as relevant for our study of growing export competition.

The theory of foreign direct investment is thus primarily focused toward the advantages of direct investments in general, while the reference plane relevant here, that is, foreign direct investment and industrial organization theory, specifically focuses on the utilization of investment incentives in imperfect markets. The theory of foreign direct investment does not discuss these advantages' limitations, which result from the overcapacities and export competition that first affected cash crops and have now affected manufactured standard products with large linkage networks. Discussions within the foreign direct investment and industrial organization theory therefore take into account only a part of the vast research on industrial organization (Stead, Curwen, and Lawer 1996; Tirole 1995), that is, the basic models of oligopolistic competition as understood by Dixit (1979), which are restricted to duopoly models.

Multi-market competition is disregarded, although the industrial organization theory takes this phenomenon into account and establishes negative external (spillover) effects (Baum and Korn 1996; van Wegberg and van Witteloostuijn 1991).

In the following section, therefore, this paper presents these approaches to multi-market competition and extends the direct investment and industrial organization theory to include the challenges posed to MNCs by overcapacity and export competition for standard products on world markets and suggests possible responses.

THE CHALLENGES TO EUROPEAN AUTOMOBILE MANUFACTURERS

European automobile manufacturers have long been strong net exporters on global markets. They are thus particularly challenged by overcapacity and export competition resulting from industrial clustering in developing countries. In order to suggest potential responses to these challenges, one first needs to extend the theory of foreign direct investment to include the negative externalities of multi-market competition as established in industrial economics research.

Extending the Theories of Foreign Direct Investment to Include the Negative External Effects Resulting from Multi-Market Competition

The advantages of international direct investments as stated in the traditional theory of foreign direct investment are offset by disadvantages resulting from overcapacity and export competition, which until now have been largely ignored. This traditional theory of foreign direct investment focuses primarily on isolated market entries, competitors' reactions to these market entries, or competition within markets. Interactions between markets in multi-market competition (van Wegberg and van Witteloostuijn 1991, 96; 1992, 441), on the other hand, are absent from previous discussions of the foreign direct investment and industrial organization theory. These interactions, however, need to be included to take into account the negative external impacts of export competition (see Figure 3.6).

Interactions between markets are not necessarily negative. Regarding multi-market supply from an industrial economic perspective, positive image (brand identity) transfers, for example, can be established between different national markets (e.g., Coca-Cola being regarded as a typical American product on world markets) or between product markets (e.g., between Boss clothing and aftershave).[9] Overcapacity and export competition for standard products, however, cause a global decline in prices and are therefore examples of negative interactions or externalities.

It would exceed the scope of this paper to provide an analytical description of multi-market competition, which in its simplest form is based on a Cournot model, with two firms in one market and a monopoly in another market (Bulov, Geanakoplos, and Klemperer 1985). Moreover, a conclusive solution in regard to multi-market competition is not available. For this reason, industrial economic research frequently distinguishes between the conditions and type of multi-market competition (Hughes and Oughton 1993, 204–8). These distinctions are also meaningful in discussions of overcapacities and export competition, as negative spillover effects in multi-market competition

Figure 3.6
Necessary Extension of the Theory of Foreign Direct Investment to Include Interactions between Markets to Take into Account Overcapacity and Export Competition

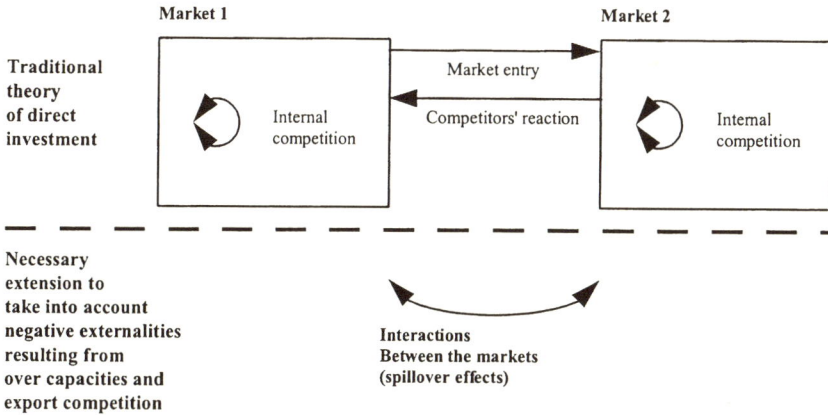

are significant for multinational corporations only if they nullify or exceed the advantages of direct investment. From a commercial perspective, then, the factors influencing the level of negative multi-market or spillover effects need to be examined.

In the discussion of multi-market competition within the framework of the industrial organization theory (Baum and Korn 1996, 256; Bulov, Geanako-plos, and Klemperer 1985, 450; van Wegberg and van Witteloostuijn 1991, 98), two factors influencing the extent of negative or spillover effects can be deduced from analytical models:

1. The substitutability or the similarity of goods on the market.

2. The quantum of multi-market contacts.

Regarding (1): The first factor influencing the level of negative external effects is the similarity of supplied products, or their substitutability. The cross elasticity of price is a good indicator of substitutability. It indicates by how many percent the sales of product 1 would vary if the price of product 2 changes by 1 percent. For the unit to be meaningful, it must pertain to comparable goods in the same market segment. As a rule, the substitutability of both products, for example an Opel Astra and a VW Golf, increases with an increase in the cross elasticity of price. This implies that the greater the negative externalities of multi-market competition, the more easily products of important competitors or subsidiaries of a concern can be substituted in a market segment. This would be applicable at least in those cases in which, for the sake of simplicity, one assumes a constant cross elasticity of price for all supplied countries. Extrapolating this to overcapacities and export competition, one can infer that if product substitution by competitors or subsidiaries on global markets can be reduced in a market segment, overcapacity and export competition will also decline.

Regarding (2): The second factor influencing the extent of negative external effects is the number of multi-market contacts, that is, the frequency with which firms meet as competing suppliers in different markets. The quantum of multi-market contacts can be measured by the total difference in turnover share of the relevant products of suppliers in various national markets at a global level. Here too, a specific market segment needs to be considered. In the automotive industry this would mean, for instance, that within the lower-middle-class segments, the significance of individual national markets is compared at a global level for the Opel Astra and the VW Golf. The argument of mutual forbearance that anticipates lower competition intensity during multi-market contacts as a result of informal arrangements (Hughes and Oughton 1993) is irrelevant for standard products in view of overcapacity and the tendency toward declining price premiums as demonstrated in Figure 3.2b, particularly for the lower market segments in global markets. Instead, negative external effects occur when there is an increase in competition due to a rising number of multi-market contacts in a market segment.

This means that overcapacity and export competition between firms or subsidiaries of the same concern will be lower when multi-market contacts in a market segment are reduced.

Both factors influencing the level of negative externalities resulting from overcapacity and export competition (substitutability of products and the number of multi-market contacts) must be regarded jointly. What emerges is that when overcapacity and export competition are pronounced enough to outweigh the advantages of direct investment, overlap between products and markets of competitors or subsidiaries of the same concern in a market segment increases. A lowering in product substitutability and a reduction in multi-market contacts provide approaches for lowering the negative externalities of overcapacities and export competition. The response of the European automotive industry must be along these lines. Both approaches can serve as the axes of a coordinate system in which one can represent the level of negative externalities arising from overcapacities and export competition (Figure 3.7). In the extreme case of very high product substitutability and the ensuing very high cross elasticity of price and a high number of multi-market contacts, overcapacities and export competition and consequently their negative external effects peak in the origin of the coordinate system. Using the example of a VW Golf and an Opel Astra, the annex shows that the adoption of both these approaches leads to a reduction in overcapacities and export competition.

Figure 3.7
Approaches for Reducing the Negative External Effects of Overcapacity and Export Competition

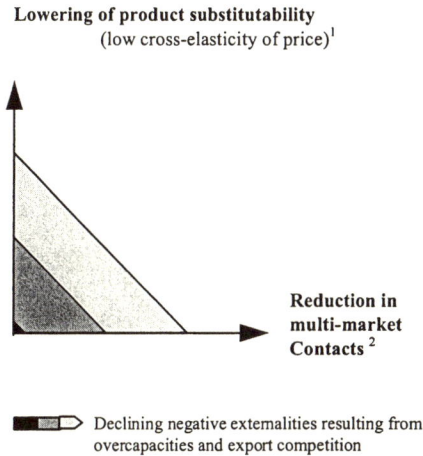

Lowering of product substitutability
(low cross-elasticity of price)[1]

Reduction in
multi-market
Contacts [2]

Declining negative externalities resulting from
overcapacities and export competition

Possible Responses of the European Automobile Manufacturers to Increasing Export Competition

Although the generally stagnant global demand for standard products cannot be influenced, there are opportunities to avoid the negative externalities of increasing overcapacities and export competition. One can distinguish among these according to the approach that is adopted to reduce the negative external effects of export competition (Figure 3.7) and according to the competitive environment, for example, on whether the exports are taking place between or within multinational corporations. This distinction according to the competitive environment is necessary, as a large portion of world trade—an estimated 25 percent to 35 percent—takes place within MNCs (Stein 1998, 35). The possible responses of European automobile manufacturers to increasing overcapacity and export competition have been presented in Figure 3.8 in the form of a matrix with both the axes (approaches to reduce negative externalities and the competitive environment).

Overcapacity and export competition within a European automobile manufacturing concern can be reduced if product substitutability resulting from internal competition is minimized, that is, if duplicate capacities for the same product at different locations are eliminated or the manufacture of specific (niche) models is concentrated at specific locations (Option 1). Within the Fiat concern, for example, the Palio Combi is manufactured only in Brazil and can be exported to global markets from there (Waelbroeck 1998). Although this strategy may not be successful for upper-class vehicles due to lack of image of the production locations, image considerations would play a sub-

Figure 3.8
Possible Responses of the European Automotive Industry to Overcapacities and Export Competition

Approaches to reducing negative externalties \ Comp. environment	Within a European automobile manufacturing concern	Between different automobile manufacturers
Lowering product substitutability	Option 1: * Reducing duplicate capacities * Focusing on one model at one location	Option 3: * Differentiation of products vis-à-vis competitors * Acquisition and cooperation
Reducing multi-market contacts	Option 2: * Arrangements and guidelines regarding market servicing * Focusing on one model at one location	Option 4: * Servicing of smaller markets (geographical differentiation) * Influence on regional integration efforts * Acquisition and cooperation

ordinate role in the case of the Fiat Palio, as the sensitivity for this aspect is lower in the lower market segments. In Figure 3.2b, however, it was demonstrated that the phenomenon of overcapacity and export competition are restricted to the entry-level segments.

Multi-market competition between products of the same concern at different locations can also be reduced if attempts are made to optimize the global production network rather than optimizing production volumes in one country. Clear arrangements or guidelines regarding the markets to be supplied can reduce the multi-market contacts between subsidiaries of the same concern (Option 2). Of course, preconditions for such a strategy are that the problem of re-imports can be avoided through harmonious pricing and that excessive export obligations are not entered into at individual locations. The latter will inevitably come into conflict with the industrialization strategies of the host countries, which European automobile manufacturers must be prepared for. In any case, these conditions are often not heeded, as the numerous hurdles to export obligations in India, for instance, demonstrate. Daimler-Chrysler in particular was left sitting on its "made in India" Mercedes.

Overcapacity and export competition between several multinational corporations can similarly be reduced by a reduction in the substitutability of competing products (Option 3). This can be achieved if, for example, while planning the production of individual models at only one location, attempts are made to differentiate the product or goods vis-à-vis the most important competitor. DaimlerChrysler's strategy of using its shareholding in Hyundai to place a "z car" in the entry level segment of Asian markets (Melfi and Rother 2000) thus makes little sense in the above context. Overcapacity and export competition can also provide the impetus for takeovers or cooperation with competitors, as export planning under Options 1 and 2 can then be structured accordingly.

A reduction in export competition can also be achieved by lowering multi-market contacts with important competitors (Option 4). In addition, European automobile manufacturers can more strongly attempt to supply small markets that have been ignored by competitors. This would help in achieving geographical differentiation as regards competitors. Suzuki has been using this strategy for some time. A precondition for supplying to smaller markets is the development of suitable marketing strategies for such markets—a competence that is difficult to acquire and is not present in many large concerns. If this is not possible, European automobile manufacturers can, under Option 4, also try to positively influence the integration efforts of member countries of regional economic blocs, as the manufacturers would then encounter their competitors in a much bigger regional market instead of several small domestic markets. This would reduce the number of multi-market contacts. Under Option 4, acquisition or cooperation as justified under Option 3 is also possible.

CONCLUSION AND FUTURE PERSPECTIVES

This chapter has attempted to examine the problem of increasing overcapacities resulting from an industrial cluster-based development approach, a problem that has received scant attention in existing literature. It was possible to demonstrate that European automobile manufacturers need to be warned about overly optimistic export planning within the framework of industrialization strategies. However, realistic possibilities do exist for the European automotive industry to reduce rising export competition on global markets. These include the concentration of individual models at one location, clear guidelines for supplying markets, avoidance of export obligations, clear differentiation with regard to competitors, supplying to smaller markets, influencing the integration moves in new regional integration zones, and acquisition or cooperation. However, as markets can only be distributed once, the production facilities being established in developing countries will in the medium term replace a part of the exports from the Triad countries, although they may at present be purely market oriented direct investments by European automobile manufacturers or planned as public sector production enterprises for manufacturing a "mass car" for the domestic market.

The prevalent line of argument that market oriented foreign direct investment does not lead to any negative impacts in Europe (Klodt and Maurer 1996, 12) can no longer be sustained in a situation in which the setting up of overcapacities results in export competition and price pressure. In this scenario, which the automotive industry is presently experiencing, a reduction in capacities in Europe is as conceivable as a de-internationalization (Oesterle 1999). Countries attempting to develop using industrial cluster-based strategies must therefore make timely adjustments to their development path. Instead of promoting traditional input-output linkages, they should attempt to provide more support to knowledge transfers in an industrial network.

NOTES

1. See Hemmer (1988, 509–21) or Marin (1992) for the significance of industrialization within the framework of export-oriented industrialization strategies.

2. Empirical studies (Athukorala, Jayasuriya, and Oczkowski 1995) have demonstrated that industry structure and the regulatory environment influence export activities more than the nationality of the firm.

3. This definition applies to price premiums in the broader sense and is well established in literature (Klein and Leffer 1981, 624). A price increase due to differentiation without equivalent performance (Rao and Monroe 1996), on the other hand, is considered a price premium in the restricted sense.

4. Author's calculation. The current issues of the "Auto Catalogue" of the specialist journal Auto Motor Sport were used as database. There was no point in going farther back in time, as most Asian manufacturers entered the market only in the 1980s.

5. An alternative development process results from development strategies without significant industrialization efforts. Instead of capital-intensive industrial production, small and medium-sized enterprises or services are viewed as the cause of an increase in per capita income (Turq 1995, 35).

This paper does not pursue this type of development process for two reasons:

1. A development strategy concentrating on services overlooks the fact that, even in industrial countries, transaction services require a direct link to the manufacturing sector (Wallis and North 1986). During the development of economic structures based on the division of labor, more and more services are procured externally by manufacturing enterprises instead of being provided internally. Without the industrial base, there would be no need for these services.

2. Small and medium-sized enterprises generate only a small number of linkages and, more importantly, do not bring about further technological development, which could lead to cost savings via economies of scale.

6. Input-output tables record all transactions between various sectors. This allows an analysis of interdependencies between sectors that make it possible to simulate the impact of structural changes through industrial policy interventions, changes in demand, or changes in production capacities.

7. In fact, the initiative for automobile assembly or production did not originate so much from the governments of these countries as from individual, globally oper-

ating automobile manufacturers from industrial countries. Their decision to locate in countries with a particularly strong purchasing power, like Brazil, was influenced more by increased market potentials than by low wages. In addition to the fact that local manufacturing costs were in any case usually higher than those in industrial countries, the share of production wages in manufacturing costs has been constantly decreasing. In 1970, 25 percent of the cost of an automobile went toward wages and salaries, while the share in the year 2000 will be approximately 15 percent (O'Brien and Karmokolias 1994, 22).

8. The entry of a competitor into one's market can be countered by investments in his local market (cross-investments). This reaction can also be understood through oligopolistic parallel conduct. Such cross-investments, however, would only be relevant to competition between suppliers from industrial countries.

9. Image and brand transfer strategies can be used to expand or transfer brand image and the recognizability factor of established brands to other product groups (Bruhn 1995, 1449). Such strategies assume an adequate transfer potential (e.g., brand image, brand strength, and innovation power).

REFERENCES

Aliber, R. A. 1970. "The Multinational Enterprise in a Multiple Currency World." In *The Multinational Enterprise*, edited by John H. Dunning. London: Allen & Unwin.

Armstrong, H., and J. Taylor. 1985. *Regional Economics & Policy*. Deddington, Oxford: P. Allan.

Athukorala, P., S. Jayasuriya, and E. Oczkowski. 1995. "Multinational Firms and Export Performance in Developing Countries: Some Analytical Issues and New Empirical Evidence." *Journal of Development Economics* 46: 120–36.

Baum, J.A.C., and H. J. Korn. 1996. "Competitive Dynamics of Interfirm Rivalry." *Academy of Management Journal* 39: 255–91.

Bea, S. 1995. *Direktinvestitionen in Entwicklungsländern: Auswirkungen von Stabilisierungsmaßnahmen und Strukturreform in Mexiko*. Frankfurt: Lang.

Beaumont, J. R. "Location-Allocation Models and Central Place Theory." In *Spatial and Location-Allocation Models*, edited by A. Gosh and G. Rushton, 21–54. New York: Van Nostrand Reinhold.

Brada, J. C., and Y. Woo. 1994. "Export Competition Between Centrally Planned Economies and Korea." *Journal of Economic Integration* 9: 29–44.

Bruhn, J. 1995. "The Real Interest Differential Hypothesis, How Did It Fare in the 1980s?" *American Economist* 39 (2): 78–86.

Bulov, J. I., J. D. Geanakoplos, and P. D. Klemperer. 1985. "Multimarket Oligopoly: Strategic Substitutes and Complements." *Journal of Political Economy* 93: 488–511.

Chow, P.C.Y. 1989. "Causality Between Export Growth and Industrial Development." *Journal of Development Economics* 31: 414–17.

DeBresson, V., and X. Hu. 1999. "Identifying Clusters of Innovative Activity: A New Approach and a Toolbox." In *Boosting Innovation: The Cluster Approach*, edited by the Organization for Economic Cooperation and Development, 27–59. Paris: OECD proceedings.

Dixit, A. 1979. "A Model of Duopoly Suggesting a Theory of Entry Barriers." *The Bell Journal of Economics* 10: 20–32.

Dunning, J. H. 1988. "The Eclectic Paradigm of International Production: A Restatement and Some Possible Extensions." *Journal of International Business Studies* 19 (1): 1–31.

Gandolfo, G. 1998. *International Trade Theory and Policy*. Berlin: Springer.

Gundlach, E., and P. Nunnenkamp. 1996. *Falling Behind or Catching up: Developing Countries in the Era of Globalization*. Kiel, Germany: Kieler Diskussionsbeiträge.

Hemmer, T. 1998. "Performance Measurement Systems, Incentives, and the Optimal Allocation of Responsibilities." *Journal of Accounting & Economics* 25: 321–47.

Hoen, H. W., and E. van Leeuwen. 1991. "Upgrading and Relative Competitiveness in Manufacturing Trade: Eastern Europe Versus the Newly Industrializing Economy." *Weltwirtschaftliches Archiv* 127: 368–79.

Holden, M. 1996. "Economic Integration and Trade Liberalization in Southern Africa." World Bank Discussion Paper 342. Washington, D.C.

Hughes, K., and C. Oughton. 1993. "Diversification, Multi-Market Contact and Profitability." *Economica* 60: 203–24.

Hymer, Stephen. 1960. *The International Operations of National Firms: A Study of Direct Foreign Investment*. Cambridge, Mass.: M.I.T. Press.

Jin, J. C. 1995. "Export-Led Growth and the Four Little Dragons." *Journal of International Trade & Economic Development* 4: 203–15.

Kindleberger, C. A. 1969. *American Business Abroad*. New Haven, Conn.: Yale University Press.

Klodt, H., and R. Maurer. 1996. "Internationale Direktinvestitionen: Determinanten und Konsequenzen für den Standort Deutschland." Kieler Discussion Paper 284. Kiel, Germany: Institut für Weltwirtschaft.

Knickerbocker, F. T. 1973. *Oligopolistic Reaction and the Multinational Enterprise*. Cambridge, Mass.: M.I.T. Press.

Krugman, P. R., and A. J. Venables. 1995. "Globalization and the Inequalities of Nations." *Quarterly Journal of Economics* 111: 857–81.

Macharzina, K. 1982. "Theorie der internationalen Unternehmenstätigkeit: Kritik und Ansätze einer integrierten Modellbildung." In *Internationalisierung der Unter-nehmen als Problem der Betriebswirtschaftslehre*, edited by W. Lück and V. Trommsdorf, 111–43. Berlin: Springer-Verlag.

Marin, D. 1992. "Is the Export-Led Growth Hypothesis Valid for Industrialized Countries?" *Review of Economics and Statistics* 74: 678–88.

McCormick, D. 1999. "African Enterprise Clusters and Industrialization: Theory and Reality." *World Development* 27: 1531–51.

McGregor, P., K. Swales, and Y. Ping Yin. 1996. "A Long Run Interpretation of Regional Input-Output Analysis." *Journal of Regional Science* 36: 479–501.

Melfi, T., and F. Rother. 2000. "Kampf an allen Fronten." *Wirtschaftswoche* 31: 46–53.

Ministry of Trade and Industry (MITI), ed. *Industrial Master Plan (Malaysia 2020)*. 1996. Kuala Lumpur.

Muscatelli, V. A., A. A. Stevenson, and C. Montagna. 1994. "Intra-NIE Competition in Export of Manufacturers." *Journal of International Economics* 27: 42–63.

O'Brien, P., and Y. Karmokolias. 1994. "Radical Reforms in the Automotive Industry." IFC Discussion Paper 21. Washington, D.C.

Oesterle, M. J. 1999. "Fiktionen der Internationalisierungsforschung: Stand und

Perspektiven einer realitätsorientierten Theoriebildung." In *Internationales Management: Auswirkungen globaler Veränderungen auf Wettbewerb, Unternehmensstrategie und Märkte*, edited by J. Engelhard and W. Oechsler, 219–45. Wiesbaden, Germany: Gabler (Klaus Macharzina zum 60. Geburtstag).

Oxelheim, L., ed. 1993. *The Global Race for Foreign Direct Investments: Prospects for the Future*. Berlin: Springer-Verlag.

Perlitz, M. 2000. *Internationales Management*. 4th ed. Stuttgart, Germany: Lucius und Lucius.

Poapongsakorn, N., and B. Fuller. 1998. "The Role of Foreign Direct Investment and Production Networks in the Development of Thai Auto and Electronic Industries." In *Can Asia Recover Its Vitality*, ed. Institute of Developing Economics, 43–61. Tokyo.

Proff, H. 1995. "Strukturanpassungsprogramme und Industrialisierung in Schwarzafrika." *Internationales Afrikaforum* 31 (1): 69–83.

———. 2000. "Hybrid Strategies as Strategic Challenge—The Case of the German Automotive Industry." *Omega. The International Journal of Management Science* 4 (3/4): 1–13.

Proff, H., and H. V. Proff. 1996. "Effects Of AFTA as a World Market Oriented Regional Integration on the Industrial Development of the Participating Countries." *Indonesian Quarterly* 24 (4): 391–404.

Proff, H. V. 1998. "Modelling a Framework for Industrial Cores During Industrialisation and Deindustrialisation." Working Paper 94. Institute of Economics, Technical University, Darmstadt.

Rao, A. R., and K. B. Monroe. 1996. "Causes and Consequences of Price Premiums." *The Journal of Business* 69 (4): 511–25.

Rother, F. W. 1999. "Wem die Stunde schlägt." *Wirtschaftswoche* 3: 36–40.

Schmitz, H. 1992. "On the Clustering of Small Firms." *IDS Bulletin* 23: 64–49.

Stead, R., P. Curwen, and K. Lawer. 1996. *Industrial Economics: Theory, Application and Policy*. London: McGraw-Hill.

Stein, I. 1998. "Die Theorien der Multinationalen Unternehmung." In *Kompendium der Internationalen Betriebswirtschaftslehre*, 4th edition, edited by S. Schoppe, 35–153. München, Wien: Oldenbourg.

Tirole, J. 1995. *Industrieökonomik*. München: Vahlen.

Turq, D. 1995. "The Global Impact of Non-Japan Asia." *Long Range Planning* 28 (1): 31–40.

van Wegberg, M., and A. van Witteloostuijn. 1991. "Multimarket Competition: Entry Strategies and Entry Deterrence When the Entrant Has a Home Market." In *Microeconomic Contributions to Strategic Management*, edited by J. Thépot and R. A. Thiétart, 91–119. Amsterdam: North-Holland.

———. 1992. "Credible Entry Threats into Contestable Markets: A Symmetric Multi-Market Model of Contestability." *Economica* 59 (4): 437–52.

Venables, A. J. 1999. "The International Division of Industries: Clustering and Comparative Advantage in a Multi-Industry Model." *Scandinavian Journal of Economics* 101: 495–513.

Waelbroeck, J. 1998. "Half a Century of Development Economics: A Review Based on the Handbook of Development Economics." *World Bank Economic Review* 12: 323–52.

Wallis, J. J., and D. C. North. 1986. "Measuring the Transaction Sector in the American Economy, 1870–1970." In *Long Term Factors in American Economic Growth*, edited by S. L. Engerman and R. E. Gallman, 95–161. Chicago: University of Chicago Press.

Welge, M. K., and D. Holtbrügge. 1998. *Internationales Management.* Landsberg, Lech: mi Verl. Moderne Industrie.

World Bank, ed. 2000. *World Development Report 2000.* Washington, D.C.

CHAPTER 4

Multinationals and Technology Development in Latin America and East Asia

Andrés López and Marcela Miozzo

INTRODUCTION

The role of multinational enterprises (MNEs) in less developed countries has been examined extensively, generating passion among the proponents of differing views. One such view is that MNEs are the most important sources of new technology, and management and organizational techniques invaluable to less developed countries. Multinational corporations (MNCs) control new technologies (reportedly based on expensive research and development [R&D] and integrated into branded products), and they are often unwilling to sell their assets to unrelated parties (because of market failures, or because they may wish to utilize those technologies as part of their competitive—or anticompetitive—strategies). They also control mature technologies used in processes integrated across several countries (such as the assembly of semiconductors for export). A correlate of this view is that different kinds of spillovers arise from the presence of MNEs, including human capital spillovers (due to the training of workers and staff engineers), productivity spillovers (as MNCs tend to increase the level of competition in the foreign market and induce local domestic national firms to enhance their competitiveness), and technology spillovers (through the greater requirements regarding the quality, price, or terms of delivery, and so forth). Thus MNEs offer a significant positive contribution to a host country's productive and technological modernization (as emphasized by Blomstrom and Kokko 1996).

The contrasting view is that host countries may not be the beneficiaries, but may be worse off as a result of the presence and the activities of MNEs. The domestic rival firms or local enterprises may be displaced in their markets. The activities of MNCs may eventually lead to job losses. That is, the exercise of oligopolistic rent-extracting power, often exercised by means of the high level of subsidiaries' profit remittances use of transfer pricing have been negative contributions to host economies. In turn, spillovers are often weak, and may even be disastrous for local firms, which may be forced to reduce their production as a result of the increasing presence of MNEs in the domestic market (Aitken and Harrison 1999). Cited earlier by Lall (1998), MNEs engage in R&D activities in developing countries, and hence the excessive presence of MNCs may impede host countries from developing national technological capabilities.

This chapter focuses on the relationship between MNEs and the process of technological learning in two sets of non-European, less developed countries. The chapter presents two contrasting experiences: the successful development process of South Korea and Taiwan and the less successful industrialization experiences of Argentina, Brazil, and Mexico. The economic success of East Asian countries as compared to Latin American countries is not only reflected in trade performance but also in industrial transformation. The latter transformation does not refer to the rapid rise of industry in total gross national product (GNP) but rather to the rise of skill-intensive, high-value-added industries that are competitive at world market standards of cost and product specifications (Miozzo 2002).

Investments in human and physical capital are not the only factors driving this industrial transformation. An emphasis solely on investment assumes that technological knowledge is fully embodied in machinery and codified in blueprints and that all that less developed countries need to do is to access these and adopt them at relatively low cost, without significant uncertainty regarding the outcome of efforts. In contrast, students of technological change stress the partly codified, cumulative nature of technology, and its imperfect tradability (Nelson and Winter 1982; Rosenberg 1982). Because only part of the technology required by less developed countries is codified in blueprints and machine manuals and much of it is tacit, it requires a painstaking and difficult process of learning by doing and using. This chapter focuses on the way East Asian countries engaged in the difficult process of technological learning from foreign technology and the relative difficulties of Latin American countries in this respect. This chapter aims to highlight how the differing approaches in both regions toward MNCs have contributed to the success of East Asia vis-à-vis Latin America.

This paper compares the different approaches toward MNCs in East Asia and Latin America across four dimensions, discussed respectively in four sections. These dimensions include the following: first, openness toward MNCs; second, the extent to which the operation of MNCs has been embedded in the national industrialization process; third, the contribution of MNCs to the absorption of modern technology; and fourth, the strategies employed by domestic firms to utilize MNCs to overcome technological and market barriers. A final section draws implications for further research.

Openness toward MNCs

The extent of restrictions on foreign investment imposed by less developed countries is considered an important factor in explaining the pace of economic growth. For example, the view espoused by the Washington Consensus (Brewer 1991; Williamson 1990) argues that Latin American countries have been forced to borrow heavily to support an inward-oriented industrialization because they imposed numerous restrictions on foreign investment. Other studies have adopted more sophisticated measurement techniques and considered the qualitative details of the range of conditions typically accompanying restrictions on foreign investment. For example, Oman (1995) argues that in the case of East Asia, it is not only the level of restrictions on foreign direct investment (FDI) that matters, but also the fact that governments encouraged mainly minority and non-equity participation in local firms rather than in wholly-owned subsidiaries, as in Latin America. Indeed, contrary to the view of the Washington Consensus, Oman argues that closer inspection shows that Latin America has displayed a relatively high degree of openness to FDI, evident in the relatively large amount of FDI hosted in Latin America (see Table 4.1).

In Latin America, mainly U.S. and also European MNCs played a key role during the import substitution industrialization (ISI) period that began in the early 1930s. They invested to exploit domestic markets protected by high tariff and nontariff barriers (that is, market-seeking strategies aimed at jumping the tariff). MNC investments, which were made mostly through subsidiaries or majority-owned affiliates, were mainly concentrated in capital intensive sectors as well as in consumer goods sectors where oligopolistic

Table 4.1

FDI Inflows by Area and Period, 1970–1999 (average annual inflows in millions of dollars and percentage of world FDI inflows)

	S. Korea		Taiwan		Argentina		Brazil		Mexico	
	$	%	$	%	$	%	$	%	$	%
1970-1974	77	.5	57	.4	10	.1	852	5.8	413	2.8
1975-1979	71	.3	79	.3	120	.4	1823	6.7	790	2.9
1980-1984	71	.2	154	.4	439	1.1	2088	5.4	1500	3.8
1985-1989	688	.5	788	.6	730	.5	1425	1.1	2178	1.6
1990-1994	840	.4	1154	.6	3026	1.5	1590	.8	5895	2.9
1995-1999	4462	.8	1764	.3	10599	1.9	18918	3.5	10603	1.9

Source: Own elaboration on the basis of data from UNCTAD.

competition prevailed. Their main competitive advantages lay in the possession of process and product technologies originally developed in their headquarters, which were transferred, often with some minor and adaptive innovations, to their affiliates in the region. Argentina, Brazil, and Mexico were the countries where ISI advanced most, both in quantitative as well as in qualitative terms; they also were (and still are) the countries with the largest domestic markets in the region. Hence, it is not surprising to find that these three countries attracted the bulk of FDI inflows to Latin America during the ISI period.

In Argentina, as well as in Brazil and Mexico, the presence of MNCs dates from the nineteenth century, when they mainly operated in export-oriented commodity sectors as well as in public utilities. Later on, as argued above, MNCs became key agents of the ISI process, through investments in sectors such as automobiles, chemicals and petrochemicals, petroleum refining, heavy machinery, consumer durables, electronics, and food and beverages, within an environment of few sectoral restrictions to MNCs. By the early 1970s, MNCs' share in industrial production reached 33 percent in Argentina (Kosacoff and Bezchinsky 1993), 40 percent in Brazil (Fritsch and Franco 1991), and 28 percent in Mexico (Peres Nuñez 1990).

Even if MNCs' affiliates had been originally established to attend the respective domestic markets, they gradually increased their exports, mainly to other Latin American countries, as a result of both the adoption of export promotion policies (such as the BEFIEX program in Brazil and the *maquila* in Mexico) and agreements that liberalized to some extent intraregional trade within Latin America (such as the ALALC). The increase in MNCs' affiliates' exports was especially significant in Brazil, where MNCs' share in manufacturing exports reached 38 percent in 1980 (Fritsch and Franco 1991). Nonetheless, MNCs' export propensities (i.e., exports/sales ratios) were generally modest, and even lower than their import propensities (which were kept in relatively low levels due to the presence of high tariffs and local content requirements). The subsidiaries' profit remittances and the MNCs' use of transfer pricing also fed perceptions that they contributed to a structural deficit problem in the region (Oman 1995).

MNCs also played a key role in recent years, when most Latin American countries engaged in structural reforms programs. The reforms included the dismantling of most of the already few existing sectoral restrictions on FDI as well as most of the other regulations on the operation of MNCs (including profit remittances and local content). In fact, in the case of Argentina and especially Brazil, the growing interest of national and local governments in attracting investment flows have led to the establishment of fiscal and other types of investment incentives mostly at regional or sectoral levels. In some cases, like in the automobile industry, this situation led to some disputes and fears of investment diversion within the region (see Chudnovsky and López 2001).

Argentina, Brazil, and Mexico were among the top FDI receivers among developing countries in the nineties. FDI inflows received by the three countries reached 62 percent of total inflows to Latin America and 22 percent of inflows to developing countries between 1990 and 1999. As a consequence, the presence of MNCs significantly increased in the three economies. In both Argentina and Brazil the sales revenue of MNCs increased between 1990 and 1998 as a proportion of the sales of one thousand leading firms in the region. However, in contrast to what happened during the ISI stage, the pattern of FDI in the nineties showed significant differences between Argentina and Brazil, on the one hand, and Mexico, on the other. In Brazil, nearly 80 percent of FDI inflows between 1996 and 1999 went to the services sector, while the industrial sector received the other 20 percent (mainly concentrated in food and beverages, automobiles, and chemicals). In Argentina, around 22 percent of FDI between 1992 and 2000 went to the manufacturing industry (concentrated in the same sectors as in Brazil), while services (public utilities and banking attracted most of these inflows both in Argentina as well as in Brazil) accounted for more than 40 percent, and oil and mining received around 35 percent. The share of Europe as the source of FDI inflows reached 60 percent in Argentina and 55 percent in Brazil, while U.S. FDI inflows share was 20 percent in both countries. According to Chudnovsky and López (2002) and Laplane et al. (2001), most FDI in Argentina and Brazil is still market seeking, although the attractiveness of each national market is now enhanced, especially for FDI in Argentina, by the perspectives of accession to the markets of MERCOSUR countries. The domestic markets have been a decisive factor not only for FDI in services, but also for the bulk of FDI in manufacturing.

Recent FDI inflows in Mexico exhibit a very different pattern. Around 60 percent of FDI inflows in Mexico in the nineties came from the U.S. Between 1994 and 1998 nearly 65 percent of FDI inflows went to the manufacturing industry. The main destination sectors were transport equipment (mainly automobiles), food and beverages, chemicals, textiles, and electronics. A large part of U.S. FDI in Mexico was attracted by the possibility of engaging in efficiency-seeking strategies where they exploit the relatively low Mexican wages to export automobiles, electronics, and textiles products to the U.S., taking advantage of NAFTA.

In spite of these differences, neither in MERCOSUR countries nor in Mexico has there been a change in contribution to deficits by MNCs' operations. In the case of Argentina, it has been shown that MNCs' operations result in a high deficit due to the fact that their import propensities are much higher than their export propensities, while obviously MNCs make significant profit remittances to their headquarters (Chudnovsky and López 2002). In Brazil, MNCs in the manufacturing sector were operating with trade deficits in the late nineties (Laplane et al. 2001). Moreover, in both countries a sort of asymmetric integration into the international economy is visible. MNCs' affiliates from Argentina and Brazil produce for the internal market and export mainly to neighboring countries, while importing inputs and final goods mainly from developed countries (Chudnovsky and López 2001). A significant part of these trade flows is intrafirm: while MNCs' affiliates within MERCOSUR exchange goods within regional division-of-labor schemes, their imports come mostly from their headquarters and from other affiliates of the same corporation in developed countries.

In Mexico, although recent FDI inflows have fostered significant export increases, the main weaknesses of this strategy are the high level of concentration of exports in one market (U.S.), the creation of a dual economy, and the limited relationships of those investments with the rest of the Mexican economy. In this scenario, it is no surprise to find that MNCs' operations in export-oriented sectors have generated high trade and current account deficits, given their weak linkages with the host economy (Dussel Peters 2000).

What happened in East Asia? In contrast with Latin America's experiences, the government in Korea had a cautious attitude to FDI. Although it relied heavily on inflows of investment resources, these have largely been in the form of debt, not equity. Between 1945 and 1962 there were virtually no equity inflows. After this, FDI began to trickle in, encouraged by the normalization of relations with Japan in 1965, and liberalization in 1969. Some equity capital entered the country's export-processing zones and there were several ambitious high-tech projects in the 1970s, but between 1970 and 1999, foreign direct investment in Korea accounted for less than 15 percent of capital inflows and a very low percentage of gross fixed capital formation (see Table 4.2).

FDI played a negligible role in Korea during the early stages of development. Korea was too small and politically risky to attract much foreign investment interest. The decade of the 1950s in Korea was characterized by the pursuit of ISI strategies, financed in large part by American aid. In the late 1950s, significant economic reforms, mainly in exchange rate and import-control systems, shifted the structure of incentives toward an export-led strat-

Table 4.2
Ratio of FDI Inflows to Gross Fixed Capital Formation for Different Periods, 1971–1998 (%)

	1971-1975	1976-1980	1981-1985	1986-1990	1991-1995	1996-1998
S. Korea	1.9	.4	.5	1.2	.7	2.8
Taiwan	1.4	1.2	1.5	3.7	2.3	2.3
Argentina	.1	2.1	5.0	11.1	12.9	13.2
Brazil	4.2	3.9	4.3	1.7	2.4	12.4
Mexico	3.5	3.6	5.0	7.5	11.6	14.5

Source: UNCTAD (2000).

egy. This was accompanied by greater openness toward FDI and new relations with foreign buyers. Despite the increasing role of foreign direct investment in the outward-oriented development, Korea's development was based on national firms. State-owned firms and heavy government support acted as a check against the domination of MNCs especially in heavy industry.

The sectoral pattern of FDI in Korea changed over the years (see Byun and Wang 1995). From 1962 to 1966, two projects, a fertilizer plant and a refinery, accounted for over 70 percent of total foreign investment. The period of export takeoff (1967–76) led to a peak of investment in textiles, clothing, and electronics assembly. Investment in electronics continued during the 1970s, but shifted away from component assembly toward consumer and industrial electronics. Textiles and clothing investment became negligible, while investments in machinery, transport equipment, and chemicals showed large increases during the 1970s. This pattern reflects the growth of investment in industries aimed at the domestic market. This shifted in the 1980s as foreign investment in light industries became unprofitable. There were major changes in the 1980s, due to difficulties arising from the negative effects of the Heavy and Chemical Industry Plan of the 1970s. The resulting plan for technological upgrading included the liberalization of foreign investment rules, which led to a rise in the share of manufacturing sectors open to FDI from 69 to 85 percent. Pressures from the U.S. resulted in additional liberalization in the service sector.

Government policy toward the import of technology through licensing arrangements was also liberalized during the late 1970s and the early 1980s, leading to increasing royalty payments (from $100 million before liberalization to over $1 billion in 1990) (Byun and Wang 1995). However, the number of cases of technology licensing has fallen since 1989, as foreign firms have become more reluctant to share technology with Korean firms. In turn, in the late 1980s and in the 1990s, the Korean government has attempted to implement policies to attract FDI, through liberalization, deregulation, the lowering of restrictions to offshore capital, the modification of laws governing land acquisition, and the protection of intellectual property (Byun and Wang 1995).

Despite the relatively small magnitude of foreign investment in Korea, however, the role of MNCs in technology transfer and upgrading was important, especially in export-processing zones. The relative importance of these declined by the mid-1970s as other specialized zones aimed at both exports and the development of heavy industry were established, mostly with extensive participation by domestic and state-owned firms. Nevertheless, at the Masan export-processing zone, according to Byun and Wang (1995), nine thousand workers and technicians were trained overseas.

FDI in Taiwan has also been very low, although its role gradually increased over time (see Table 4.1). In the 1960s and 1970s the overseas Chinese accounted for 29 percent of FDI, falling to an average of 10 percent during

1981–88. During this period, Japan headed the list of non-Chinese investors (with a 30 percent share of all foreign investment), followed by the U.S. (28 percent) and Europe (15 percent). There were great fluctuations in the 1980s with Japanese and U.S. shares of investment. During the 1980s, U.S. investments increased as firms turned away from the disappointing Chinese market, while the rising yen prompted Japan to relocate some manufacturing industry to lower-cost Taiwan (OECD 1991).

Until the late 1980s, over 90 percent of FDI in Taiwan went to manufacturing, partly because of restrictions to entry into other sectors, such as finance and insurance. Between 1952 and 1986 the largest share of investment was in electrical and electronic appliances (30 percent of the total), followed by chemicals (15 percent); services (11 percent); machinery, equipment, and instruments (10 percent); basic metals and metal products (7 percent); nonmetallic minerals (6 percent); and banking and insurance (5 percent). Electronics, chemicals and machinery, equipment and instruments, have been the most important sectors for non-Chinese foreign investment, while overseas Chinese investment is relatively large in services such as hotels and construction, as well as in textiles and garments (OECD 1991). Having built competitive export industries, Taiwan started attracting some of the biggest foreign MNCs to invest in Taiwan to supply Taiwanese firms. For example, one $235-million chemical plant was set up by Imperial Chemical Industries to produce a chemical to make polyester for the Taiwanese makers of polyester fiber.

Indeed, one of the key contrasts between East Asia and Latin America is the emphasis that the former region made on the promotion of new forms of investment (NFI), including majority locally owned joint ventures, licensing, subcontracting, and other contractual arrangements between local and foreign firms. The tendency to promote NFI over wholly- or majority-owned FDI emerged in Latin America as well, but was significantly more marked in East Asia, favored by the smaller presence of U.S. investment and the strong propensity of Japanese firms in industries undergoing restructuring in their home economy to relocate in East Asia through NFI. Furthermore, in East Asia, emphasis was placed on NFI as a means to build up local firms' manufacturing export capabilities. In Latin America, where accumulated FDI in manufacturing was considerably greater, NFI tended to be more oriented to serving the local market, and the promotion of manufactured exports tended to rely more on FDI-related fiscal incentives and performance requirements. One NFI promoted in East Asia was the technical cooperation agreement. In the case of Taiwan, the sectoral distribution of agreements follows the pattern of industry concentration, with electrical and electronics appliances taking the lead, followed by chemicals, machinery, equipment and instruments, and basic metals and metal products. Most of the technical cooperation agreements involved foreign investors as technology licensors and were for developing new products, improving product quality, cutting costs, increasing exports, increasing local content, and improving management.

Overall, therefore, this section has shown that East Asia imposed greater restrictions on MNCs than Latin America. East Asia also encouraged NFI rather than wholly owned subsidiaries. Moreover, a problem in the operation of MNCs in Latin America is that they have tended to contribute to trade and current account deficits. The next section will examine a closely related theme—the extent to which the FDI that is allowed into these regions has been embedded in the national development strategy.

MNCs AS ENABLING OR HINDERING THE DIRECTION OF NATIONAL INDUSTRIALIZATION

In this section, we explore the extent to which the dominance of MNCs represents a constraint on the ability of the state in less developed countries to direct the industrialization process. It appears that despite a strong export orientation, East Asian countries have not been fully integrated with the world economy from their early stages of development. Rather, integration has been strategic, tailored to specific sectoral needs and their level of industrial and economic development, and sequenced accordingly. Particularly in Korea, and to a lesser extent in Taiwan, the state has played a much more restrictive role vis-à-vis foreign capital and technology than has generally been the case in Latin America, subordinating foreign investment to national development strategy.

As we have seen, FDI was not such a significant factor in Korea or Taiwan as in Latin America. In sectors where FDI has played a significant role, for example, in textiles and electronics, government policy has been a major influence, promoting joint ventures, screening imported technologies, and bargaining over local content agreements. Such practices have firmly embedded MNCs within a national industrialization strategy. Also, the more dynamic Japanese FDI and technology, which was incorporated in the form of minority capital or non-equity participation in domestic firms, was a very important mechanism to ensure technological upgrades in East Asia.

Korea is perhaps the archetypal case of a country where export-led industrialization has been overwhelmingly directed and controlled by nationals (Amsden 1989; Chang 1993; Jenkins 1991). The Korean government combined selective ISI with forceful export promotion, protecting and subsidizing targeted industries. As a key part of this strategy, it stimulated the development of large domestic private firms, the *chaebol*, to enter into scale-intensive, midtechnology areas (historically, electrical machinery, basic chemicals, automobiles, consumer electronics, and commodity semiconductors more recently), to build endogenous technological capabilities and develop an international image to facilitate exports.

Korean policy makers regarded the assimilation of advanced technology as vital for industrial upgrading. To them, this meant tight state control over FDI, allowing FDI only when other means of accessing technology were unavailable. The persistent savings gap had to be filled, but Korean policy makers preferred (state-guaranteed) foreign loans to foreign direct investment. As a result, the share of FDI in total foreign capital inflow (except foreign aid) in 1962–83 was a mere 5 percent (Chang 1993). There was careful screening of foreign investment, widespread government interference, and extensive reporting requirements and control required from MNCs. MNCs were induced to sell their equity to local firms once technology transfer was completed (UNCTAD 1999). Although such restrictions weakened in the late 1980s, foreign majority ownership was practically banned, with some rare exceptions, outside the export processing zones. The fact that only 6 percent of MNCs in Korea are wholly-owned subsidiaries, compared to 50 percent in Mexico and 60 percent in Brazil in the early 1990s, suggests a substantial degree of state control over foreign direct investment in relation to ownership (Chang 1993).

In order to upgrade industry, industrial policy targeted key sectors that had priority in acquiring subsidized credits and rationed foreign exchange, state investment funds, preferential tax treatment import protection, and entry restrictions. The state has been willing and able to withdraw support whenever productive performance has lagged and to force inefficient firms into mergers, sales, and liquidations (e.g., after the investment boom of the late 1970s there was a reorganization of the heavy and chemical industries, the car industry, the naval diesel engine industry, and heavy electrical machinery; and later in 1984–88 there was reorganization in the declining shipping, overseas construction, and fertilizer sectors). The state encouraged firms to build plants of efficient production scale in high productivity sectors, which compelled them to start exporting as soon as possible in order not to incur losses due to low capacity utilization (Chang 1993).

Although Taiwan's policy toward foreign capital has been less restrictive than that of Korea, it has also been selective in its approach toward FDI (Wade 1990). The government evaluates foreign investment proposals in terms of how much they open new markets, contribute to increasing exports, and transfer technology. Two landmark cases are cited by Wade (1990) that set a pattern for future agreements between the government and MNCs. In one, the government allowed Singer Sewing Machine Company to set up a plant in 1963 despite the objection of local assemblers and suppliers. The government imposed that Singer locally procure 83 percent of its required parts one year after start-up and assist local components producers to meet its specifications. Singer did not in fact meet such a stringent local requirement but contributed satisfactorily to the transfer of technology and the upgrading of local industry. In the other case, in the 1960s, the government required the U.S. National Distiller and Chemical Corporation, five years after start-up, to transfer half its shares to Chinese nationals (i.e., to create a 50/50 joint venture). It also forbade it to establish production facilities in downstream sectors and obliged it to export any surpluses over domestic needs.

Key sectors of the economy are controlled in Taiwan by the state and a decentralized network of small and medium-sized firms. A number of large state-owned firms dominate the large scale capital-intensive sectors (such as steel). A multitude of smaller enterprises, set up with family and cooperative savings and supported by bank credit, focus on the export trade in consumer goods. Overall, their share and the share of manufacturing output and exports accounted for by MNCs are similar to those of Korea.

Korea and Taiwan offer good illustrations of the way governments act to discipline business groups and domestic firms in order to encourage them to be the agents of industrialization rather than the MNCs. Licenses to expand the scale of production of firms in Korea were granted only as long as firms could prove satisfactory performance in exports, R&D, and in the introduction of new products (Amsden 1989). Taiwan has relied more on fiscal incentives, administered selectively to promote industrial priorities. Subsidies to export, however, were also tied to targets such as R&D spending and personnel training (Wade 1990).

In contrast, in Latin America the transition toward a more advanced ISI stage in the 1950s was accompanied by strong efforts to attract foreign capital, technology, and entrepreneurial capabilities through FDI. Foreign capital was granted equal national treatment with local capital, and in some cases even got preferential treatment. These policies were applied mainly in a nonselective way, and led to most of the dynamic, high-growth, high-profit sectors during the secondary import-substitution period being dominated by foreign capital. As a result, foreign capital played a much more significant role in Latin America than in East Asia, both in terms of industrial output and exports (see Table 4.3). During the ISI, MNCs' affiliates showed higher efficiency and productivity levels than their local competitors and were closer to the international frontier in terms of technologies and scale (Peres Nuñez 1990; Sourrouille, Lucángeli, and Kosacoff 1985; Wilmore 1993). However, they often employed obsolete product and process technologies, and their scales were far from those of their headquarters or from those of the affiliates in developed countries, since Latin American domestic markets were relatively small. In turn, they operated with higher levels of vertical integration than their counterparts in developed countries due to the lack of qualified domestic suppliers and the high tariff barriers (Katz and Kosacoff 1989).

These characteristics of FDI during the ISI are not surprising given the incentives structure that arose from the economic policy regime of that period. Latin American industrialization was driven by the objective of transforming the economic structure in order to make it less dependent on natural resources, but little emphasis was placed on the need to promote or upgrade industries progressively and to ensure international competitiveness. Thus, in contrast to East Asia, the level of competition in the domestic markets was not intense and the industrial policies did not contain instruments aimed at guaranteeing that the subsidies received by the manufacturing firms were tied

Table 4.3
Share of FDI Inflows in Manufactured Exports and Output (%)

Country	Exports	Output
Korea (1978)	23	19
Taiwan (1980)	21	<25
Argentina (early 1980s)	27	33[a]
Brazil (1980)	38	40[a]
Mexico (late 1970s)	36	28[a]

Note: [a]Data for the early 1970s.
Sources: Jenkins (1991); Fritsch and Franco (1991); Peres Nuñez (1990); Azpiazu (1992); Kosacoff and Bezchinsky (1993).

to effective performance requirements. Many explanations have been offered by Auty (1994) and other writers.

However, in the three Latin American countries that we are examining in this chapter there were also large state enterprises in sectors such as steel, petroleum, and petrochemicals, as well as a growing presence of domestic conglomerates, which were fostered by state policies, especially in Brazil and Mexico. For instance, since the late 1960s, the Brazilian state promoted joint ventures between MNCs, domestic conglomerates, and public enterprises in sectors such as petrochemicals and telecommunications equipment, with the objective of encouraging the transfer of technological and productive assets from MNCs to the local agents. However, state support to local business groups in Brazil and Mexico has been constrained by income distribution considerations (Amsden 2001). Latin American business groups, especially in Argentina, have also been associated with rent-seeking behavior and the support they received from the state often lacked the quid pro quo or reciprocity control mechanisms that had been the norm in East Asian countries. Furthermore, few of them advanced to high-tech or skilled labor-intensive sectors (although Brazilian groups were relatively ambitious in this regard), and when they did, the rate of success was not particularly high due to the lack of adequate government stimulus and the weaknesses of the domestic science and technology infrastructure.

It is therefore no surprise to find that by the mid-nineties Latin American business groups were dominant in nondurable consumer goods or scale intensive and resources-based industries (such as beverages, textiles, agroindustry, petrochemicals, pulp and paper, glass, steel and cement), while they had a low presence in high-tech activities such as informatics and telecommunications equipment (see Evans 1995), biotechnology, or fine chemicals as well as in the automotive industry (see Garrido and Peres 1998). Furthermore, some business groups that had acquired significant productive and technical competences in sectors such as auto parts were acquired by MNCs in the nineties. Domestic business groups have also faced increasing difficulties in

competing in sectors where marketing capabilities and the possession of international brands are key competitive assets. Hence, domestic business
groups in Latin America have been far from playing the same role as their
East Asian counterparts. Even if many of them have made significant investments abroad (see Chudnovsky and López 2000), they have not led the process
of technological and productive modernization of their home economies. As
a result, it is MNCs that have been dominant in most of those sectors where
significant R&D or technical skills, as well as international brands, are the key
elements of market competition.

In summary, both Latin America and East Asia regarded the assimilation
of advanced technology as important for industrialization. However, in Korea
(and to a lesser extent in Taiwan) this meant tight control and selectivity
toward MNCs. In these countries, domestic business groups and networks of
small firms, respectively, were the agents of industrialization, encouraged by
subsidies and performance targets. MNCs were embedded in these countries'
strategies of industrial transformation. In contrast, in Latin America, MNCs
played a more significant role in industrial output and exports. The limited
efficiency of their operations acted as an obstacle against their serving as a
competitive stimulus for domestic firms.

MNCs' CONTRIBUTION TO THE ABSORPTION OF MODERN TECHNOLOGY

The success of East Asia compared to Latin America is not only reflected
in trade performance but also in industrial transformation. Even if East Asian
countries began as importers of technology, they adopted a selective strategy
for technology transfer, prioritizing those channels that could open the way
to domestic learning processes, and they consistently tried to enhance domestic absorption capabilities in order to make more efficient use of the imported technologies (Nelson and Pack 1999). In this way, they could enter
progressively into more technology-intensive industries.

Taiwan and Korea employed a number of mechanisms to acquire foreign
technology. In Taiwan an important mechanism was the information provided
by purchasers of their exports, in particular, the continuous transfer of knowledge to Taiwanese firms by importers desiring lower cost, higher quality products in the 1960s and 1970s (Pack 2001). The purchasers of exports in the
U.S. and other industrialized countries (especially Sears, Roebuck and Co.;
Kmart; and JCPenney) transferred considerable knowledge of production engineering and quality control to local firms. In a number of cases they specified
the equipment to be acquired and laid out the production process for new
products. Also, in the process of production for export, firms utilized familiar
techniques used for production in the domestic market, rather than shifting
to the much more capital-intensive techniques used, for example, in Latin
America. Also, in Taiwan and Korea, the use of nonproprietary information

or reverse engineering during much of its early industrialization contributed to the absorption of technology. Taiwan and Korea employed older machinery and manufactured standardized products that were not subject to proprietary restrictions (Amsden 1989; Pack 2001). Knowledge about how to improve the utilization of this equipment as well as how to introduce modifications of product specifications was readily available at low cost in trade literature and engineering publications, and from independent consultants. Third, Taiwan in particular obtained knowledge from nationals who were educated abroad and had been employed in firms in industrial countries for a considerable period. This became a more important mode of technology transfer as industrialization shifted to more capital and technology-intensive sectors in which products and specialized equipment were protected by patents and characterized by tacit knowledge (Pack 2001).

The development of the Korean steel industry is a good illustration of how Korea succeeded in an explicit strategy of accumulating indigenous technological capability through importing technology not only related to investment capability but also to production capability. The initial involvement of foreign companies and engineers was high as Korea possessed little knowledge about modern steel-making methods. Subsequently, the government increased local participation ensuring that foreign equipment supplier firms partnered with domestic ones (D'Costa 1994). One of the distinguishing characteristics of the turnkey transfer was the degree to which local engineers actively participated in it, learning what was being taught them by Japanese and Austrian counterparts, assimilating what was not being taught them directly (Amsden 1989). Thus, MNCs in Korea and Taiwan have played an important role in the transfer of technology to Taiwan and Korea both directly and indirectly.

In contrast, during the ISI, the governments in Latin American countries chose FDI as the main vehicle of technology transfer. They did little to stimulate endogenous R&D efforts (it was in Brazil where those efforts reached a relatively higher level), the domestic technological infrastructure was mostly weak, and little emphasis was placed on developing absorption capabilities aimed not only at adopting, adapting, and using efficiently the imported technologies, but also as a basis for the development of an evolutionary process of endogenous technological learning. It must be acknowledged that even if they rarely engaged in formal R&D activities, MNCs' affiliates have generated spillovers through human resource policies of training and of developing local suppliers. Blomstrom (1986) found evidence of positive spillovers. MNCs' affiliates also had to develop engineering teams dedicated to adapting the product and process technologies of their headquarters to the idiosyncratic features of the host countries (Dahlman 1984; Katz 1999). However, due to the lack of incentives to attain world competitiveness standards, the weak domestic technological infrastructure, and the limited absorption capabilities of most local firms, technology spillovers from MNCs were often limited.

In the nineties, FDI was again a major channel of technology transfer in Latin America. MNCs in the manufacturing sector operate in an environment where competitive pressures are higher than in the past, while privatized utilities are under regulations that push for quality and efficiency enhancements. Hence, it is not surprising to find that MNCs' affiliates' product and process technologies are now closer to the international frontier than during the ISI period, and that significant efficiency and productivity gains have been obtained by those affiliates in the nineties.

However, in the case of Argentina and Brazil, the spillovers from this modernization process seem to be weak (see Miozzo 2000 for the role of MNCs in the Argentine auto industry in the nineties). First, MNCs' affiliates have tended to replace domestic suppliers by imported inputs and capital goods, taking advantage of the trade liberalization process. Second, the increased presence of MNCs, instead of acting as a stimulus for domestic competitors to update their technological, productive, and managerial assets, made many local entrepreneurs go out of business and/or sell their plants to foreign investors. Third, affiliates seldom engage in significant R&D activities, while their technological interactions with domestic firms and institutions are weak. For instance, Brazilian MNCs' subsidiaries have significantly reduced their local technological and innovative activities in the 1990s, productive and innovative networks are being disarticulated, and there is no new significant integration between the recent investments and the local R&D infrastructure (Cassiolato et al. 2001). In turn, even if MNCs' affiliates present higher rates of innovative performance and technological intensity than their national counterparts, most of their technological activities are about the adaptation of products and processes originated abroad (Costa and Queiroz 2001; Quadros et al. 1999).

Nonetheless, the FDI sectoral distribution and the MNCs' trade patterns reflect the structural differences among MERCOSUR countries. Brazil clearly appears as the country that attracts more FDI in scale-intensive and high-tech sectors. State policies that grant fiscal incentives to investments in sectors such as informatics, electronics, and telecommunications equipment have contributed to attracting significant FDI inflows. In order to receive those incentives, MNCs must commit to spend at least 5 percent of their sales in R&D activities (and 40 percent of those expenditures must be made through R&D agreements with local universities and research institutions). In turn, in some sectors, Brazilian subsidiaries of MNCs are participating in global product development networks in niche products that are sold in Brazil as well as in other developing countries. Hence, Brazil is seemingly being consolidated as a peripheral product development center in specific areas of product design (Carneiro Dias and Ribeiro Galina 2000; Quadros et al. 2000). In some cases, for instance in the automobile industry, this trend has been accompanied by the dismantling of adaptive innovation activities which were performed in Argentinean affiliates, some of which now depend upon Brazilian affiliates in that area (Kosacoff and Porta 1997). However, even in Brazil the bulk of goods with high value added and/or technological sophistication are exported to MERCOSUR and to the rest of Latin America. At the same time, similar, but presumably more complex, goods are imported (parts, components, capital goods, inputs, or final goods) from industrialized countries (Laplane et al. 2001).

In the case of Mexico, much of the FDI in the nineties was attracted to high-tech sectors, including TV receivers and computers. However, these investments had a very limited impact on the Mexican economy, since most of the parts and components were imported. Given time, these kinds of investments could increase their linkages with the host economy. Nonetheless, previous experience does not allow for much optimism, since the government has tried to increase the linkages of the *maquila* since its start in the sixties without having much success (Dussel Peters 2000). Hence, FDI in high-tech sectors are mostly an enclave in the Mexican economy.

Overall, East Asia has put in place mechanisms to ensure the acquisition and assimilation of foreign technology (information from purchasers of their exports, nonproprietary technology, returning nationals, partnering with foreign firms). In contrast, little emphasis was placed in Latin America on developing absorption capabilities.

LEARNING STRATEGIES OF DOMESTIC FIRMS

In East Asia, domestic firms exploited their relations with MNCs to their advantage, learning production methods, reverse engineering products, and accumulating design skills. While in Korea these strategies relied on the scale and financial power of the large *chaebol*, in Taiwan the key was the speed and agility of hundreds of local entrepreneurs, in both cases doing incremental process and product improvements on borrowed technology on the shop floor (Amsden 1989; Wade 1990).

Hobday (1994, 1995) focuses on the strategies of domestic firms in East Asia to utilize foreign connections to overcome technology and market barriers in electronics. Foreign buyers, MNCs, OEM (original equipment manufacture) arrangements, and joint ventures and licenses were exploited by domestic firms to progress from simple assembly tasks to more sophisticated product design and development capabilities. East Asian firms travel backwards along the product life cycle, from the standardized market and technology stages to the more uncertain, early design-intensive and complex innovation stages.

In Korea, large vertically integrated firms used the needs of demanding export customers as a focusing device to upgrade their technology. During the mid-1960s U.S. MNCs entered Korea to assemble products using cheap labor, while importing most inputs. As Korean firms acquired sufficient skills, leading Japanese MNCs formed joint ventures in the late 1960s and early

1970s with Korean firms. OEM was used as an alternative to joint ventures. Under OEM, MNCs helped train engineers, select equipment, and supply materials and capital goods to domestic Korean firms. OEM enabled Korean firms to export large volumes of goods under foreign brand names and distribution channels, but it was also a training school for Korean firms to learn skills from Japanese and American MNCs. Hence, Korean firms were able to expand into more sectors, overcome barriers to entry, and access Japanese-controlled channels of distribution into Western markets. OEM and licensing were important for products that were new to Korea (advanced computer terminals, large telecommunications exchanges, and semiconductors). As products matured and capabilities were learned, OEM became less important (such as in audio and TV). However, the lack of high-quality international brand images was felt by many Korean firms to be a long-term constraint on growth. The strategy of larger firms was to invest heavily in R&D and brand awareness campaigns. The results of these strategies are still unfolding, with some firms retreating to OEM (called ODM—own-design manufacture—in Taiwan) in the early 1990s after sustaining heavy losses in own-brand investments.

By the late 1980s, many of the goods purchased were designed and specified, as well as manufactured, by the local firm, while foreign buyers simply branded the ready-made product. Korean firms carried out some or all of the product and process tasks, according to a general design layout provided by the MNCs. This signified more advanced design skills and often new production technologies. As large firms approached the technology frontier, other learning mechanisms became important, particularly in-house R&D efforts to develop new products and to assimilate advanced foreign technologies. Also, strategic partnerships with foreign firms, with Korean firms using their technological and other assets to bargain for leading edge technologies, and access to markets in area sectors such as consumer electronics and telecommunications, became important. Also, during the 1980s, Korean firms began investing heavily in overseas high-tech firms.

The story is similar in Taiwan, with industry benefiting considerably from investment by MNCs, joint ventures, and foreign buyers. In contrast to Korea, however, industrial development relied on a multitude of small and medium-sized firms and FDI continued to play a central role throughout the 1980s and 1990s. Under OEM and ODM, exports focused domestic learning efforts and helped to pull Taiwan's competitive capabilities forward. The Taiwanese case shows how hundreds of tiny latecomer firms clustered together behind the electronics frontier to exploit market opportunities, indicating that the large-scale mass market approach followed by the *chaebol* is not the only route for less developed countries. In electronics, sewing machines, footwear, bicycles, and other fast-growing export industries, small firms made themselves indispensable to foreign buyers and MNCs and forged backward links to other industries. In sectors of low capital intensity such as electronics assembly and textile manufacturing, the government intervened less than in large-scale, complex technological fields and intermediate goods. In the latter, direct intervention and financial support from the government enabled state-owned enterprises (in petrochemicals, shipbuilding, and automobiles) to prosper in the 1960s.

As firms became internationally competitive, they found joint ventures and licenses insufficient. The latest vintage of technology was not available from the innovators. They had to import technology by going into new arrangements (franchising or OEM) and/or by investing in their own R&D to build upon foreign technology. Some firms became outward investors to engage in alliances or take over innovative firms abroad.

In Latin America the extent to which domestic business groups utilized MNCs to climb the ladder in technology and market access has been clearly lower than in East Asia. Take for instance the petrochemical sector, where local firms made significant inroads in the three countries under study. It was only in Brazil, through the so-called tripartite model in which state funds were invested along with domestic and foreign firms—a three-way joint venture—where those firms traveled though a technological learning process that allowed them to gradually, but not totally, reduce their dependence on foreign technology providers (see Chudnovsky and López 1997). However, even in Brazil this was more the exception than the rule.

In turn, in the nineties, part of the FDI operations was made through joint ventures with local Latin American partners. However, many of these operations have ended in the total acquisition of the domestic firm by the foreign partner. Hence, seldom have they been a stimulus for technological, productive, and marketing learning processes in domestic business groups.

In sum, domestic firms in East Asia used their relations with MNCs, OEM, and licenses to develop technology and marketing capabilities in contrast with Latin American firms. More recently, East Asian are investing in in-house R&D and marketing efforts.

CONCLUSIONS AND FURTHER RESEARCH ISSUES

This chapter has compared and contrasted the role of multinationals in Latin America and East Asia. It has reviewed the history and recent experience of multinationals in both regions in the context of different development strategies. The presence of multinationals has been and remains stronger in Latin America than in Taiwan or Korea. This is not to say that multinationals have not played an important role in the favorable economic performance of East Asian countries, where the state has played a substantial degree of control, embedding MNCs in a national industrialization strategy. Also, domestic firms used their involvement with multinationals in East Asia in an explicit strategy of accumulating indigenous technological capability.

In contrast, in Latin America during the ISI, MNCs did little to integrate host countries into the world economy, and their technology and productive spillovers were weak in a scenario of excessively inward-looking economic policies and poor technological and scientific domestic infrastructures. In the 1990s, in an environment of more open trade regimes, MNCs' affiliates had to operate closer to the international efficiency frontier, but in Argentina and Brazil they kept mainly focused on domestic markets (while reducing their linkages with local suppliers and science and technology institutions), while in Mexico significant export-oriented investments were undertaken, but with weak linkages to the host economy. In sum, MNCs' contributions to the economic development of Latin American countries have been weaker than what was expected by proponents of greater openness toward FDI.

Besides exploring in more depth the reasons that are behind the contrasting roles of MNCs in East Asia and Latin America, two areas of research should receive further attention in a research agenda on multinationals in less developed countries. First, the privatization of many state-owned firms operating in manufacturing and services is creating new business opportunities for multinationals. The role of multinationals in the privatization process, the extent to which multinationals contribute to the performance and efficiency of privatized firms, and the ways in which this contribution can be evaluated should be one of the priorities in future research.

Also, much less attention has been devoted to investment by multinationals in the service sector of less developed countries. The present round of international trade liberalization negotiations has some important new features, linked to the particular impact of technical change in the service sector (Miozzo and Soete 2001). These issues raise new research and policy questions on the operations and business practices of MNCs in less developed countries.

REFERENCES

Aitken, B., and A. Harrison. 1999. "Do Domestic Firms Benefit from Direct Foreign Investment? Evidence from Venezuela." *American Economic Review* 89: 605–18.

Amsden, A. 1989. *Asia's Next Giant: South Korea and Late Industrialization.* New York: Oxford University Press.

———. 2001. *The Rise of "The Rest": Challenges to the West from Late-Industrializing Economies.* New York: Oxford University Press.

Auty, R. M. 1994. "Industrial Policy Reform in Six Large Newly Industrializing Countries: The Resource Curse Thesis." *World Development* 22 (1).

Azpiazu, D. 1992. "Las empresas transnacionales en una economía en transición: la experiencia argentina en los años ochenta." Paper prepared for the Simposio de Alto Nivel sobre la Contribución de las Empresas Transnacionales al Crecimiento y el Desarrollo de América Latina y el Caribe, Santiago de Chile.

Blomstrom, M. 1986. "Foreign Investment and Productive Efficiency: The Case of Mexico." *Journal of Industrial Economics* 35 (1).

Blomstrom, M., and A. Kokko. 1996. "Multinational Corporations and Spillovers."

Working Paper Series in Economics and Finance, no. 99. Stockholm: Stockholm School of Economics.

Brewer, T. 1991. *Foreign Direct Investment in Developing Countries: Patterns, Policies, and Prospects.* Washington, D.C.: The World Bank.

Byun, H., and Y. Wang. 1995. "Technology Transfer and Multinational Corporations: The Case of South Korea." *Journal of Asian Economics* 6 (2): 201–16.

Carneiro Dias, A. V., and S. Ribeiro Galina. 2000. "Global Product Development: Some Case Studies in the Brazilian Automotive and Telecommunication Industries." Paper prepared for the Fourth International Conference on Technology Policy and Innovation, Curitiba, Brazil.

Cassiolato, J, H. Lastres, M. Szapiro, and M. A. Vargas. 2001. "Local Systems of Innovation in Brazil, Development and Transnational Corporations: A Preliminary Assessment Based on Empirical Results of a Research Project." Paper prepared for the Nelson and Winter Conference, Danish Research Unit for Industrial Dynamics (DRUID), Aalborg, Denmark, June.

Chang, H. J. 1993. "The Political Economy of Industrial Policy in Korea." *Cambridge Journal of Economics* 17: 131–57.

Chudnovsky, D., and A. López. 1997. *Auge y ocaso del capitalismo asistido. La industria petroquímica latinoamericana.* Buenos Aires: CEPAL/IDRC/Alianza Editorial.

———. 2000. "A Third Wave of FDI from Developing Countries. Latin American Multinationals in the 1990s." *Transnational Corporations* 9 (2).

———. 2001. "La inversión extranjera directa en el MERCOSUR: Un análisis comparativo." In *El boom de inversion extranjera directa en el MERCOSUR*, edited by D. Chudnovsky. Madrid: Siglo XXI.

———. 2002. "Estrategias de las empresas transnacionales en la Argentina de los años 90." *Revista de la CEPAL* 76 (April).

Costa, I., and S. Queiroz. 2001. "FDI and Technological Capabilities in the Brazilian Industry." Fifth International Conference on Technology Policy and Innovation, Delft, Netherlands.

Dahlman, C. 1984. "Foreign Technology and Indigenous Technological Capability in Brazil." In *Technological Capability in the Third World*, edited by M. Fransman and K. King. Hong Kong: Macmillan.

D'Costa, A. 1994. "State, Steel, and Strength: Structural Competitiveness and Development in South Korea." *The Journal of Development Studies* 31 (1): 44–81.

Dunning, J. 1994. "Re-evaluating the Benefits of Foreign Direct Investment." *Transnational Corporations* 3 (1).

Dussel Peters, E. 2000. "La inversión extranjera en México." Serie Desarrollo Productivo, no. 80. Santiago, Chile: CEPAL.

Enos, J. L., and W. H. Park. 1988. *The Adoption and Diffusion of Imported Technology: The Case of Korea.* London: Croom Helm.

Evans, P. 1995. *Embedded Autonomy: States and Industrial Transformation.* Princeton: Princeton University Press.

Fritsch, W., and G. Franco. 1991. *Foreign Direct Investment in Brazil: Its Impact on Industrial Restructuring.* Paris: Development Centre Studies, OECD.

Garrido, C., and W. Peres. 1998. "Las grandes empresas y grupos industriales latinoamericanos en los años noventa." In *Grandes empresas y grupos industriales latinoamericanos*, edited by W. Peres. Madrid: Siglo XXI-CEPAL.

Hobday, M. 1994. "Export-Led Technology Development in the Four Dragons: The Case of Electronics." *Development and Change* 25: 333–61.

———. 1995. "The Asian Latecomer Firms: Learning the Technology of Electronics." *World Development* 23 (7): 1171–93.

Jenkins, R. 1991. "The Political Economy of Industrialization: A Comparison of Latin American and East Asian Newly Industrializing Countries." *Development and Change* 22 (2): 197–231.

Katz, J. 1999. "Reformas estructurales y comportamiento tecnológico: reflexiones en torno a la naturaleza y fuentes del cambio tecnológico en América Latina en los años noventa." Serie Reformas Económicas, no. 13 (February). Santiago, Chile: CEPAL.

Katz, J., and B. Kosacoff. 1989. *El proceso de industrialización en la Argentina: evolución, retroceso y prospectiva.* Buenos Aires: CEPAL.

Kosacoff, B., and G. Bezchinsky. 1993. "De la sustitución de importaciones a la globalización. Las empresas transnacionales en la industria argentina." In *El desafío de la competitividad: La industria argentina en transición*, edited by B. Kosacoff. Buenos Aires: CEPAL/Alianza.

Kosacoff, B., and F. Porta. 1997. "La inversión extranjera directa en la industria manufacturera argentina." Estudios de la Economía Real, no. 3 (December). Buenos Aires, CEP.

Lall, S. 1998. "The Investment Development Path: Some Conclusions." In *Foreign Direct Investment and Governments: Catalysts for Economic Restructuring*, edited by J. Dunning and R. Narula. London: Routledge Studies in International Business and the World Economy.

Laplane, M., F. Sarti, C. Hiratuka, and R. Sabatini. 2001. "El caso brasileño." In *El boom de inversion extranjera directa en el MERCOSUR*, edited by D. Chudnovsky. Madrid: Siglo XXI.

Miozzo, M. 2000. "Transnational Corporations, Industrial Policy, and the 'War of Incentives': The Case of the Argentine Automobile Industry." *Development and Change* 31 (3): 651–80.

———. 2002. "Sectoral Specialisation in East Asia and Latin America Compared." *Brazilian Journal of Political Economy.* Forthcoming.

Miozzo, M., and L. Soete. 2001. "Internationalisation of Services: A Technological Perspective." *Technological Forecasting and Social Change* 67 (2): 159–85.

Nelson, R., and H. Pack. 1999. "The Asian Miracle and Modern Growth Theory." *Economic Journal* 109 (457): 416–39.

Nelson, R., and S. Winter. 1982. *An Evolutionary Theory of Economic Change.* Cambridge, Mass.: Harvard University Press.

OECD. 1991. *Foreign Investment and Industrialisation in Malaysia, Singapore, Taiwan, and Thailand.* Paris: OECD

Oman, C. 1995. "Emerging Policy Issues for the Dynamic Non-Member Economies: Trends in Global FDI and Latin America." In *Foreign Direct Investment: OECD Countries and Dynamic Economies of Asia and Latin America.* Paris: OECD.

Pack, H. 2001. "The Role of Acquisition of Foreign Technology in Taiwanese Growth." *Industrial and Corporate Change* 10 (3): 713–34.

Peres Nuñez, W. 1990. *Foreign Direct Investment and Industrial Development in México.* Paris: Development Centre Studies, OECD.

Quadros, R., A. Furtado, R. Bernardes, and E. Franco. 1999. "Technological Innovation in Brazilian Industry: An Assessment Based on the São Paulo Innovation Survey." Paper prepared for the Third International Conference on Technology Policy and Innovation, Austin.

Rosenberg, N. 1982. *Inside the Black Box*. Cambridge, Mass.: Cambridge University Press.

Sourrouille, J., F. Gatto, and B. Kosacoff. 1984. "Inversiones extranjeras en América Latina. Política económica, decisiones de inversión y comportamiento económico de las filiales." Buenos Aires: INTAL/BID.

Sourrouille, J., J. Lucángeli, and B. Kosacoff. 1985. *Transnacionalización y política económica en Argentina*. Buenos Aires: Centro de Economía Transnacional-CEAL.

UNCTAD. 1999. *World Investment Report: Foreign Direct Investment and the Challenge of Development*. Geneva: UNCTAD.

Wade, R. 1990. *Governing the Market: Economic Theory and the Role of Government in East Asian Industrialization*. Princeton, N.J.: Princeton University Press.

Williamson, J., ed. 1990. *Latin American Adjustment: How Much Has Happened*. Washington, D.C.: Institute for International Economics.

Wilmore, L. 1993. "The Comparative Performance of Foreign and Domestic Firms in Brazil." In *Transnational Corporations and Economic Development*, edited by S. Lall. United Nations Library on TNCs, vol. 3. London: Routledge.

CHAPTER 5

Supranational Rules on Strategy Context: Embraer and Brazil's Aerospace Program

Thomas C. Lawton and Steven M. McGuire

INTRODUCTION

We develop a case study of the commercial rivalry between two global aircraft manufacturers, Canada's Bombardier and Brazil's Embraer, in order to demonstrate the growing importance of supranational regulation—the ways in which the World Trade Organization (WTO) can have a positive impact upon the policy context and strategy choices of Brazilian multinational corporations.

The interaction of business and its environment has long been a subject of scholarly enquiry. Much of the early interest was in foreign direct investment, an interest that remains salient today (Graham 1997). However, relatively little of this work concerns the growth and development of international organizations like the WTO or explores how that institution's rules shape national economic policies. Instead, where firm-government relations are concerned, much of the focus remains on national governments in their capacity as home or hosts for foreign direct investment. Sanyal and Guvenli (2000) note that "more and more governments" have accepted liberal economic policies, yet they fail to recognize that this liberalism has an institutional manifestation in the WTO. Rugman and Verbeke (1998) note that the WTO may become increasingly important, but regard the international regulation of investment policies as a more pressing matter on the regulatory agenda. In her review of the government-business relations literature, Getz (1997) argues that as international business expands, it is reasonable to expect that international regulation will become more salient for scholars and practitioners. However, she does not attempt to develop either theoretical frameworks or case studies to pursue this point. Dunning (1997a), similarly, raises the potential importance of supranational or international regulation in his work on business-government relations. He notes that the expansion of international commercial activity challenges states to reconsider their governance of economic affairs. Dunning also stops well short of examining the actual interaction of business and international institutions like the WTO. The international business literature therefore suggests that there is something important about international organizations like the WTO, but no consensus has emerged on how to proceed.

This is particularly true where developing country multinationals are concerned. While antiglobalization protesters received the headlines, the Seattle meeting was somewhat of a watershed for developing countries in respect to their participation in the WTO. The Uruguay Round agreements represented a major extension of liberal economic policies around the world. They also represented an enormous burden for developing states in terms of the logistics of agreement implementation and the challenge to reconcile liberalism with economic and social development. As Finger notes, developed countries pressed for—and received—acceptance by developing states of a variety of commitments for intellectual property rights, services trade, and transparency in government procurement, all of which had enormous implications for their domestic economies (2001, 1098). In sum, a trade agreement actually ended up shaping the internal economic practices of developing states. The Doha Round of negotiations, begun in late 2001 and called, symbolically, the Development Round, reflects developing state concerns that the Uruguay Round was a bad deal. For many, it burdened them with vast amounts of new regulations and constrained their ability to pursue domestic policies (pharmaceutical pricing and health policy is the most prominent example), yet did not give them the promised market access to the developed world.

Brazil represents an interesting case in developing country interaction with the international trading regime. The country has long viewed full-blown liberalization with caution, arguing that free trade would merely lock in the advantages enjoyed by developed countries (Caldas 1998). As such, Brazil opposed efforts in the early 1980s to relaunch the liberalization process through a new round of the General Agreement on Tariffs and Trade (GATT). Although Brazil's major concern was services liberalization, as Caldas notes, Brazil's infant industry programs in a variety of sectors—especially information technology—would be vulnerable to new international disciplines (1998, 128). However, this desire for protection was increasingly difficult to reconcile with the demand from those domestic lobbies that did enjoy a comparative advantage (agriculture and extractive industries) for further integration into the GATT/WTO system. Brazil has continually tried to juggle this discord between the political need to protect and promote some sectors while embracing liberalization more generally.

This chapter does not argue that the WTO is the only important environmental variable for international business, nor is it the most powerful (however one determines relative power in the international system). We do argue, however, that the organization's potential impact on the conduct of international commerce—including that originating in developing countries—is understudied. The business and management literature has generally not grappled with the details of WTO decisions—in contrast to the legal literature—but has concentrated on the WTO's place within the international regulatory system (Lenway 1985; Rugman 2000). A proper assessment of the WTO's influence—or lack of—on international business can be gained only by a careful examination of actual cases. The case developed in this chapter is intended merely to add some empirical leverage to the argument that the WTO matters to developing country multinational corporations (MNCs). Significant further work needs to be done in this area. Our aim is to illustrate how WTO decisions may affect firms through shaping national-level industrial and technology policies.

The chapter begins by outlining the development of the WTO as a supranational authority. From there, it examines the Brazilian aerospace program and the emergence of Embraer as a successful multinational enterprise (MNE). It then considers the WTO dispute involving Canada and Brazil. The case is interesting because it focuses attention on one of the more contested areas of international trade: government subsidies to firms. The case helps illuminate how government intervention on behalf of home firms is an intrinsic element of the global competitive dynamics in the aerospace industry, and how WTO rules might affect this in the future. The implications of the WTO's reasoning in the case go beyond the aircraft industry. WTO decisions are cumulative: later case law builds on earlier ones. Thus, understanding the aircraft case is important for many industries, especially those where government subsidies feature prominently.

SUPRANATIONALISM AND THE WTO

Supranationalism refers to a level of political authority above the nation-state. It implies a shift in sovereignty away from states and toward an international institution. The European Union (EU) is the best example of a supranational authority: the European Commission is, for instance, able to make and ultimately enforce laws on EU member states. The WTO is nowhere near as strong as the European Commission, but it would be a mistake to argue that it does not constrain states.[1] The WTO is a much more robust institution than the General Agreement on Tariffs and Trade, which it replaced. The key institutional innovation of the WTO is the binding disputes process. When a trade dispute is taken to the WTO, the parties face a panel process not unlike a court proceeding. The panel, having heard arguments from the parties, issues a report and recommends action. Parties to the dispute can appeal the result to a standing appellate body. The decision of the appellate body is final: no further appeals are allowed. Crucially, final reports are adopted by the WTO council—and so are binding on the losing states—unless there is a consensus against adoption. Mustering a consensus against a decision is effectively impossible: reports of the appellate process are, in essence, binding and final. States must comply with the WTO recommendations or face trade sanctions. Since compliance with WTO decisions may require changes in domestic law, firms can be affected.

Some WTO decisions have caused considerable public anger, and this reflects the fact that the disputes process places states in the position of complying with decisions—by changing domestic law if necessary—or run the risk of trade sanctions. While some of the more controversial decisions concerned environmental protection, other cases centered on firms. The Kodak-Fuji dispute, for example, centered on the question of fair access for Kodak to Japan's retail film market. There was considerable anger in congress when the American government—and hence Kodak—lost the case. The case that we will examine here, the regional aircraft dispute between Brazil and Canada, is similar to the Kodak case in that the world of trade policy became blurred with corporate strategy. As Baron (1995) has noted, corporate strategy involves not only market activities like product development, finance, and marketing, but also nonmarket issues like government aid, regulatory policy, and trade policy. Early cases in the WTO should serve as a warning to managers that the Geneva-based institution can have an important role in shaping corporate strategy by affecting the economic regulatory environment where firms operate.

As suggested above, international regulation of subsidies faces several problems, not least of which is the question of how liberalized markets can be reconciled with the desires of developing states for government intervention in the economy in the form of industrial policy. While liberalism has been embraced by developing states as part of the answer to development questions, that does not mean that they eschew state intervention altogether. Indeed, one of the key points of contention in both the Uruguay and Doha Rounds of WTO negotiations is the scope of rules.

The agreement, negotiated in 1993, does something that the GATT subsidies code never did—define subsidy. A subsidy is a financial contribution by a state in which it transfers funds or liabilities (e.g., loans or loan guarantees); foregoes revenue (e.g., tax credits); provides goods and services other than that for general infrastructure; or entrusts a private body to conduct the above and in doing so confers a benefit.[2] The subsidy must also be specific, in the sense that it is aimed at a particular firm or industry. As Trebilcock and Howse (1999) note, in this sense the agreement on subsidies and countervailing measures (ASCM) follows U.S. countervail law; its inclusion in the WTO text represents a significant victory for U.S. efforts to develop international subsidy disciplines.

However, the agreement does not ban subsidies; in some respects its disciplines on government funding are very liberal. This too owes much to the U.S. During the Uruguay Round, European diplomats were among those who expected a fight with the U.S. over subsidies regulation. For years, the U.S. had complained that its firms were competing against foreign firms that made extensive use of government money. However, the expected fight over government subsidies did not materialize. The Uruguay Round marked a significant shift in U.S. policy regarding subsidy (Kleinfeld and Kaye 1994). This arose from the Clinton administration's view that, rather than complain about foreign subsidy programs, the best response was to have the U.S. develop its own. "Expand" might be a better term than "develop" as the U.S. has always subsidized its firms—particularly in the defense sector (Lawton 1997). Clinton's acceptance of the role of the state came in the wake of influential academic work that detailed the strengths of Japanese and to a lesser extent European, research and development (R&D) programs (Kleinfeld and Kaye 1994; Tyson 1993).

As Hoekman and Kostecki note, making multilateral subsidy rules is complicated by the fact that subsidies may be a desirable form of government intervention, rather than merely the product of protectionist business lobbies (2001, 171). Thus, WTO regulations concerning subsidies are themselves complex and in no way constitute a prohibition on subsidy. Instead, the ACSM seeks to, "refine, clarify, and enforce previously murky distinctions between subsidies that distort trade and those that do not" (Kleinfeld and Kaye 1994, 43). Three categories of subsidy are delineated in the agreement: prohibited, actionable, and permitted. Prohibited subsidies include all types of export subsidies or those that have the effect of discriminating against imported goods. Actionable subsidies are in the first instance permitted provided they do not cause serious injury to other WTO members. The final category of subsidy is the permitted category. These, non-actionable subsidies

could either be non-specific subsidies, or specific subsidies involving assistance to industrial research and pre-competitive development activity, assistance to disadvantaged regions, or certain types of assistance for adapting existing facilities to new environmental requirements imposed by law/or regulations.[3]

However, as the analysis below illustrates, the type of subsidy is not as important to panel decisions as the purpose of the aid.

Decisions made by WTO panels do affect firms, though it is true that firms do not have standing at the organization; that is, they cannot be actors in the disputes process. This does not diminish the importance of the organization to international business. The WTO is an international regime, a bundle of regulations and norms of behavior. Regimes are important in that they constrain and shape, in various ways, the policy preferences of actors, including firms and governments. This chapter contributes to an emerging debate about firms, and the role of the WTO in shaping and constraining national industrial policy.

BRAZILIAN INDUSTRIAL POLICY: THE SUCCESS OF EMBRAER[4]

Brazil, like its neighbor Argentina, has failed to live up to observers' expectations about economic growth as periodic but severe economic downturns remain a feature of the regional political economy (Phillips 2000). The country has seen repeated bouts of hyperinflation, which have exacerbated already extreme income inequalities. This economic volatility both gives rise to and results from, political instability; Brazil has endured periods of authoritarian rule and its democracy remains fragile. A 1964 military coup brought the generals control of the country, which they only relinquished in 1985. Yet, it was during this period of military rule that a company that would become *the* success story of the 1990s was born.

Embraer was created in 1969 as a joint project of the military and the state aeronautical research and development establishment, Centro Technico Aeronautica (CTA) (Goldstein 2002, 524). The military was loath to cede control of military aircraft production to foreign firms; neither was it interested in buying foreign aircraft. As a result, the military was happy to see Embraer run with a degree of managerial autonomy, provided that it maintained close links with the government and military interests. The company was able to source sophisticated components from abroad, rather than try to manufacture them itself. In aerospace, however, the assembly process is so complex that the systems integration skills of the manufacturer are themselves highly prized competences. Thus, unlike other industries, where final assembly has low value added, in aerospace, it is a key competitive advantage. In addition, the firm developed linkages with other, domestic Brazilian firms in a good example of spillover effects. As Patibandla and Petersen (2002) observed in their study of the Indian software industry, the creation of these linkages is vital to the success of the domestic industry, not just the individual firm. Moreover, the government understood that there was no trade-off between Embraer being a key military supplier and an exporter of aircraft: indeed, export sales were encouraged as they eased the burden on the treasury. Embraer thus carved out a successful niche as a producer of light, turboprop aircraft—the Tucano series (Goldstein 2002). In short, what was remarkable about Embraer's early success was that, in spite of macroeconomic policies that emphasized autarky, import substitution, and government control, at the firm level the picture was rather different. Embraer enjoyed government support and patronage, but was also given considerable operational freedom.

Embraer could not, however, cope with the economic slump of the late 1980s and by 1994 the company had posted a large loss. It was during this time that civilian rule was restored, but initially this did little to help the economy. Indeed, both presidents Collor and France prevaricated on the structural issues facing the Brazilian economy. Of these, perhaps the biggest was the increasing international pressure for privatization. Embraer's success notwithstanding, the state-controlled sectors of the Brazilian economy were ripe for an injection of private-sector management and financing. From the 1980s onward, though with a quickening pace in the late 1990s, some 170 state enterprises with combined revenues of $83 billion were sold off (Pinheiro 2002, 5). This was not always done out of a sudden embrace of the free market, but rather a stark assessment of the parlous finances of the Brazilian state (ibid).

Brazilian authorities' eagerness to support post-privatization Embraer, through both industrial and trade policies, cannot be understood in isolation from the dramatic evolution of the Brazilian economy from discredited import substitution policies to the belated embrace of market reforms in the 1990s (Goldstein 1999; Phillips 2000; Reinhardt and Peres 2000). In addition to being less than true believers in economic liberalization, politically, Brazilian elites were reluctant to make decisions about which parts of Brazilian society would bear the inevitable adjustment costs associated with the fiscal austerity demanded by the international markets. Historically, this choice had been avoided by recourse to inflationary fiscal policy; the post-1994 Real Plan represented a break with this tradition (Amann and Baer 2000, 1805). Economically, there remained concerns about the swamping of domestic producers by foreign multinationals. Operating in their large but protected domestic market Brazilian firms had stagnated and fallen behind foreign competitors. Some businesspeople did oppose liberalization and worked to stop it, but liberalization in no sense represented a defeat for Brazilian businesses. Many firms saw an opportunity to break out of the domestic market and increase profitability via exports.[5] There has been significant export growth, signaling that firms are indeed grasping the nettle of international competition.

Market opening was blended with active policies, for instance, incentives to foreign firms to transfer technology and skills (Dedrick et al. 2001, 1204). However, export growth has occurred mainly in slow-growth sectors such as mining, coffee, edible oils, and sugar and there is little evidence that firms are shifting resources out of these areas and into more technologically intensive sectors (Reinhardt and Peres 2000, 1556–57). In short, liberalization might be reinforcing rather than reducing the region's traditional reliance on commodities. The exception here is Embraer; it is one of the few Latin American firms to have succeeded in leveraging foreign technology and indigenous managerial expertise for international success. Business support to a market-friendly government rests on how well Brazilian firms cope with the restructuring that liberalization brings. Embraer has succeeded more than any other Brazilian MNC and that status makes it valuable to the state, both for its economic success and its symbolic value. This importance helps explain why Brazil was so keen to defend its interests in the WTO against Canada, even though it risked subjecting its own state subsidy regime to supranational scrutiny.

The Competitive Dynamics of the Regional Aircraft Sector

A regional aircraft is an airplane that can seat between 30 and 100 people, travel up to 1,500 miles, and is powered by either turboprops or jets. The market for these aircraft expanded dramatically during the 1990s. This expansion was particularly marked for jet-powered regional aircraft. For much of the 1990s, two firms dominated the market for these jets: Embraer of Brazil and Canada's Bombardier. These two companies, while bitter rivals, show remarkable similarities in both corporate and product development (see Table 5.1 for the latter).

Both companies are to some degree chosen instruments of national governments wishing to develop a domestic aerospace industry, though the firms used very different strategies to expand their operations. Bombardier did not begin life as an aerospace firm but rather moved into the sector via a string of acquisitions.

Embraer's development stands in stark contrast to its Canadian rival. Bombardier has always been a private company; Embraer, in contrast, was state-owned from its creation in 1969 until privatization in 1994 (Embraer 2000). The firm's existing product lines of light, propeller-driven, and jet aircraft provided the key competencies needed for entry into the regional airliner market. The company entered this civil market with the 50-seater EMB-145 in 1992.

Although Bombardier and Embraer evolved differently and came at the market from different directions, internationalizing their operations produced

Table 5.1
A Comparison of Models

Model	No. of Passengers	Wing span (ft.)/Wing area (sq.ft.)	Cruise speed (mach)	Range (miles)
Bombardier CJ200/ER/LR	50	69.7/560	0.77	1134/1893/2307
Embraer ERJ-145ER/LR	50	65.8/551	0.78	1186/1771

Source: Data from *Aviation Week and Space Technology*, Aerospace Source Book, 17 January 2000, pp. 70–71.

a convergence in strategy. The regional aircraft market places pressure on firms to implement very similar strategies. A series of environmental conditions makes product differentiation difficult and forces firms to compete on price and service quality. This sensitivity to price has a major role in explaining the key role of government subsidy in the sector. Pressures for convergence exist on both the demand and supply side of the market and the rapid development of the regional jet market in particular represents a positive interaction of technology and market demand conditions.

The civil aircraft industry generally is a sector characterized by incremental technological change (McGuire 1999). Unlike the computer industry, for example, the basic technologies underlying civil aircraft, particularly in airframe design and construction and propulsion, have remained relatively stable since the development of the jet engine in the 1940s. The fact of this arises for two reasons: cost of new product development and certification procedures. The civil aircraft industry is a highly R&D intensive industry with typical research and development spending equal to 10–15 percent of revenues (Department of Trade and Industry 1997). Launching an entirely new product is incredibly risky. Boeing was nearly bankrupted by the development costs for the 747 airliner, designed in the 1960s (Rodgers 1996). In short, the uncertainty associated with new product development makes firms reluctant to introduce revolutionary technologies; incremental changes to a design are a preferred option.

This caution is reinforced by the arduous certification procedures for new aircraft. Certifying a new airliner requires a minimum amount of flying to demonstrate the reliability of the aircraft and its systems in a variety of conditions. This process can take years and firms will not introduce new technologies unless they are already robust enough to withstand the certification regimen. Thus, competing aircraft makers tend to introduce products that are remarkably alike in basic technologies and performance. Commercial rivalries tend to manifest themselves as competitions among relatively undifferentiated aircraft. Embraer developed products that differed little in basic performance and design.

The development of the regional aircraft niche into which Bombardier and Embraer belong also demonstrated the demand side pressures that force strategic convergence. A key pressure was the growth of hub-and-spoke routing systems among major airlines, particularly American ones, in the wake of U.S. airline deregulation in 1978. Hub-and-spoke systems work by funneling large numbers of passengers through large, hub airports like Chicago, Dallas, or London Heathrow. Smaller planes perform the vital role of linking these hub airports with smaller regional centers. Traditionally, propeller-driven aircraft performed this function. However, customer surveys showed that customers prefer jet-powered aircraft, perhaps viewing them (correctly or not) as safer airplanes (Shifrin 1998). Airlines had to wait until technological progress in the small jet sector provided engines that were both quiet enough to fly in and out of local airports without causing noise pollution and efficient enough to make the routes economical (Sparaco 1998, 1). Once this was achieved in the late 1980s, regional jet orders began to soar. By 1998, the 80 member airlines of the European Regions Airlines Association (ERA) had ordered almost 1,000 regional jets (Sparaco 1999, 2).

The argument we make here is that in an environment where environmental pressures make differentiation strategies difficult, government intervention on behalf of domestic firms can be key to competitive success. Brazil sought to use state aids as a way of reducing the cost of their firms' products. For its part, Embraer was not shy in articulating the need for extensive government support for their product development and sales. However, national provision of state aids is subject to multilateral disciplines. Thus, the success of corporate strategy depended, partly at least, on how the WTO chose to interpret its subsidy provisions.

Bombardier was the first to market, introducing the 50-seat Canada Regional Jet (CRJ)-100 in 1992. Embraer's offering, the EMB-135 followed two years later. Although Bombardier was the first to market, it did not enjoy a first mover advantage. Embraer stunned its Canadian competitor in 1996 by announcing large orders from two American regional airlines: Continental Express and American Eagle. Both air carriers ordered in excess of 100 Brazilian regional jets each. Bombardier began to complain that Embraer's success was the result of Brazilian government support. The Brazilian government had developed an exchange rate subsidy scheme, Proex, to assist exporters. Under the scheme a bank lending funds for the purchase of an Embraer aircraft received two payments. The first was from the airline purchasing the aircraft; the second was from the Brazilian government. Whatever the interest rate attached to the loan, the program allowed the Brazilian government to pay 3.8 percentage points. Hypothetically, if an airline negotiated a loan at say, 7 percent, Brazil's subsidy effectively reduced that interest rate—and hence payments—to 3.2 percent. Crucially, Embraer would secure the agreement of the Brazilian government to fund the subsidy *before* concluding the sale. The company could thus enter a bidding contest with Bombardier knowing that the Brazilian state would agree to the funding (WTO 1999a, 2). Trade press reports suggested that Embraer aircraft were enjoying a $2 million price advantage in bidding contests. For its part, Bombardier claimed that the program provided an effective subsidy of $4.5 billion to Embraer (Bombardier Corporation 1999).

However, Bombardier itself had secured government support for its product development programs. In 1992, the Canadian government offered the company a Can$38 million loan to support development costs of the first CRJ model. Then, in 1996, Ottawa pledged Can$87 million of funding for a new, 70-seat CRJ model. This second subsidy, which would be paid back on a royalty basis, was delivered under the auspices of the Canadian government's Technology Partnerships Canada (TPC) program (TPC 1996). Canadian government assistance to the aerospace sector in general, however, came to Can$631 million. While not all of this money went to support regional aircraft production, some did go to support the development of subsystems with possible applications on Bombardier aircraft (TPC 2000, 2).

The rivalry became increasingly bitter through 1997. Bombardier pressed the Canadian government to take a case to the WTO, but withdrew the request when the possibility of a negotiated settlement appeared. Neither firm was able to develop a product strategy that would break the impasse: the firms were offering technologically similar solutions and price competitiveness was the key element in the rivalry.

THE WTO DECISION AND ITS IMPACT

A situation therefore emerged where Canada and Brazil had national champion firms locked in an increasingly bitter contest—and since both governments offered financial support for this, the dispute had economic implications beyond aerospace. In an attempt to avoid a confrontation in the WTO, Brazil and Canada held bilateral consultations through 1998. In the event, both countries essentially countersued each other in the WTO after failing to agree on a bilateral negotiated compromise. On April 14, 1999, a WTO disputes panel found that some Canadian subsidy programs supporting Bombardier violated the ASCM (WTO 1999b). These were the debt-financing scheme, the Canada Account, and the Technology Partnerships Canada program designed to support regional aircraft production. For its part, Brazil was found to have afforded Embraer an illegal subsidy with its Proex scheme of interest rate subsidies to purchasers of Brazilian aircraft. Brazil and Canada appealed sections of the panel reports. On August 2, 1999, the appellate body issued its report (WTO 1999c), which essentially upheld the initial findings. The regional aircraft case clarified the WTO's position on the nature and scope of permitted support for the aircraft industry. More importantly, it provides insight into emerging international disciplines on subsidization that may affect other firms and industries in the future.

Brazil's defense of its Proex scheme rested on two arguments: that as a developing country it enjoyed looser disciplines on subsidy than Canada, and that it was entitled to subsidize Embraer so as to cancel out the beneficial effect of Canada's support to Bombardier (WTO 1999d). In the appeals process, the developing country argument was dropped. In any event, the latter defense is the more analytically interesting, as firms often use a level-playing-field defense as a reason for receiving state support. However, the WTO rejected this argument; to admit that countries may subsidize firms so as to retaliate for foreign subsidization, was to invite a spiral of counter subsidy and a race to the bottom in international subsidy disciplines (WTO 1999d, 51). Moreover, as the Proex interest subsidy was fixed at 3.8 percent, it could not be the case that Brazil simply sought to match Canada's subsidization: matching in one case might have demanded a larger subsidy, and in another case a smaller amount. The Proex program was thus not designed to merely cancel out state aid to Bombardier, but to provide Embraer with a price advantage.

When the appellate body review upheld Canada's argument that the Proex-based contracts with airlines had to be unwound, Brazil's argument was that Embraer could not renege on its legal obligations—such as, on binding contracts with airlines for some 900 aircraft with a value of $3 billion. As one industry observer noted, asking Embraer to comply with the ruling and unwind the contracts was essentially asking the company to put itself out of business (Alden and Collitt 2000, 12). Some observers, however, have noted that Brazil's problems in defending its commercial interests in international organizations relates to the commitment of its diplomatic body to ideologies opposite to free trade itself (Pio 2001). In mid-2001, trade policy competences were centralized in a new body (Câmara de Gestão do Comércio Exterior, or Gecex) and the Ministry of Foreign Affairs started a reorganization process in view of improving diplomats' skills in trade promotion. Gecex arbitrates between the often conflicting positions of the Finance Ministry and the more heterodox and developmentalist Câmara de Comércio Exterior (Camex) (Goldstein and McGuire 2002). Interestingly, concerns in business circles have come less from exporters to Canada than from other heavy users of Proex who feared that the excessive publicity given to the scheme could alert competitors.[6]

Equally important, Brazil has also tried to widen its support base by acting as a champion of developing countries' rights. In this it purports to be supplying a public good, just like Canada does when arguing that not to enforce the WTO decision would be detrimental to the global trading system. The main claim made by Brazil is that the ASCM unfairly allowed countries to use only export credit rates that complied with the Organization for Economic Cooperation and Development (OECD) arrangement, which the Brazilian government contends are not suited to the needs and specificities of developing countries or of any nonparticipant. The criticism runs on two levels. On the one hand, it questions the fairness of imposing OECD norms on countries that did not sit at the negotiating table. On the other hand, it casts doubt on the use of OECD methods for calculating subsidy when financial markets have now developed much more sophisticated instruments for export financing (Goldstein and McGuire 2002). Competitors from industrial countries can count on both direct loan and subsidy programs and indirect insurance and guarantees ones managed by independent and specialized export credit agencies. Other developing countries, such as India, Tanzania, and Jamaica, have recently taken the argument one step further and proposed that developing countries be authorized to use subsidies for regional development, export diversification, and technological upgrading that are currently prohibited by the ASCM (Goldstein and McGuire 2002)

As a result of the appeals process, both Canada and Brazil had to alter their state aids. The Brazilian case was complicated by the binding contracts that the firm had signed with airlines. The WTO ruled that the Proex scheme was an unfair, trade-distorting subsidy. However, asking the Brazilians to withdraw the funding within 90 days of the issue of the report raised a complication: did that mean that contracts between Brazil, Embraer, and an airline, which had been signed but not executed, were to be terminated? This raised a difficult legal issue; Embraer argued that it could not be asked to break legally binding contracts with customers. Bombardier insisted that it do so, arguing that some $3.7 billion in illegal supports would otherwise go through. In May 2000, the WTO ruled in favor of Canada, judging that the Proex-based sales could not proceed. The number of aircraft involved was staggering: some 900 units. The enormity of the penalty had serious implications for both Embraer and Brazil. As one observer noted, Embraer is by far Brazil's most successful high-technology exporter and this decision was about whether or not Brazil has a high-technology industry (Alden and Collitt 2000). In August 2000, a WTO arbitration panel ruled that Canada was entitled to impose tariffs on Brazilian goods worth $230 million per year until a bilateral accord on the Proex-based sales was agreed upon (Williams et al. 2000, 10).

Negotiations to conclude this agreement were ongoing at the time of writing. Canada had found it relatively easy to comply with the ruling, but the contractual issue remains a difficult problem for Embraer. Simply, the penalty seems disproportionate to the trade affected, a point legal scholars are now raising with increasing concern. Canada increased the pressure in 2001 by supplying soft loans to Bombardier to clinch a sale to Air Wisconsin. Remarkably, Canadian officials were quite candid about the dubious legality of the loans: they fully expected to lose the case in the WTO. Brazil took the matter to the WTO and won a victory in late 2001. Canada dropped the loan scheme, but the sale went ahead anyway. Canada justified its actions, citing Brazil's refusal to comply with the original WTO ruling.

Since WTO treaties have the status of international law, and since WTO panel decisions are meant to form a corpus of law to guide future decisions, the Bombardier-Embraer case could have repercussions in a variety of industries. We argue that there are two key issues for firms. First, the case established that governments may not subsidize their own firms, simply because other states are doing so. Second, the market reference test developed in the case may prove troublesome. Government subsidies are often justified by structural conditions in a sector, such as long payback periods or appropriability problems, that make private capital markets unwilling to invest. Yet, the market reference test seems to argue that, unless a government loan is substantially commercial in its structure, it is vulnerable to trade action.

This decision may affect types of strategic rent-seeking behavior where governments seek to position their firms competitively relative to foreign firms via state aid. Crucially, it calls into question the viability of corporate strategies where government support is a key component of either product-specific R&D or foreign direct investment decisions. It is worth recalling that the TPC was a research and development program. That, however, did not insulate it from the WTO. It is also worth noting that both the U.S. and EU governments participated in the regional aircraft hearings and that the British government, to cite one example, was concerned that its own regional economic development programs might be affected by the WTO's developing jurisprudence on subsidies.[7] In short, as the WTO reaches into domestic economies, corporate strategies will be affected as, in the Rugman and Verbeke formulation (1998), the degree of national responsiveness that can be offered to firms is constrained.

AN EMERGING RESEARCH AGENDA

We argue that the Embraer case is merely an early example of what may confront more and more internationalized firms from developing countries: the importance of supranational regulation for corporate strategy. This process is indirect; WTO decisions apply to governments and their domestic legislation or state aid policies. In the aircraft case, lack of product differentiation made government intervention a key element in the competitive struggle. WTO subsidy regulations have forced Canada, Brazil, and its firms to reassess their funding plans and strategies. However, the effects may reach far beyond the aircraft sector. Since the Proex scheme was supposed to assist various Brazilian exporters, the WTO decision may make the task of numerous Brazilian firms more difficult. International business scholars, unlike international lawyers (such as Bronckers 1999; Mattoo and Subramanian 1998; Trebilcock and Howse 1999), have been slow to comprehend the changed environment and hesitant to acknowledge the increased market relevance of supranational institutions. In a review of the literature, Getz (1997) calls on scholars to apprehend that international institutions are natural targets for corporate political activity as their importance in regulating international business grows.

In sum, it is time to emphasize the significance of supranational regulation to national industrial policy and, indirectly, the strategic direction of modern multinationals. Supranationalism is still in its infancy and there is widespread disagreement about the appropriate scope of international-level regulation (Trebilcock and Howse 1999). There is a rich literature on the input side of trade policy making and strategy: that is, on the role of companies in lobbying for specific policies to be adopted by their governments, or inserted into WTO treaties. What we currently lack at the international level are output-side studies that examine what the WTO decided and how it decided it (Hocking and McGuire 2002). Further down that line, we also lack studies of the actual adjustments made by firms and states to WTO rulings (Capling 2000). This chapter represents a small attempt to redress this imbalance.

NOTES

1. Consider the text of the WTO panel report on U.S. foreign sales corporations, where the U.S. argued that taxation policy was outside the WTO's purview: "[The] United States is free to maintain a worldwide tax system, a territorial tax system or any other type of system it sees fit. This is not the business of the WTO. *What it is not free to do* is to establish a regime of direct taxation, provide an exemption from direct taxes specifically related to exports, and then claim that it is entitled to provide such an export subsidy because it is necessary to eliminate a disadvantage to exporters created by the U.S. tax system itself." WTO, *United States—Tax Treatment of "Foreign Sales Corporations": Report of the Panel* (Geneva: WTO, 1999), p. 282. Italics added.

2. WTO, *Agreement on Subsidies and Countervailing Measures*, Art.1.1, p. 1.

3. WTO, *Summary of the Final Act of the Uruguay Round*, http://www.wto.org/wto/legal/ursum_wp.htm, March 1998.

4. This section draws heavily from Andrea Goldstein and Steven McGuire, "The Political Economy of Strategic Trade Policy: The Canada-Brazil Export Subsidies Saga Explained," unpublished paper, 2002.

5. Goldstein and Schneider (2001). Doctor (2001) presents an interesting case study of conflicting business interests in the area of port reform.

6. "Itamaraty S/A," *Istoé*, 31 July 2000.

7. McGuire acknowledges the insights of an official from the Department of Trade and Industry, personal communication, Bristol, England, 17 November 1998.

REFERENCES

Alden, Edward, and Raymond Collitt. 2000. "Canada and Brazil Seek Subsidies Deal." *The Financial Times*, 12 May: 12

Amann, Edmund, and Werner Baer. 2000. "The Illusion of Stability: The Brazilian Economy under Cardoso." *World Development* 28 (10): 1805–19.

Barney, J. B. 1991. "Firm Resources and Sustained Competitive Advantage." *Journal of Management* 17 (1): 99–120.

Baron, D. 1995. "Integrated Strategy: Market and Nonmarket Components." *California Management Review* 37 (2): 47–65.

———. 1997. "Integrated Strategy, Trade Policy, and Global Competition." *California Management Review* 39 (2): 145–69.

Bartlett, C., and S. Ghoshal. 1989. *Managing across Borders: The Transnational Solution.* Boston: Harvard Business School Press.

Bombardier Corporation. 1999. "Bombardier Welcomes WTO Final Decision on Proex Subsidy." Press Release, August 2, 1999. http://www.bombardier.com/.

Bronckers, M. 1999. "Better Rules for a New Millennium: A Warning against Undemocratic Developments in the WTO." *Journal of International Economic Law* 2 (4): 547–66.

Caldas, R. W. 1998. *Brazil in the Uruguay Round of the GATT.* Aldershot, England: Ashgate.

Capling, A. 2000. "The American Way? Aggressive Bilateralism in Australian Trade

Policy." Chap. 7 in *Havana to Seattle: Australia and the Global Trade System*, by A. Capling. Cambridge: Cambridge University Press.

Day, G. S. 1990. *Market Driven Strategy, Processes for Creating Value*. New York: The Free Press.

Dedrick, Jason, Kenneth L. Kraemer, Juan Palacios, Paulo Bastros Tigre, and Antonio Jose Junqueira Botelho. 2001. "Economic Liberalization and the Computer Industry: Comparing Outcomes in Brazil and Mexico." *World Development* 29 (7): 1199–214.

Department of Trade and Industry. 1997. "R&D Intensity in Manufactured Products for Years between 1986 and 1995." http://www.dti.gov.uk/ost/SETstats97/sect.4/4tabs/4_8tabs.htm.

Doz, Y. 1986. *Strategic Management in Multinational Companies*. Oxford: Pergamon Press.

Dunning, J. 1997a. "Introduction." In *Governments, Globalization, and International Business*, edited by John Dunning, 1–28. Oxford: Oxford University Press.

———. 1997b. "Governments and the Macro-Organization of Economic Activity: A Historical and Spatial Perspective." In *Governments, Globalization, and International Business*, edited by J. H. Dunning, 29–72. Oxford: Oxford University Press.

Embraer, S. A. 2000. *Embraer Update*. Corporate Press Release, March 2, 2000. http://www.embraer.com/.

Finger, M. 2001. "Implementing the Uruguay Round Agreements: Problems for Developing Countries." *The World Economy* 24 (9): 1097–108.

Foss, N. 1999. "Research in the Strategic Theory of the Firm: 'Isolationism' and 'Integrationism.'" *Journal of Management Studies* 36 (6): 725–55.

Getz, K. 1997. "Research in Corporate Political Action: Integration and Assessment." *Business and Society* 36 (1): 32–72.

Globerman, S., and D. Shapiro. 1999. "The Impact of Government Policies on Foreign Direct Investment: The Canadian Experience." *Journal of International Business Studies* 30 (3): 513–32.

Goldstein, A. 1999. "Brazilian Privatization: The Rocky Path from State Capitalism to Regulatory Capitalism." *Industrial and Corporate Change* 8 (4): 673–712.

———. 2002. "The Political Economy of High-Tech Industries in Developing Countries: Aerospace in Brazil, Indonesia, and South Africa." *Cambridge Journal of Economics* 26: 521–38.

Goldstein, A., and S. McGuire. 2002. "The Political Economy of Strategic Trade Policy: Explaining the Canada-Brazil Export Subsidies Saga." Unpublished paper.

Goldstein, A., and B. S. Schneider. 2002. "Big Business in Brazil: States and Markets in the Corporate Reorganization of the 1990s." In *Brazil and Korea*, edited by Edmund Amann and Ha-Joon Chang. London: Palgrave.

Graham, E. 1997. "Should There Be Multilateral Rules on Foreign Direct Investment?" In *Governments, Globalization, and International Business*, edited by J. H. Dunning. Oxford: Oxford University Press.

Grant, R. M. 1991. "The Resource-Based Theory of Competitive Advantage: Implications for Strategy Formulation." *California Management Review* (spring): 114–35.

Hocking, B., and S. McGuire. 2002. "Government—Business Strategies in EU-U.S.

Economic Relations: The Lessons of the Foreign Sales Corporation Issue." *Journal of Common Market Studies* 40 (3): 449–70.

Hoekman, B., and M. Kostecki. 2001. *The Political Economy of the World Trading System: The WTO and Beyond.* Oxford: Oxford University Press.

Kay, J. 1993. *The Foundations of Corporate Success.* Oxford: Oxford University Press.

Kleinfeld, G., and D. Kaye. 1994. "Red Light, Green Light? The 1994 Agreement on Subsidies and Countervailing Measures, Research, and Development Assistance, and U.S. Policy." *Journal of World Trade* 28 (6): 43–64.

Lawton, T. C. 1997. *Technology and the New Diplomacy: The Creation and Control of EC Industrial Policy for Semiconductors.* Aldershot, England: Avebury.

Lenway, S. A. 1985. *The Politics of U.S. International Trade: Protection, Expansion, and Escape.* Boston: Pitman.

Levitt, T. 1983. "The Globalization of Markets." *Harvard Business Review* (May/June): 92–102.

Mattoo, A., and A. Subramanian. 1998. "Regulatory Autonomy and Multilateral Disciplines: The Dilemma and a Possible Resolution." *Journal of International Economic Law* 1 (2): 303–22.

Maxwell, J., S. Rothenberg, F. Briscoe, and A. Marcus. 1997. "Green Schemes: Corporate Environmental Strategies and Their Implementation." *California Management Review* 39 (3): 118–34.

McGuire, S. 1999. "Sectoral Innovation Patterns and the Rise of New Competitors: The Case of Civil Aerospace in Asia." *Industry and Innovation* 6 (2): 153–70.

———. 2002. "Between Pragmatism and Principle: Legalization, Political Economy, and the WTO's Subsidy Agreement." *International Trade Journal* 16 (3): 319–43.

Mercer, D., ed. 1992. *Managing the External Environment: A Strategic Perspective.* London: Sage.

Mintzberg, H. 1990. "Strategy Formation: Schools of Thought." In *Perspectives on Strategic Management*, edited by J. Frederickson. New York: Harper and Row.

Mowery, D., and N. Rosenberg. 1998. *Paths of Innovation.* New York: Cambridge University Press.

Ohmae, K. 1989. "Managing in a Borderless World." *Harvard Business Review* (May/June): 152–61.

Ott, J. 2000. "Airbus Eclipses Boeing, Sets Order Book Record." *Aviation Week and Space Technology*, 10 January, 44–46.

Patibandla, M., and B. Petersen. 2002. "Role of Transnational Corporations in the Evolution of a High-Tech Industry: The Case of India's Software Industry." *World Development* 30 (9): 1561–77.

Phillips, N. 2000. "The Future of the Political Economy of Latin America." In *Political Economy and the Changing Global Order*, eds. R. Stubbs and G. Underhill, 284–96. 2d ed. Oxford: Oxford University Press.

Pinheiro, A. C. 2002. "The Brazilian Privatization Experience: What's Next?" Working Paper CBS-30-02, Brazilian Studies Centre, Oxford University.

Pio, C. 2001. "Diplomatic Immunity." Letter to *The Economist*, February 22.

Porter, M. E. 1979. "How Competitive Forces Shape Strategy." *Harvard Business Review* (March/April).

———. 1980. *Competitive Strategy: Techniques for Analyzing Industries and Competitors.* New York: The Free Press.

————. 1985. *Competitive Advantage: Creating and Sustaining Superior Performance.* New York: The Free Press.

————. 1990. *The Competitive Advantage of Nations.* London: Macmillan.

Power, T., and M. Doctor. 2002. "The Resilience of Corporatism: Continuity and Change in Brazilian Corporatist Structures." Working Paper CBS-29–02, Brazilian Studies Centre, Oxford University.

Prahalad, C. K., and G. Hamel. 1990. "The Core Competences of the Corporation." *Harvard Business Review* (May/June): 79–91.

Reinhardt, Nola, and Wilson Peres. 2000. "Latin America's New Economic Model: Micro Responses and Economic Restructuring." *World Development* 28 (9): 1543–66.

Rodgers, E. 1996. *Flying High: The Story of Boeing and the Rise of the Jetliner Industry.* New York: Atlantic Monthly Press.

Rugman, A. 2000. *The End of Globalization.* London: Random House.

Rugman, A., and A. Verbeke. 1990. *Global Corporate Strategy and Trade Policy.* London/ New York: Routledge.

————. 1998. "Multinational Enterprises and Public Policy." *Journal of International Business Studies* 29 (1): 115–36.

Sanyal, Rajib, and Turgut Guvenli. 2000. "Relations between Multinational Firms and Host Governments: The Experience of American-Owned Firms in China." *International Business Review* 9 (2000): 119–34.

Sell, Susan. 1999. "Multinational Corporations as Agents of Change: The Globalization of Intellectual Property Rights." In *Private Authority and International Affairs,* edited by A. Claire Cutler, Virginia Haufler, and Tony Porter, 169–97. Albany, N.Y.: SUNY Press.

Shaffer, B., and A. J. Hillman. 2000. "The Development of Business-Government Strategies by Diversified Firms." *Strategic Management Journal* 21 (2): 175–90.

Shifrin, C. 1998. "Upswing in Jet Sales Boon to Regional Aircraft." *Aviation Week and Space Technology,* May 18, http://www.awst.com/.

Smith, B. 1999. "WTO Rules on RJs: Final Impact Unclear." *Aviation Week and Space Technology,* August 9, http://www.awst.com/.

Sparaco, P. 1998. "Fairchild Dornier Seeks Big Role for Small 328JET." *Aviation Week and Space Technology,* March 2, http://www.awst.com/.

————. 1999. "Competition Escalates in the Twinjet Market." *Aviation Week and Space Technology,* October 11, http://www.awst.com/.

Stalk, G., P. Evans, and L. E. Schulman. 1992. "Competing on Capabilities: The New Rules of Corporate Strategy." *Harvard Business Review* (March/April): 57–69.

Story, J. 1999. *The Frontiers of Fortune.* London: FT Pitman.

Taylor, L., and B. Pearson. 2000. "WTO Rulings Force Review." *Australian Financial Review,* 2 March, 3.

Technology Partnerships Canada (TPC). 1996. "Federal Government Lays the Foundation for Jobs in Montreal." Industry Canada Press Release, October 21, 1996.

————. 1999. "Canada Announces Measures to Comply with WTO Ruling on Regional Aircraft Subsidies." Industry Canada Press Release, November 18, 1999.

————. 2000. "Current Statistics." Industry Canada, January 31, 2000. http://strategis.ic.gc.ca/SSG/tp00175e.html.

Teece, D., G. Pisano, and A. Shuen. 1990. *Firm Capabilities, Resources, and the Concept of Strategy: Four Paradigms of Strategic Management.* CCC Working Paper, December.

Trebilcock, M., and R. Howse. 1999. *The Regulation of International Trade.* 2d ed. London: Routledge.

Tyson, L. 1993. *Who's Bashing Whom? Trade Conflict in High-technology Industries.* Washington, D.C.: Institute for International Economics.

Webster, F. 1994. *Market Driven Management: Using the New Marketing Concept to Create a Customer-Oriented Company.* New York: Wiley.

Williams, F., et. al. 2000. "Canada Given Go-Ahead for Sanctions Against Brazil." *Financial Times,* 23 August, 10.

WTO. 1999a. *Agreement on Subsidies and Countervailing Measures.* Geneva: WTO.

———. 1999b. *Canada—Measures Affecting the Export of Civilian Aircraft: Report of the Panel.* 14 April 1999. Geneva: WTO.

———. 1999c. *Canada—Measures Affecting the Export of Civilian Aircraft: Report of the Appellate Body.* 2 August 1999. Geneva: WTO.

———. 1999d. *Brazil—Export Financing Programme for Aircraft: Report of the Appellate Body.* 2 August 1999. Geneva: WTO.

———. 1999e. *United States—Tax Treatment of "Foreign Sales Corporations": Report of the Panel.* 8 October 1999. Geneva: WTO.

PART II

Changing Contexts

CHAPTER 6

Initial Trust of Joint Venture Partners in Emerging Nations

Kwong Chan, W. Harvey Hegarty, and Stewart R. Miller

INTRODUCTION

As multinational enterprises (MNEs) expand into emerging markets, scholars and practitioners need to develop a better understanding of trust as MNEs interact with host-country governments, and local partners. This is reflected in the increasing attention the concept of trust is receiving from practitioners and scholars in a variety of disciplines (e.g., Gambetta 1988; North 1990; Rousseau et al. 1998; Wicks, Berman, and Jones 1999; Williamson 1993). In interorganizational relationships, trust is an insatiable good for firms and markets, facilitating cooperation (Mayer, Davis, and Schoorman 1995), through reduced agency and transaction costs (Jones 1995), and an ability to promote smooth and efficient market transactions (Arrow 1981). Complementary views have also attributed explicit competitive advantages to trust (Barney and Hansen 1994). It has become increasingly apparent, however, that excessive trust can have unfortunate consequences, including inappropriate resource allocation and the assumption of unnecessary risk (Wicks, Berman, and Jones 1999). Similarly, insufficient trust can lead to missed opportunities to reduce costs or develop organizational capabilities. Determining optimal trust in an interorganizational relationship is thus crucial to organizational effectiveness.

Trust has become increasingly important in studies of interorganizational relationships; yet researchers have yet to unanimously embrace a definition of trust (Deutsch 1962; Gambetta 1988; Mayer, Davis, and Schoorman 1995; Rousseau et al. 1998). For example, Mayer, Davis, and Schoorman defined trust as "the willingness of a party to be vulnerable to the actions of another party based on the expectation that the other will perform a particular action important to the truster, irrespective of the ability to monitor or control that other party" (1995, 712). Rousseau et al. (1998) proposed the following definition: "a psychological state comprising the intention to accept vulnerability based upon positive expectations of the intentions of another" (1998, 395). Another aspect of trust deals with "when parties first meet or interact," referred to as *initial trust* (McKnight, Cummings, Cherveney 1998, 473).

Wicks, Berman, and Jones contend "optimal trust exists when one creates (and maintains) prudent economic relationships biased by a willingness to trust. That is, agents need to have stable and ongoing commitments to trust so that they share affect-based belief in moral character sufficient to make a leap of faith, but they should also exercise care in determining whom to trust, to what extent, and in what capacity. Optimal trust is an embedded construct, suggesting that it is determined in context and shaped by a variety of factors, such as the trustworthiness of the agent, local and broader social norms regarding trust, and other features of the relevant social structure(s)" (1999, 103). These authors focused primarily on matching trust levels and interdependence and the effect on firm performance.

Although scholars have begun to focus on trust in cross border activities (Aulakh, Kotabe, and Sahay 1997; Doney, Cannon, and Mullen 1998; Dyer and Chu 2000; Hagen and Choe 1998), the concepts of *initial trust* (McKnight, Cummings, and Chervany 1998) and optimal trust have yet to be explored in an international context. An inability to comprehend the appropriate level of initial trust with local firms in an emerging market may result in operational ineffectiveness and, perhaps the failure of the venture. In addition, a growing number of scholars are examining the institutional environment in an international context, including emerging nations (Delios and Henisz 2000; Meyer 2001), yet there has been little consideration of the institutional environment as it relates to the development of trust in an international setting.

In the present study, we aim to contribute to the literature by developing a framework of ideal levels of initial trust for an MNE considering a joint venture in an emerging nation. In doing so, we build on the work of McKnight, Cummings, and Chervany (1998) and Wicks, Berman, and Jones (1999) by unifying and internationalizing their concepts of initial trust and optimal trust, respectively. By focusing on the institutional environment in emerging nations, we extend a research stream that recognizes the utility of applying institutional theory to the study of multinational enterprises (Delios and Henisz 2000; Kostova 1999; Kostova and Zaheer 1999; Meyer 2001; Westney 1993). While the institutional perspective played a role in the McKnight, Cummings, and Chervany (1998) study, which partly based initial trust on institutional cues, reference to structural safeguards such as legal recourse may not be a realistic assumption in emerging markets with institutional uncertainty (Meyer 2001).

There are two additional reasons for investigating optimal initial trust in emerging nations. The first reason focuses upon the importance of signals emitted and received. Upon the commencement of a business relationship, firms naturally seek a partner who will not behave in an opportunistic manner. To establish this intent, both partners must necessarily signal a willingness to trust, which can lead to a synergistic, mutually trustworthy business relationship, or an exploitative asymmetric economic outcome. Poor signaling during this phase can have repercussions for the development of cooperation between the two firms throughout their relationship. Receiving signals can be problematic when the sender is from a different institutional environment. The second reason underscores embeddedness of local firms. Foreign partners need to understand the local partner's network and manner of conducting business, relative to its own network. It is also becoming increasingly evident that network considerations are vital during initial trust formation (e.g., McKnight, Cummings, and Chervany 1998). Assessment of interfirm network compatibility facilitates planning and effective negotiations between firms, highlighting the boundaries of cooperation and laying a clear foundation for initial trust. Essential to this process is the accumulation of relevant knowledge, without which initial trust is more problematic (Inkpen and Li 1999).

CONCEPTUAL FRAMEWORK

In developing a framework of optimal initial trust, we focus on the joint venture in emerging nations. Different levels of trust are linked to different types of interorganizational relationships (Barney and Hansen 1994; Das and Teng 1998). By holding the relationship constant, we are able to probe deeper into the roles of the institutional environment and firm-specific resources. The consideration of two firms from different networks emphasizes the compatibility aspect between the home and host business networks. In establishing optimal initial trust with a potential foreign partner, emerging markets present unique institutional environments that may influence assessments of initial trust. An accurate assessment of this level of initial trust can increase the chance of venture success.

The framework described below draws upon institutional theory and the resource-based view of the firm to predict the optimal initial trust that an MNE must consider during the initial stages of an International Joint Venture (IJV) in an emerging nation. To examine the factors that influence an MNE's assessment of initial trust in a potential JV partner we develop propositions of three kinds. Factors that influence optimal initial trust primarily through the institutional environment represent the first kind of proposition. The second kind of proposition examines the more traditional firm-specific factors that influence optimal initial trust. The third kind represents the interaction effect of institutional and firm-specific resources upon trust. These propositions utilize the inherent differences between firms that come from different countries to precipitate the confounding factors an MNE may encounter in an emerging market. Consideration of these firm-specific resources makes the framework more complete, contrasts the difference relative to institutional factors, and demonstrates the interaction effect of institutional factors and firm-specific resources upon optimal initial trust. The key concepts included in the following propositions are represented in Figure 6.1.

INSTITUTIONAL THEORY

Institutions represent the "rules of the game in a society" (North 1990, 3). Institutional theory underscores the ability of institutions to influence organizations to conform to practices, policies, and structures that are consistent with institutional preferences (Meyer and Rowan 1977). According to DiMaggio and Powell (1983), highly institutionalized environments are strongly influenced by coercive, mimetic, and normative isomorphism. Institutional scholars have conjectured that a firm is more inclined to survive if it has external legitimacy (Baum and Oliver 1991; DiMaggio and Powell 1983; Meyer and Rowan 1977; Meyer and Scott 1983). This is because external legitimacy improves an organization's status and facilitates resource acquisition in the local environment, while attenuating evaluations of its capabilities (Oliver 1991). The relevance of the institutional environment to MNEs has been highlighted by research that has adapted institutionalization to MNE theory (Kostova 1999; Kostova and Zaheer 1999; Meyer 2001; Rosenzweig and Singh 1991; Westney 1993).

Figure 6.1
A Conceptual Framework of Initial Trust of Joint Venture Partners in Emerging Nations

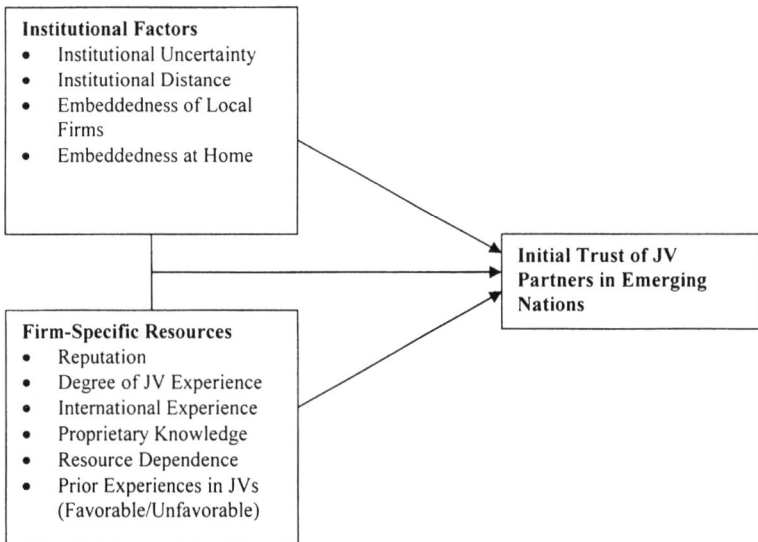

An MNE seeking to operate in an emerging nation may face multiple challenges stemming from the institutional environment. First, the MNE may encounter institutional uncertainty (Meyer 2001) that limits the advantages that may be gained from local partners and encounter high costs when searching for information regarding local partners and the legal system of the emerging market.[1] Second, even when operating in emerging nations with established institutions, an MNE may face challenges due to differences in regulatory systems, cognitive abilities and normative institutions (Kostova and Zaheer 1999). Third, local firms may have uniquely embedded networks. Institutional uncertainty, institutional distance, and embeddedness, represent key external factors that can have important implications for the assessment of optimal initial trust of an MNE in an emerging nation.

Institutional Factors

Institutional Uncertainty

Hoskisson et al. (2000) noted that emerging nations are heterogeneous, even within the same geographic region. Heterogeneity arises from differences in starting points of transition, paths of transition, and degrees of progress that collectively result in the degree and nature of institutional uncertainty being different across countries. The protection of intellectual property rights for example tends to be weak in emerging nations when it comes to enactment and enforcement (Rawski 1994). An MNE's technological capabilities may thus be compromised without the requisite institutional structures. Several scholars have suggested that an MNE can compensate for this kind of uncertainty by maintaining higher control of its local operations.

Uncertainty arising from institutional factors acts as *noise* in the foreign market that makes it harder to interpret signals from a firm, and alters the behavior needed to achieve mutual trust longitudinally (Bendor, Kramer, and Stout 1991). In the context of a potential international joint venture, more information is needed about the foreign firm to overcome this noise. In emerging nations with high institutional uncertainty, we anticipate that the MNE will exhibit lower trust levels. Therefore:

Proposition 1: In an emerging nation with high institutional uncertainty, an MNE is inclined to establish low initial trust with a local JV partner, ceteris paribus.

Institutional Distance

Institutional distance between two countries refers to the degree of congruence between the regulatory, cognitive, and normative institutions of two countries (Kostova and Zaheer 1999). In general, the greater the political, legal, socio-cultural and economic differences between the home and host countries, the greater the costs of doing business abroad. Consequently, institutional distance should reduce the ability of a new foreign entrant to comprehend host country institutional guidelines. We contend that high institutional distance makes comprehension of the foreign network difficult and, thus, it is difficult to make accurate assessments of the trustworthiness of the local partner. This degree of uncertainty makes it difficult for a local firm in the emerging market to appear legitimate to an MNE. Firms in the emerging market accordingly incur higher costs when attempting to demonstrate integrity to other parties (Eden and Miller 2002). High levels of trust will thus be difficult to establish in an emerging market. Therefore:

Proposition 2: If the level of institutional distance between an MNE's home country and an emerging nation is high, then the MNE will establish low initial trust with a potential local partner, ceteris paribus.

Embeddedness

Embeddedness reflects the degree to which economic transactions take place through relationships that use social and noncommercial criteria to govern business dealings (Marsden 1981). A high degree of embeddedness in a business network leads to the exclusion of firms that are unable to establish comparable ties (Granovetter 1973), higher entry barriers (Bower 1987), and makes the demarcation between network insiders and outsiders more apparent. High embeddedness can also be a barrier to firms not from the emerging market network when trying to acquire information, increasing the cost of information acquisition for MNEs. Thus, in host countries with highly embedded firms the MNE has a greater need for a local partner in order to penetrate local networks and lessen the risk of discriminatory treatment. However, the MNE may find network members either unwilling or unable to share relevant information because of reputation concerns or legal obligations, suggesting that low initial trust is optimal when a local firm is part of a highly embedded network. Therefore:

Proposition 3a: In an emerging nation with local firms that are highly embedded, an MNE is inclined to establish low initial trust with a local JV partner, ceteris paribus.

Punishment in an embedded network   Social capital in a business network plays a prominent role in establishing the incidence of opportunism and hence trust levels appropriate to a business venture.[2] As a form of normative governance, social capital arises from the embedded nature of a business network that requires the actions of firms to occur in continued simultaneous consideration with the other firms to which it is linked. These interfirm linkages form the basis for an opportunistic constraint through the imposition of sanctions against opportunistic firms (Hagen and Choe 1998). As a result, embedded

local firms that are penalized for opportunistic behavior may encounter reduced interaction with network members in future periods, as other firms
restrain themselves from dealing with an untrustworthy firm.

The existence of penalties for opportunistic behavior provides a valuable
signal for firms new to the business network in an emerging nation. In such
an environment, a local firm with social capital is less likely to behave opportunistically because of the potential loss of social capital that can increase
operating costs and preclude synergistic benefits from developing. This is
insufficient to establish the probability that the foreign partner will behave
opportunistically; however, it must also be known if betrayal between this
host partner and the foreign multinational will indeed result in negative reputation effects and a loss of social capital in the host partner's network. It is
possible that the culture of the network will not punish the host partner for
betrayal, or even admire the firm for being able to *better* the larger foreign
multinational entity. Thus mere existence of an embedded network is insufficient to establish likely opportunism, as the nature of the network must also
be known. In a study of firms exporting to Asia, distributors in Indonesia were
far more likely to behave opportunistically than Japanese firms despite having
a high degree of embeddedness, as opportunistic behavior was less likely to
be punished (Dowling et al. 2001).[3] Therefore:

Proposition 3b: In a host country with highly embedded local firms, an MNE
is inclined to exhibit high initial trust if the embedded network punishes opportunistic behavior, ceteris paribus. If the host country does not punish opportunistic behavior, an MNE is inclined to exhibit low initial trust, ceteris
paribus.

RESOURCE-BASED VIEW

A model of how firms build and sustain competitive advantage, known as
the *Resource Based View* (RBV) of the firm, has assumed an increasingly important position in the strategic management literature (Barney 1986, 1991;
Peteraf 1993; Rumelt 1984; Rumelt, Schendel, and Teece 1991; Wernerfelt
1984). Resources that are distinct and costly to imitate may form the basis of
sustainable competitive advantage (Andrews 1971; Barney 1986; Peteraf
1993). A key assumption of the RBV is the notion of resource heterogeneity
where resource bundles and capabilities underlying production differ across
firms (Barney 1991) with some resources being superior to others. In the
context of the present study, we focus on distinctive resources that may influence optimal initial trust in joint ventures located in emerging nations. Distinctive resources enhance an MNE's ability to understand local network
capabilities, interpret and emit signals, as well as, reduce the possibility of
opportunism. Prior studies have considered an MNE's reputation (Dollinger,
Golden, and Saxton 1997; Dyer 1996; Houston and Johnson 2000), interna-

tional experience (Anderson and Gatignon 1986, Johanson and Vahlne 1977), proprietary knowledge (Luo 2001), prior experiences in JVs (Roath, Miller, and Casvusgil 2002), and resource interdependence (Cook and Emerson 1978; Pfeffer and Salancik 1978; Zaheer and Venkatraman 1995).

Firm-Specific Resources

Reputation of a Multinational

Reputation can have an effect on opportunistic behavior (Houston and Johnson 2000), as a firm with a reputation for being trustworthy is attractive to potential partners (Dyer 1996). Furthermore, the host network in the emerging market is likely to be more open to a well-regarded MNE, and potential local partners will more readily provide information concerning their activities to demonstrate their superior competence and positive intent. Strong home reputation effects for the MNE are in fact a special case of network comprehensibility, as members in the host network are able to interpret the MNEs network enough to observe positive reputation effects. The *language* of the MNE's home country network is thus recognizable enough to host country firms for them to interpret the MNE's signals quite accurately. Therefore:

Proposition 4: An MNE with a favorable reputation is inclined to establish high initial trust with a local JV partner, ceteris paribus.

International Experience

A number of studies have highlighted the role of the firm's international experience in accumulating market knowledge (Johanson and Vahlne 1977), and determining the optimal entry mode (Anderson and Gatignon 1986). It can be argued that an MNE with extensive international experience possesses sufficient knowledge of the host market and the organizational practices of potential JV partners and therefore, would be better able to interpret signals concerning a potential JV partner. Furthermore, an experienced MNE is well positioned to anticipate circumstances and select ideal relational governance mechanisms (Roath, Miller, and Casvusgil 2002). Thus:

Proposition 5: An MNE with high (low) international experience is likely to establish high (low) initial trust with a local JV partner, ceteris paribus.

Proprietary Knowledge

The protection of knowledge is one of the most important elements in successful joint ventures (e.g., Hennart 1989; Zander and Kogut 1994), as overexposure of knowledge to the local partner can erode an MNE's competitive advantage (Luo 2001). JV scholars have argued that as an MNE's level of proprietary knowledge increases, there is a greater need for control in order to prevent knowledge leaks (Harrigan 1985; Yan and Gray 1994). In the context of the present study, an MNE can protect its knowledge resources by employing hierarchical governance mechanisms that have the unfortunate effect of lowering the level of initial trust with a local partner in an emerging market. Therefore:

Proposition 6: An MNE with a high level of proprietary knowledge is inclined to establish low initial trust with the local JV partner, ceteris paribus.

Prior Experience in IJVs

Several studies have cited the importance of prior negative or positive experiences with regard to current business relationships (Roath, Miller, and Casvusgil 2002). An MNE that has encountered opportunistic behavior in a previous interorganizational relationship, especially with local firms from emerging nations, will be less inclined to trust a local JV partner than an MNE with favorable previous experiences with partners in emerging nations. While favorable or unfavorable prior experience may affect assessments of trustworthiness in the potential partner positively or negatively, on balance, past experience should equip the MNE with skills that facilitate interaction and interpretation of the foreign network. Thus:

Proposition 7: The more positive (negative) the prior IJV experiences of an MNE, the more inclined it is to establish high (low) initial trust with a local partner, ceteris paribus.

Resource Interdependence

Interdependence between two firms leads to a situation whereby the outcomes or the payoff for both parties depends upon the actions of each (Pfeffer and Salancik 1978). The interdependence (especially when it is symmetrical) creates mutual safeguards for both parties because it discourages the development and expression of behaviors that may be detrimental to the relationship (Cook and Emerson 1978; Williamson 1985). Moreover, interdependence provides both parties with incentives to make the relationship work and endure (Buchanan 1992). Accordingly, they are likely to increase interaction, share information, and create a mutual understanding regarding their obligations to each other (Ring and Van de Ven 1992). Therefore:

Proposition 8: If resource interdependence between a local firm and an MNE is expected to be high and symmetrically distributed, the MNE is inclined to establish high initial trust with the local JV partner, ceteris paribus.

INTERACTIONS

We contend that interactions between institutional factors and firm-specific resources are theoretically relevant for an MNE dealing with an emerging nation. For instance, an MNE's level of optimal initial trust in an emerging nation with institutional distance or embedded local firms can be affected by its firm-specific resources: international experience, prior JV experiences, reputation, and even home-country factors such as home-country embeddedness, which may form the basis of a distinctive resource for an MNE.

As social systems, business networks develop their own character and customs that are the result of cultural, institutional, and historical factors. Divergent networks that evolve in different countries or cultures possess unique customs that form their individual language. While similarities between social systems almost always exist, firms from outside the system inevitably face communication difficulties such as an inability to signal and interpret signals in the foreign network. We expect these difficulties to become more pronounced as institutional distance increases. The more difficult it is for potential venture partners to interpret each other's business network (i.e., the higher the institutional distance), the harder it is to assess trustworthy characteristics. Needless to say, firms familiar with structuring business transactions in their own environment may encounter difficulties in emerging countries where the methods of dealing with government bodies and legal problems differ greatly. All of these factors may be mitigated by a firm's international experience in emerging markets. An MNE that has dealt with foreign firms in emerging markets previously, is more likely to be able to interpret the language of a foreign network and be able to handle real and implied hazards in the host-country environment (Delios and Henisz 2000). Likewise, a host-country partner with prior experience concerning foreign MNEs is also better equipped to read and provide signals that will reduce the chance of misunderstanding (Luo 1997). Thus:

Proposition 9: In an emerging nation with high institutional distance, the greater the degree of international experience in emerging nations by an MNE, the more likely it is to establish high initial trust with a local partner, ceteris paribus.

The efficacy of prior experience in understanding a network is tempered by the extent to which prior encounters with partners have been positive. Both MNEs and firms in emerging markets that have had negative encounters in the past will be more cautious when entering new agreements. This level of caution mediates the extent to which network familiarity can be relied upon to build trust. Therefore:

Proposition 10: In an emerging nation with high institutional distance, the more positive the prior emerging market IJV experiences of an MNE, the more inclined it is to establish high initial trust with a local partner, ceteris paribus.

As we noted earlier, reputation effects reduce opportunistic behavior. But when a potential local partner is embedded, word of opportunist behavior would spread throughout the network leading to unfavorable consequences such as loss of future business dealings with the network (Hennart 1989; Williamson 1985). In emerging nations with highly embedded firms that penalize opportunism, we infer that an MNE with a favorable reputation will initiate even higher levels of initial trust with a local partner than a rival MNE without such a reputation. Therefore:

Proposition 11a: In an emerging nation with local firms that are highly embedded, the more favorable the reputation of the MNE, the more inclined it is to establish high initial trust with a local partner, ceteris paribus. If the embedded network penalizes opportunistic behavior, then an MNE with a favorable reputation is inclined to exhibit very high initial trust, ceteris paribus.

One overlooked element in the study of initial trust is the importance of the home-country environment. MNEs from highly embedded home countries are able to leverage their home country experience in host countries (especially if opportunism is penalized in the home environment) through better interpretation of signals from a potential partner, and understanding of embedded network customs. For example, in the United States, where "firms rarely trust each other" enough to establish a relationship, firms often fail to establish trust when dealing with foreign firms that value normative embeddedness. But in Japan normative interfirm relationships are strong (Ouchi 1981, 16) and trust in Japanese cooperative relationships has been attributed with reducing the costs of doing business in Japan (Dore 1987). Scholars conclude that the Japanese trust-based, interorganizational system can be transplanted effectively to other countries (Hagen and Choe 1998; Nishiguchi 1994), suggesting that embeddedness of both local firms and the MNE's home-country market structure need to be assessed when evaluating trust (Eden and Miller 2002). Thus:

Proposition 11b: In an emerging nation with local firms that are highly embedded, an MNE from a home-country with high embeddedness is inclined to establish higher initial trust with a local JV partner than an MNE from a home country with low embeddedness, ceteris paribus.

The above propositions are summarized in Figure 6.1 that categorizes the factors that affect optimal initial trust into institutional and firm-specific factors. Explicit in the framework, is the key role institutional and resource-based factors have for levels of initial trust. In addition to the direct influence institutional differences have upon optimal initial trust. Firm-specific resources such as the MNE's prior experiences are necessarily moderated by the difference in institutions between the country from which the MNE is based, and the emerging market in which the local partner comes from. This institutional perspective emphasizes the embedded nature of firms and the need to consider the nature of embeddedness when organizations from different countries meet.

CONCLUSION

A consideration of optimal initial trust in an emerging market has important distinguishing characteristics. The development of long-term trust and commitment necessarily begins with an initial encounter. This initial encounter has been proven to be crucial to building long-term trust between social actors (Axelrod 1984). The present study extends prior research on initial trust (McKnight, Cummings, and Cherveney 1998), and optimal trust (e.g., Parkhe and Miller 2000; Wicks, Berman, and Jones 1999) by developing an optimal initial trust framework that integrates both institutional factors and firm-specific resources in an emerging market. Moreover, it extends a growing body of literature that has applied institutional theory to emerging nations (e.g., Delios and Henisz 2000; Hoskisson et al. 2000; Meyer 2001).

The framework can be useful to managers of MNEs that are considering a joint venture as a mode of entry into an emerging nation. For example, during the initial contact stage, the MNE must account for the network characteristics surrounding the potential JV partner together with the internal characteristics of the local firm. Furthermore, international managers must understand the firm-specific resources and network characteristics of their respective MNEs in order to realize where inconsistencies and opportunities for cooperation may exist. If trust is unlikely to be established with a local firm in the emerging market, the MNE must then consider alternative ventures that involve a different firm, investigate avenues for overcoming the barriers to trust, such as teaming with a more reputed MNE or a third-country firm, or evaluate other permissible modes of entry, such as a wholly-owned subsidiary.

We recognize that scholars have yet to embrace a single definition of trust (e.g., Sheppard and Sherman 1998). In fact, optimal trust consists of both trust and distrust (Wicks, Berman, and Jones 1999).[4] Others have debated the relationship between trust and opportunism contending that neither trust nor opportunism can be stated to be exclusively bad or good in any given circumstance (e.g., Barney and Hansen 1994). While insufficient trust in a business relationship can result in a sub-optimal outcome, excessive trust can place a firm at risk of opportunistic behavior by its business partner. Opportunism may be similarly viewed, as an absence of opportunism removes an important competitive force in market transactions and can result in inefficiencies arising from a lack of knowledge regarding alternatives. The benefit of hindsight has also allowed the field of interorganizational relationships to realize a somewhat counterintuitive linkage between trust and opportunism. It is necessary to first have trust in a relationship before true opportunism may occur (Elangovan and Shapiro 1998). Nevertheless, we point out that our objective was to focus specifically on the concept of optimal initial trust. As such, future research may consider a dynamic analysis of optimal trust or integrate the concept of distrust. Lastly, the present study focused on joint ventures in emerging nations. However, trust is relevant to other organizational relationships in other contexts. A logical theoretical extension to this line of research is to consider alternative forms of operation in a variety of markets that have marked institutional differences.

NOTES

1. In addition, MNEs may face inertia as employees cling to work-related practices that were embedded in the centrally-planned system, (e.g., shirking).

2. Williamson defined opportunism as "self-interest seeking with guile" (1975: 47).

3. In contrast, negative behavior is, at time, considered evidence of business competence in parts of the Indonesian importing network, as the local Indonesian firm demonstrated its ability to "outdo" the foreign company (Dowling et al. 2001). Similar reputation rewards have been observed in India where nationalization or interference in the affairs of foreign owned businesses is often viewed in a patriotic light such as in Enron Development Corporation's experience (Inkpen 1996).

4. Lewicki, McAllister, and Bies (1998) argue that trust and distrust should not be considered as polar opposites along a single dimension as both may be simultaneously present in a relationship. Distrust as applied by Lewicki, McAllister, and Bies is analogous to opportunism but better captures the notion of attributing intent to an individual rather than a singular action. Thus distrust implies a lack of trustworthiness in an individual, who is more likely to undertake opportunistic actions. Lewicki, McAllister, and Bies observed that an individual may be trustworthy in some respects and untrustworthy in others.

REFERENCES

Anderson, E., and H. Gatignon. 1986. "Modes of Foreign Entry: A Transaction Cost Analysis and Propositions." *Journal of International Business Studies* 17: 1–26.

Andrews, K. 1971. *The Concept of Corporate Strategy.* Homewood, Ill.: Irwin.

Arrow, K. 1981. *The Limits of Organizations.* New York: Norton.

Aulakh, P., M. Kotabe, and A. Sahay. 1997. "Trust and Performance in Cross-Border Marketing Relationships." In *Cooperative Strategies: Vol. 1. North American Perspectives*, edited by P. Beamish and J. Killing. San Francisco: New Lexington Press.

Axelrod, R. 1984. *The Evolution of Cooperation.* New York: Basic Books.

Barney, J. 1986. "Strategic Factor Markets: Expectations, Luck, and Business Strategy." *Management Science* 42: 1231–41.

———. 1991. "Firm Resources and Sustained Competitive Advantage." *Journal of Management* 17: 99–120.

Barney, J., and M. Hansen. 1994. "Trustworthiness as a Source of Competitive Advantage." *Strategic Management Journal* 15: 175–90.

Baum, J., and C. Oliver. 1991. "Institutional Linkages and Organizational Mortality." *Administrative Science Quarterly* 36: 187–218.

Bendor, J., R. M. Kramer, and S. Stout. 1991. "When in Doubt . . . Cooperation in a Noisy Prisoner's Dilemma." *Journal of Conflict Resolution* 35 (4): 691–719.

Bower, J. 1987. *When Markets Quake*. Boston: Harvard Business School Press.

Buchanan, L. 1992. "Vertical Trade Relationships: The Role of Dependence and Symmetry in Attaining Organizational Goals." *Journal of Marketing Research* 29: 65–75.

Cook, K. S., and R. M. Emerson. 1978. "Power, Equity, and Commitment in Exchange Networks." *American Sociological Review* 43: 721–39.

Das, T., and B. S. Teng. 1998. "Between Trust and Control: Developing Confidence in Partner Cooperation in Alliances." *Academy of Management Review* 23: 491–512.

Delios, A., and W. Henisz. 2000. "Japanese Firms' Investment Strategies in Emerging Economies." *Academy of Management Journal* 43 (3): 305–23.

Deutsch, M. 1962. "Cooperation and Trust: Some Theoretical Notes." *Nebraska Symposium on Motivation*. Lincoln, Nebr.: Nebraska University Press.

DiMaggio, P., and W. Powell. 1983. "The Iron Cage Revisited: Institutional Isomorphism and Collective Rationality in Organization Fields." *American Sociological Review* 48: 147–60.

Dollinger, M., P. Golden, and T. Saxton. 1997. "The Effect of Reputation on the Decision to Joint Venture." *Strategic Management Journal* 18: 127–40.

Doney, P., J. Cannon, and M. Mullen. 1998. "Understanding the Influence of National Culture on the Development of Trust." *Academy of Management Review* 23 (3): 601–20.

Dore, R. 1987. *Taking Japan Seriously*. Stanford, Calif.: Stanford University Press.

Dowling, P., P. Liesch, J. Flint, S. As-Saber, P. Innes, and K. Chan. 2001. "Management Strategies of Firms Exporting to Asia." *Journal of the Australian and New Zealand Academy of Management* 6 (2): 1–19.

Dyer, J. 1996. "Does Governance Matter? Keiretsu Alliances and Asset Specificity as Sources of Japanese Competitive Advantage." *Organization Science* 7: 649–66.

Dyer, J., and W. Chu. 2000. "The Determinants of Trust in Supplier-Automaker Relationships in the U.S., Japan, and Korea." *Journal of International Business Studies* 31: 259–85.

Eden, L., and S. R. Miller. 2002. "Multinationals and the Costs of Doing Business Abroad: An Organizational Legitimacy Approach." Texas A&D University. Unpublished.

Elangovan, A. R., and D. L. Shapiro. 1998. "Betrayal of Trust in Organizations." *Academy of Management Review* 23 (3): 547–66.

Gambetta, D. 1988. *Trust: Making and Breaking Cooperative Relations*. New York: Basil Blackwell.

Granovetter, M. 1973. "The Strength of Weak Ties." *American Journal of Sociology* 81: 1287–1303.

Hagen, J., and S. Choe 1998. "Trust in Japanese Interfirm Relations: Institutional Sanctions Matter." *Academy of Management Review* 23: 589–600.

Harrigan, K. 1985. *Strategies for Joint Ventures*. Lexington, Mass.: Lexington Books.

Hennart, J.-F. 1989. "Can the 'New Forms of Investment' Substitute for the 'Old Forms?' A Transaction Cost Perspective," *Journal of International Business Studies* 20: 211–34.

Hoskisson, R., L. Eden, C. M. Lau, and M. Wright. 2000. "Strategy in Emerging Economies." *Academy of Management Journal* 43 (3): 249–67.

Houston, M., and S. Johnson. 2000. "Buyer-Supplier Contracts Versus Joint Ventures: Determinants and Consequences of Transaction Structure." *Journal of Marketing Research* 37: 1–15.

Inkpen, A. 1996. "Case Study: Enron Development Corporation." In *Strategic Management: Competitiveness and Globalization.* Cincinnati: South-Western College Publishing.

Inkpen, A., and K.-Q. Li. 1999. "Joint Venture Formation: Planning and Knowledge-Gathering for Success." *Organizational Dynamics* 27 (4): 33–47.

Johanson, J., and J.-E. Vahlne. 1977. "The Internationalization Process of the Firm—A Model of Knowledge Development and Increasing Foreign Market Commitments." *Journal of International Business Studies* 8: 23–32.

Jones, T. 1995. "Instrumental Stakeholder Theory: A Synthesis of Ethics and Economics." *Academy of Management Review* 20: 404–37.

Kostova, T. 1999. "Transnational Transfer of Strategic Organizational Practices: A Contextual Perspective." *Academy of Management Review* 24: 308–24.

Kostova, T., and S. Zaheer. 1999. "Organizational Legitimacy Under Conditions of Complexity: The Case of the Multinational Enterprise." *Academy of Management Review* 24: 64–81.

Lewicki, R. J., D. J. McAllister, and R. J. Bies. 1998. "Trust and Distrust: New Relationships and Realities." *Academy of Management Review* 23 (3): 438–58.

Luo, Y. 1997. "Partner Selection and Venturing Success: The Case of Joint Ventures with Firms in the People's Republic of China." *Organization Science* 8 (6): 648–62.

———. 2001. "Entry Mode Selection during International Expansion: The Case of MNEs in an Emerging Market." *Journal of Management Studies.* Forthcoming.

Marsden, P. 1981. "Introducing Influence Processes into a System of Collective Decisions." *American Journal of Sociology* 86: 1203–35.

Mayer, R., J. Davis, and D. Schoorman. 1995. *Taking Risks: The Management of Uncertainty.* New York: Free Press.

McKnight, D. H., L. L. Cummings, and N. L. Chervany. 1998. "Initial Trust Formation in New Organizational Relationships." *Academy of Management Review* 23 (3): 473–90.

Meyer, J., and B. Rowan. 1977. "Institutionalized Organizations: Formal Structure as Myth and Ceremony." *American Journal of Sociology* 83: 340–63.

Meyer, J., and W. R. Scott. 1983. "Centralization and the Legitimacy Problems of Local Government." In *Organizational Environments: Ritual and Rationality,* edited by J. Meyer and W. R. Scott. Beverly Hills, Calif.: Sage Publications.

Meyer, K. 2001. "Institutions, Transaction Costs and Entry Mode Choice in Eastern Europe." *Journal of International Business Studies* 32: 357–67.

Nishiguchi, T. 1994. *Strategic industrial sourcing.* London: Oxford University Press.

North, D. C. 1990. *Institutions, Institutional Change, and Economic Performance.* New York: Cambridge University Press.

Oliver, C. 1991. "Strategic Responses to Institutional Processes." *Academy of Management Review* 16: 145–79.

Ouchi, W. 1981. *Theory Z.* New York: Avon.

Parkhe, A., and S. R. Miller. 2000. "The Structure of Optimal Trust: A Comment and Some Extensions." *Academy of Management Review* 25: 10–11.

Peteraf, M. 1993. "The Cornerstones of Competitive Advantage: A Resource-Based View." *Strategic Management Journal* 14 (3): 179–91.

Pfeffer, J., and G. R. Salancik. 1978. *The External Control of Organizations: A Resource Dependence Perspective.* New York: Harper and Row.

Rawski, T. 1994. "Chinese Industrial Reform: Accomplishments, Prospects, and Implications." *The American Economic Review* 84 (2): 271–75.

Ring, P. S., and A. H. Van de Ven. 1992. "Structuring Cooperative Relationships Between Organizations." *Strategic Management Journal* 13 (7): 483–98.

Roath, A., S. R. Miller, and S. T. Cavusgil. 2002. "A Conceptualization of Relational Governance in International Relationships." *International Business Review* 11(1): 1–16.

Rosenzweig, P., and J. Singh. 1991. "Organizational Environments and the Multinational Enterprise." *Academy of Management Review* 16: 340–61.

Rousseau, D., S. Sitkin, R. Burt, and C. Camerer. 1998. "Not So Different After All: A Cross-Disciplined View of Trust." *Academy of Management Review* 23: 393–404.

Rumelt, R. 1984. "Towards a Strategic Theory of the Firm," In *Competitive Strategic Management*, edited by R. Lamb. Englewood Cliffs, N.J.: Prentice-Hall.

Rumelt, R., D. Schendel, and D. Teece. 1991. "Strategic Management and Economics." *Strategic Management Journal* 12: 5–29.

Sheppard, B. H., and D. M. Sherman. 1998. "The Grammars of Trust: A Model and General Implications." *Academy of Management Review* 23 (3): 422–37.

Wernerfelt, B. 1984. "A Resource-Based View of the Firm." *Strategic Management Journal* 5 (2): 171–80.

Westney, D. E. 1993. "Institutionalization Theory and the Multinational Corporation." In *Organizational Theory and the Multinational Corporation*, edited by S. Ghoshal and D. E. Westney. New York: St. Martin's Press.

Wicks, A., S. Berman, and T. Jones. 1999. "The Structure of Optimal Trust: Moral and Strategic Implications." *Academy of Management Review* 24: 99–116.

Williams, M. 2001. "In Whom We Trust: Group Membership as an Affective Context for Trust Development." *Academy of Management Review* 26: 377–96.

Williamson, O. 1975. *Market and Hierarchies: Analysis and Antitrust Implications.* New York: Free Press.

———. 1985. *The Economic Institutions of Capitalism.* New York: Free Press.

———. 1993. "Calculativeness, Trust and Economic Organization." *Journal of Law and Economics* 30: 131–45.

Yan, A., and B. Gray. 1994. "Bargaining Power, Management Control, and Performance in United States-Chinese Joint Ventures." *Academy of Management Journal* 37: 1478–1517.

Zaheer, A., and N. Venkatraman. 1995, "Relational Governance as an Interorganizational Strategy: An Empirical Test of the Role of Trust in Economic Exchange." *Strategic Management Journal* 16 (5): 373–93.

Zander, U., and B. Kogut. 1994. "Knowledge and the Speed of the Transfer and Imitation of Organizational Capabilities." *Organization Science* 6: 76–92.

CHAPTER 7

Family Conglomerates: Key Features Relevant to Multinationals

*Destan Kandemir, Daekwan Kim, and
S. Tamer Cavusgil*

Recently the Hyundai Group, one of the top five family conglomerates (*chaebols*) in South Korea, experienced a financial crisis that prompted the Korean government, and Hyundai's major creditors, to provide well over $400 million in assistance, including credit extension and short-term loans, to secure some of the major business units of the group from bankruptcy. It is not easy for most small and medium-sized firms to obtain that type of assistance in Korea, but the family-owned and operated Hyundai Group had no great difficulty (Chung 2000). Historically, the group was led by its founder, Joo Young Chung, in all strategic moves, which included diversifying into many different industries, but the business is in the process of transitioning to the second generation (Drozdow and Carroll 1997). The recent crisis resulted from a battle for power by the founder's two sons, and the bailout reflects the heavy dependence of the Korean economy on this major family conglomerate (FC) (Chung 2000; Donga 2001; Hwang 2000).

Several months earlier, the Daewoo Group, another top *chaebol* and FC, also experienced a severe financial crisis and was restructured. Creditors and the government sought a buyer for one of the group's major business arms, Daewoo Motors. Despite successful expansion at home and abroad, the group's persistent inefficiency and exuberant business expansion—financed largely by loans (Chung 2000; Hwang 2000)—drove the conglomerate to the brink of ruin (Donga 2001; Khanna and Palepu 1999; Nachum 1999).

Large, diversified family-owned businesses are not unique to Korea. Indeed, such dominant players are part of the economic landscape in most emerging markets (EMs). Whether they are known as *chaebols* in Korea, business houses in India, holding companies in Turkey, *bumiputra* in Malaysia, or *groupos* in Latin America, FCs are some of the most prevalent business structures. Its role in EMs is significant. For example, the top 30 conglomerates (FCs) in Korea generate more than 46 percent of the entire industry's revenue while their total assets account for 47 percent of the whole economy. Their origins and growth can be attributed to a special relationship with government and with the economy itself. Because FCs play such a significant role in Korea and other emerging markets, it is critical for Western companies contemplating business in such markets to understand that role. Our objective in this research is to provide a better understanding of the FCs' roles in emerging markets. The 19 family conglomerates we investigated in this study originate from eight emerging markets: India, Indonesia, Korea, Mexico, the Philippines, Taiwan, Thailand, and Turkey, as shown in Table 7.1.

FAMILY CONGLOMERATES IN EMERGING MARKETS

EMs have high growth potential in the evolving world economic order and present a mixture of opportunities and risks for Western companies (Cavusgil 1997; Garten 1997a; Kock and Guillen 2001). The attractiveness of these markets lies not only in cheap raw materials and labor but also in the potential to generate revenues. Companies in industrialized countries depend on overseas markets for both economies of scale and profits.

Yet, there are risks to doing business in EMs. These include an inadequate marketing infrastructure, such as poorly developed distribution systems; limited communication channels; lack of regulatory discipline and frequent regulatory changes; a high level of product diversion; various market failures; and political and economic instability (Arnold and Quelch 1998; Garten 1997a; Khanna and Palepu 1997). In many EMs, Western companies have poor market information, and sometimes regulation misguides foreign businesses (Khanna and Palepu 1997). Consequently, strategic alliances are an important entry strategy in these markets (Kock and Guillen 2001; Lane and Beamish 1990; Osborn and Hagedoorn 1997). Western companies can use these alliances to share risk and resources, gain local market knowledge, and obtain access to markets (Kock and Guillen 2001).

FCs that can be potential allies to Western companies are a universally observed ownership type across EMs (Khanna and Palepu 1997; Kock and Guillen 2001). In this study, we use several defining measures to describe FCs. A typical FC is owned and controlled by a family (Ben-Porath 1980), and has a single founder who dominates, although family members may serve as executives in the business (Church 1993; Drozdow and Carroll 1997). Traditionally, the family holds the majority of the controlling rights of FCs in EMs (Church 1993; Khanna and Palepu 1999; Kock and Guillen 2001). Therefore, FCs are not the same as business groups because the ownership of a business group is not necessarily shared by a family (Granovetter 1995). Business

Table 7.1
Demographic Profiles of the Family Conglomeration

Group Name	Country of Origin	Founder	Current CEO	Year Started	Number of Employees	Annual Sales	Major industry (% of total sales)	Number of industries	Number of Subsidiaries	Number of JV	Number of Foreign Markets	Mode of Internationalization	Competitors	Year for Transition to Professional Management
Hyundai	Korea	Ju Young Chung	Mong Koo Chung	1947	200,000 ('97)	$49 bill. ('97)	Automotive (32.6), Finance and Service (23.2), Heavy (15.0), Construction (14.2)	7	41 ('99)		100+	Subsidiary	Deere, Ford, Honda, Toyota, GM, IBM, NEC, Siemens	1990 (2nd Gen)
Daewoo	Korea	Woo Choong Kim	Woo Choong Kim	1967	265,000 K ('97)	$71bill. ('97)	Automotive (32.6), Finance and Service (23.2), Heavy (15.0), Construction (14.2)	8	30+(97, domestic) 400+(Overseas)		130+	Subsidiary	Ford, GM, Sony, Toshiba, Toyota, Volkswagen	n.a.
LG	Korea	In Hwoi Koo	Bon Moo Koo	1947	126,000 ('97)	$46bill. ('97)	Chemical, Energy, Electronics	9	55 ('99)		120+ (hv)	Alliances	Motorola, Dow Chemical, GE, Toshiba, Sharp, Sony	1995 (3rd Gen)
Samsung	Korea	Byung Chull Lee	Kun Hee Lee	1936	267,000 ('97)	$72 bill ('98)	Electronics (27%), Financial (27%), Machinery (7%)	9	47 ('99)		70 (hv)	Acquisition	Compaq, DuPont, Matsushita, NEC, Sharp, Sony, Toshiba	1987 (2nd Gen)
Siam Cement	Thailand	Rama VI (Vajiravudh)	Chirayu Isarangkun Na Ayuthaya	1913	5,600 (ca. '97)	$2.9 bill. ('98)	Trading (41%), Petrochemicals (26%), Cement (21%), Paper (20%)	9	64		12	Subsidiary	Taiheyo Cement Corp., Sumitomo Osaka Cement Co., Ssanyyong Cement Industrial Co.	
Ayala	Philippines	Domingo Roxas and Antonio de Ayala	Jaime Zobel de Ayala	1834	24,000 ('99)	$858 mil. ('98)	Real Estate (29%), Food/Agriculture (30%), Electronics/IT (10%)	8	42		not significant	n.a.	Grasim Industries, Indian Rayon And Industries, Century Textiles and Industries	
San Miguel	Philippines	Don Enrique Barretoy de Ycaza	Eduardo M. Cojuangco Jr.	1890	15,900 (ca. '98)	$1.9 bill. ('98)	Beverages & Food (61%) Agribusiness (29%), Packaging (10%)	4	23		24	Export, Off-shore Production	Tsingtao Brewery, Murree Brewery, Tyson Food, PepsiCo, Heineken	
Astra	Indonesia		Rini Mariani Suarno Soewandi	1957	123,000 ('96)	$1.5 bill. ('98)	Automotive (76%), Financial (11%), Electronics (9%), Agricultural (3%)	7			not significant	n.a.	Keyo Co., Laox Co., Aichi Toyota Motor	
Formosa Plastics	Taiwan	Yung Ching Wang	Yung Ching Wang	1932	4,800 ('97)	$1.2 bill. ('98)	Chemical & Plastics, Power Supplier, Electronics	4	9			Export, Acquisition	Shanghai Petrochemical, Amoco, BASF AG, Dow Chemical, Eastman Chemical	
Tatung	Taiwan	Shan-Chih Lin	Tingsheng Lin	1918	19,600 ('97)	$3.0 bill. ('98)	Electronics, Telecom Equip, PCs	4	12			JV, Export, Subsidiary	Compaq, Dell Daewoo, Hitachi, Sharp, Sony, Matsushita, NEC	
ALARKO Group	Turkey	Ishak Alaton & Uzeyir Garh	Uzeyir Garh	1954	6,000 ('98)	$0.85 bill.	Contracting	n.a.	5	1	13	Contractual agreements, Exporting	STFA, ENKA	n.a.
KOC Group	Turkey	Vehbi Koc	Rahmi Koc	1926	37,178 ('98)	$5.8 bill. ('98)	Automotive (21%), Consumer Goods & Retailing (7 %), Financial Sevices (18%)	9	88	23	50	Export, Manufacturing, Distributor	Sabanci, Dogus, Anadolu Group, Cukurova Holding	1963 - Koc Holding Inc. created

(continued)

Table 7.1
Continued

Group Name	Country of Origin	Founder	Current CEO	Year Started	Number of Employees	Annual Sales	Major industry (% of total sales)	Number of industries	Number of Subsidiaries	Number of JV	Number of Foreign Markets	Mode of Internationalization	Competitors	Year for Transition to Professional Management
SABANCI Group	Turkey	Haci Omer Sabanci	Sakip Sabanci	1925	30,500 (n.a.)	$5.2 bill.	Tires and Tire Reinforcements, Textile, Automotive	8	53	16	10	Joint Venture, Foreign Investments, Export	Koc Group, Dogus , Anadolu Group, Cukurova Holding	1967 - Haci Omer Sabanci Holding Inc. established (second generation)
Desc	Mexico	Liberto Senderos	Fernando Senderos Mestre	1905	28,347 (n.a.)	$2.15 bill.	Auto parts (43%), Food (23%), Chemicals & Petrochemicals (16%)	5	4	13	50	Export		
Alfa	Mexico	n.a.	Dionisio Garza Medina	1974	36,254 ('98)	$3.641 bill.	Petrochemical & Synthetic Fibers (36.8%), Steel (47.7%), Food (16.4%), Auto Components & Construction, Telecom (12.20%)	7	22	20	n.a.	Subsidiaries	Desc, Grupo Carso	n.a.
Vitro	Mexico	n.a.	Jose Antonio Lopez M.	1909	33,320 ('97)	$2.51 bill.	Flat Glass (34%), Containers (30%), Household Goods (18%)	5+		15	70	Export		
Tata	India		Ratan Tata	1,945	262,000 (n.a.)	$8.8 bill.	Metals (82%), Automobiles, Energy, Chemicals, Finance	12				Export, Turnkey Projects		
Reliance	India				16,640 ('97)	$1.8 bill.	Chemicals, Polyester, Fibre, Textiles, Oil & Gas	4		10	6	Export	Tata Chemicals Ltd., Indian Petrochemicals Co. Ltd.	
Mahindra	India	J.C. & K.C. Mahindra	Keshub Mahindra	1947	17,000 ('97)	$0.76 bill.	Automotive Division (54%), Tractor Division (38%), Parts and Components (4%)	8		12	6	Export	Tata Engineering, Hero Honda Motors Ltd.	1963

groups may include firms linked by personal relationships stemming from similar personal, ethnic, and regional backgrounds (Granovetter 1995; Leff 1978). In the second and third generations, owners may become more removed from management, and this gap may gradually widen (Drozdow and Carroll 1997). Eventually, few family members actually work in the company, but the family still controls the board of directors. FCs have been operating for many years and have a substantial history (Ben-Porath 1980). They are highly dominant in their home market (Granovetter 1995) and have significant investments in a large number of businesses. They usually use internally generated capital as well as government loans for expansion and growth.

The FCs can add value to their national economy in several ways (Granovetter 1995; Khanna and Palepu 1999; Kock and Guillen 2001; Nachum 1999). For example, in 2000, the total number of subsidiaries of the top 30 Korean conglomerates exceeded 600. In addition, the aggregated firm value of the top five Korean conglomerates amounted to 5 percent of the total value of firms listed in the Korean Stock Exchange Market. Therefore, the conglomerates in Korea, which are mostly FCs, provide a significant contribution to Korean economy in terms of both number and impact (Hwang et al. 2000).

FCs have several advantages over foreign companies intending to enter their markets. They have a well-established local distribution network that would take years for Western companies to replicate. Longstanding relationships with government officials are not available to foreign companies (Kock and Guillen 2001; "Links" 1994). Their distinctive products appeal to local tastes (Ger 1999). FCs also have access to natural resources or labor that can give them a cost advantage (Dawar and Frost 1999) and competitive prices (Prahalad and Lieberthal 1998). Usually, FCs become aware of a Western company's new product strategy long before the brand is launched in the local market and can adjust its product line accordingly. FCs play an important role in the industrialization of their country and, therefore, are ideal partners for Western companies because they tend to have valuable local market data and understand local preferences (Kock and Guillen 2001).

An FC can use its group name to enter into new businesses (Khanna and Palepu 1997). Hyundai, Samsung, and Koc are examples. The use of a name that symbolizes world-class quality and customer service (Khanna and Palepu 1999) helps FCs compete with well-established multinational brands (Prahalad and Lieberthal 1998). In contrast, Western companies face a high cost to build a credible brand in markets with a relatively poor communication infrastructure (Khanna and Palepu 1997; Kock and Guillen 2001).

In this article, we address three basic questions: Why are FCs so important to their respective economies? What advantages do FCs offer Western companies? What may happen to FCs in the future? This study provides a better understanding of the concept of FCs and identifies patterns as well as differences with respect to their origins, governance, drivers, foreign partnerships, internationalization, and transition to professional management.

THE STUDY

Content Analysis

A replicable experiment is essential for a reliable and objective analysis, and categorizations should be consistent with the applied rules to avoid researcher bias (Holsti 1968). Since this is an exploratory study, we specified the scale and scope of this study, in advance, to a set of qualitative and quantitative factors. First, the scope of this study excluded nonfamily conglomerates, which are publicly owned and/or state owned. For example, in some emerging markets such as China or Africa, a majority of the conglomerates are owned by the government. Second, FCs and emerging markets were selected based on quantitative factors such as economic, financial, and business-related indicators.

Major emerging markets include the following: Argentina, Brazil, Chile, China, Colombia, Czech Republic, Egypt, Hungary, Hong Kong, India, Indonesia, Israel, Malaysia, Mexico, Peru, the Philippines, Russia, Singapore, South Africa, South Korea, Taiwan, Thailand, Turkey, Venezuela, and Poland ("Emerging Market Indicators" 2001). These countries were ranked based on their growth in GDP, industrial production, and consumer prices. For the current study, eight markets were selected from the list: India, Indonesia, Korea, Mexico, the Philippines, Taiwan, Thailand, and Turkey. The selection criteria were as follows (Garten 1997b): a large population and resource base; a major participant in critical political, economic, and social activities; being among the world's fastest expanding markets; and an increasing GDP.

The FCs were selected based on their origins, revenues, diversification, foreign partnerships, and internationalization figures. The following criteria were used: founded by a family, holds a number of subsidiaries and businesses, year-end sales figures for 1998, mode of market entry, and number of subsidiaries, joint ventures, and foreign markets. In each emerging market, we selected one to four FCs that were usually among the top 10 companies in their country. Thus, 19 FCs were investigated in depth in eight emerging markets. In our exploratory analysis, first we classified them according to their different stages (introduction, growth, and maturity) based on some indicators (e.g., sales, number of products, etc.). Then, we verified the drivers in each stage for each individual company and determined the drivers.

Secondary Research

The Web sites, annual reports, and financial records of the companies were analyzed. Biographies of founders, which provided some important insights into an FC's evolution, were also investigated. Directories consulted included the following: Wright Investors' Service, Hoover's *Handbook of World Business, International Public and Private Companies, International Directory of Company Histories, Principal International Business*, and *Asia's 7,500 Largest Companies.*

Business periodicals, journals, and newspapers were examined, including *Harvard Business Review*, *The Economist*, and the *Wall Street Journal*. Exploratory research into the literature on emerging markets, FCs, and international business also was conducted.

THE FORMATION OF FAMILY CONGLOMERATES

Founders

The critical role of the FC founder has been observed. Some characteristics in their biographies are noteworthy. They usually started the business with some capital when they were young. Through foresight and strategic decision-making ability they became market leaders (Drozdow and Carroll 1997), although in most cases they were not highly educated. Generally, they were entrepreneurs and risk takers, who became nationally prominent (Mariussen, Wheelock, and Baines 1997). Within the organization, they are hardly challenged while positioned as a ruler (Steers et al. 1989). The following case illustrates their power in the organizations.

Ethnically Chinese, Mr Kuok spent several of his eight decades collecting bitter memories of abuse by the Malay majority in his native Malaysia. So Mr Kuok, like most of South-East Asia's huaqiao, or overseas Chinese, early on made it his aim in life to build a better future for his children. This meant amassing wealth, spreading it across countries and industries to reduce risk, and above all keeping quiet about it. He began in the 1950s and 60s by cornering the markets for flour, palm oil and sugar in Malaysia. He then branched out into practically everything, from manufacturing to property, from hotels to media. Today, he commands a sprawling empire, managed by sons, nephews and in-laws. Its headquarters have been, at various times, in Malaysia, Singapore, Indonesia and Hong Kong. To protect himself, he likes to be everywhere in the region and nowhere; exposed to every industry and reliant on none. Gregarious and chatty, Mr Kuok nonetheless ensures that virtually nothing of substance is known about him. A few years ago, a big international investigative agency probed deeply into the Kuok empire and produced a report that included this profile of the patriarch: name—Robert Kuok; political affiliation—unknown; adversaries—none identified; litigation—nothing known; ambitions—not known. His Confucian management style is equally legendary. At a recent lunch he hosted, one of his guests put a question to Mr Kuok's fortysomething, western-educated son Ean, who runs Hong Kong's main English-language newspaper. But just as Ean started to answer, his father noted that it was time for another helping of garoupa, Mr Kuok's favourite fish, and sent his son out of the room to order more. The incident left little doubt about who did the talking in the family. ("Empires Without Umpires" 2001, 4)

They assumed social responsibilities by endowing schools, cultural and sports centers, and health care facilities ("The Import-Import" 1997). They also played an inspirational role in the advancement of business groups (Dent and Randerson 1997). Typical founders are Joo Young Chung of Hyundai, Byung

Chull Lee of Samsung, Vehbi Koc of Koc, and Haci Omer Sabanci of Sabanci; they are well known for their creativity, proactive and arduous efforts, aggressive and anticipatory decision making, and successful achievements.

Country-Specific Factors

Each country is a unique combination of factors (Woodall 1998): evolutionary stage of the economy, political system, government influence, natural resources, work ethic, financial resources, and endowments in land and labor (Kock and Guillen 2001; Nachum 1999). Some of these factors may cause the decay of family businesses ("Manila" 1982), some may foster their growth (Khanna and Palepu 1999), and each may play a different role in various evolutionary stages of a business.

DRIVERS OF FAMILY CONGLOMERATES

We analyzed FCs through the stages of introduction, growth, and maturity. We then identified major drivers influential in each stage of evolution, as shown in Figure 7.1. We also determined the relative importance of these drivers in each stage, as listed in Figure 7.1. The following sections are organized chronologically, that is, according to drivers that are prominent in the early, middle, and late stages of FC development.

Early Mover Advantages

At the introduction stage, FCs must understand the needs and wants of consumers when making new investments and creating new enterprises. FCs are generally the first manufacturers in many industries to serve the local market. Being an early mover enables the FC to capture a high market share and build brand equity ahead of competitors. For example, in Turkey, Koc was the first producer of automobiles, washing machines, and refrigerators; it played an important role in the country's industrialization and in the development of those sectors. Mahindra and Mahindra was the first manufacturer of tractors in India and currently has the largest facility. Hyundai Group, one of the early movers among current Korean automobile manufacturers, now has the largest share of the Korean auto market (Guillen 2001). The early mover advantage establishes market position for many FCs in various sectors throughout the subsequent growth stage. Typical sectors are auto-related industries, electronics, construction, information technology, confectionery, beverages, retailing, exporting, and importing.

Government Protection

In emerging markets, the government is heavily involved in business decisions (Granovetter 1995; Kock and Guillen 2001; Steers et al. 1989). In some

Figure 7.1
Drivers of Family Conglomerate's Evolution

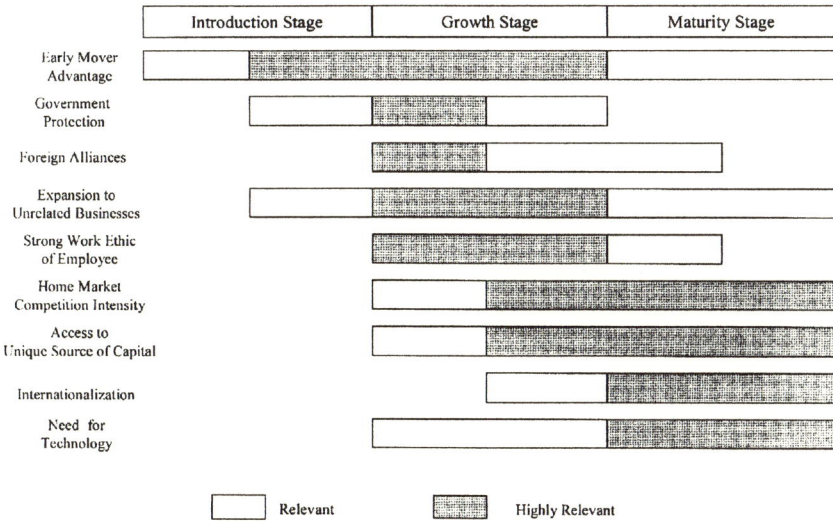

	Introduction Stage	Growth Stage	Maturity Stage
Early Mover Advantage			
Government Protection			
Foreign Alliances			
Expansion to Unrelated Businesses			
Strong Work Ethic of Employee			
Home Market Competition Intensity			
Access to Unique Source of Capital			
Internationalization			
Need for Technology			

☐ Relevant   ▦ Highly Relevant

Note: The gray area (highly relevant) indicates higher relative significance of the driver across the time line, not across drivers within each stage.

cases, it even initiates the FC. Siam Cement Group in Thailand is an example, as are the Indonesian FCs of Salim, Astra, and Lippo (Shin 1993). Government protection may take the form of special loans, subsidies, market entry barriers, and tax incentives among others (Jones and Rose 1993). For example, the Indian government regulates commodity price, raw material imports, and business exit. In most of the countries we examined, government protection has played a significant role in the growth of FCs. LG group in Korea benefited from elevated import barriers until the government opened up its toothpaste market in the 1980s. Until that time, LG made and marketed toothpaste products without any major competition in the domestic market. That for family conglomerates need to maintain a good working relationship with their government for their ongoing success is widely known as in Indonesia, South Korea, Turkey and elsewhere. The following cases in Indonesia and South Korea are illustrative.

Since the 1950s, the success of a particular business group in Indonesia has been closely linked to political elite. The national logistics board (Bulog) controls the price and supply of basic commodities. Bulog also spurs private business groups. One such group was Salim Group, a vast conglomerate. It is owned by an individual, a long time friend of President Suharto. Since 1969, The Group has ventured deeply in wheat milling and distribution, and has emerged as one of the world's largest producer. Much of its success has been ascribed to Bulog. The Group in turn expresses its gratitude (hutang budi) to Suharto. There is clear quid pro quo in this context, not an uncommon feature of the emerging markets. (Inside Indonesia, 1999)

Among South Korean chaebol, Kukje was seventh-largest. In 1985, it was forced into bankruptcy, for even though it had 38,000 employees and a sales revenue of more than $1.5 billion, it has had excess debt. In addition to its financial problem, Kukje evidently offended the government of President Chun. Under Chun's auspices was founded the New Village Movement. Businesses normally made contributions or quasi-taxes. Kukje President Yang Chang Mo, it was alleged did not contribute enough and did not show enough support to the Movement. In December 1984, the disssension culminated in Korea First Bank refusing to honor Kukje's checks, followed by finance companies calling up their debts. The end result was the forced bankruptcy of Kukje. (Steers et al. 1989)

As FCs grow, the effort of maintaining government relationships declines (Khanna and Palepu 1997; Kock and Guillen 2001). Experience and connections with officials give FCs an advantage in managing their business. Although government protection is an important driving force in the growth stage, it is less frequently observed in the introduction or maturity stages of FC evolution.

Foreign Alliances

Foreign alliances or collaborations are very important for FCs in the growth and early maturity stages. The need for expansion, access to resources, and organizational learning opportunities leads them to form joint ventures, international alliances, and licensing agreements with Western companies (Kock and Guillen 2001). Because of poorly developed financial markets, weak institutions for capital distribution, and volatility in economic development, FCs need access to capital at a reasonable cost (Hitt et al. 2000). FCs also may desire access to multiple forms of technological capability and may seek partners so they can learn from the experience and knowledge of others (Amsden and Hikino 1994; Kock and Guillen 2001). For example, joint ventures between Ford and Koc, Vitro, and Alfa as well as DuPont joint ventures with Sabanci, seek complementarities of benefit to each party. Mahindra and Mahindra is also licensed by Peugeot to produce automobile parts.

Through the maturity stage of FCs, the need to enhance managerial capabilities is another reason for foreign alliances. These capabilities and decision-making processes are not always well developed in FCs. Hitt et al. (2000) suggest that the need to compete in market-oriented economies and with more managerially sophisticated competitors prompts FCs to seek partners. In the initial stage of the partnership, FCs supply a dealer network, market information, and institutional knowledge about local regulations and laws, as well as language competency. The Western company needs local know-how, and the FC needs advanced technology or industry know-how (Kock and Guillen 2001). The usual progression is for the Western company to increase involvement with the FC, from licensing agreements to joint ventures, and then to wholly owned subsidiaries as uncertainty about the market decreases.

Expansion Strategy to Unrelated Businesses

Companies grow in many different ways. In the process of their evolution, FCs tend to invest in unrelated businesses and create fairly diversified businesses. This may happen partially because of the entrepreneurial orientation of the owners. Some expand production capacity to meet excess demand, enter new markets, develop new products, or form mergers or acquisitions (Hwang 2000). Others diversify within an industry, whereas still others expand across sectors. Although patterns depend on the unique business environment (Kock and Guillen 2001; Markides 1997), they also may be a function of internal factors, such as the founder's business philosophy, financial soundness, and latent connections with other businesses. The following case concerns the LG group in Korea.

My father and I started a cosmetic cream factory in the late 1940s. At the time, no company could supply us with plastic caps of adequate quality for cream jars, so we had to start a plastic business. Plastic caps alone were not sufficient to run the plastic-molding plant, so we added combs, toothbrushes, and soapboxes. This plastic business also led us to manufacture electric fan blades and telephone cases, which in turn led us to manufacture electrical and electronic products and telecommunication equipment. The plastic business also took us into oil refining, which needed a tanker-shipping company. The oil refining company alone was paying an insurance premium amounting to more than half of the total revenue of the largest insurance company in Korea. Thus, an insurance company was started. This natural step-by-step evolution through related businesses resulted in the Lucky-Goldstar group (now LG) as we see it today. (Koo Cha-Kyung, son of the LG founder, as quoted in Milgroms and Roberts 1992, 542–43)

There is some question as to whether FCs tend to overdiversify in their home markets (Church 1993; Hwang 2000; Kock and Guillen 2001), but it is clear that an expansion strategy is one of the most important drivers of their growth (Amsden and Hikino 1994; Kock and Guillen 2001). Even though expansion occurs in the early and late stages, it is a major driver in the growth stage. FCs have a tendency to deepen their involvement in one industry during the early stage, whereas they expand into different industries in the late growth and maturity stages (Amsden and Hikino 1994). For example, Daewoo began as a textile exporting company and expanded into clothing manufacturing, garnering Sears, J.C. Penney, and Montgomery Ward as accounts. As the Korean economy took off, it entered construction and heavy industries, then automobile manufacturing and financial services.

In emerging markets, FCs tend to expand as a way to cope with a poor communication structure, misguided regulations, and inefficient judicial systems (Khanna and Palepu 1997) and to realize some economic benefits from internalizing transactions (Hwang 2000). In addition, they have to perform the basic functions of several institutions in order to do business effectively. Sabanci in Turkey, for example, has its own private bank and university. Another reason for expansion is exit barriers in EMs. Most FCs, including the Tata Companies, continue to stay in business to leverage their large scale and wide scope.

As for the relationship between investment in unrelated businesses and FC performance in EMs, Khanna and Palepu (2000) report a curvilinear relationship with Chilean business groups. That is, performance declines until unrelated diversification increases to a certain threshold, beyond which point further increases will result in improvements in firm performance. Surprisingly, Hwang (2000) reports that failed *chaebols* tend to have a higher level of related diversification than do successful FCs in Korea, which implies that the problem may be with a lack of institutional infrastructure and competence of an individual *chaebol* (Khanna and Palepu 1999), rather than unrelated diversification.

Home Market Competition Intensity

In the late growth and maturity stages, FCs face a number of domestic and even some foreign competitors. As the market begins to saturate and mature, FCs must serve customers better than competitors do, create new markets, and develop their own technologies (Kock and Guillen 2001). They diversify and internationalize their businesses, seeking a competitive edge in the global arena. Goldstar, now part of the LG group, enjoyed an early mover position in the Korean electronics market until Daewoo and Samsung entered the industry. As the competition grew fierce, Goldstar merged with Lucky, and the new group acquired Zenith, a major TV manufacturer in the United States, in order to penetrate the North American market.

Strong Work Ethic of Employees

A cornerstone of Korean FCs seems to be the work ethic of employees. For instance, during the 1980s and 1990s, Korean workers were willing to work overtime to achieve assigned goals in a shorter period than expected and to put the employer first. Biggart (1991) describes this phenomenon as institutionalized patrimony. Work ethic has contributed to the growth of FCs in most Asian countries.

Access to Unique Source of Capital

Unique sources of capital also play an important role in the formation of FCs, including loans at very favorable interest rates and unique investment opportunities (e.g., land and/or real estate investments with extremely high annual returns). Special loans are one fruit of the FC-government relationship (Dent and Randerson 1997; Nachum 1999). In Korea, cross-equity investments and cross-debt guarantees are widely used to finance FC business expansions (Hwang 2000). Some Mexican FCs, such as Desc and Alfa, listed their stock on the New York Stock Exchange to obtain financing. All the FCs that we analyzed in Korea, plus Koc and Sabanci in Turkey, Vitro in Mexico, and Astra in Indonesia, have their own financial arms (e.g., insurance, banking, and securities brokerage), which are sources of capital (Granovetter 1995). Even though the capital sources cannot be identified for all FCs, all have various types of financial resources available to them. In addition, unique capital markets in each country contribute to the formation and growth of FCs in various ways, too.

Internationalization

As a business grows, it will participate to some degree in international activities. Some companies such as born globals take on internationalization early on, but many others take the gradual approach. Figure 7.2 indicates typical internationalization activities in various stages of FC growth.

In the introduction stage, the main activity involves importation of raw materials, followed in the growth stage by technology transfer, licensing, and franchising by a foreign business partner (Sarkar and Cavusgil 1996). However, as Johanson and Wiedersheim-Paul (1975) assume that internationalization is a consequence of developments in the domestic market, FCs accumulate expertise from foreign alliances that can help them develop their own technologies (Kock and Guillen 2001). Another strategic purpose of such alliances is to compete more effectively with firms outside the relationship (Kock and Guillen 2001; Walker & Poppo 1991). The CEO of Vitro claims that international partnering and exporting helped the company grow faster and are crucial to future growth. Intensified competition in a maturing local market often forces FCs to seek new business opportunities abroad. Exporting can be the first step in the process; for example, Sabanci and Tata have their own trading companies in London. For most Korean FCs, exporting was a core business that grew rapidly in the 1970s and 1980s. FCs may use intermediaries initially, such as import agents and sales subsidiaries, but they tend to assume the business themselves as they reach maturity.

In the growth and maturity stages, FCs may become direct investors and increase their level of international holdings. Activities in foreign markets deepen, and major modes of entry are wholly owned subsidiaries, turnkey projects, and joint ventures. Hyundai, Daewoo, and Samsung have a larger number of wholly owned subsidiaries in foreign markets compared to Ayala in the Philippines, Astra in Indonesia, and Siam Cement in Thailand. In the late growth stage, the switch from exporting to direct investment in overseas operations is a crucial decision. The major obstacles to internationalization are a lack of knowledge and resources. As FCs learn about foreign markets, the perceived risk of investment decreases and internationalization is simulated. In the late growth stage and maturity stages, FCs increase the level of resources committed abroad and change the mode of market servicing. Licensing and joint venture agreements are examples of intermediate moves toward direct investment, such as wholly owned subsidiaries.

Need for Technology

Technology is not a main driver in the introduction and early growth stages of most FCs because the initial focus is on production capacity to meet customer demand. When foreign businesses enter the market, however, there is a pressure to adopt new technology in order to increase efficiency and remain competitive. FCs seek know-how and technology through licensing arrange-

Figure 7.2
Internationalization of Family Conglomerates

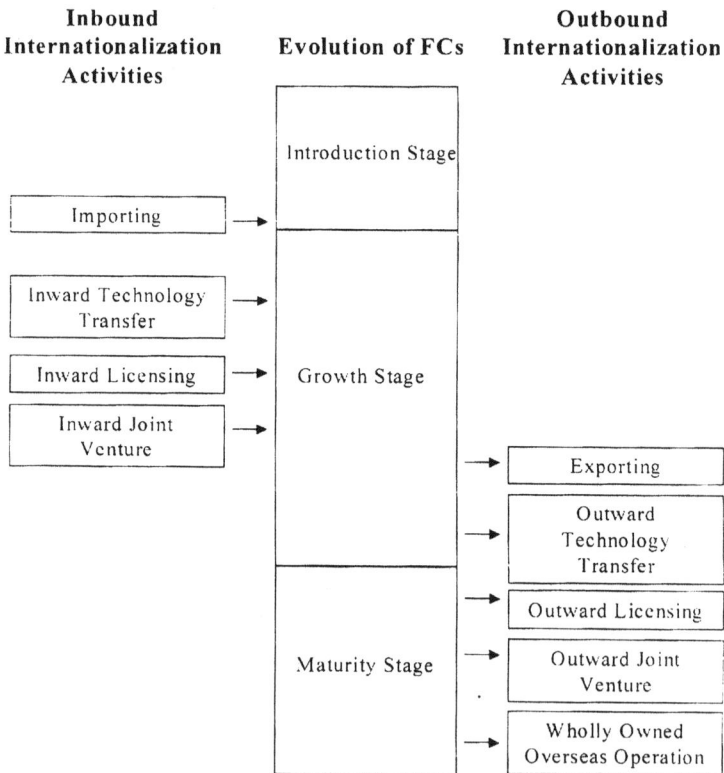

ments and joint ventures with foreign partners who have cutting-edge technology. The following case illustrates how the Sabanci Holding in Turkey started producing synthetic fibers.

In Turkey, the industry was developing and the consumption of polyester fibers was increasing steadily during the 1960s. Turkey was obliged to import them with its scarce foreign currency. Sabanci holding started the idea of setting up a plant for the production of polyester thread and fibres. At that time, the most important problem was the foreign currency. Foreign currency for such plants was allocated by the Association of Chambers. When Sabanci Holding brought its proposal about the polyester fiber factory, it obtained a license for DM220,000. Now another problem was to get a license. In those times, it was the first time for Sabanci bargaining about a license. The managers did not even know either how to make a know-how contract or the procedures for paying for the license. Finally, Sabanci signed the licensing and technology agreement with ICI, the British firm, and the SASA company was established. The ICI provided the machinery, but could only provide short-term experts. Over time, Sabanci learned to train qualified people, increased the capacity of SASA, expanded its product lines and produced polyester filament yarn, and brought in new technologies. (Sabanci, 1988)

In the maturity stage, FCs are more likely to start high-tech businesses based on their accumulated knowledge and to build their own research and design (R&D) centers (Amsden and Hikino 1994; Kock and Guillen 2001). Companies such as Alfa, Koc, and Mahindra and Mahindra are gearing themselves to meet competition through rapid modernization and expansion of manufacturing technologies. Samsung and Hyundai are focusing on high-tech industry more than ever before.

HOW FAMILY CONGLOMERATES EVOLVE

Based on our study, we can delineate a typical growth pattern as explained behavior. At the introduction stage, a single founder with some capital realizes what is needed in the economy and responds. The Koc Group in Turkey, for example, was an early mover after the War of Independence. Government support is an important factor at this stage, as in the case of Siam Cement in Thailand.

The growth stage begins when FCs expand and gain synergies through expansion into untapped industries, which often provides a strong advantage over competitors (see stage I and II of Kock and Guillen 2001). Foreign alliances may be formed to counter foreign competition and obtain technological know-how. As expansion continues in terms of the number of industries as well as subsidiaries, many FCs acquire financial institutions to meet capital needs. As members of the second or third generation, who are usually highly educated, become involved in the business, they may start to hire professional managers from outside the family (Jones and Rose 1993). A new organizational structure may be needed to meet the challenges of expansion and global competition, and holding companies may be established to identify strategies and to control and coordinate activities.

In the maturity stage, expansion declines or ceases (see stage III of Kock and Guillen 2001), and FCs focus on competition with major domestic rivals and/or seek out new business opportunities in foreign markets to gain economies of scale and scope. The usual pattern (Dent and Randerson 1997) is to move gradually from exporting and/or importing of raw materials and components, to domestic joint ventures with a foreign partner, and/or to importing of subcontracted components, contract manufactured goods, and licensed or OEM products. Finally, FCs tend to enter cooperative agreements related to technical know-how, production, marketing, and purchasing (Luostarinen and Hellman 1994). Some, by creating wholly owned subsidiaries and joint ventures in foreign markets, imitate world-class companies. As technology becomes critical to retaining competitive advantage, they develop their own technologies (Kock and Guillen 2001) and build R&D centers to compete globally.

Due to their management experience and capital resources, some mature FCs can be counted among the largest industrial and financial conglomerates, not only at home but also abroad. The following Hyundai case reveals how FCs evolve over time.

Joo Young Chung, the former chairman of Hyundai group, was born to a poor, rural farming family in 1915. With little formal education, he learned various manual labor skills and in the 1940s established a truck and motor service business. In 1947 he formed Hyundai Engineering and Construction Company, focusing on the construction of dams, roads, harbors, and housing projects. As the first Korean construction company to win overseas contracts, Hyundai undertook highway projects in Thailand, harbor dredging in South Vietnam and Australia, bridges in Alaska, and housing complexes in Guam. The company became increasingly adept at larger and more complex projects and could successfully compete internationally because it used cheap, hardworking labor and had a tradition of timely completion dates. In 1968 Chairman Chung decided to enter the automobile industry and established Hyundai Motor Company to assemble Ford passenger cars for sale locally. With this experience, Hyundai designed and produced (with technical assistance from Mitsubishi) Korea's first integrated passenger car, the Pony. In 1983 the midsized Steller model was introduced, and by 1988 Hyundai was producing a luxury sedan, the Grandeur, under license from Mitsubishi. A redesigned version of the Pony Excel was introduced first into Canada in 1986 and into the United States a year later. The Steller has also been sold in Canada. More recently, a newly designed Hyundai Sonata has been introduced to the North American market. The Sonata is designed as a more up-scale medium-sized car to compete with many of the Japanese imports, such as the Honda Accord and the Toyota Camry. (Adapted from Steers, Shin, and Ungson 1989, 51)

WHAT DOES THE FUTURE HOLD FOR FAMILY CONGLOMERATES?

Will FCs in emerging markets continue to prosper as family-owned businesses? The optimistic view is that family influence will remain strong due to accumulated wealth and stockholder power (Chung 2000; Hwang 2000). Although ownership of the conglomerates will be dispersed so that one person is unable to control a conglomerate, it is highly likely that a family as a strong collective owner can control a conglomerate utilizing the majority ownership realized through the cross investment. For instance, according to Korean Fair Trading Committee, the average cross investment within a conglomerate is above 35 percent among 30 major Korean conglomerates while the average ownership of each individual family member is around 3.3 percent ("Hyundai's" 2001). Under this circumstance, conflicts with the founder's family could weaken the collective ownership of a conglomerate and the recent financial crisis of Hyundai Group in Korea has proven the importance of collective ownership of a founder's family through cross investment. Likewise, even though some subsidiaries of FCs in EMs are becoming publicly held, the founder's family still has significant influence and control on management.

Especially as the second or third generation inherits the business, however, more FCs are expected to hire professional managers, and family members are likely to play a less direct role (Hwang 2000). The founder's death or transfer of power to the next generation often marks the transition to professional management and the addition of outsiders to the board. As FCs enter phases where second or third generations take over, one may speculate that management at the FCs will become more participative as well as more professional. For example, the Koc family holding in Turkey and the Vitro Groupo in Mexico have executives from Western companies on their board.

The pessimistic view is that FCs will face pressure from government as well as domestic and international markets to reduce the number of core businesses in order to improve efficiency. Also, a leadership vacuum may occur in the second or third generation (Church 1993). In addition, as the Hyundai and Daewoo cases illustrate, FCs seem to have some degree of inefficiency due to family ownership (Hwang 2000; Khanna and Palepu 1999, 2000; Kock and Guillen 2001; Schulze et al. 2001), usually because of the lack of professional management (Kao 1993; Khanna and Palepu 1999; Nachum 1999). Allegiance to owners is a characteristic of FCs (Drozdow and Carroll 1997; Hayashibara 1997) but not always good for business. A good illustration is the Samsung Group, whose founder long dreamed of having an automobile-manufacturing arm. He did not achieve his hope before his death, but the group continued to pour financial resources into the plan. The expansion was undertaken at a financial risk that probably would never be assumed by professional managers and despite government and industry concerns about overcapacity. The new unit was taken over by a competitor during the restructuring that followed the Korean economic crisis a few years ago.

Even though more and more FCs are hiring professional management, the family influence on business operations can still affect strategic moves (Drozdow and Carroll 1997). To most Western companies that have been professionally managed for decades, the inefficiencies in FCs seem to be a waste of time and resources. Global pressures may accentuate those inefficiencies and reduce FCs to a few small businesses in the future.

ENTRY STRATEGIES FOR WESTERN COMPANIES TARGETING EMERGING MARKETS

FCs represent both a potential and challenge for Western companies (Kock and Guillen 2001; Prahalad and Lieberthal 1998). Strategic alliances have become an important tool for entry into emerging markets, and in many cases the likeliest candidate is an FC. What the Western company wants from the ally is not product knowledge but local market knowledge and experience, established networks with suppliers and distributors, and government contacts (Kock and Guillen 2001). Market knowledge is organized and structured information specific to a particular environment (Li and Calantone 1998). It can be acquired through experience in that market, and is comprised of macro and micro factors. The former includes economic, political, financial, cultural, and legal conditions; the latter involves knowledge about customers, competitors, and suppliers. Davidson (1980) notes the importance of long-term experience in a particular market; as familiarity increases, firms become more comfortable with local differences and more confident in their ability to capitalize on local expertise (Shetty 1979), and are more willing to accept risks and commit resources. For their part, FCs are mainly interested in the technological capabilities or know-how of Western companies to produce and/or sell a product or service.

Strategic alliances between FCs and Western companies can take several forms, such as joint ventures, licensing agreements, distribution and supply agreements, research and development partnerships, and technological exchanges (Inkpen 1998). The local market knowledge of the FC and the technical knowledge of the Western company may determine the type of alliance (Dawar and Frost 1999). Modes of entry depending upon the parties' needs are shown in Figure 7.3.

Western companies may form alliances in emerging markets for various reasons. A Western company may be seeking a market for its products, a production site, source materials, components, or technology. Product marketing, for example, requires warehousing, transportation, and retailing, and the FC may be able to supply facilities, vehicles, and a sales force. If the Western company is interested in penetrating the market in a relatively short time, the business network and/or consumer recognition of the FC is very important (Arnold and Quelch 1998; Ger 1999; Kock and Guillen 2001). Consequently, a Western company may not be willing to license its technol-

Figure 7.3
**Appropriate Market Entry Strategies for Western Companies in Emerging
Markets**

	Low	High
High	Technology Licensing	Joint Ventures
Low	Wholly owned Investment	Distribution and Supply Agreements

Family Conglomerate's Need for Technical Knowledge

Western Company's Need for Market Knowledge

ogy at the initial stages of entry, so the appropriate partnership may be distribution and supply agreements with an FC, whose need for technical
knowledge is low. In this type of partnership, learning is minimal in the FC,
whereas the Western company will be more active in gaining knowledge.

In 1988, for example, Ford Motor formed a partnership with Kia, a *chaebol*,
to introduce the Sable into Korea. Ford was interested in Kia's distribution
and after-service network; Kia Motors was interested in a premium model to
complement its product line at a time when technology transfer for producing
the car was not feasible and too costly for Kia. In 1994, Digital Equipment
Corporation designated Tatung, a Taiwanese FC and market leader in computers, as the main distributor of its workstations and related client-server
products. With the agreement, Digital took advantage of Tatung's local experience and distribution network, and Tatung gained the benefit of carrying
a technologically advanced product ("Tatung" 1994).

Depending upon the business scale of FCs and their unique relationship
with the local market, Western companies should consider carefully whether
a partnership is the appropriate entry mode (Harrigan 1984; Kock and Guillen
2001). In the case of production, the Western company may want to protect
its technical knowledge and property rights, in which case, it will look for an
FC whose need for technical knowledge is high. When the Western company
needs market knowledge and the FC needs technical knowledge, entry
through a joint venture may be appropriate.

In 1997 Sabanci Holding entered a 50-50 equity joint venture with Danone
Company, a European leader in dairy products and owner of the Evian brand
of bottled water. Danone has high technical knowledge in packaging and bot-
tling and a reputation for healthy and environmentally friendly products, but
lacked information on the Turkish market. Sabanci is a leader in Turkey with
its bottled water, Hayat, and is knowledgeable about customers, retailers, and

distributors. The collaboration with Danone to market Hayat made this brand the market leader in the following year. Danone then introduced its dairy products into Turkey through Sabanci.

Joint ventures have been used to exploit markets and technologies, and they can be very important in maintaining a firm's competitive advantage. Alestra is a joint venture in telecommunications formed by ALFA in Mexico, AT&T, and Bancomer-Visa. Through the collaboration, AT&T wanted to address the opportunities of worldwide markets, and ALFA provided a network in Mexico and gained access to AT&T's advanced technical knowledge.

In other cases Western companies enter the local market without an ally and put pressure on domestic FCs. For example, India became a major export base for auto components when the economy was deregulated. The entry of multinational automobile giants forced Mahindra and Mahindra to meet the challenge through a rapid upgrade of manufacturing technology. The company built an R&D center to speed the design of products to meet customer needs. It also formed a partnership with Peugot, which licensed its technology, to manufacture diesel engines. In another case, Sabanci founded Temsa to provide boilers, ventilation, and heating systems but, later agreed with Mitsubishi Motors to produce buses in Temsa plants, using Mitsubishi engines.

A Western company may gain a good understanding of a local market through previous alliances and then pursue its own wholly owned venture. For example, as Ford Motors gained local market knowledge through its experience with Kia, it launched a wholly owned subsidiary, Ford Motor Company of Korea, in 1996. Another example is BMW AG, the Germany automotive company, which announced the establishment of a wholly owned subsidiary in Indonesia, where market knowledge was gained through a partnership with Astra International although Astra will continue to handle importing, assembling, and retailing activities ("BMW" 2001).

A general practice in operating as a foreign company in emerging markets is to establish strategic alliances with local partners in order to reduce risks and legal/bureaucratic barriers. Also partnerships are seen as keys to success by foreign investors, especially in nationalistic countries such as Turkey. The foreign partner should understand cultural differences and economic policies before entering an emerging market. The following case concerns how the relationship between the Uzan family, owner of Telsim, and Motorola and Nokia, failed.

In 2000 Motorola and Nokia signed an agreement with Telsim for the supply of a third generation mobile network worth almost $3 billion. Telsim is Turkey's second largest mobile phone operator, owned and privately managed by the Uzan family, as an affiliate of Rumeli Holding with a 66% stake. The Turkish telecom service operators relied on foreign companies for equipment and infrastructure for mobile services. The agreement also entailed vendor financing or supplier credit. Telsim agreed to pay in installments. However, Telsim in January 2002 was unable to make the installment payment. Motorola and Nokia jointly sued the Uzan family under the RICO Act (Racketeer Influenced and Corrupt Organizations Act, a law often used to indict mobsters) claiming that Uzans never intended to repay the loans. There were claims and counter claims. More importantly, the feud emerged as a vital issue of political concern to both governments of Turkey and the United States.

The special feature of FCs is that they are owned and controlled by a family. There are several factors that exist in shaping the family business. The main factors are national culture and economic policies (Ward 2000). The evolution of a family business is closely related to the economic evolution in emerging markets. On the other hand, cultural context is an important determinant of ownership and leadership vision of FCs. FCs could offer Western companies several opportunities in emerging markets, because FCs are composed of firm-specific resources such as market knowledge, government relations, and network strength (Manikutty 2000). Western companies entering an emerging market should do the extensive work required to learn about the FCs in the market, as well as the national culture and economic policy of that particular emerging market. Then, they should determine whether complementarities exist, and decide whether an alliance should be formed. Certainly, there are more factors to consider than the need for technical and local market knowledge. Financial needs, first-mover advantages, and business networks are among the other aspects that either Western companies or FCs may want to examine.

CONCLUSION

Large and diversified family-owned businesses represent a remarkably common feature of many high-growth economies. Family conglomerates exhibited much resilience over the years, their ownership transcending several generations. Their stronghold in their respective economies implies much political clout in governmental relations, and recognition and franchise with customers. Interestingly, many FCs seem to have successfully transformed themselves over time in order to sustain their competitiveness. Many are responsible for introducing new technologies and new products to their respective economies.

Despite variations in organizational and national cultures surrounding these companies—including government protection, capital resources, and employee work ethic—FCs from different countries tend to evolve in much the same way. Market expansion strategies such as diversification and internationalization are widely adopted, and FCs benefit from and adapt to their business environment. Given their unique competencies in their respective economies, Western companies targeting these markets ought to familiarize themselves with FCs. As competitors, FCs will be formidable rivals for Western firms. As collaborators and business partners, FCs can take much of the hassle and difficulty out of entering and succeeding in emerging markets.

Indeed, FCs have much to offer Western companies: a local business network, government contacts, consumer recognition, and established channels, among others. In turn, FCs also stand to gain from the new business opportunities and know-how that Western companies may bring to the arrangement. By identifying the complementarities that FCs offer, Western companies should enjoy more frictionless entry into emerging markets.

REFERENCES

Amsden, Alice H., and Takashi Hikino. 1994. "Project Execution Capability, Organizational Know-How, and Conglomerate Corporate Growth in Late Industrialization." *Industrial and Corporate Change* 3 (1): 111–47.

Arnold, David J., and John A. Quelch. 1998. "New Strategies in Emerging Markets." *Sloan Management Review* 40 (1): 7–20.

Asia's 7,500 Largest Companies. 1999. London: ELC International.

Ben-Porath, Yoram. 1980. "The F-Connection: Families, Friends, and Firms and the Organization of Exchange." *Population and Development Review* 6 (1): 1–30.

Biggart, Nicole W. 1991. "Institutionalized Patrimonialism in Korean Business." In *Comparative Social Research*, edited by C. Calhoun. Vol. 12, *Business Institution.* Greenwich, Conn.: JAI Press.

"BMW AG Forms Subsidiary." 2001. *Jakarta Post*, 30 January.

"Business: Beware Turks bearing phones." 2002. *The Economist*, 2 February: 67.

Cavusgil, S. Tamer. 1997. "Measuring the Potential of Emerging Markets: An Indexing Approach." *Business Horizons* 40 (1): 87–91.

Chung, Y. Peter. 2000. "Corporate Governance System in Korea: What Questions Should We Ask for Future Recommendations?" Presented at Transforming Korean Business and Management Culture Conference organized by Michigan State University, 19–20 September.

Church, Roy. 1993. "The Family Firm in Industrial Capitalism: International Perspectives in Hypotheses and History." *Business History* 35 (4): 17–43.

Davidson, William H. 1980. "The Location of Foreign Investment Activity: Country Characteristics and Experience Effects." *Journal of International Business Studies* 11 (fall): 9–22.

Dawar, Niraj, and Tony Frost. 1999. "Competing with Giants: Survival Strategies for Local Companies in Emerging Markets." *Harvard Business Review* (March/April): 119–29.

Dent, Christopher M., and Claire Randerson. 1997. "Enter the Chaebol: The Escalation of Korean Direct Investment in Europe." *European Business Journal* 9 (4): 31–40.

Drozdow, Nancy, and Vincent P. Carroll. 1997. "Tools for Strategy Development in Family Firms." *Sloan Management Review* 39 (1): 75–88.

Dunning, J. H. 1988. *Explaining International Production.* London: Unwin Hyman.

"Emerging Market Indicators." 2001. *The Economist* (August): 82–84.

"Emerging Multinationals: Enter the Lippo-potamus." 1994. *The Economist*, 16 July: 61.

"Empires Without Umpires." 2001. *The Economist,* 7 April: S4–S7.

Garten, Jeffrey E. 1997a. "Troubles Ahead in Emerging Markets." *Harvard Business Review* 75 (3): 38–50.

———. 1997b. *The Big Ten: The Big Emerging Markets and How They Will Change Our Lives.* Basic Books: New York.

Ger, Guliz. 1999. "Localizing in the Global Village." *California Management Review* 41 (4): 64–83.

Granovetter, Mark. 1995. "Case Revisited: Business Groups in the Modern Economy." *Industrial and Corporate Change* 4 (1): 93–129.

Guillen, Mauro F. 2000. "Business Groups in Emerging Economies: A Resource-Based View." *Academy of Management Journal* 43 (3): 362–80.

———. 2001. *The Limits of Convergence: Globalization and Organizational Change in Argentina, South Korea, and Spain.* Princeton, N.J.: Princeton University Press.

Handbook of World Business. 1999. Austin, Tex.: Hoover's Business Press.

Harrigan, Kathryn Rudie. 1984. "Joint Ventures and Global Strategies." *Columbia Journal of World Business* 14 (2): 36–64.

Hayashibara, Mariko. 1997. "From Family Business to Multinational." *Asian Business,* 19 November.

Hitt, Michael A., M. Tina Dacin, Edward Levitas, Jean-Luc Arregle, and Anca Borza. 2000. "Partner Selection in Emerging and Developed Market Contexts: Resource-Based and Organizational Learning Perspectives." *Academy of Management Journal* 43 (3): 449–67.

Holsti, Oli R. 1968. "Content Analysis." In *The Handbook of Social Psychology: Research Methods,* edited by G. Lindzey and E. Aronson, vol. 2. Reading, Mass.: Addison-Wesley.

Hwang, Inhak. 2000. "Diversification and Restructuring of the Korean Business Groups." Presented at Transforming Korean Business and Management Culture Conference organized by Michigan State University, 19–20 September.

Hwang, Inhak, Inkwon Lee, Chunghwan Seo, Byungkee Lee, and Hyunok Han. 2000. *Chaebol Structure and Chaebol Policy: Evaluation and Recommendations.* Seoul: The Korea Economic Research Institute.

"Hyundai Group's Financial Crisis." 2001. *Donga Daily Newspaper,* 9 January. http://www.donga.com/docs/issue.html.

"The Import-Import." 1997. *The Economist,* 29 November: 70.

Inkpen, Andrew C. 1998. "Learning and Knowledge Acquisition through International Strategic Alliances." *Academy of Management Executive* 12 (4): 69–80.

International Directory of Company Histories. Chicago: St. James Press.

International Public and Private Companies. Version 5. New Providence, N.J.: LexisNexis Group.

Johanson, Jan, and Finn Wiedersheim-Paul. 1975. "The Internationalization of the Firm: Four Swedish Case Studies." *Journal of Management Studies* (October): 305–22.

Jones, Geoffrey, and Mary B. Rose. 1993. "Family Capitalism." *Business History* 35 (4): 1–16.

Kao, John. 1993. "The Worldwide Web of Chinese Business." *Harvard Business Review* (March/April): 24–38.

Khanna, Tarun, and Krishna Palepu. 1997. "Why Focused Strategies May Be Wrong for Emerging Markets." *Harvard Business Review* 75 (4): 41–51.

————. 1999. "The Right Way to Restructure Conglomerates in Emerging Markets." *Harvard Business Review* 77 (4): 125–34.

————. 2000. "The Future of Business Groups in Emerging Markets: Long-Run Evidence from Chile." *Academy of Management Journal* 43 (3): 268–85.

Kock, Carl J., and Mauro F. Guillen. 2001. "Strategy and Structure in Developing Countries: Business Groups as an Evolutionary Response to Opportunities for Unrelated Diversification." *Industrial and Corporate Change* 10 (1): 77–113.

Lane, Henry W., and Paul W. Beamish. 1990. "Cross-Cultural Cooperation Behavior in Joint Ventures in LDCs." *Management International Review* 30: 87–102.

Leff, Nathaniel H. 1978. "Industrial Organization and Entrepreneurship in the Developing Countries: The Economic Groups." *Economic Development and Cultural Change* 26 (July): 661–75.

Li, Tiger, and Roger J. Calantone. 1988. "The Impact of Market Knowledge Competence on New Product Advantage: Conceptualization and Empirical Examination." *Journal of Marketing* 62 (October): 13–29.

"Links with the first family." 1994. *Asiamoney* (October): 36.

Luostarinen, Reijo, and Harri Hellman. 1994. *The Internationalization Processes and Strategies of Finnish Family Firms.* Helsingin Kauppakorkeakoulun Kuvalaitos, Helsinki: HSE Press.

Manikutty, S. 2000. "Family Business Groups in India: A Resource-Based View of the Emerging Trends." *Family Business Review* 13 (4): 279–92.

"Manila Moves in on the Family Conglomerates." 1982. *Business Week*, 17 May, 51–53.

Mariussen, Age, Jane Wheelock, and Susan Baines. 1997. "The Family Business Tradition in Britain and Norway, Modernization, and Reinvention." *International Studies of Management and Organization* 27 (3): 64–85.

Markides, Constantinos C. 1997. "To Diversify or Not to Diversify." *Harvard Business Review* 75 (6): 93–99.

Milgroms, Paul, and John Roberts. 1992. *Economics, Organization, and Management.* Englewood Cliffs, N.J.: Prentice Hall.

Mulholland, J. P. and K. Thomas. 1999. "The Price of Rice." *Inside Indonesia*, no. 58.

Nachum, Lilach. 1999. "Diversification Strategies of Developing Country Firms." *Journal of International Management* 5: 115–40.

Osborn, R. N., and J. Hagedoorn. 1997. "The Institutionalization and Evolutionary Dynamics of Interorganizational Alliances and Networks." *Academy of Management Journal* 40 (2): 261–78.

Prahalad, C. K., and Kenneth Lieberthal. 1998. "The End of Corporate Imperialism." *Harvard Business Review* 76 (4): 68–79.

Principal International Business. 1998–99. London: Dun and Bradstreet Incorporation.

Sabanci, S. 1988. *This is My Life.* Avon, U.K.: Bath Press.

Sarkar, Mitra Barun, and S. Tamer Cavusgil. 1996. "The Trends in International Business Thought and Literature: A Review of International Market Entry Mode Research: Integration and Synthesis." *International Executive* 38 (6): 825–48.

Schulze, William S., Michael H. Lubatkin, Richard N. Dino, and Ann K. Buchholtz. 2001. "Agency Relationships in Family Firms: Theory and Evidence." *Organization Science* 12 (2): 99–116.

Shetty, Y. K. 1979. "Managing the Multinational Corporation: European and American Styles." *Management International Review* 19 (3): 39–48.

Shin, Yoon Hwan. 1993. "Modern Form of Capital Accumulation: A Study about the Formation of Indonesian Family Conglomerates." *Korean Political Science Review* 27 (2): 251–74.

Steers, Richard M., Yoo Keun Shin, and Gerardo R. Ungson. 1989. *The Chaebol: Korea's New Industrial Might.* New York: Harper and Row:

"Tatung as Main Distributor." 1994. *Dow Jones International News,* 26 July.

Walker, Gordon, and Laura Poppo. 1991. "Profit Centers, Single-Source Suppliers, and Transaction Costs." *Administrative Science Quarterly* 36 (1): 66–87.

Ward, John L. 2000. "Reflections on Indian Family Groups." *Family Business Review* 13 (4): 271–78.

Woodall, Pam. 1998. "Survey: East Asian Economies: How Many Paths to Evolution." *The Economist* 346 (8058): S14–S17.

———. 1997. "The Emerging Asian Competitors." *Harvard Business Review* 75 (5): 64–65.

Wright Investors' Service, Inc. 2000. Corporate Information, http://profiles.wisi.com/profiles/Comsrch.htm.

CHAPTER 8

International Joint Venture Control: An Integrated Framework

Yan Zhang and
Haiyang Li

INTRODUCTION

Recent studies have paid increasing attention to international joint ventures (IJVs) in emerging economies, such as China, Russia, and Eastern European countries (e.g., Hitt et al. 2000; Steensma and Lyles 2000; Zhang and Li 2001). IJVs in emerging economies differ significantly from their counterparts in market economies. Relative to those in market economies, IJVs in emerging economies tend to have parent firms (foreign parents versus local parents), who have different resource endowments and different objectives for the joint venturing. As Child and Faulkner (1998, 297) stated, "when one of the partners . . . come from an emerging country and the other from a highly developed economy, their configuration of objectives . . . will almost certainly differ from that in the case of partners from two developed countries." Parent firms' differences in resource endowments and objectives will further increase the possibility that these firms are exposed to the risk of opportunism of their partners in the IJVs (at least in their perceptions). Thus, control becomes a particularly important issue in these IJVs.

Although there have been a large number of studies on IJV control, there are still two important gaps that constrain our understanding of this issue. First, prior literature tends to assume that all parent firms want to control the IJVs to the same extent. However, we raise the possibility that parent firms may vary in their desired level of control, depending upon their task interdependence with the IJVs. Second, prior research has indicated that IJVs are transitional organizations with dynamic natures (Franko 1971; Harrigan 1986). Although several factors that affect IJV reconfiguration have been identified in previous studies (Gomes-Casseres 1987; Hamel, Doz, and Prahalad 1989; Inkpen and Beamish 1997), how the control structure of IJVs evolves over time remains unclear (c.f., Zhang and Li 2001). In this chapter our goal was to develop an integrated framework of IJV control, which would include its antecedents, consequences, and evolution. The framework was developed based upon the organization economics theory and our comprehensive inter-view data of eight China-Japan IJVs operating in China. The framework addresses two important control issues: (1) from the organization economics perspective, what is the relationship between parent firms' task interdependences with an IJV and their levels of control over the IJV? and (2) from an evolution perspective, how does the relationship between IJV control and performance evolve over time?

The remainder of this chapter is organized as follows. First, we briefly describe our framework. Then we discuss the research methodology, including sampling, codification of key constructs, approach of data analysis, and the description of the eight cases. We then present the findings of our comparative case studies. Specific hypotheses are also developed in this section. The chapter concludes with a discussion of the implications of the whole framework and our findings.

AN INTEGRATED FRAMEWORK OF IJV CONTROL

IJV control can be generally conceptualized into various types: *ownership control*, which is determined by parent firms' equity shares in the IJV (Blodgett 1991; Buckley and Casson 1988; Hennart 1988), *specific control*, which refers to parent firms' control over specific operational activities of the IJV (Geringer and Hebert 1989; Mjoen and Tallman 1997; Schaan 1983), and *strategic control* (or overall control and management control), which refers to parent firms' control of IJVs' key strategic decision making (Killing 1983; Mjoen and Tallman 1997; Yan and Gray 1994). In this chapter, we focus on parent firms' strategic control of IJVs. As Mjoen and Tallman (1997) argued, control seems to be a direct managerial function closely related to strategic direction rather than ownership. Strategic control over an IJV may ensure the most effective use of strategic resources shared by parent firms and the IJV, and it may prevent leakage of proprietary knowledge. Specifically, Demirbag and Mirza (1996) suggested that in developing countries (e.g., China, the current research context) where local parents depend heavily on foreign parents' expertise and knowledge, the parents' influence on the IJVs' strategy formulation and implementation is a better measure of control than the parents' equity share in a joint venture.

Killing (1983) has formally classified IJV control structure into three categories according to which parent is the main decision maker: dominant parent IJVs (where only one parent firm is heavily involved in decision making while the others are silent), shared management IJVs (where both parent firms actively make strategic decisions), and independent IJVs (where the IJVs' management has substantial decision power while none of the parent firms are actively involved in decision making). Killing's classification has been adopted and validated by several studies (e.g., Beamish 1984; Lecraw 1984; Yan and Gray 1994). In the current study we draw upon this conceptualization of IJV control and examine the antecedents and consequences of different types of controls. Our integrated framework of control in IJVs is depicted in Figure 8.1.

Antecedents of IJV Control

We adopted an organizational economics (OE) perspective to examine the antecedents of IJV control. The OE perspective has been widely used in research on organizations (Barney and Ouchi 1986; Hesterly, Liebeskind, and Zenger 1990). This paradigm aims to address the key determinants of the shape and function of organizations. In the IJV literature, some scholars (e.g., Shenkar and Zeira 1992) have suggested that an IJV is an organizational form that sits just in the middle of the market-hierarchy continuum. We extend this argument and suggest that there exists a set of organizational arrangements available to govern the IJVs and that these arrangements can be represented along a market-hierarchy continuum. Which arrangement is chosen to govern a particular IJV largely depends upon the task interdependence between the IJV and its parent firms.

Thompson (1967) conceptualized task interdependence between subunits of a firm into three forms: pooled, sequential, and reciprocal. *Pooled interdependence* refers to a situation in which each unit renders a discrete contribution to the whole and each is supported by the whole. *Sequential interdependence* is

Figure 8.1
An Integrated Framework of IJV Control

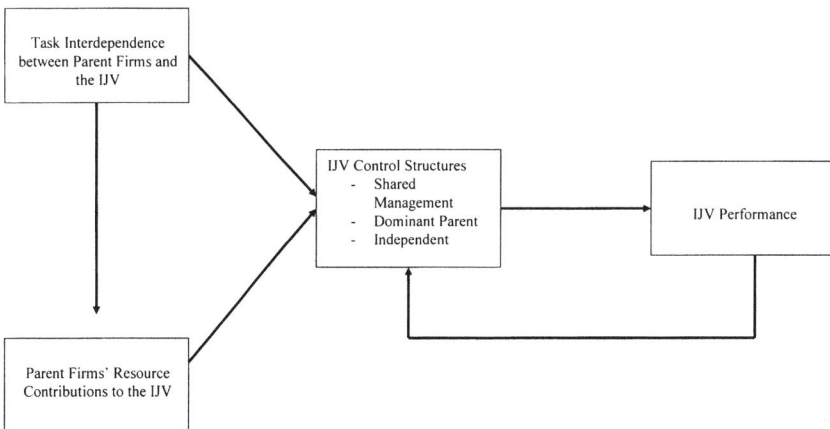

a serial form of interdependence, with one unit producing parts that become inputs for another unit's operation. *Reciprocal interdependence* is a situation in which the outputs of each unit become the inputs for the others, so that each unit is penetrated by the other. According to Thompson (1967), the sequence from pooled, through sequential, to reciprocal interdependence represents an increasing level of task interdependence.

We used Thompson's (1967) conceptualization to analyze the relationships between the parent firms and the IJVs. We argue that there exist three types of task interdependence between an IJV and its parent firms. First, an IJV that is an unrelated diversification of one parent firm has pooled interdependence with this parent firm. In this situation, the IJV and the parent firm have few business linkages and task coordination activities. Second, when an IJV's operations are upwardly or downwardly integrated into one parent firm's value adding chain, the two firms have sequential interdependence. In this situation, the IJV represents an extension of the parent firm's value adding chain. Finally, when an IJV is horizontally related to one parent firm, the two have reciprocal interdependence. In this situation, the IJV is formed to widen one or several parts of the parent's value chain.

From the OE perspective, different levels of task interdependence between an IJV and a parent firm require the parent firm to control the IJV differently, along the market-hierarchy continuum. As the level of task interdependence increases, the parent needs to position the IJV closer to the hierarchy pole rather than the market pole of the continuum. Specifically, in pooled interdependence, actions in the IJV can proceed without regard to actions in the parent's operations as long as the IJV remains viable, so that the parent can position the IJV at the market pole of the continuum. In reciprocal interdependence, the actions of each player, including the IJV's actions, must be adjusted to the actions of one or more others in the whole parent-IJV relationship. High task interdependence causes the exchanges between the IJV and the parent to be more frequent, to last for a longer time, to be associated with higher specific asset investment, and to involve greater uncertainty. Therefore, the parent will have to position the IJV in its hierarchy rather than in the market, in order to reduce the risk and uncertainty (Barney and Ouchi 1986). Sequential interdependence is somewhere between pooled interdependence and reciprocal interdependence. It represents a situation in which the parent's operations must be adjusted if the IJV acts improperly or fails to meet the parent's expectations. Because of this, the parent tends to position the IJV in the middle between market and hierarchy.

In summary, we propose that a parent firm will choose the level of control over an IJV along the market-hierarchy continuum in accordance with its task interdependence with the IJV. The higher the task interdependence, the higher level of control the parent firm will choose, by the positioning of the IJV within the parent's hierarchy, rather than in the market. Further, the combinations of the (two or multiple) parent firms' task interdependencies with the IJV will determine the IJV's control structure. For example, if both parents (we only use the example of an IJV with two parents for simplicity) position the IJV in their hierarchies, the IJV will be a shared-management IJV. If both parents position the IJV in the market, the IJV will be an independent IJV. When one parent positions the IJV in the market while the other positions it in its hierarchy, the IJV will be a parent-dominant IJV.

Previous studies (Blodgett 1991; Yan and Gray 1994) have suggested that parent firms' resource contributions determine their relative control in the joint venture. However, as Inkpen and Beamish (1997) argued, parent firms' resource contributions to the IJV will not happen voluntarily because they have options with regard to what and how much to contribute to the IJV. We argue that while task interdependence determines a parent firm's objective of control over an IJV, its resource contributions to the IJV constitute its power, which helps realize the parent firm's control objective. Thus, we expect a consistent pattern among parent firms' task interdependencies with the IJV, their resource contributions to the IJV, and their relative control over the IJV.

IJV Control and Performance

In the IJV literature, empirical findings on the control-performance relationship are not consistent. For example, in a sample of 37 IJVs from developed countries, Killing found that the 13 dominant-parent IJVs and 4 independent IJVs outperformed the 20 shared-management firms in terms of perceived success by the IJV managers. The underlying argument is that shared-management IJVs involve more management difficulties and bargaining costs, because both parent firms play active roles in the decision making. As Killing (1983, 23) further noted, "the more equally the parents share the management of a venture, the worse it will perform." In a sample of IJVs in five developing Asian countries, Lecraw (1984) investigated the relationship between parent control and performance from the perspective of multinational corporations (MNCs). This study found that the success rate was low when overall control was roughly divided between the MNC and the local parents.

However, other studies have produced contradictory findings. Beamish (1984) utilized Killing's design and performance measures on 12 IJVs in less-developed Caribbean countries. He found that dominant control by foreign firms is negatively related to IJV performance, while dominant control by local firms and shared control are not. Yan and Gray (1994) argued that the inter-partner relationship in the IJV is embedded in divergent and competitive self-interests and objectives. They found that partner firms' relative control in the IJV predicts the extent to which they achieve their objectives. In particular, among four IJVs operating in China, they found that shared-management IJVs demonstrated better performance than dominant and independent ones.

We argue that these inconsistent findings may be partially attributed to the static approach used in the prior research. It is our belief that an evolution perspective should help us understand the complex nature of such relationships because IJVs are always under reconfiguration. Several studies have focused on how IJV performance affects IJV reconfiguration. Killing (1983) observed that the parent firms might loosen or strengthen control over the IJV as a response to the IJV's ongoing performance. When an IJV shows superior performance, the parents tend to loosen control, since the IJV's management team has proven its expertise. Yan (1999) proposed that undesirable performance prompts structural instability because poor performance implies that at least one of the parent firms failed to achieve its objectives, thus creating stimuli for changing the existing structure. In addition, it is argued that IJVs have the potential to develop strategies of their own and to make autonomous decisions (Butler and Sohod 1995). The evolution toward autonomy may lead to improved performance. As Killing (1983) noted, the more the IJV managers are left alone, the better they will perform. So, the relationship between IJV control and performance is not unidirectional but reciprocal.

RESEARCH METHODOLOGY

Sample and Data Collection

The cases analyzed in this study consisted of eight China-Japan joint ventures in manufacturing industries operating in China. We limited the cases to manufacturing industries because IJVs in service industries may significantly differ from those in manufacturing industries in the complexity of technology, structures, and the processes and procedures of management (Chowdhury 1988). Further, the cases were restricted to China-Japan IJVs so that the extraneous variation (Eisenhardt 1989) that might be derived from studying IJVs with different national cultures would be minimized. Because of geographical convenience, Japanese businesses had concentrated their investments along the eastern coast of China. In this sample, four cases were located in Tianjin (a large city in the northeast) and the other four were in Nantong (a medium-sized city in the southeast).

Data were collected mainly through in-depth interviews conducted in mid-1995. The interviews were guided by a semi-structured questionnaire to assure that similar procedures were carried out in each case. Examples of the interview questions are included in the Appendix. In order to address the dynamics in these IJVs, we asked the informants to describe the history of the IJV, with special attention paid to the IJV formation stage, significant reconfigurations, and the current situation. Five of the eight IJVs had been operating for over eight years at the time of interview, so this sample enabled us to examine control evolution in these IJVs. In addition, all informants had worked in these IJVs since their formation, so they were able to provide relevant information.

To make the interviewees feel comfortable, the interviews were not tape recorded, but extensive notes were taken. We used the local general manager of each joint venture as the key informant for data collection. General managers were considered the appropriate informants because they were the most knowledgeable people about their ventures and were involved in strategic decision making (Geringer and Hebert 1991). A practical consideration was that there exist tremendous barriers to collecting data from multiple informants in the IJVs in China. The companies have been disguised to ensure confidentiality. The major characteristics of the eight cases are summarized in Table 8.1.

Key Constructs and Measurements

IJV Control

We used Killing's (1983) categories to identify IJV control. Our sample had demonstrated all three types of IJV control structures in Killing's categorization: shared-management IJVs, dominant-parent IJVs, and independent IJVs. Our data also suggested that management appointment, particularly to the position of general manager of an IJV, was an important mechanism for parent control. In our sample, in a typical shared-management IJV, both parent firms were highly involved in the IJV's operations, and the IJV's general management positions were split between the two parents. In an IJV with a dominant parent, only the dominant parent was highly involved in the IJV's operations, and the IJV's general manager acted as a middle manager in the parent firm's hierarchy. In an independent IJV, neither parent was highly involved in the IJV's operations, and the general manager was the top decision maker in the IJV.

Task Interdependence

Task interdependence between the IJV and its two parent firms was coded according to two criteria: the overlap in the IJV's and parent firms' business domains and the parents' strategic objectives in the IJV. An IJV and a parent firm had pooled interdependence if they had no overlap in their business domains and the parent's main objective was to get profit from the IJV (e.g., in case 1 the IJV had pooled interdependence with its Chinese parent). An IJV and a parent firm had sequential task interdependence if the IJV's business domain was upwardly or downwardly related to the parent's business domain and the parent's strategic objective was to gain access to low-cost raw materials/ products or to local market channels (e.g., in case 3 the IJV had sequential interdependence with its Japanese parent). In two cases (cases 2 and 8), the Chinese parent firms were transformed into the IJVs after the Japanese parents pooled part of their resources. In these cases, the IJVs and the Chinese

Table 8.1
A Summary of Major Characteristics of the Cases

Characteristics	Case 1	Case 2	Case 3	Case 4	Case 5	Case 6	Case 7	Case 8
Product	Men's suits	Plastic materials for shoes, belts	Retail shoes	Capacitors	Medicine and intravenous solutions	Panty shields	Syringes, infusion sets, hemodialysis equipment	Printing ink
Formation	1993, Nantong	1986, Nantong	1982, Nantong	1994, Nantong	1981, Tianjin	1987, Tianjin	1986, Tianjin	1993, Tianjin
Total Investment [a] Japan-China	2.5	6.7	1.4	7.0	5.0	1.0	7.85	48.0
Equity Shares	50/50	40/60	60/40	60/40	50/50	50/50	47/53	70/30
Product Market	95% export	10% export	100% export	70% export	30% export	100% local	70% export	10% export
Supply Source	100% local supply	100% local supply	40% import	60% import	15% import	40% import	60% import	20% import

Note: [a]The unit is in millions of U.S. dollars.

parent firms referred to the same identities, and thus they were codified as having reciprocal interdependence.

Parent Resource Contribution

This referred to the parent firms' contributions of resources and capabilities to the IJV (Yan and Gray 1994). Parent resource contribution was assessed along three dimensions: the parent's equity shares, noncapital contributions, and the overall evaluation of their contributions.

IJV Performance

We got information on IJV performance via three steps. First, the key informant was asked to answer performance questions by referring to the triangular relationship between the IJV, the local parent(s), and the foreign parent(s). Our interviews suggested that such a reference might help the informant incorporate both the parent firms' perspectives and the IJV's perspective in assessing performance. Second, we asked the informants to evaluate their IJVs' performance by using their own criteria. We believed that by using open-ended questions we would allow the respondents to evaluate their IJVs' performance realistically and multidimensionally. Finally, we used a single-item perceptual measure to provide an overall evaluation of IJV performance. Each IJV's overall performance was assessed using a scale ranging from good to satisfactory to poor.

Approach of Data Analysis

We analyzed the data following the procedures of comparative case studies suggested by Ragin (1994) and Eisenhardt (1989). The goal of comparative analysis is to determine the causal conditions or combinations of causal conditions that differentiate sets of cases (Ragin, 1994). Three steps were adopted: First, a within-case analysis was conducted for each case. The purpose of this analysis was to provide an adequate explanation for each case that permitted a comparative analysis. According to the theoretical discussion above, key variables were identified. Second, data were analyzed by comparing the presence or absence of causal conditions with the presence or absence of the outcomes. Third, the results of the examination of similarities and differences between cases were then compared with the theoretical debates. Consistency among cases and between the empirical results and the theoretical debates led to the conclusions.

Case Description

Case 1

This IJV was formed in 1993 between a Chinese textile manufacturer and a Japanese clothing producer. At its founding, the IJV was dominated by the

Japanese parent, although it only held 50 percent of the equity share. Ninety-five percent of the IJV's end products—clothes—were exported to Japan, and 85 percent of the raw materials were imported from Japan through the Japanese parent. Thus, the Japanese parent had a stronger influence than the Chinese parent on the IJV's activities. While both parents, especially the Japanese one, were satisfied with the IJV's performance, the IJV's local managers were not satisfied and attempted to seek independence from the Japanese parent's control for two reasons. First, the Japanese parent could not provide enough orders to the IJV, and thus parts of the IJV's production facilities were wasted. Second, the exporting price was very low, and targeting the local market seemed more profitable than exporting. Therefore, the IJV's local managers were attempting to establish the IJV's own brand in the Chinese market and were looking for local suppliers.

Case 2

This IJV was transformed from a Chinese state-owned enterprise in 1986, and the other two parent firms were a Chinese financial company and a Japanese trade company with equity shares of 35 percent, 25 percent, and 40 percent, respectively. The IJV had its own independent businesses, led by the general manager from the Chinese state-owned enterprise. Neither of the parents was involved in its businesses. Despite the difficulties the IJV faced at its founding (e.g., high debt ratio), it had achieved satisfactory performance in past years, paying off debts and building new workshops.

In 1995, the Japanese parent proposed to restructure the IJV by buying 60 percent of the equity shares held by the Chinese parents. The reason for this proposal was to integrate all of the Japanese parent's businesses in China, including this IJV. However, the proposal was strongly opposed by the local IJV general manager. The manager said, "I don't agree with this reconfiguration proposal. It will damage the interests of our company and the employees. Anyway, the proposal cannot be passed without my approval in the board." In fact, the manager had called for all employees not to cooperate with the consultant team sent by the Japanese headquarters for restructuring. The conflict between the local general manager and the Japanese headquarters resulted in losses for the IJV for the first time in the last six years.

Case 3

The IJV, formed in 1982, was jointly owned by a Japanese shoe company, a Chinese local government, and a Chinese financial institute with 60 percent, 30 percent, and 10 percent of the equity shares, respectively. This IJV represented a dominant-parent IJV because only the Japanese parent was involved in the IJV's daily operations. The IJV focused on only one value-adding activity: producing shoes. The Japanese parent bought 100 percent of the venture's products and supplied 40 percent of raw materials needed by the

IJV. Major decisions were made by the Japanese headquarters rather than by the IJV's board of directors.

The IJV has achieved good performance since its formation, meeting the Japanese parent's objective of providing low-cost shoes for Japanese markets and the Chinese parents' objective of setting up a model enterprise for potential foreign investors. Thus, none of the parents wanted to reconfigure the venture. Although the Japanese IJV general manager complained that the Japanese headquarters controlled the IJV too much, he had no intention of trying to free the IJV from the Japanese parent's control because he would not have a career in China.

Case 4

This IJV was formed in 1994 by Chinese and Japanese parents that both operated in the capacitor industry. The IJV focused on a single value-adding activity: producing capacitors. Its production capacity was split between the two parents: 70 percent belonging to the Japanese parent and 30 percent belonging to the Chinese parent.[1] The parents benefited from the IJV's dividend as well as product sales.

However, the two parents had achieved unbalanced benefits from the IJV. The Japanese parent was a multinational corporation and had large overseas markets and high sales prices. Thus, this parent mainly benefited from selling the IJV's products and wished to keep the venture's ex-factory price at a low level. The Chinese parent, as a local company, had limited local markets, and its sales price was quite low. Thus, this parent mainly benefited from the IJV's dividends and wished to set the venture's ex-factory price at a high level. Since the IJV's ex-factory price was fixed at a low level, the IJV had almost no profit, and the Chinese parent could not benefit from dividends. Therefore, the Chinese parent was considering ending the partnership. As the IJV's local general manager said, "I think that the Japanese parent is making use of us. We are being cheated. The venture can no longer exist unless both parents can benefit from it."

Case 5

This IJV, established in 1981, was jointly owned by a Chinese governmental bureau in charge of medicine quality and distribution (50 percent of the equity share) and a Japanese medicine producer (50 percent of the equity share). At its founding, this IJV was a dominant-parent venture, with the Japanese parent providing technology and equipment and being involved in the IJV's daily operations, while the Chinese parent only provided access to local market channels. The IJV had achieved satisfactory performance because its products were competitive in the Chinese market. Its performance improved after the Japanese general manager was replaced by a Chinese manager, who emphasized exploiting the local market and learning technology from the Japanese parent.

At the beginning of the 1990s, the Japanese parent proposed to reinvest in the venture to increase its equity share. However, this request was rejected by the local parent because it did not want to lose control over the venture. Then, the Japanese parent invested in other regions in China, and thus the importance of this IJV to the Japanese parent decreased. Even with reduced support from the Japanese parent, the IJV was still very successful in the Chinese market because it had learned technology know-how from the Japanese parent, and its products were very competitive in the local market. Further, since the IJV had penetrated the local market, it did not rely on exporting through the Japanese parent. The IJV's superior performance gave the local IJV managers greater bargaining power with the Japanese headquarters, and under the leadership of the Chinese general manager, it became very independent. The Chinese general manager expected that there would be no expatriates in the firm after 1997.

Case 6

This IJV had two Chinese parents and two Japanese parents. The largest Chinese and Japanese parents had 40 percent and 48.5 percent equity shares, respectively. The IJV had been an independent venture since its founding. None of the parents was familiar with the venture's businesses. The Japanese parent was an equipment producer that aimed to use the IJV as a "window" to show its products to potential Chinese customers, while the Chinese parent was a paper producer that had little to do with the IJV's businesses. Thus, neither of them could integrate the IJV's activities into their own value-adding chains. Also, since the IJV was small and its operations were of a little importance to the parents, the parents would have obtained little benefit from controlling it. The board of directors was the top decision maker. The IJV had performed well from the beginning, and its superior performance had strengthened the local IJV managers' autonomy.

Case 7

This IJV, a shared-management venture, was established in 1986. All the management positions were split between the managers from the Chinese parent and those from the Japanese parent. According to the partnership contract of 1986, 50 percent of the venture's products would be exported to Japan. However, the venture failed to do this because of poor product quality and high costs. Thus, both parents were dissatisfied with the venture's performance.

In 1991, the Japanese parent reinvested in a new assembly line for the venture and increased its equity share from 40 percent to 67 percent. After that, Japanese expatriates controlled the IJV's operations, and the local IJV managers were excluded from decision making. Although the Japanese parent was criticized as having cheated the IJV through internal transfer pricing, the overall performance of the IJV greatly improved. Its new product was more competitive in overseas markets, which further increased the sales of the IJV's other products. The local general manager stated that they had tried to free themselves from the Japanese parent's control but that it was very difficult because the Japanese parent controlled the exporting channels of the venture's products.

Case 8

This IJV was transformed in 1993 from a large Chinese state-owned firm in the printing ink business with more than 1,700 employees. The initial equity share between the Chinese and Japanese parents was 50/50. This IJV was an independent venture with a complete value-adding chain, and the board of directors was the final decision maker. The IJV's performance was satisfactory, though it sustained losses after the joint venture was formed. However, accounting losses did not result from the operation failures but from increases in employee compensation and the change in the depreciation calculation after the IJV was formed. The main reason that the state-owned enterprise formed the IJV was to facilitate its R&D (research and development) and exports. In fact, the IJV had developed more than ten new products and had expanded its exporting channels with the help of the Japanese parent in the two years since the venture's founding.

In 1994, the Japanese parent reinvested in a raw material supply base in the IJV and increased its equity share from 50 percent to 70 percent. The board composition changed as well. In the past, the board had had five Chinese directors and five Japanese directors, but now it had seven Japanese directors and five Chinese directors. Despite the changes in equity structure and board composition, the IJV still remained independent and was led by the Chinese general manager. The Chinese general manager had been in the state-owned firm for more than 10 years, and his authority had been institutionalized during that time. This was a large and old Chinese firm, and thus it would have been difficult for a Japanese manager to manage it effectively. It was stipulated that a decision could be passed in the board only when more than two thirds of the directors agreed. Thus, the Japanese parent could not control the venture by simple majority.

FINDINGS OF COMPARATIVE CASE STUDIES: ANTECEDENTS OF IJV CONTROL

In this section, we will present the findings of our comparative case studies related to the antecedents of IJV control. We have argued that task interdependence between a parent firm and an IJV represents a primary motive for the parent firm to control the IJV and that the parent's resource contributions help achieve the parent's desired level of control over the IJV. Table 2 presents the two major parents' (one Chinese and one Japanese parent) task interdependences with the IJV, their resource contributions to the IJV, and IJV control for each of the eight cases. Among the eight IJVs, two were shared-management IJVs (cases 4 and 7), three were dominant-parent IJVs (cases 1, 3, and 5, all dominated by Japanese parent firms), and three were independent IJVs (cases 2, 6, and 8).

The data have suggested various business linkages between the IJVs and their parent firms. While all the IJVs in this study were manufacturing firms, their parent firms consisted of local government bureaus (or local economic development authorities), trade companies, and manufacturing firms. These parent firms exhibited different strategic objectives for joint venturing, including technology acquisition, local market access, profit generation, and simply using the IJV as a "window" to show the foreign parent's products to potential local customers. We also observed considerable differences in these parent firms' resource contributions to the IJVs. Chinese parents usually contributed access to local market channels and local government support, and Japanese parents contributed technology, equipment, and access to export channels.

Table 8.2 demonstrates clear patterns between task interdependence and IJV control. When an IJV had pooled interdependence with both parents, it was an independent IJV, with both parents positioning the IJV in the market (case 6). When an IJV had sequential interdependence with both parents, it was a shared-management IJV, with the parents positioning the IJV in the

Table 8.2
The Patterns of Task Interdependence, Resource Contributions, and Control

Case	IJV's Task Interdependence with: CP[a] JP[b]	Relative to JP, CP's Resource Contributions:	IJV's Initial Control Structure
1	Pooled < Sequential	Moderately lower	Dominated by J P
2	Reciprocal > Pooled	Moderately higher	Independent IJV [c]
3	Pooled < Sequential	Lower	Dominated by J P
4	Sequential = Sequential	Approximately equal	Shared-management IJV
5	Pooled < Sequential	Moderately low	Dominated by J P
6	Pooled = Pooled	Approximately equal	Independent IJV
7	Sequential = Sequential	Approximately equal	Shared-management IJV
8	Reciprocal > Sequential	Higher	Independent IJV [c]

Notes: [a]CP denotes Chinese parents; [b]JP denotes Japanese parents; [c]In these two cases, the IJVs were transformed from the Chinese parent firms.

hierarchy (cases 4 and 7). When an IJV had asymmetric interdependence with the two parents, it was dominated by the parent that had higher interdependence with the IJV. Three of the eight cases (cases 1, 3, and 5) were dominated by Japanese parent firms. In these cases, the Japanese parent firms had sequential interdependence with the IJVs, whereas the Chinese parent firms had pooled interdependence with the IJVs. In two other cases (cases 2 and 8), the Chinese parent firms had reciprocal interdependence with the IJVs, while the Japanese parents had pooled interdependence or sequential interdependence. These two IJVs were dominated by local Chinese managers, as predicted. In addition, in these two cases, the Chinese parents were transformed into the IJVs, and the Chinese parent firms, as an entity, did not exist any more. Hence, we categorized these two cases as independent IJVs, led by local Chinese managers, rather than IJVs dominated by the Chinese parent firms.

The data also demonstrated clear patterns between the parent firms' relative task interdependences with the IJV and their relative resource contributions to the IJV. In IJVs where the parent firms had asymmetric task interdependences with the IJV, the parent that had a higher level of interdependence tended to contribute more resources to the IJV (cases 1, 2, 3, 5, and 8) than the parent with a lower level of interdependence. In IJVs that had symmetric task interdependences with the two parents, the parents tended to contribute approximately equally to the IJVs (cases 4, 6, and 7). Based on these findings, we propose the following propositions:

Proposition 1: From a single parent firm's view, a parent firm's task interdependence with the IJV determines its resource contributions to the IJV and the level of its control over the IJV.

Proposition 2: From an inter-parent view, the parent firms' relative levels of task interdependences with the IJV determine their relative resource contributions to the IJV and their relative levels of control over the IJV.

FINDINGS OF COMPARATIVE CASE STUDIES: CONSEQUENCES OF IJV CONTROL

Initial Control Design and Performance

Table 8.3 presents the IJVs' initial control, initial performance, current control, and current performance. Comparing initial control (column 2) and initial performance (column 3), we found that the two shared-management IJVs (cases 4 and 7) had poor performance, while the other types of IJVs had satisfactory or good performance. Closer examination of cases 4 and 7 provided insights into why shared-management IJVs tends to have poor performance. In case 4, the venture's production capacity was split between the two parent firms. Its management positions were also split between Japanese expatriates, who were in charge of production and product quality, and Chinese managers who were in charge of personnel and public relations. However, the Chinese and Japanese parents had conflicting interests. The Chinese parent wanted to set up a higher ex-factory price in order to benefit more from the venture's dividends, while the Japanese parent preferred a lower ex-factory price in order to benefit more from selling products. The Chinese parent felt that it was being cheated because the current price was fixed at a lower level. Also, the Japanese expatriates always arranged the orders from the Japanese parent prior to those from the Chinese parent, and they often made free use of the production capacity belonging to the Chinese parent.

Case 7 initially was a shared-management venture. For each senior management position, there was a Chinese manager with formal authority and a Japanese manager as a consultant to that position. Although this arrangement was intended to reduce inter-parent opportunistic behaviors, it created bargaining and influence problems. No decision could be made unless both managers agreed. In addition, while the IJV's strategy was to export 50 percent of its end products to the Japanese market, the Chinese managers dominated the production processes. The Japanese headquarters believed that product quality could not meet the standards of the Japanese market and refused to export the products. Hence, the IJV almost could not survive at the beginning. It was not surprising that, later on, the Japanese parent increased its equity share, monopolized the decision making, and exported 70 percent of the end products to the Japanese market.

These cases suggest that managers in shared-management IJVs tend to form subgroups based on their organizational affiliations. They view themselves as safeguards of their parent organizations' interests in the IJV, and they lack confidence in the other group's goodwill in cooperation. The achievement of one group's objectives automatically causes the other group to feel that it has been cheated (a typical response would be, "How can they achieve so much if they do not make use of us?"). Moreover, the fact that both subgroups are involved in decision making in shared-management IJVs increases the chance that members of different subgroups will compare their relative achievements and perceive intergroup conflicts and politics.

The Evolution of IJV Control and Performance

We examined the evolution of IJV control by comparing columns two, three, and four in Table 8.3. We observed that shared-management and dominant-parent IJVs (cases 1, 4, 5, and 7) tended to evolve, while independent types remained stable (case 2, as an exception, will be discussed later). More specifically, shared-management IJVs tended to evolve toward the dominant parent type (case 7), and dominant-parent IJVs tended to evolve toward the independent type (cases 1 and 5). We did not observe design reconfiguration in case 4 because of its short history at the time of interview.

Table 8.3
The Dynamic Relationships between IJV Control and Performance

Case	Initial Control	Initial Performance	Current Control	Current Performance
4	Shared	Poor	To be liquidated	Poor
7	Shared	Poor	Dominant	Satisfactory
3	Dominant	Good	No evolution	Good
1	Dominant	Satisfactory	Independent	Satisfactory
5	Dominant	Satisfactory	Independent	Good
6	Independent	Good	No evolution	Good
8	Independent	Satisfactory	No evolution	Satisfactory
2	Independent	Satisfactory	Dominant	Poor

Note: Performance ranking: Good > Satisfactory > Poor.

We observed that IJV performance has an important feedback impact on the evolution of IJV control. Shared-management/dominant-parent IJVs are more likely to be reconfigured over time if they have poor or satisfactory performance (cases 1, 4, 5, and 7). In contrast, an IJV with good performance tends to be stable over time even if it is a dominant-parent IJV (case 3). Our data (except case 2) demonstrated that stable IJVs tend to be: those that have good performance, regardless of their control structure; and those that are independent, regardless of their performance. The overlap of these two sets of IJVs is the independent IJVs with good performance, which represent the ultimate destination of the evolution of IJV control. The results suggest that the evolution of IJV control has a strong tendency toward independence, evolving along a continuum from a shared-management IJV, through a dominant-parent IJV, to an independent IJV. Moreover, poor IJV performance tends to accelerate this process, and good IJV performance may delay the process. The finding that independent IJVs with good performance serve as the end point of IJV evolution indicates that the purpose of IJV evolution is to build the IJV as a successful independent firm operating in the Chinese market.

To examine the performance consequences of the evolution of IJV control, we compared columns four (IJV evolution) and five (current performance) in Table 8.3. Across the seven cases (except case 2), we found that the evolution of IJV control had resulted in similar or better performance. For example, case 7 evolved from a shared to a dominant type, which increased performance from a poor to a satisfactory level. Case 5 evolved from a dominant to an independent type, resulting in increased performance from a satisfactory to a good level. Although the evolution of case 1 from a dominant to an independent type did not increase the firm's performance significantly, it still maintained its performance at a satisfactory level. The cases (cases 3, 4, 6, and 8) where no evolution occurred remained at their original performance levels.

Case 2 represented an exception in our data. This venture started with an independent IJV led by a Chinese general manager and satisfactory performance. Later, the Japanese parent attempted to reconfigure the firm into a dominant-parent IJV, but this attempt raised conflicts between the Chinese general manger and the Japanese headquarters, which resulted in reduced (from satisfactory to poor) performance (see Table 8.3). During the interview, the Chinese general manager was very emotional in discussing the reconfiguration issues. He claimed that, "I cannot accept the reconfiguration plan. I have called for all employees to resist the consulting team sent from the Japanese headquarters. I will fight them in board meetings." We interpreted the general manager's reaction in two ways. First, this reconfiguration attempt was emotionally unacceptable to him because he viewed the IJV as his and the employees' firm, not the Japanese headquarters' subsidiary. Second, he might have been afraid of losing power in the venture if it were reconfigured into a dominant-parent IJV in which the Japanese headquarters would dominate the decision making and into which Japanese expatriate managers would come. The case suggested that the local manager's autonomy in an IJV has little elasticity. Once local managers are empowered, it would be difficult to take away their power later on. Based upon the previous discussions, we summarize the dynamic relationship between IJV control and performance into the following propositions:

Proposition 3: Shared-management IJVs tend to have worse performance than dominant-parent IJVs and independent IJVs.

Proposition 4: Successful IJVs tend to be stable over time. The poorer the IJV performance, the more likely that its control structure will evolve over time.

Proposition 5: IJV control structure tends to evolve over time along a continuum from a shared-management type, through a dominant-parent type, toward an independent type, with successful and independent IJVs as the ultimate end of the evolution path.

Proposition 6: IJVs that evolve along the proposed evolution path tend to have better performance, while IJVs that evolve against the path tend to have poorer performance.

DISCUSSIONS OF THE INTEGRATED FRAMEWORK OF IJV CONTROL

A Portrait of IJV Control

Our analyses of the eight China-Japan IJVs suggest an interesting portrait of IJV control. Our findings support the notion that parent firms vary in their intent to control their IJVs. This is probably because control of IJVs has both benefits and costs. On the one hand, tightly controlling an IJV has the benefits of determining how best to use the IJV's resources for the parent firm's purposes (Mjoen and Tallman 1997) and for protecting the parent firm from premature exposure of its technologies to the other parent (Geringer and Hebert 1989). On the other hand, tight control of an IJV may also result in increased bureaucratic costs—which can be viewed as the transaction costs associated with hierarchy (Jones and Hill 1988).

The bureaucratic costs of control depend upon the achievement of economies of scale in the parent firms' management skills (Buckley and Casson 1988). When the parent firm is related horizontally to the IJV (a situation involving reciprocal interdependence), required management skills for the parent firm and the IJV are quite similar. The parent can thus achieve economies of scale in its management abilities. In contrast, when the IJV is unrelatedly diversified from the parent (a situation involving pooled interdependence), the parent is less likely to be familiar with the IJV's domains. It may lead to managerial diseconomies arising from the scale and diversity of the resultant firm when the parent firm attempts to closely control the IJV (Buckley and Casson 1988). Thus, we argue that the prevailing assumption in the prior literature that the parent firms struggle for control of the IJVs is incomplete at best. Instead, parent firms may choose the optimal level of control over the IJVs in accordance with their task interdependence with the IJVs. Control struggle occurs only if both parent firms want to tightly control the IJV.

Our data also suggest a consistent pattern among parent firms' relative task interdependences with the IJVs, their relative resource contributions to the IJVs, and their relative control over the IJVs. These results support Inkpen and Beamish's (1997) argument that parent firms' resource contributions to the IJV do not occur automatically. Our results suggest that parent firms' resource contributions to the IJV are triggered by their task interdependence with the IJVs, with the purpose of helping achieve the parent firms' desired level of control over the IJVs.

Our results also suggest that parent firms' control over IJVs represents a double-edged sword to the IJVs (Zhang and Li 2001). On the one hand, parent firms' control reduces the IJV managers' autonomy in decision making, and it may even lead to poor performance (Killing 1983). On the other hand, a high level of control by a parent firm is associated with a high level of resource contributions from the parent. For example, during the first several years of operation, case 5 was dominated by the Japanese parent that supplied technology, equipment, and raw materials to the IJV. The success of this IJV at the early stage depended heavily upon the foreign parent's support with products and technology. As the venture freed itself from the foreign parent's control to become an independent firm, the support from this parent also decreased.

Similarly, in case 6, the local general manager enjoyed extreme autonomy in decision making, but he could not get support from the parent firms. He complained that, "we need capital to expand the production capability and promote the products. But none of the parent firms has an interest in reinvesting in the venture. We have to solve these problems by ourselves." These findings indicate that IJV managers should balance parent firms' control and their pursuit of autonomy, especially at the early IJV stage.

Evolution of IJV Control

Our findings about the evolution of the IJV control structure coincide with the failure cycle in shared-management IJVs identified by Killing (1983). He found that there existed a common pattern of shared-management IJVs in decline: poor venture performance leads to the parent firms monitoring the IJVs' activities closely, which lowers the autonomy of IJV managers. Low autonomy of IJV managers and high intervention from the parents are likely to slow and confuse the decision making process in the IJVs, which may cause performance to worsen further. This in itself encourages the parents to become even more closely involved, and so the downward cycle continues.

The current study and Killing's work (1983) have revealed a critical issue in IJV management: independence (or autonomy) and success are twins in IJVs from a dynamic view. Indeed, these two studies describe the same coin from different sides. While Killing (1983) found that low autonomy may cause failure and that failure further lessens autonomy, our study suggests that high independence will lead to success and that success further enhances independence. However, our study has advanced Killing's (1983) study by addressing how an IJV evolves across the three types of IJV control structures, while his study focused on shared-management IJVs.

Our results suggest that successful and independent IJVs represent the ultimate IJV control evolution. This finding is somehow contradictory to the view that IJVs (or strategic alliances in general) are temporary organizational arrangements between two (or more) organizations, which may be terminated once the parent firms have achieved (or cannot achieve) their objectives. This view has been developed mainly in examining IJVs/alliances between firms in developed countries. In these IJVs/alliances, the managers are likely to have their careers within their parent firms rather than in the IJVs/alliances. Hence, these managers tend to emphasize the achievements of their organizations' objectives over the IJVs/alliances' growth and independence. In contrast, in IJVs in an emerging economy, local managers are unlikely to pursue their careers in the foreign parent's organization. Most local parent firms of these

IJVs are state-owned enterprises or local government agencies, where these local managers do not want to or cannot pursue their future careers. These local managers will pursue their careers within the IJVs or in other firms in the local labor market. Therefore, developing the IJVs into successful and independent entities in the local market will be in the interest of these local managers. Thus, managers (especially the local managers) of IJVs in an emerging economy tend to be very entrepreneurial and to be committed to the IJVs rather than to the parent firms.

In conclusion, based upon the data from eight international joint venture (IJVs) operating in China, we have developed an integrated framework for IJV control, which tries to answer questions such as: When do parent firms want to control an IJV? How does an IJV's control structure evolve over time? and What is role of performance in such an evolution? We believe that our study will contribute to the IJV literature by providing a more comprehensive and dynamic view of IJV control, particularly in the context of an emerging economy.

Appendix
Examples of Interview Questions

Interview Category	Example
Dominance of the parent firms	1. How much was the total investment in this venture? How was the ownership split between parent firms? 2. What did each parent firm invest in the venture (e.g., capital, equipment, or technology)? 3. How many directors are on the board, and how is the board membership split between parent firms? 4. What decisions are made within the venture, and what decisions should be referred to the headquarters of parent firms?
The IJVs' value adding chain	1. What are the major businesses of the venture? 2. What are the major businesses of each parent firm? 3. What were the main objectives of each parent firm in the venture? 4. What percentage of your venture's products is sold by each parent firm, and what percentage of your venture's raw materials is provided by each parent firm?
Organizational affiliation of the general manager	1. Who is the general manager of your venture? Is this person a Chinese or a Japanese? 2. Who appointed this person, and who pays him?
Performance	1. How would you assess the performance your venture? 2. What are the major problems your venture has solved? 3. What are the major problems your venture is facing now? 4. How would you evaluate the relationship between your venture and the parent firms? 5. Has overall performance reached initial expectations?

NOTE

1. The split of the IJV's production capacity between the two parents did not parallel their equity shares because the IJV wanted to qualify for some priority treatments from the Chinese government. The priority treatments were given only to IJVs that exported 70 percent or more of their products.

REFERENCES

Barney, J. B., and W. G. Ouchi. 1986. *Organizational Economics: Toward a New Paradigm for Understanding and Studying Organizations.* San Francisco: Jossey-Bass.

Beamish, P. W. 1984. "Joint Venture Performance in Developing Countries," Ph.D. dissertation, University of Western Ontario.

Blodgett, L. L. 1991. "Parent Contributions as Predictions of Equity Share in International Joint Ventures." *Journal of International Business Studies* (First Quarter): 63–78.

Buckley, P. F., and M. Casson. 1988. "A Theory of Cooperation in International Business." In *Cooperative Strategies in International Business.* edited by F. J. Contractor and P. Lorange. Lexington, Mass.: Lexington Books.

Butler, R. J., and S. Sohod. 1995. "Joint-Venture Autonomy: Resource Dependence and Transaction Costs Perspectives." *Scandinavian Journal of Management* 11 (2): 159–75.

Child, J., and D. Falkner. 1998. *Strategies of Cooperation.* Oxford, England: Oxford University Press.

Chowdhury, M. A. J. 1988. "International Joint Ventures: Some Interfirm-Organization Specific Determinants of Success and Failure—A Factor Analytic Exploration." Doctoral Dissertation, Temple University, Philadelphia. Unpublished.

Demirbag, M., and H. Mirza. 1996. *Inter-Parent Reliance, Exchange of Resources and Parents' Influence on Joint Venture's Strategy.* University of Bradford Management Centre, U.K.: Asia Pacific Research and Development Unit Discussion Paper Series.

Eisenhardt, K. M. 1989. "Building Theories from Case Study Research." *Academy of Management Review* 14 (4): 532–50.

Franko, L. G. 1971. *Joint Venture Survival in Multinational Corporations.* New York: Praeger.

Geringer, J. M., and L. Hebert. 1989. "Control and Performance of International Joint Ventures." *Journal of International Business Studies* 22: 249–63.

———. 1991. "Measuring Performance of International Joint Ventures." *Journal of International Business Studies* (Second Quarter): 246–63.

Gomes-Casseres, B. 1987. "Joint Venture Instability: Is It a Problem?" *Columbia Journal of World Business* (Summer): 97–107.

Hamel, G., Y. Doz, and C. K. Prahalad. 1989. "Collaborate with Your Competitors and Win." *Harvard Business Review* 67 (1):133–39.

Harrigan, K. R. 1986. *Managing for Joint Venture Success.* Lexington, Mass.: Lexington Books.

Hennart, J. 1988. "A Transaction Cost Theory of Equity Joint Ventures." *Strategic Management Journal* 9: 361–74.

Hesterly, W. S., J. Liebeskind, and T. R. Zenger. 1990. "Organizational Economics:

An Impending Revolution in Organizational Theory?" *Academy of Management Review* 15: 402–20.

Hitt, M. A., M. T. Dacin, E. Levitas, J. L. Arregle, and A. Borza. 2000. "Parent Selection in Emerging and Developed Market Contexts: Resource-Based and Organizational Learning Perspectives." *Academy of Management Journal* 43: 449–67.

Inkpen, A. C., and P. W. Beamish. 1997. "Knowledge, Bargaining Power, and the Instability of International Joint Ventures." *Academy of Management Review* 22 (1): 177–202.

Jones, G. R., and C. W. L. Hill. 1988. "Transaction Cost Analysis of Strategy-Structure Choice." *Strategic Management Journal* 9: 159–72.

Killing, J. P. 1983. *Strategies for Joint Venture Success*. New York: Praeger.

Lecraw, D. J. 1984. "Bargaining Power, Ownership, and Profitability of Transnational Corporations in Developing Countries." *Journal of International Business Studies* 15 (1): 27–43.

Mjoen, H., and S. Tallman. 1997. "Control and Performance in International Joint Ventures." *Organization Science* 8 (3): 257–74.

Ragin, C. C. 1994. *Constructing Social Research*. Thousand Oaks, Calif.: Pine Forge Press.

Schaan, J.-L. 1983. "Parent Control and Joint Ventures Success: The Case of Mexico." Doctoral dissertation, University of Western Ontario. Unpublished.

Shenkar, O., and Y. Zeira. 1992. "Role Conflict and Role Ambiguity of Chief Executive Officers in International Joint Ventures." *Journal of International Business Studies* 1: 55–75.

Steensma, H. K., and M. A. Lyles. 2000. "Explaining IJV Survival in a Transition Economy through Social Exchange and Knowledge-Based View." *Strategic Management Journal* 21: 831–51.

Thompson, J. D. 1967. *Organizations in Action: Social Science Bases of Administrative Theory*. New York: McGraw-Hill

Yan, A. 1999. "Structural Stability and Reconfiguration of International Joint Ventures." *Journal of International Business Studies* 29 (4): 773–96.

Yan, A., and B. Gray. 1994. "Bargaining Power, Management Control, and Performance in International Joint Ventures: Development and Test of a Negotiation Model." *Academy of Management Journal* 37 (6): 1478–1517.

Zhang, Y., and H. Li. 2001. "The Control Design and Performance in International Joint Ventures: A Dynamic Evolution Perspective." *International Business Review* 10: 341–62.

CHAPTER 9

An Analysis of Joint Venture Activities in Southeast Asia

Daniel C. Indro and Malika Richards

INTRODUCTION

The study reported in this chapter empirically examines a sample of joint ventures established in Southeast Asia between 1990 and 1999. Our focus is on the type of activity in which a joint venture engages. We address the following questions: What factors determine the choice of joint venture activities in Southeast Asia? How does membership in the World Trade Organization affect the types of joint venture activities in these countries?

Studies in foreign direct investment generally focus on the mode of entry into a country (Buckley and Ghauri 1993). For example, Pan and Tse (2000) suggest that a firm can choose an equity or non-equity mode of entry. In the equity mode, the choice is between establishing a wholly owned subsidiary and setting up a joint venture. In the non-equity mode, a firm can choose between exporting its products and a contractual agreement. Studies on the modes of entry use Williamson's (1985) transaction costs theory to explain why a particular entry mode is chosen (Anderson and Gatignon 1986; Beamish and Banks 1987; Erramilli and Rao 1993; Kogut and Singh 1988). Unlike the choice of entry modes, the choice of joint venture activities has not received much attention. However, it is an important issue, as pointed out by Buckley and Casson (1998).

In addition, the entry of the Southeast Asian countries into the World Trade Organization (WTO) can alter the attractiveness of these countries as venture locations. The WTO agreements include commitments by individual members to lower tariffs and other trade barriers and to open or keep open markets for services. The WTO agreements also cover dispute resolution procedures.

As such, one can expect to see differences in the types of joint venture activity conducted before and after a country joined the WTO.

We make five important contributions to the joint venture literature. First, we capture changes in joint venture activity as a result of entrance into the WTO. Five of the six countries in our sample joined the WTO on January 1, 1995. Second, we go beyond the basic joint venture location decision and examine the operational types of joint ventures that are established in the context of partner-specific and country-specific factors. Third, we operationalize the role of human capital in joint ventures by using educational attainment of the population in the country in which the joint ventures were established. Fourth, our sample period is unique. The Southeast Asian economies enjoyed remarkable growth in the early half of the sample period and experienced a severe crisis towards the end of the sample period. Lastly, our study is valuable because it covers joint ventures in emerging economies. Moreover, our sample is not limited to only large multinationals or to companies in one industry or one country.

JOINT VENTURES

Joint ventures are collaborative arrangements in which two or more partners create an entirely new entity. Each partner has equity in the venture. Because of the ownership sharing arrangement, a joint venture is more formal than a contractual alliance and involves more commitment from the partners. In addition, because joint ventures are organizationally interdependent, they are complex organizations that are difficult to manage. Companies engage in such organizational modes if they see a long-term perspective and significant benefits. As Hagedoorn (1993) shows, joint ventures cover a large share of the normal business ventures of companies.

Buckley and Ghauri (1993) indicate that joint ventures have become an important component of a firm's global strategy. Extant empirical studies on joint ventures have generally documented positive stock market reactions to announcements of new joint ventures (Koh and Venkataraman 1991; McConnell and Nantel 1985; Woolridge and Snow 1990). These positive stock market reactions to the joint venture announcements, however, may mask challenges faced by the joint venture partners following the formation and announcement of the venture. Indeed, Lane and Beamish (1990) argue that poor implementation and lack of management attention after the venture has started operating often cause joint ventures in developing countries to fail. Moreover, such defects tend to stem from unresolved conflicts between partners due to misunderstandings of cross-cultural behavior.

The transaction costs literature (Williamson 1985) highlights the potential for opportunistic behavior by partners in joint ventures. Transaction costs theory suggests that the terms and types of joint ventures depend on the level of opportunism and uncertainty surrounding the transaction. The theory assumes that companies will choose the least costly mode of organization and take into account the effects of production and transaction costs. There are both partner/company-specific and country-specific factors that joint venture partners take into account.

Partner-Specific Factors

It is possible for one partner in a joint venture to take knowledge from the other without adequately paying for this resource. It is costly for a company to monitor its joint venture partner. The presence of partner trust lowers the monitoring and transaction costs involved in a joint venture.

Gulati (1995) defines trust as "a type of expectation that alleviates the fear that one's exchange partner will act opportunistically." Trust in alliances has been examined in various settings, and the general conclusion is that successful alliances exhibit trust between the partners (Koza and Lewin 1998). Trust has been operationalized by the number of prior alliances by the same pair of firms, whether they were domestic or international, and the number of partners involved (Gulati 1995). Several studies suggest that partner selection and experience with the partner are important considerations because they ultimately affect firm performance (Baum, Calabrese, and Silverman 2000; Merchant and Schendel 2000; Stuart, Hoang, and Hybels 1999). Ring and Van de Ven (1992) develop a set of theoretical propositions concerning the structure of cooperative relationships, one of which relates to the building of trust between companies through experience that encourages relational contracts, such as an alliance. Zaheer and Venkatraman (1995) found evidence for a significant social component (trust) in the determination of relational governance. In Glaister and Buckley's (1997) study of joint ventures in the United Kingdom, the most important partner-related selection criteria were reputation, trust between the top management teams, and relatedness of the partner's business. Barkema and Vermeulen (1997) found that cultural differences between joint venture partners have a significantly negative relationship with international joint venture survival. Furthermore, there is evidence that entry success diminishes when firms deal with both country and partner national culture differences (Barkema, Bell, and Pennings 1996). Similarly, Buckley and Casson (1996) contend that cultural differences increase transaction costs by causing misunderstandings that occur between partners from different cultural backgrounds.

However, empirical studies have not extensively examined joint ventures in terms of their specific functions and how these functions are related to joint venture partner characteristics. Partner familiarity is related to trust and perceived risk. If a firm is familiar with its partner, whether through prior joint venture experience or because of cultural similarity, it will be more willing to invest in a more risky project with this partner. There will be lower "transactions" costs—less likelihood of opportunistic behavior and lower monitoring costs. Manufacturing and R&D facilities involve more risk than do marketing joint ventures because of the intellectual property and physical plant and equipment involved. We therefore propose the following hypotheses:

H1a: The likelihood that a joint venture will engage in R&D activities is positively related to the frequency of the partners' prior joint venture experience with each other.

H1b: The likelihood that a joint venture will engage in manufacturing activities is positively related to the frequency of the partners' prior joint venture experience with each other.

H2a: The likelihood that a joint venture will engage in R&D activities is negatively related to the cultural distance between its parents.

H2b: The likelihood that a joint venture will engage in manufacturing activities is negatively related to the cultural distance between its parents.

Country-Specific Factors

The partner-specific factors described above capture the characteristics of the joint venture and the venture partners. In addition to partner-specific factors, there are country-specific factors that impact the level of opportunism and uncertainty surrounding a joint venture transaction.

Country risk refers to the extent to which a country's economic and political situation is unstable. Country volatility negatively impacts a joint venture's profitability as well as the day-to-day execution of its business. Transaction costs literature proposes that lower levels of country risk will help in the achievement of a venture's potential because firms will be operating in less risky environments. This sustains partners' contributions because firms will need to expend less managerial resources to counter political uncertainties (Merchant and Schendel 2000). Lower levels of country risk increase the chances that a venture will achieve its goals, as the collaboration is not exposed to the negative effects of government-driven disturbances (Root 1988). Instability creates uncertainty.

Multinationals tend to shun equity modes of investment when there is a high level of host country risk (Contractor and Kundu 1998). Tatoglu and Glaister (1998) found that perceived country risk, market attractiveness, and availability of qualified labor played a role in firms' decisions to invest in Turkey. In addition, Selzer (1994) noted that intellectual property protection in a developing host country is more important for high-tech industries than for sales and distribution outlets.

A joint venture limits exposure to the risks of entering a new market, as compared with a wholly owned subsidiary. In many of the Southeast Asian countries, although outright government misappropriation is not much of a threat, "creeping expropriation" is a significant factor. For example, a government may impose restrictive policies, such as limitations in the repatriation of profits, import controls, local content requirements, or a refusal to provide expatriate work visas. Government officials may engage in extortion or dishonesty by changing or canceling contractual agreements. The impact of country risk is potentially more severe in manufacturing and R&D joint ventures than in marketing ones. There may be lax enforcement of patent and trademark protection laws. The chances that new knowledge may be expropriated increases with political instability. On the other hand, five of the six Southeast Asian countries joined the WTO on January 1, 1995. Because the WTO provides a forum for dispute resolution, the entry of these countries into the organization may reduce their perceived risk and enhance their attractiveness as joint venture locations.

There is much evidence that the decision to invest and the overall entry mode are related to country risk factors (Buckley and Ghauri 1993). This study, however, will focus on the next level. It will examine whether there is a relationship between the type of joint venture (marketing, manufacturing, or R&D) and country risk factors. While manufacturing facilities require a considerable investment in equipment, R&D facilities also involve intellectual property. The least risky option is a marketing joint venture; thus we offer the following hypotheses:

H3: The likelihood that a joint venture will engage in R&D activities is positively related to a host country population's education level.

H4a: The likelihood that a joint venture will engage in R&D activities is negatively related to a host country's misappropriation risk.

H4b: The likelihood that a joint venture will engage in manufacturing activities is negatively related to a host country's misappropriation risk.

H5a: The likelihood that a joint venture will engage in R&D activities is positively related to a host country's membership in the WTO.

H5b: The likelihood that a joint venture will engage in manufacturing activities is positively related to a host country's membership in the WTO.

METHODOLOGY

Sample Selection

This study focuses on joint venture agreements between two partners. Our data comes from six different sources, namely: Barro and Lee (2000), *Euro-*

money, the Heritage Foundation, Hofstede (1980, 2001), the IMF Statistical Appendix, and the Securities Data Corporation. To identify joint venture agreements, we used the Securities Data Corporation's joint venture database. The information in this database is gathered from publicly available sources, including trade publications, news and wire sources, and SEC filings. Other studies using this database have found the information on industry and type of joint venture agreement to be reliable (Anand and Khanna 2000). The unit of our analysis is the joint venture agreement. To be included in the sample, each joint venture agreement must have information with respect to the partner- and country-specific factors mentioned earlier. We provide a brief description of these factors below.

Sample Characteristics

Table 9.1 shows summary statistics of our final sample of 522 global joint venture agreements that were announced between 1990 and 1999. We originally planned to include Brunei, Burma, Cambodia, and Laos in this study, but found so few joint ventures reported that we could not include them in the final sample of Southeast Asian joint ventures. When a country becomes too risky, firms avoid investment altogether. Malaysia has the largest number of joint ventures, followed by Vietnam and Thailand, with the Philippines having the smallest number. The majority of manufacturing joint ventures are in Vietnam, Malaysia, and Thailand. Singapore, Malaysia, and Thailand command a larger share of marketing joint ventures in the Southeast Asia region. R&D joint ventures took place primarily in Malaysia and Singapore.

Table 9.1 also shows that the number of joint ventures where one of the

Table 9.1
Southeast Asian Joint Venture Sample Description (N = 522)

JV Characteristic	Indonesia	Malaysia	Philippines	Singapore	Thailand	Vietnam
Number of joint ventures	81	122	47	73	97	102
Manufacturing activity only	56	65	35	31	63	77
Marketing activity only	1	15	5	18	14	5
R & D activity only	3	9	0	9	3	2
JV size (average cost in millions of dollars)	244	1,018	223	125	219	85
JV is in high-tech industry	32	39	10	37	30	36
One parent and JV have same 4-digit SIC	20	33	20	21	23	26
Both parents but not JV have same 4-digit SIC	6	13	5	1	5	4
Both parents and JV have same 4-digit SIC	4	1	2	2	10	14
Neither parents nor JV have same 4-digit SIC	51	75	20	49	59	58
At least one parent is in *Fortune* Global 500	18	21	12	19	25	24
Parents are both public firms	15	30	9	17	24	4
Parents are both private firms	16	27	8	4	10	25
One or more parent is government-owned	10	21	6	16	11	40
Purely local JV parents	2	28	2	8	6	4
One local and one Southeast Asian parent	18	7	8	4	6	16
One local and one Chinese (PRC/HK/ROC) parent	3	5	3	5	4	5
One local and one Jananese or Korean parent	26	18	11	7	28	29
One local and one "other" MNE parent	19	41	10	30	37	34
Parents have prior JV experience	3	3	3	7	6	12

parent companies shares the same four-digit Standard Industrial Classification (SIC) code as the joint venture is about equal across the six countries. Similarly, except for Malaysia and the Philippines, there is an approximately equal number of joint ventures in which the SIC codes of the parents and joint ventures are different. Malaysia has the most joint ventures in which both parents share the same SIC code, but this SIC code is different from that of the joint venture. Thailand and Vietnam have the most joint ventures in which both parents and the joint venture share the same SIC code.

Table 9.2 provides the means, standard deviations, and pairwise correlation coefficients between independent variables.

Measures

Dependent Variable

Types of Joint Venture Activity.   The Securities Data Corporation provided information about the activity of a joint venture. Out of the 522 joint venture agreements in our sample, 327 (63%) involve only manufacturing, 58 (11%) involve only marketing, and 26 (5%) involve only R&D. One hundred joint ventures involve both marketing and manufacturing, five joint ventures involve both marketing and R&D, three joint ventures involve both manufacturing and R&D, and three joint ventures involve manufacturing, marketing, and R&D. To test hypotheses 1–5, we omitted joint ventures that involve multiple activities. We followed Kogut's (1991) classification and created three dichotomous variables to indicate three types of mutually exclusive joint venture activities: manufacturing only, marketing only, and research and development only. Joint ventures involving marketing only in country j announced during year t were coded as 0, while those that engaged in research and development and manufacturing activities were coded as 1 and 2, respectively.

Independent Variables: Partner-Specific Factors

Prior Joint Venture Experience.   Prior joint venture experience between the two partners is a proxy for partner familiarity, as suggested by Chi and McGuire (1996). Prior joint venture experience can be thought of as a measure of the partner's tendency to behave opportunistically. As such, this is a *partner*-specific measure of trust between partners. For each joint venture agreement in a given year, we examined the Securities Data Corporation database back to 1979 to identify whether the two partners had any previous joint venture experience with each other. We summed the number of prior joint venture experiences for a given pair of partners. Out of the 522 joint venture agreements in our sample, 34 are between partners with prior joint venture experience. The maximum number of prior collaborations in our sample is seven.

Cultural Distance.   Cultural distance between the two joint venture partners is a proxy for partner uncertainty. Based on Hofstede's (1980, 2001) four

Table 9.2
Descriptive Statistics and Correlations between Independent Variables (N = 522)

	Mean	S.D.	1	2	3	4	5	6	7	8	9	10	11	12	13	14	15
1. Marketing activity	0.11	0.31															
2. Manufacturing activity	0.63	0.48	-0.46**														
3. R&D activity	0.05	0.26	-0.10**	-0.36**													
4. Joint venture size [a]	4.15	1.63	0.03	0.10*	-0.11*												
5. SIC Technology	0.35	0.48	-0.11*	0.04	0.11*	0.05											
6. Global 500	0.23	0.42	-0.03	-0.01	0.01	0.11	0.13**										
7. Government	0.20	0.40	-0.04	0.08	0.01	-0.02	-0.01	-0.03									
8. Prior experience freq	0.11	0.55	-0.04	0.05	0.00	0.03	0.06	0.15**	0.18**								
9. Partial bus overlap [b]	0.27	0.45	-0.01	-0.06	-0.02	-0.03	-0.03	0.09*	-0.06	-0.02							
10. Complete bus overlap [c]	0.13	0.33	0.01	0.04	-0.04	0.03	-0.02	-0.00	-0.19**	-0.04	-0.24**						
11. All MNE partners	0.19	0.39	-0.00	-0.01	0.04	0.06	0.12**	0.15**	-0.20**	0.04	0.02	-0.02					
12. Pure local partnership	0.10	0.29	-0.01	-0.06	0.04	-0.06	-0.12**	-0.07	0.07	-0.04	-0.07	0.07	-0.16**				
13. Cultural distance	1.92	1.41	0.08	-0.12*	0.07	-0.00	0.14**	0.05	-0.02	-0.05	0.10*	-0.08	-0.21**	-0.45**			
14. Country risk	31.12	17.85	-0.17**	0.21**	-0.18**	0.02	-0.10*	-0.00	0.16**	0.13**	0.03	0.09*	-0.06	-0.15**	-0.11**		
15. Post-second educ attain	5.45	3.68	0.09*	0.02	-0.03	0.11*	-0.08	0.03	-0.12**	-0.06	0.07	-0.01	0.05	0.03	-0.06	-0.15**	
16. WTO membership	0.44	0.50	-0.01	-0.01	0.10*	0.09	-0.01	0.01	-0.08	-0.51	-0.01	-0.06	-0.00	0.07	-0.02	-0.34**	0.37**

Notes: [a]Measured in natural logarithm of the joint venture cost.
[b]This group contains joint ventures in which the primary SIC code of *one* of the parents is the same as that of the joint venture.
[c]This group contains joint ventures in which the primary SIC codes of *both* parents are the same as that of the joint venture and ventures in which both parents are direct competitors.

$*p <; 0.05.$
$**p < 0.01.$

dimensions: power distance, uncertainty avoidance, masculinity/femininity, and individualism/collectivism, we computed, for each joint venture agreement, the cultural distance between the two joint venture partners by using the Kogut and Singh (1988) method. The usefulness of Kogut and Singh's cultural distance index has been validated in numerous studies on joint ventures (Barkema and Vermeulen 1997; Hennart and Larimo 1998; Morosini, Shane, and Singh 1998; Park and Ungson 1997). Unlike prior joint venture experience, cultural distance can be thought of as a *culture*-based measure of trust between two partners from two different cultural backgrounds. From their experiments, Glaeser et al. (2000) indeed found that the tendency to cheat one another increases when partners have national and racial differences. On average, the cultural distance between joint venture partners in our sample is 1.92.

Joint Venture Parent Company Size (Global 500).   The size of joint venture parents is a measure of the partner's reputation (Fombrun and Shanley 1990). When partners have an incentive to maintain a good reputation, they are unlikely to engage in opportunistic behavior. Because the joint venture parents in this sample include both private and public firms, it was impossible to obtain financial data on each. Therefore, we created a dummy variable whereby a joint venture parent was coded 1 if it was a member of the Fortune Global 500 list during the year the joint venture was formed, and 0 otherwise. In our sample of 522, there are 119 (23%) joint ventures in which at least one parent is a member of the *Fortune* Global 500. Table 9.1 shows that there are approximately equal numbers of joint ventures in which at least one parent is a member of the *Fortune* Global 500 in each of the six Southeast Asian countries.

Type of Joint Venture Parent: Government versus Company.   It was necessary to consider the possibility that one or both of the joint venture parents were governments. In some instances, such as transportation or defense industries, a government may not allow complete private ownership. In addition, while partnership with a government may provide the venture with operating stability, governments in emerging economies can also change rapidly and without notice. When a new government regime takes power, the operating stability of a venture that was created through a partnership with the previous regime may be in jeopardy. A dummy variable was coded as 1 if one or both parents were governments, and otherwise as 0. In this study there are 104 joint ventures in which one or both parents are governments. Table 9.1 indicates that Vietnam has the highest number of joint ventures in which a government is involved as a partner. Vietnam also has the smallest number of joint ventures in which both parents are publicly traded firms.

Type of Joint Venture Parent: MNC versus Local.   One of the motivations for a multinational to establish operations overseas is to exploit technological competence, particularly if the firm's home market is saturated. One reason for a local firm to partner with a multinational is to obtain technology. In turn, the local firm provides knowledge about the local marketplace. Because each party brings a unique contribution to the venture, such a partnership is mutually beneficial. In this study, we therefore control for whether each partner is local or a foreign MNC. Each joint venture parent was classified according to whether it was a local or a multinational (foreign) firm in that host country. This information was obtained from the Securities Data Company. Then, three dummy variables were created to indicate three types of joint venture partnerships: (1) between two foreign MNCs, (2) between a local firm and an MNC, and (3) between two local firms.

For descriptive purposes, Table 9.1 also classifies each joint venture parent according to whether it is a local, a Southeast Asian, a Chinese (PRC, Hong Kong, ROC), a Japanese/Korean, or an "other" foreign multinational in that host country. There are 50 joint ventures in which both parents are local firms. There are 59 joint ventures in which one parent is local and one is another Southeast Asian firm. There are 25 joint ventures in which one parent is local and the second is Chinese. There are 119 joint ventures in which one parent is local and the other is Japanese or Korean. There are 171 joint ventures in which one parent is local and the second is a Western multinational. The remaining 98 joint ventures were established by two foreign multinationals.

Figure 9.1 illustrates the changes in partner characteristics for three types of joint ventures—manufacturing, marketing, and R&D—before and after five of the six Southeast Asian countries joined the WTO on January 1, 1995. There is a general increase in the number of R&D joint ventures established involving a local partner. After January 1995, there are more marketing joint ventures between local and Japanese or Korean partners and between local and Southeast Asian partners, but fewer marketing joint ventures established between two local partners, between local and Chinese partners, and between two Japanese or Korean partners. The number of Western MNE–local marketing joint ventures remains high and constant. With regard to manufacturing joint ventures, there appears to be a particularly large increase in the number of manufacturing joint ventures established between a local partner and a Western MNE after January 1995. The number of manufacturing joint ventures established between the other categories of partnerships also increased, but to a lesser extent. Overall, both before and after January 1995, there are more local–Western MNE partnerships than any other kind. Local-Japanese/Korean partnership makes up the second largest number of manufacturing and marketing joint ventures.

Independent Variables: Country-Specific Factors

Misappropriation Risk (Country Risk).   Similar to Barkema and Vermeulen (1998), Mudambi (1998), and O'Donnell (2000), we used the *Euromoney* annual country risk ratings as a proxy for environment uncertainty in the country where the joint venture operates. To generate an overall country risk score, *Euromoney* assigns a weighting to nine risk categories, which include political risk and various indicators of economic performance. The country risk scores

Figure 9.1
Description of Southeast Asian Joint Ventures, by Partner Type

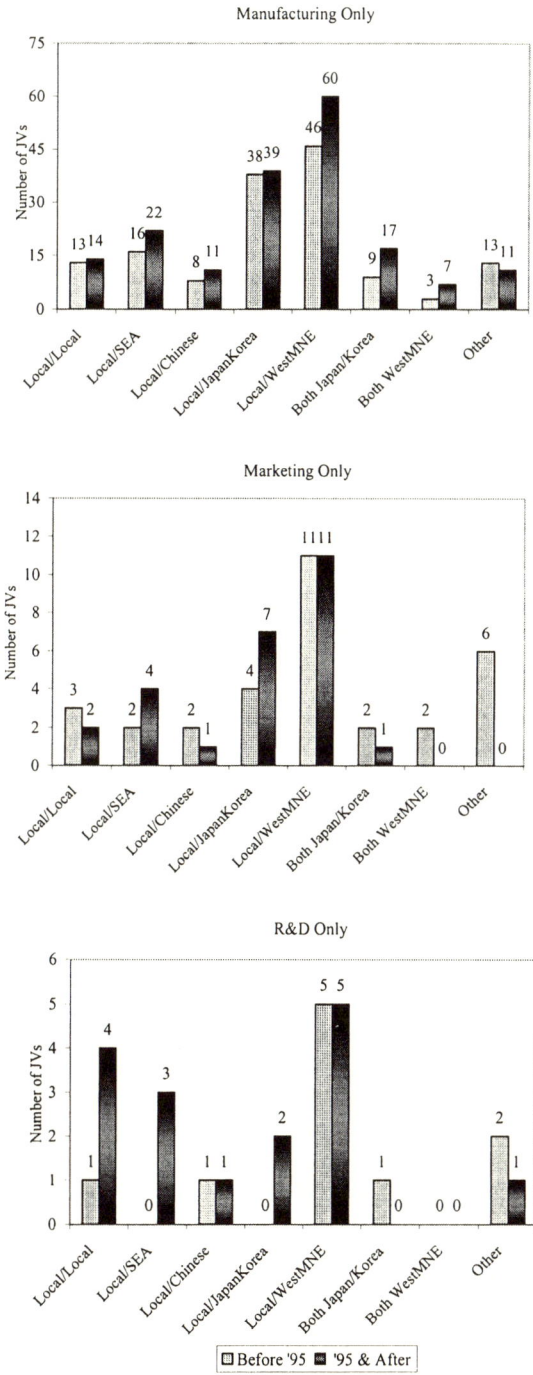

Manufacturing Only

Marketing Only

R&D Only

□ Before '95   ■ '95 & After

range from 0 to 100. For ease of interpretation, we reverse-coded the score so that a higher country risk score indicates greater risk. Because the *Euromoney* risk rating measures creditworthiness, an MNC is exposed to a greater likelihood of capital misappropriation when investing in a country with a high country risk score.

Misappropriation Risk (Property Rights Protection).   As a proxy for misappropriation of property rights, we used a component of the Index of Economic Freedom, constructed by the Heritage Foundation. This component scores the degree to which private property rights are protected and the degree to which the government enforces laws that protect private property.[1] Each country is given a score from one to five, with lower scores indicating a better protection. A score of one means that private property is guaranteed by the government, an efficient court system enforces contracts, the justice system punishes those who unlawfully confiscate private property, and expropriation is unlikely. A score of five suggests that property protection is nonexistent in a country. Property rights protection depends on a government's ability to enforce law and order. We used the Heritage Foundation measure because the International Country Risk Guide's political risk rating, while containing an assessment of corruption, law and order, and government stability, does not explicitly incorporate a property rights protection index. The property rights protection measure is highly correlated (at 86%) with the country risk score. Our test results are similar when we used the two proxies for misappropriation risk interchangeably.

Educational Attainment.   As Tatoglu and Glaister (1998) show, an MNC's decision to invest in a country is influenced by the availability of a qualified labor pool in that country. It is quite likely that the skills requirement varies across different types of joint ventures. A joint venture involved in R&D activities is more likely to require a labor force with more technical skills than one involved in marketing activities. For each year the joint venture was formed, we obtained data on the percentage of post-secondary education completion for the population aged 25 and older in each Southeast Asian country. This information came from Barro and Lee (2000). The average rate of post-secondary education completion is 5.45 percent.

WTO Membership.   This categorical variable signifies whether or not a joint venture was established in a nation belonging (at *that* time) to the WTO. A joint venture was coded as 1 if it was established in a country after the country joined the WTO. Indonesia, Malaysia, the Philippines, Singapore, and Thailand all became members of the WTO on January 1, 1995. The WTO membership variable also captures the dimension of time. While none of the countries were WTO members before January 1, 1995, all except Vietnam were members afterwards. Two hundred and thirty joint ventures (44% of total ventures) were established during and after the year these countries joined the WTO.

To show how membership in the WTO may affect the distribution of joint venture activities in Southeast Asia, Figure 9.2 provides a breakdown of three types of joint ventures—manufacturing, marketing, and R&D—by country for the period before January 1, 1995, and thereafter. In all countries except Malaysia there were more manufacturing joint ventures after these countries joined the WTO. Except for Indonesia, the Philippines, and Thailand, there was generally a decline in the number of marketing joint ventures. Similarly, more R&D joint ventures were established in Indonesia, Malaysia, and Thailand after these countries joined the WTO.

Independent Variables: Control Variables

Joint Venture Size.   Joint venture size is defined as the expected total investment (cost) to both partners to establish the venture. We computed the natural logarithm of each venture's cost. When the joint venture partners have more investment in the venture, they are more likely to make a strong, long-term commitment to the venture to ensure its success. On the other hand, it may also pay to make a small initial investment instead of a larger one because a joint venture has an option to expand in the future. This option to expand can later be exercised when the opportunity materializes (Bowman and Hurry 1993). Data on joint venture size is available from the Securities Data Corporation. On average, the size of joint ventures in our sample is 371.2 million U.S. dollars. Table 9.1 indicates that the average size of joint venture investment is much larger in Malaysia than in any other Southeast Asian country. Vietnam has the smallest average joint venture investment.

Industry Effects (SIC Technology).   In studies of alliance formation, Osborn and Baughn (1990) suggest that a firm's primary industry is an objective measure of its environment. Non-equity arrangements are the most common form of technology partnership in the high technology sectors. Indeed, Hagedoorn and Narula (1996) found a negative relationship between the use of joint ventures and the technological intensity of the industry. Using Hagedoorn and Narula's definition of high-technology sectors, we control for industry effects by creating a dummy variable that takes a value of 1 if the joint venture agreement is in the high-technology sectors, and 0 otherwise. There are 184 (35%) joint ventures in high-technology sectors. Of the six countries, the Philippines has the smallest number of technology-intensive joint ventures.

Business Similarity.   A joint venture is generally formed to enhance the economic interests of the parent companies. When the nature of their businesses is similar, not only can joint venture partners more effectively monitor each other for any signs of opportunistic behavior (Alchian and Demsetz 1972; Merchant and Schendel 2000), but they may also more fully realize their transactional gains because their business similarity facilitates production and allows them to communicate better. On the other hand, partners in the same line of business are direct competitors. They may seek synergies and be more willing to share knowledge with a partner in a different industry. We measured

Figure 9.2
Description of Southeast Asian Joint Ventures, by Country

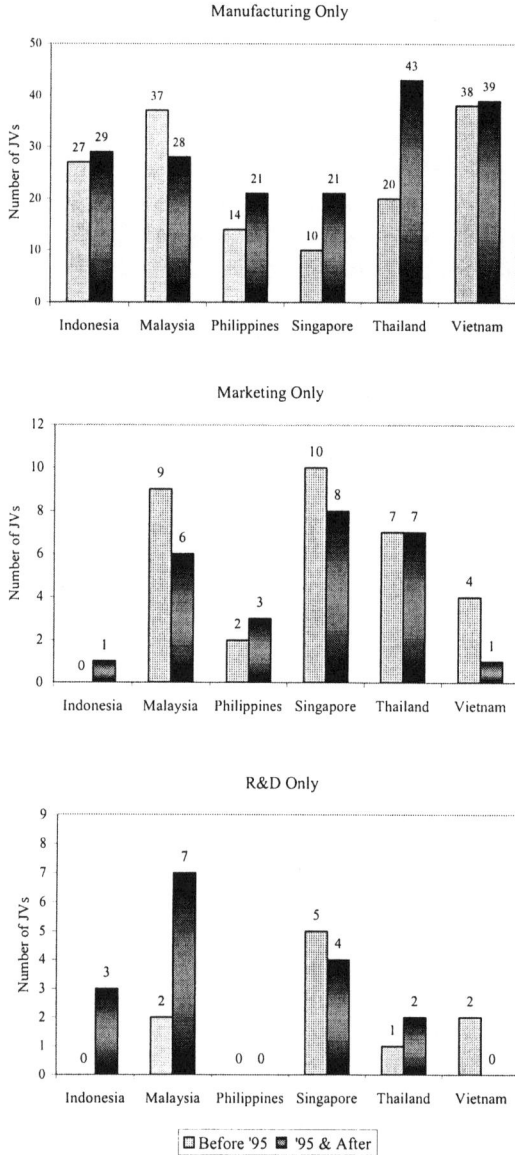

Manufacturing Only

Marketing Only

R&D Only

☐ Before '95 ▨ '95 & After

business similarity by looking at the primary SIC codes of the partners and the joint venture SIC code at the four-digit level. Following Reuer and Koza (2000), we used four dummy variables to indicate these cases of business similarity: (1) when both partners and the joint venture share the same primary SIC codes; (2) when both partners' primary SIC codes are the same but the joint venture has a different SIC code; (3) when the joint venture SIC code is the same as the primary SIC code of *only one* of the partners, and the partners do not have the same SIC codes; and (4) when both partners and the joint venture do not share the same SIC codes. Case (1) describes a situation where the business environment of the partners completely overlaps with that of the joint venture. There are a total of 33 joint ventures that fall into Case (1). Case (2) is a venture between direct competitors, of which there are 34 in the sample. Case (3) involves a partial business overlap. In case (4), all entities operate in different industries. There are 143 and 312 joint ventures that fall into Cases (3) and (4), respectively.

RESULTS

We used logistic regression models to examine the effect of partner-specific and country-specific variables on the likelihood that a joint venture engages in R&D or manufacturing relative to marketing activity. The results are reported in Table 9.3.

Model 1 in Table 9.3 reports the effect of control and partner-specific variables on the likelihood that a joint venture engages in R&D or manufacturing relative to marketing activity. R&D and manufacturing joint ventures are significantly more likely than marketing joint ventures to be in high-tech industries (significant at the 0.01 level and 0.05 levels respectively). When there is a greater cultural distance between partners, they tend to engage more in marketing than in manufacturing joint ventures (significant at the 0.10 level).

Model 2 in Table 9.3 examines the effects of country-specific variables on the likelihood that a joint venture engages in R&D or manufacturing relative to marketing activity. In locations with high levels of post-secondary educational attainment, joint ventures are significantly less likely to engage in R&D than in marketing (significant at the 0.05 level). In countries with high levels of misappropriation risk, as measured by property rights protection, joint ventures are more likely to engage in manufacturing than in marketing (significant at the 0.01 level). Also, in WTO-member countries, the joint ventures are significantly more likely to engage in R&D and manufacturing than in marketing (significant at the 0.10 level).

Model 3 in Table 9.3 combines the variables in Models 1 and 2 to explain the impact of partner-specific and country-specific variables on the choice of joint venture activities. The results indicate that the same relationships found in Models 1 and 2 continue to hold in this comprehensive analysis. As an additional test, we created a dummy variable that takes a value of one of the

Table 9.3

Results of Multinomial Logistic Regressions Examining the Determinants of ASEAN Joint Venture Activities (N = 411)

| | Model 1 | | Model 2 | | Model 3 | |
| | Activity is | | Activity is | | Activity is | |
	R&D	Manufacturing	R&D	Manufacturing	R&D	Manufacturing
Constant	-0.71	2.27***	0.41	-0.30	0.76	0.59
Control variables:						
Joint venture size [a]	-0.22***	-0.01	-0.25	0.02	-0.21	-0.02
SIC technology	1.53***	0.89**	1.31**	0.87***	1.51**	0.96***
Partial business overlap [b]	-0.25	0.10	-0.32	-0.05	-0.29	-0.01
Complete business overlap [c]	-0.26	0.14	1.48	0.59	-0.06	-0.02
Partner-specific variables:						
Prior experience frequency	0.35	0.31			0.58	0.33
Cultural distance	-0.08	-0.37***			-0.17	-0.29**
Global 500	0.33	0.18			0.34	0.12
Government	0.58	0.41			0.51	0.14
Purely local partnership	0.80	-0.85			0.60	-0.49
All partners are MNC	-0.71	-0.54			-0.95	-0.39
Country-specific variables:						
Property rights misappropriation risk			-0.22	0.65***	-0.30	0.58***
Post-secondary education attainment			-0.21**	-0.01	-0.22*	-0.01
WTO membership			1.17**	0.60*	1.03*	0.55*
Log likelihood	-229.18		-216.96***		-212.89***	
χ²	27.31		51.75***		59.90***	

[a]Measured in natural logarithm of the joint venture cost.

[b]This group contains joint ventures in which the primary SIC code of *one* of the parents is the same as that of the joint venture.

[c]This group contains joint ventures in which the primary SIC codes of *both* parents are the same as that of the joint venture and ventures in which both parents are direct competitors.

*$p < 0.10$.

**$p < 0.05$.

***$p < 0.01$.

joint ventures announced between 1996 and 1999. We used this dummy variable to capture the changes in the joint venture activity as a result of the 1997 Asian crisis. Our result indicates that the Asian crisis had no impact on the types of joint venture activity in the region. To conserve space, this result is not reported.

Overall, our results indicate that country-specific factors are a more important determinant of joint venture activity than joint venture- or partner-specific factors (Table 9.3). Table 9.4 presents a summary of the results.

DISCUSSION AND CONCLUSION

We find inconclusive evidence to support the predictions of transactions costs theory regarding the impact of partner familiarity on the choice of joint venture activities. Although there is a positive relationship between the frequency of the partners' prior joint venture experience and the likelihood that a joint venture engaged in R&D or manufacturing activities, it is not significant (Hypotheses 1a and 1b). Also, while there is a negative relationship between joint venture parents' cultural distance and the likelihood that a joint

Table 9.4
Summary of Results

H1a:	The likelihood that a joint venture will engage in R&D activities is positively related to the frequency of the partners' prior joint venture experience with each other.	Not supported *(not sig.)*
H1b:	The likelihood that a joint venture will engage in manufacturing activities is positively related to the frequency of the partners' prior joint venture experience with each other.	Not supported *(not sig.)*
H2a:	The likelihood that a joint venture will engage in R&D activities is negatively related to the cultural distance between its parents.	Not supported *(not sig.)*
H2b:	The likelihood that a joint venture will engage in manufacturing activities is negatively related to the cultural distance between its parents.	Supported
H3:	The likelihood that a joint venture will engage in R&D activities is positively related to a host country population's education level.	Not supported *(the opposite)*
H4a:	The likelihood that a joint venture will engage in R&D activities is negatively related to a host country's misappropriation risk.	Not supported *(not sig.)*
H4b:	The likelihood that a joint venture will engage in manufacturing activities is negatively related to a host country's misappropriation risk.	Not supported *(the opposite)*
H5a:	The likelihood that a joint venture will engage in R&D activities is positively related to a host country's membership in the WTO.	Supported
H5b:	The likelihood that a joint venture will engage in manufacturing activities is positively related to a host country's membership in the WTO.	Supported

venture engages in R&D activities, it too is not significant (Hypothesis 2a). However, when the cultural distance between two joint venture partners is high, they tend to engage in joint marketing rather than manufacturing activity, supporting Hypothesis 2b.

The evidence regarding the impact of country uncertainty on the choice of joint venture activities is also mixed. We expected that firms would try to minimize their exposure to host country risk. However, both Hypotheses 4a and 4b are not supported. Greater host country risk does not affect the likelihood that R&D joint ventures will be established relative to marketing joint ventures. In addition, manufacturing joint ventures are more likely than marketing joint ventures to be established in *riskier* countries. Indonesia, the Philippines, and Vietnam are the three riskiest countries in this sample. They also happen to be the countries with the lowest labor costs per worker in manufacturing. Singapore is the least risky, but also has the highest labor costs. Perhaps it makes sense to locate marketing joint ventures in locations where local customers are sophisticated and relatively well off. The manufacturing joint ventures in Indonesia and Vietnam may be export-oriented and they are established in these countries simply to take advantage of low labor costs.

On the other hand, both Hypotheses 5a and 5b are supported. There is a greater likelihood that an R&D or manufacturing joint venture is established when a country is a WTO member. Because the WTO agreement also covers dispute resolution procedures, a membership in the WTO signifies a commitment by member countries to abide by multilateral trade agreement and decision making by consensus. Moreover, as the Asian financial crisis has shown, the rules and disciplines of the WTO help restrain protectionist pressures and can reduce the severity of a downturn (World Trade Organization 2001). As a result, membership in the WTO may alter the risk profile of a country, and hence its attractiveness as a venture location. The negative correlation between country risk and WTO membership in Table 9.2 supports the notion that a membership in the WTO is associated with a lower country risk score.

Foreign Direct Investment theory predicts that multinationals are attracted to locations with resources, such as an educated workforce. However, this study found that a host country population's education level is *negatively* related to the likelihood that a joint venture engages in R&D activities. Hypothesis 3 is not supported. A finding that may help explain the above is that joint ventures in high-tech industries are more likely to engage in manufacturing and R&D than in marketing. Therefore, it could be that while low-tech firms are drawn by the low labor costs of Indonesia and Vietnam, the high-tech firms establish *combined* manufacturing and R&D operations in Malaysia and Singapore. Although Malaysia and Singapore each have only 7 pure R&D joint ventures (Table 9.1), this number increases to 14 each when R&D is combined with Manufacturing or Marketing in a joint venture.

In conclusion, although one may think it best to establish R&D joint ventures in nations with highly educated populations, marketing joint ventures are more often established in such nations in Southeast Asia. The sophistication of the local market may be more critical for marketing joint ventures. At the same time, when the local populations are more educated, they are also more likely to earn higher incomes and can afford a higher level of consumption. The greater purchasing power of the local population creates fertile ground for the creation of marketing joint ventures. On the other hand, export markets may be the driving force behind many manufacturing joint ventures. In addition, to the extent that manufacturing joint ventures are established in the riskier countries to take advantage of their low labor costs, there might be government stipulations that such joint ventures involve some transfer of production process or technology. These factors may help to explain why manufacturing joint ventures are more likely than marketing joint ventures to be established in risky countries.

Membership in the World Trade Organization has affected the type of joint venture activities in Southeast Asia. There was a significant shift in the kinds of joint ventures established. There was a general decrease in the number of marketing joint ventures. The number of R&D and manufacturing joint ventures increased. The increase in manufacturing joint ventures was primarily due to local–Western MNC partnerships. Also, there was a relatively large increase in purely local R&D joint ventures formed. This was driven primarily by Malaysia and Singapore.

It is interesting to note, though, that despite not joining the WTO, Vietnam has a large number of manufacturing joint ventures. Most of these are local–Western MNE and local-Japanese/Korean partnerships. One may speculate that multinationals are investing in low-tech labor-intensive manufacturing joint ventures in Vietnam to take advantage of low labor costs. Misappropriation of technology would not be such a concern in a low-tech venture. However, after January 1995, five of the Vietnamese manufacturing joint ventures are high-tech (13%). This compares with nine in Singapore (43%), five in Indonesia (17%), four in Malaysia (14%), six in Thailand (14%), and two in the Philippines (10%). Aside from Singapore, which clearly has a significant amount of high-tech manufacturing, Vietnam has approximately the same percentage of high-tech manufacturing joint ventures as do the other Southeast Asian countries, although the others are members of the WTO.

Our research identifies a challenging issue faced by foreign multinational corporations and government policy makers. The lack of a labor pool with sufficient technical skills in a country presents a multinational corporation with a dilemma. On the one hand, the relatively lower labor costs in the Southeast Asian countries provide an attractive opportunity for the multinational corporation to establish a joint venture there. On the other hand, the scarcity of qualified labor with sufficient technical skills implies that the multinational corporation may have to provide elaborate training to the local labor pool and send more expatriates than would be necessary had sufficiently qualified labor been available, both of which are costly undertakings. The same issue is also important for government policy makers. Improvements in educational quality may be called for, or the government may have to create an atmosphere that reduces brain drain. These initiatives can help a country enlarge its pool of well-qualified labor, which will eventually enhance not only the country's attractiveness as a joint venture location, but also the standard of living of its citizens.

ACKNOWLEDGMENTS

Earlier versions of this paper were presented at the Ninth Southeast Asia Business Research conference at the University of Michigan Business School in May 2002 and the 2002 British Academy of Management conference. The authors would like to thank LeBow College of Business, Drexel University, for research support.

NOTE

1. The specific variables encompassed in the property rights factor are: the presence of commercial code defining contracts, sanctioning of foreign arbitration of contract disputes, corruption within the judiciary, delays in receiving judicial decisions, freedom from government influence over the judicial system, government expropriation of property, and legally granted and protected private property.

REFERENCES

Alchian, A., and H. Demsetz. 1972. "Production, Information Costs and Economic Organization." *American Economic Review* 62: 777–95.

Anand, B. N., and T. Khanna. 2000. "Do Firms Learn to Create Value?: The Case of Alliances." *Strategic Management Journal* 21: 295–315.

Anderson, E., and H. Gatignon. 1986. "Modes of Foreign Entry: A Transaction Cost Analysis and Proposition." *Journal of International Business Studies* 11: 1–26.

Balakrishnan, S., and M. Koza. 1993. "Information Asymmetry, Adverse Selection and Joint Ventures: Theory and Evidence." *Journal of Economic Behavior and Organization* 20: 99–117.

Barkema, H. G., J.H.J. Bell, and J. M. Pennings. 1996. "Foreign Entry, Cultural Barriers and Learning." *Strategic Management Journal* no. 17: 151–66.

Barkema, H. G., and F. Vermeulen. 1997. "What Differences in the Cultural Backgrounds of Partners Are Detrimental for International Joint Ventures?" *Journal of International Business Studies* 28: 845–64.

———. 1998. "International Expansion Through Start-Up or Acquisition: A Learning Perspective." *Academy of Management Journal* 41: 7–26.

Barro R. J., and Lee. 2000. *International Data on Educational Attainment: Updates and Implications*. Harvard University Manuscript.

Baum, J., T. Calabrese, and B. Silverman. 2000. "Don't Go It Alone: Alliance Network

Composition and Startups' Performance in Canadian Biotechnology." *Strategic Management Journal* 21: 267–94.

Beamish, P., and J. C. Banks. 1987. "Equity Joint Ventures and the Theory of the Multinational Enterprise." *Journal of International Business Studies* 18 (summer): 1–16.

Blodgett, L. L. 1991. "Partner Contributions as Predictors of Equity Share in International Joint Ventures." *Journal of International Business Studies* 21: 63–78.

———. 1992. "Factors in the Instability of International Joint Ventures: An Event History Analysis." *Strategic Management Journal* 13: 475–81.

Bowman, E. H., and D. Hurry. 1993. "Strategy Through the Option Lens: An Integrated View of Resource Investments and the Incremental-Choice Process." *Academy of Management Review* 18: 760–82.

Buckley, P. J., and M. Casson. 1996. "An Economic Model of International Joint Venture Strategy." *Journal of International Business Studies* 27: 849–76.

———. 1998. "Analyzing Foreign Market Entry Strategies: Extending the Internationalization Approach." *Journal of International Business Studies* 29 (3): 539–61.

Buckley, P. J., and P. N. Ghauri. 1993. *The Internationalization of the Firm: A Reader.* London: Academic Press.

Chi, T., and D. J. McGuire. 1996. "Collaborative Ventures and Value of Learning: Integrating the Transaction Cost and Strategic Option Perspectives on the Choice of Market Entry Modes." *Journal of International Business Studies* 27: 285–307.

Contractor, F. J., and S. K. Kundu. 1998. "Modal Choice in a World of Alliances: Analyzing Organizational Forms in the International Hotel Sector." *Journal of International Business Studies* 29 (2): 325–57.

Contractor, F. J., and P. Lorange. 1988. "Why Should Firms Cooperate? The Strategy and Economic Basis for Cooperative Ventures." In *Cooperative Strategies in International Business,* edited by F. J. Contractor and P. Lorange, 3–30. Lexington, Mass.: Lexington Books.

Cosset, J. C., and J. Roy. 1991. "The Determinants of Country Risk Ratings." *Journal of International Business Studies* 21: 135–42.

Das, T. K., and B. S. Teng. 1998. "Between Trust and Control: Developing Confidence in Partner Cooperation in Alliances." *Academy of Management Review* 23: 491–512.

Erramilli, M. K., and C. P. Rao. 1993. "Service Firms' International Entry Mode Choice: A Modified Transaction Cost Analysis Approach." *Journal of Marketing* 57 (July): 19–38.

Fagre, N., and L. T. Wells Jr. 1982. "Bargaining Power of Multinationals and Host Countries." *Journal of International Business Studies* 12: 9–24.

Fombrun, C., and M. Shanley. 1990. "What's in a Name? Reputation Building and Corporate Strategy." *Academy of Management Journal* 33: 233–58.

Geringer, J. M., and L. Hebert. 1989. "Control and Performance of International Joint Ventures." *Journal of International Business Studies* 19: 235–54.

Glaeser, E. L., D. I. Laibson, J. A. Sheinkman, and C. L. Soutter. 2000. "Measuring Trust." *Quarterly Journal of Economics,* 115: 811–46.

Glaister, K. W., and P. J. Buckley. 1997. "Task-Related and Partner-Related Selection Criteria in U.K. International Joint Ventures." *British Journal of Management* 8 (3): 199–222.

Gomes-Casseres, B. 1996. *The Alliance Revolution: The New Shape of Business Rivalry*. Cambridge: Harvard University Press.

Gulati, R. 1995. "Does Familiarity Breed Trust? The Implications of Repeated Ties for Contractual Choice in Alliances." *Academy of Management Journal* 38: 85–112.

Hagedoorn, J. 1993. "Understanding the Rationale of Strategic Technology Partnering: Interorganizational Modes of Cooperation and Sector Differences." *Strategic Management Journal* 14 (5): 371–85.

Hagedoorn, J., and R. Narula. 1996. "Choosing Organizational Modes of Strategic Technology Partnering: International and Sectoral Differences." *Journal of International Business Studies* 27: 265–84.

Hennart, J. F. 1988. "A Transaction Costs Theory of Equity Joint Ventures." *Strategic Management Journal* 9: 361–74.

Hennart, J. F, and J. Larimo. 1998. "The Impact of Culture on the Strategy of Multinational Enterprises: Does National Origin Affect Ownership Decision?" *Journal of International Business Studies* 29: 515–38.

Hofstede, G. 1980. *Culture's Consequences: International Differences in Work-Related Values*. Beverly Hills, Calif.: Sage Publications.

———. 2001. *Culture's Consequences: Comparing Values, Behaviors, Institutions and Organizations Across Nations*. Thousand Oaks, Calif.: Sage Publications.

Kogut, B. 1991. "Joint Ventures and the Option to Expand and Acquire." *Management Science* 37: 19–33.

Kogut, B., and H. Singh. 1988. "The Effect of National Culture on the Choice of Entry Mode." *Journal of International Business Studies* 19 (3): 411–32.

Koh, J., and N. Venkatraman. 1991. "Joint Venture Formation and Stock Market Reactions: An Assessment in the Information Technology Sector." *Academy of Management Journal* 34: 869–92.

Koza, M. P., and A. Y. Lewin. 1998. "The Co-Evolution of Strategic Alliances." *Organization Science* 9 (3): 255–64.

Lane, H. W., and P. W. Beamish. 1990. "Cross-Cultural Cooperative Behavior in Joint Ventures in LDCs." *Management International Review* 30: 87–102.

McConnell J., and T. Nantel. 1985. "Corporate Combinations and Common Stock Returns: The Case of Joint Ventures." *Journal of Finance* 40: 519–36.

Merchant, H., and D. Schendel. 2000. "How Do International Joint Ventures Create Shareholder Value?" *Strategic Management Journal* 21: 723–37.

Morosini, P. 1999. *Managing Cultural Differences*. New York, N.Y.: Pergamon.

Morosini, P., S. Shane, and H. Singh. 1998. "National Cultural Distance and Cross-Border Acquisition Performance." *Journal of International Business Studies* 29: 137–58.

Mudambi, R. 1998. "The Role of Duration in Multinational Investment Strategies." *Journal of International Business Studies* 29: 239–62.

O'Donnell, S. W. 2000. "Managing Foreign Subsidiaries: Agents of Headquarters, or an Interdependent Network?" *Strategic Management Journal* 21: 525–48.

Osborn, R. N., and C. C. Baughn. 1990. "Forms of Interorganizational Governance for Multinational Alliances." *Academy of Management Journal* 33: 503–19.

Pan, Y., and D. K. Tse. 2000. "The Hierarchical Model of Market Entry Modes." *Journal of International Business Studies* 31 (4): 535–54.

Park, S. H., and M. V. Russo. 1996. "When Competition Eclipses Corporation: An

Event History Analysis of Joint Venture Failure." *Management Science* 42: 875–90.

Park, S. H., and G. R. Ungson. 1997. "The Effect of National Culture, Organizational Complementarity, and Economic Motivation on Joint Venture Dissolution." *Academy of Management Journal* 40: 279–307.

Reuer, J. J., and M. P. Koza. 2000. "Asymmetric Information and Joint Venture Performance: Theory and Evidence for Domestic and International Joint Ventures." *Strategic Management Journal* 21: 81–88.

Ring, P. S., and A. Van de Ven. 1992. "Structuring Cooperative Relationships Between Organizations." *Strategic Management Journal* 13: 483–98.

Root, F. 1988. "Some Taxonomies of International Cooperative Agreements." In *Cooperative Strategies in International Business*, ed. F. J. Contractor and P. Lorange, 69–80. Lexington, Mass.: Lexington Books.

Selzer, R. 1994. "Intellectual Property Rights: Risk Cuts Flow of Investment, Technology." *Chemical and Engineering News* 72 (11): 6–7.

Stuart, T., H. Hoang, and R. Hybels. 1999. "Interorganizational Endorsements and the Performance of Entrepreneurial Ventures." *Administrative Science Quarterly* 44 (2): 315–49.

Tatoglu, E., and K. W. Glaister. 1998. "Western MNC's FDI in Turkey: An Analysis of Location-Specific Factors." *Management International Review* 38 (2): 133–59.

Williamson, O. E. 1985. *The Economic Institutions of Capitalism*. New York, N.Y.: Free Press.

Woolridge J., and C. Snow. 1990. "Stock Market Reaction to Strategic Investment Decisions." *Strategic Management Journal* 11: 353–63.

World Trade Organization. 2001. *Annual Report, 2001.*

Zaheer, A., and N. Venkatraman. 1995. "Relational Governance as an Inter-Organizational Strategy: An Empirical Test of the Role of Trust in Economic Exchange." *Strategic Management Journal* 16 (5): 373–92.

CHAPTER 10

National Culture in China and Multinationals' Performance

Ji Li

INTRODUCTION

National culture has been defined as the values, beliefs, and assumptions learned in early childhood that distinguish people in one nation from those in another (e.g., Beck and Moore 1985; Hofstede 1991). Researchers have been trying to conceptualize and measure differences in national culture since the 1960s (e.g., Haire, Ghiselli, and Porter 1963; Hofstede 1980, 1983, 1984, 1991; Laurent 1983, 1986; Trompennaars 1993). Past research has shown that national culture can influence managerial decision making (e.g., Schneider and Demeyer 1991), leadership style (e.g., Dorfman and Howell 1988; Puffer 1993), and human resource management practices (e.g., Luthans, Welsh, and Rosenkrantz 1993). In addition, the greater relative importance of national culture compared with other levels of culture, such as organizational culture, has also been demonstrated. For example, national culture has been found to have a greater impact on employees than does the organizational culture of the firm (Adler 1986). Numerous studies have suggested that, in business organizations, management practices that reinforce the values of the employees' national culture are more likely to yield desired behaviors (Wright and Mischel 1987), higher self-efficacy (Earley 1994) and stronger performance (Earley 1994).

Insufficient empirical research, however, has been conducted on the effects of MNEs' (multinational enterprises) home country culture or national culture on the behavior of MNEs' subsidiaries in their host countries. In other words, when studying multinational enterprises from different industrialized countries, little research tested the effects of MNEs' home country culture on the behavior of their subsidiaries overseas. Testing this issue will be of significance because it can improve our understanding on the effects of home country culture on MNEs' international operations. For example, if home country culture does not have any significant effects on MNEs' international operations, the firms may not need to consider the issue of cultural distance when deciding in which country to invest. According to research, cultural distance can be defined as the difference between the home country and a foreign market with respect to the level of development, education, business language, everyday language, cultural values, and the extent of connections between the home and foreign market (Carlson 1975). Carlson (1975) showed that the buying preferences of Swedish firms correlated negatively with cultural distance, and another Swedish study reported by Carlson concluded that Swedish firms were more likely to invest in "culturally nearby countries" first.

In spite of the research on cultural distance, the effect of this culturally-nearby-countries-first policy on MNEs' performance remains unclear. Testing the effects of home country culture will help understand this issue. If the effect of home country culture is not significant on MNEs' behavior and performance, cultural distance may not be a significant issue, and MNEs may not need to invest in culturally nearby countries first. However, if the effect of home country culture is indeed significant on MNEs' behavior and performance in their host countries, cultural distance should be considered as an major issue when the MNEs invest internationally; and the MNEs may have to adopt the culturally-nearby-countries-first policy.

This article deals with this issue by testing the effects of home country culture on MNEs' behavior and performance in China. In the following sections, I first offer a brief review of previous research on national culture and consider its effects on MNEs' behavior and performance in their host countries. Based on that, I present several testable research hypotheses and describe a study I conducted to empirically test those hypotheses. Finally, the results of this study are reported and the implications of these findings are discussed.

LITERATURE REVIEW

Some authors have studied the effects of national culture on the behavior and performance of MNEs in their host countries. For example, Hennart (1988) studied the strategy of MNEs in the United States and showed that their strategy was influenced by cultural distance between the home base of the investor and the target country. On the other hand, Dunning and Bansal (1997) studied the effects of national culture on international firms and their joint ventures. The author suggested that home country culture could have effects on the strategies of MNEs. For example, low individualism or high collectivism, together with a perception of high transaction costs, in a firm's home country may lead to the firm's preference for joint ventures rather than other forms of investment (10).

National culture can influence the selection of an MNE's competitive strategy (e.g., Bluedorn and Lundgren 1993; Jelinek and Litterer 1988; Kotter and Hestkett 1992). For example, Bluedorn and Lundgren (1993) suggested that large power distance and high uncertainty avoidance were more compatible with the so-called defender strategy, which concentrates on protecting current markets and serving current customers only (Miles and Snow 1978). On the other hand, small power distance and low uncertainty avoidance are more congruous with the so-called prospector strategy, which stresses risk-taking, flexibility, and aggressively searching for new products, new markets, and new growth opportunities (Miles and Snow 1978).

Research has also suggested that national culture may influence MNEs' selection of investment location (Creel 1953). For example, according to a group of Australian government researchers, over 60 percent of the investment in China by overseas Chinese capital has been in only 2 of the 30 provinces on mainland China, namely, Guangdong or Fujian, where the majority of the overseas Chinese have ancestral origins (East Asia Analytical Unit 1995). Li, Khatri, and Lam (1999) studied the investment by overseas Chinese in China's electronics industry. They found that overseas Chinese investors invested heavily in some sectors of China's electronics market, such as semiconductor device, television sets, display parts, and hard disk driver, regardless of the slow market growth, fierce market competition, and negative industrial profitability in the market sectors for those products. However, in some other fast-growing and much more profitable sectors, such as communications equipment repairs and TV equipment repairs, overseas Chinese established much less businesses than firms from Western countries. After considering several critical factors, such as market potential and profit margin, the authors concluded that the most important factor explaining the investment locations of the overseas Chinese was their kinship relationships.

Finally, national culture can also influence a firm's competitive advantage. Porter (1990) pointed out that the competitive advantages of firms could be derived from the most rapid accumulation of specialized assets and skills, sometimes due solely to greater commitment. Dunning and Bansal (1997) further suggested that this greater commitment might well be based on cultural values observed in some countries and not in others. When a national culture offers its firms advantages over those of others, then that nation can be considered as having a cultural competitive advantage. Specifically, many individualistic cultures (e.g., U.S. culture) may have an advantage in technological assets, whilst many collectivistic cultures (e.g., Japanese culture) may benefit in the ways that they organize their workforce and establish relationships among contractors, suppliers, and joint-venture partners (Dunning and Bansal 1997).

Based on the research and theorizing outlined above, it can be argued that national culture may influence an MNE's behavior and performance overseas. This can be summarized in the following research hypothesis.

First, national cultures in individualistic countries, such as the United States and western European countries, may lead to an advantage in technological research and development. On the other hand, many collectivist national cultures, such as that in Japan, may result in an advantage in workforce organization, quality control of products and service, and establishment of good relationships among contractees, suppliers, and customers (Dunning and Bansal 1997). Because of this difference in organizing workforce, the firms from collectivistic cultures may be more likely to adopt a labor-intensive human resource management (HRM) practice. Accordingly, it is predicted,

Hypothesis 1. Among MNEs in China, there is a positive relationship between collectivistic home country culture and the adoption of a labor-intensive HRM practice.

Also, comparing the culture in East Asia with those in Western countries, some authors show that East Asian culture is characterized by its long-term orientation (e.g., Hofstede 1991, Chap. 7). According to Hofstede (1991), for example, long-term orientation refers to future-orientation, or focusing on the future. With this long-term orientation, people in a nation are more likely to emphasize education and training, practice persistence and thriftiness, and delay immediate gratification. Long-term orientation may also influence firms' employment system. For example, some authors have suggested that nations with long-term orientation are more likely to adopt a system of long-term employment (e.g., Selmer 1997). In other words, the long-term cultural perspective is consistent with the long-term employment system often adopted by Oriental organizations. Accordingly, it is predicted,

Hypothesis 2. Among MNEs in China, there is a positive relationship between collectivistic home country culture and the adoption of a long-term employment system.

In addition, according to research, Oriental cultures are characterized by collectivism, which can be defined as a preference for a tightly knit social framework in which individuals can expect their clan or organization members to look after them, in exchange for unquestioning loyalty (e.g., Hofstede 1984). Influenced by this cultural value, Oriental firms may adopt a pay system that maximizes collective rather than individual interests. Therefore, it is predicted,

Hypothesis 3. Among MNEs in China, there is a positive relationship between collectivistic home country culture and the adoption of a pay system that maximizes collective interests.

Finally, given the differences in HRM, or managerial practices, MNEs from different cultures may have different financial or accounting performance in

China. However, there has been insufficient research testing the effect of home country culture on MNEs' financial performance in host countries. Because of insufficient research evidence, this paper proposes no hypotheses on this issue but tests it in an exploratory study.

METHOD

Sample

The sample for this study consisted of firms invested in by MNEs in a southern China province (N = 85). Specifically, this sample consisted of 38 Japanese investments, 32 U.S. investments, and 15 investments from western European countries. These firms were operating in two industries, the electronics (N = 50) and the clothes and shoes industries (N = 35). These firms were randomly selected from a list of firms covered by a recent Chinese industrial survey, which showed the firms' addresses and detailed accounting information about the firms' performance (see Li, Lam, and Qian 2001 for more information about this data set). This sample made it possible to test the effects of home country cultures on MNEs operating in a host country.

To collect more information about the firms' operations and performance, student assistants hired from a major southern China university were sent to conduct structured interviews in these firms. The main task of these assistants was to ask three middle managers from each firm in our sample to respond to a list of questions, which will be discussed in the next section.

Measurement

The measurement of factors in the current study consisted of both questionnaire data and secondary government survey data. Below is a detailed discussion of these two sets of measurements.

Questionnaire Data

Some dependent variables were measured with items selected from a measuring instrument developed by House and his GLOBE research team (see House et al. 1999). The main reason to use these items was that the items were developed jointly by scholars from different cultures, including those from Chinese cultures, such as those from China, Hong Kong, Taiwan, and Singapore. Since 1995, the Chinese version of the items had been tested and showed high reliability and validity. Therefore, using the items could save some resources in doing back-translation and developing the items.

Two key dependent variables were tested with the items. These variables were *long-term employment system* and *collective pay system*. Specifically, long-term employment system was measured by three items: (1) In this organization, managers are mainly promoted from inside the organization rather than recruiting from outside the organization. (2) In this organization, employees will not lose their jobs if they don't make major mistakes. (3) People in this organization can enjoy a long-term employment policy. On the other hand, collective pay system was tested by two items: (1) The pay and bonus system in this organization is designed to maximize collective interests. (2) In this organization, managers encourage group loyalty even if individual goals suffer. A pretest among a class of MBA students in southern China showed that the items of the two factors had reliabilities alphas .75 and .71, respectively. Also, the reliability alphas among the three sets of data from each firm in our sample ranged between .69 and .91.

Secondary Survey Data

In this study, I measured several factors based on the secondary industrial survey data from the Chinese Statistical Bureau in 1997, described as follows. (1) *Labor intensiveness* was tested by a ratio of equipment value to total number of employees. The smaller this ratio, the higher the labor intensiveness. (2) *Profitability*, i.e., a firm's return on assets (ROA), was computed by dividing the total after-tax profit of the firm by its total assets. (3) *Firm productivity* was tested by computing the average annual sales generated by each employee in a given firm. (4) *Asset growth* was tested by the average annual growth of assets of a firm since it was established. (5) *Home country culture* was tested as a dummy with one being the Japanese culture and zero the Western culture. Finally, (6) *Firms' export ratio* was the proportion of exporting among a firm's total sales. Finally, industry was measured as a dummy also with one being an electronic firm and zero otherwise.

Results

Table 10.1 reports the means, standard deviations, and zero-order correlations of all variables tested in the study. A negative and significant correlation was found between a Japanese home culture and the firms' long-term employment policy. On the other hand, a positive and significant correlation was found between Japanese home culture and the firms' labor intensiveness. These results seem surprising and I will discuss this issue in later sections.

To further test the effects of home country culture, hierarchical blocked regressions were adopted as the primary statistical approach to further test the hypotheses. Separate analyses were conducted for the dependent variables (i.e., labor intensiveness, long-term employment, and collective pay system). Specially, I first tested the effects of the independent factors on the factor labor intensiveness. In this analysis, the two independent variables (i.e., Japanese home culture and industry) were first entered as independent variables (Model 1). After that, I tested the effects of the control variable, meaning, the firm size (Model 2). With the same approach, I also tested the effects of the

Table 10.1
Descriptive Statistics

Variables	M.	S.D.	1	2	3	4	5	6	7	8	9	10
1 Japan Home Culture	0.447	0.311	1									
2 Industry	0.588	0.466	-0.062	1								
3 Exporting or Not	0.492	0.276	0.05	-0.191**	1							
4 Firm Size	299.237	560.362	0.097	-0.057	0.122*	1						
5 Employment Policy	11.273	4.196	-0.244**	-0.013	0.029	-0.124*	1					
6 Labor Intensity	0.33	0.234	0.371**	-5.06**	0.356**	0.28**	-0.258**	1				
7 Collective Pay	7.406	2.495	0.07	-0.043	-0.045	-0.063	-0.034	0.068	1			
8 Asset Growth	2.895	4.274	-0.103	0.074	-0.097	0.053	0.131*	-0.295**	-0.098	1		
9 Return on Asset	0.204	0.633	-0.063	0.006	-0.062	0.122	0.006	-0.21**	-0.024	0.688**	1	
10 Productivity	252	376	-0.321**	-0.116	-0.204**	0.156*	-0.226**	0.25**	0.069	-0.003	-0.042	1

Note: $^*p < 0.05$; $^{**} p < 0.01$; $^{***} p < 0.001$.

two independent variables on long-term employment and collective pay system.

Table 10.2 shows the results of the analyses. One can observe a positive and significant B value from the test for labor intensiveness, which suggests the effect of the Japanese home country culture on labor intensiveness ($p < .001$). This result supports hypothesis 1. Also, there is a negative and significant B value from the test for long-term employment ($p < .001$), which is surprising and different from the prediction of hypothesis 2. In other words, it seems that the MNEs from the West are more likely than those from Japan to adopt a policy of long-term employment. This result suggests two possibilities. First, it is possible that the Japanese home culture may not always influence the HRM practice of their MNEs in other countries, especially in developing countries. One major purpose of Japanese investment in China is to take advantage of the low-cost labor to produce for export markets. To reduce their labor costs, the Japanese firms may find it more beneficial to adopt a short-term employment policy. Another possibility is that the Japanese home culture itself changed already after over 10 years of economic recession in Japan. There have been reports and studies showing that many Japanese firms in their home country have given up their long-term employment system (e.g., Ornatowski 1998). This issue will be discussed further in the next section.

Finally, the effect of industry was significant on labor intensiveness, suggesting that the MNEs in the electronics industry were less labor-intensive than those in the clothes and shoes industry. However, the effect of home country culture on collective pay system was not supported as the B value from the test was not significant.

I also conducted hierarchical blocked regression to test the effects of home country culture on firm performance. Again separate analyses were conducted for three dimensions of firm performance: assets growth, employee productivity and return on assets (ROA). Specially, I first tested the effects of the

Table 10.2
Effect of Home Country Culture on MNEs' Behavior in China

	Labor Intensity		Long-term Employment		Collective Pay System	
	Model 1	Model 2	Model 1	Model 2	Model 1	Model 2
Independent Variables						
Japanese Home Culture	.322***	.289***	-.331***	-.317***	.076	.082
Industry Effect	-.371***	-.391***	-.054	-.046	-.097	-.094
Control Variables						
Size of Firm		.209***		-.124*		-.050
Overall Model F	42.0***	37.6***	10.8***	9.3***	1.214	1.062
Adjusted R-Square	.345	.385	.103	.115	.003	.001
Standard Error	.189	.183	3.912	3.886	2.413	3.415

Note: $^*p < 0.05$; $^{**}p < 0.01$; $^{***}p < 0.001$.

independent factors on the factor assets growth. In this analysis, four independent variables—Japanese home culture, collective pay, long-term employment and labor intensiveness—were first entered as independent variables (Model 1). After that, two control variables, firm size and industry effects, were entered (Model 2). With the same approach, I also tested the effects of the independent variables on employee productivity and ROA.

Table 10.3 shows the results of the analyses. The data suggest that home country culture does not have any direct significant effects on any dimensions of the firm performance tested. Neither does the factor collective pay. However, long-term employment has a positive effect on employee productivity ($p < .01$). Finally, firms' HRM practice, being labor-intensive or not, affects all three dimensions of firm performance negatively ($p < .01$).

SUMMARY AND IMPLICATIONS

Consistent with the past research on the effects of national culture, the data in the current study partially support the effects of home country culture on MNEs' behavior and performance. The findings in this study suggest several interesting points.

First, the data suggest some effects of home country culture on MNEs' behavior and performance in their host countries. For example, compared with Western MNEs, Japanese MNEs are more likely to adopt the policy of labor intensiveness. However, the hypothesis about the effect of home country culture on collective pay system was not supported. This result may suggest that some MNEs from the West also adopt a collective pay system. According to research, many European MNEs are different from U.S. ones in terms of their pay systems. Specifically, while U.S. firms often adopt a pay system that

Table 10.3
Effect of Home Country Culture on MNEs' Performance in China

	ASSETS GROWTH		PRODUCTIVITY		ROA	
	Model 1	Model 2	Model 1	Model 2	Model 1	Model 2
Independent Variables						
Japanese home culture	.025	.024	-.116	-.119	-.003	-.003
Collective pay	-.076	-.071	0.081	-.068	-.017	-.012
Long term employment	.059	.060	.186**	.163*	.051	.053
Labor intensiveness	-.279***	-.079***	-.198**	-.252**	-.214**	-.355***
Controlled Variables						
Firm size		.159*		.199**		.205**
Industry effect		-.112		-.149		-.167*
Overall Model F	5.812***	5.229***	4.854**	4.826***	2.554*	4.004**
Adjusted R Square	.078	.100	.063	.091	.026	.073
Standard Error	4.138	4.088	469.655	462.576	.630	.614

Note: $*p < 0.05$; $**p < 0.01$; $***p < 0.0001$.

maximizes individual interests and increases the gap between high-pay and low-pay employees, the European firms often adopt a system similar to that of the Japanese that emphasizes collective interests and narrows the gap between the high-pay and the low-pay. This may explain why the effect of the Japanese home country culture was not significant in this test.

Interestingly, the effect of Japanese home culture has a negative effect on the selection of a long-term employment system in this study. Although this finding is different from the prediction of hypothesis 2 and, therefore, surprising, this finding is in fact consistent with many empirical observations reported in China in recent years. Japanese firms were often reported to sign only a two-year contract with their employees in China. Yet even these two-year contracts may be terminated. For example, a Japanese electronic firm in Zhuhai city, one of the Special Economic Zones in South China, signed a two-year contract with one of its employees at the end of 1999. However, on January 3, 2000, the employee was told that his contract would be terminated on February 3, 2000, and he was given only one-month basic salary as compensation ("Illegal" 2000). All these suggest that MNEs' human resource management system is not merely influenced by their home country cultures. Other factors, such as their competitive strategy, may also influence their HRM policy. When Japanese firms adopt a labor-intensive policy in China, reducing labor costs as much as possible may become their priority. Given an abundance of skilled labor in China, these Japanese may ignore their home country culture or tradition and adopt a short-term employment system in their host country.

Second, the effect of home country culture on MNEs' performance is another interesting issue. The data in the current study seem to suggest that home country culture has no direct effects on the three dimensions of firm performance. However, according to the data, a long-term employment system has a direct positive effect on employee productivity; and labor intensiveness had negative effects on all three dimensions of firm performance, namely, assets growth, employee productivity, and return on assets (ROA). Theses results seem to suggest that, in terms of their effects on firms' performance, firms' strategies are more significant than firms' home country cultures.

Finally, assuming that a labor-intensive strategy means adopting a lower level of technology, one may also argue that this study suggests the important effects of advanced technology on MNEs' performance in China. Many recent reports or studies have provided consistent findings on this issue (e.g., Li, Lam, and Qian 2001). According to these studies, in the Chinese market, firms that have no advanced technological resource or are unwilling to use the resource seem to have some great disadvantages. Given the competition among all major MNEs in China today, Chinese customers in China will be unlikely to pay a high price for products with less advanced technology. Very often they may not even purchase those less advanced products. Selling out-of-date products will also make a firm more vulnerable in its competition with local firms. The local firms have their own valuable resources, such as good connections and familiarity with the local culture. If a foreign firm decides to compete with them in labor-intensive or low-tech product markets, there might be little chance that this foreign firm can win the competition. Finally, without the backup of advanced technological resources, foreign firms will be less likely to obtain support and cooperation from governments in a developing country such as China. Yet these supports and cooperation are often critical to business successes in those economies. All these seem to explain the significant negative effects of the labor-intensive strategy presented in Table 10.3. In other words, it seems that advanced technology rather than home country culture is the most important factor predicting the successes of MNEs in China today.

REFERENCES

Adler, Nancy J. 1986. *International Dimensions of Organizational Behavior.* Boston: Kent Publishing, 46–48.

Beck, B.E.F., and L. F. Moore. 1985. "Linking the Host Culture to Organizational Variables." In *Organizational Culture,* edited by P. J. Frost et al., 335–54. Beverly Hills, Calif.: Sage.

Bluedorn, A. C., and E. F. Lundgren. 1993. "A Culture-Match Perspective for Strategic Change." *Research in Organizational Change and Development* 7: 137–79.

Carlson, S. 1975. *How Foreign Is Foreign Trade?* Acta Universitatis Upsaliensis.

Creel, H. G. 1953. *Chinese Thought, from Confucius to Mao Tse-tung.* Chicago: The University of Chicago Press.

Dorfman, P. W., and J. P. Howell. 1988. "Dimensions of National Culture and Effective Leadership Patterns: Hofstede Revisited." In *Advances in International Comparative Management,* edited by R. N. Farmer and E. G. McGoun. vol. 3, 127–50. New York: JAI.

Dunning, J. H., and S. Bansal. 1997. "The Cultural Sensitivity of the Eclectic Paradigm." *Multinational Business Review* (winter): 1–16.

Earley, P. C. 1994. "Self or Group? Cultural Effects of Training on Self-Efficacy and Performance." *Administrative Science Quarterly* 39: 89–117.

East Asia Analytical Unit (Dept. of Foreign Affairs and Trade, Australia). 1995. "Singapore's Investment in China." In *Overseas Chinese Business Networks in China.* Melbourne: AGPS Press: 240.

Haire, M., E. E. Ghiselli, and L. W. Porter. 1963. "Cultural Patterns in the Role of the Manager." *Industrial Relations* 2: 95–117.

Hennart, J. 1988. "A Transaction Costs Theory of Equity Joint Ventures." *Strategic Management Journal* 9: 361–74.

Hofstede, G. 1980. *Cultural Consequences: International Differences in Work Related Values.* Beverly Hills, Calif.: Sage.

———. 1983. "National Culture in Four Dimensions." *International Studies of Management and Organisation* 13 (2): 46–74.

———. 1984. "Cultural Dimensions in Management and Planning." *Asia Pacific Journal of Management* 6 (January): 81–99.

———. 1991. *Cultures and Organizations*. London: McGraw-Hill.

House, R. J., P. J. Hanges, S. A. Ruiz-Quintanilla, P. W. Dorfman, M. Javidan, M. W. Dickson, and V. Gupta. 1999. "Cultural Influences on Leadership and Organizations: Project GLOBE." In *Advances in Global Leadership*, edited by W. Mobley, vol. 1., 175–233. Stamford, Conn.: JAI Press.

"Illegal Termination of Employee Contracts among Overseas Investment in China." 2000. *Singtao Daily*, 8 February, 7.

Jelinek, M., and J. A. Litterer. 1988. "Why OD Must Become Strategic." In *Research in Organizational Changes and Development*, edited by W. A. Pasmore and R. W. Woodman, vol. 2, 135–62. Greenwich, Conn.: JAI Press.

Kotter, J. P., and J. L. Hestkett. 1992. *Corporate Culture and Performance*. New York: Free Press.

Laurent, A. 1983. "The Cultural Diversity of Western Conceptions of Management." *International Studies of Management and Organizations* 13: 75–96.

———. 1986. "The Cross-Cultural Puzzle of International Human Resource Management." *Human Resource Management* 25: 91–102.

Li, J., N. Khatri, and K. Lam. 1999. "Changing Strategic Postures of Overseas Chinese Firms in Asian Emerging Markets." *Management Decision* 37: 445–56.

Li, J., K. Lam, and G. Qian. 2001. "Does Culture Affect Behaviour and Performance of Firms: The Case of Joint Venture in China." *Journal of International Business Studies* 32: 1–18.

Luthans, F., D. B. Welsh, and S. A. Rosenkrantz. 1993. "What Do Russian Managers Really Do? An Observational Study with Comparisons to U.S. Managers." *Journal of International Business Studies* 24: 741–61.

Miles, R. E., and C. C. Snow. 1987. *Organizational Strategy, Structure and Process*. New York: McGraw-Hill.

Ornatowski, G. 1998. "The End of Japanese-Style Human Resource Management?" *Sloan Management Review* 39 (3): 73–84.

Porter, M. E. 1990. "The Competitive Advantage of Nations." *Harvard Business Review* 68: 73–94.

Puffer, S. M. 1993. "A Riddle Wrapped in an Enigma: Demystifying Russian Managerial Motivation." *European Management Journal* 11: 473–80.

Schneider, S. C., and A. Demeyer. 1991. "Interpreting and Responding to Strategic Issues: The Impact of National Culture." *Strategic Management Journal* 12: 307–20.

Selmer, J. 1997. *Vikings and Dragons, Swedish Management in Southeast Asia*. Hong Kong: The David C. Lam Institute for East-West Studies, Hong Kong Baptist University, Kowloon Tong.

Trompennaars, F. 1993. *Riding the Waves of Culture*. Chicago: Irwin.

Vanderwerf, P., and J. F. Mahon. 1997. "Meta-Analysis of the Impact of Research Methods on Findings of First-Mover Advantages." *Management Science* 43: 510–19.

Wright, J. C., and W. Mischel. 1987. "A Conditional Approach to Dispositional Constructs: The Local Predictability of Social Behaviour." *Journal of Personality and Social Psychology* 53:1159–77.

CHAPTER 11

Entering Emerging Markets: Ignorance and Discovery

Jan Johanson and Martin Johanson

INTRODUCTION

It is generally acknowledged that lack of knowledge is an obstacle when firms enter and operate in foreign markets (Barkema, Bell, and Pennings 1996; Delios and Beamish 2000). They have to learn how to do business in new institutional and cultural settings (Blomstermo and Sharma 2002; Luo 1999). There seems also to be general agreement that learning about markets and operations to a great extent occurs through experience from activities in the market (Erramilli 1991; Johanson and Vahlne 1977; Yu 1991). Given that emerging markets usually are quite different from the domestic markets of most multinational firms there is reason to expect the problems associated with lack of knowledge are particularly difficult. However, activities during foreign market entry and expansion might be viewed as a journey of discovery into the unknown, an attempt to discover new ways to do things better than they have been done before (Hayek 1980). However, we do not know very much about how various market activities contribute to experiential learning. The objective of this paper is to contribute to our understanding of the processes that underlie such learning in connection with market entry into and expansion in emerging markets.

Following a number of researchers saying that learning is a process starting with discovery, we focus on the role of discovery in experiential learning about foreign markets and operations (Epple, Argote, and Devadas 1991; Huber 1991; Levitt and March 1988; Moorman and Miner 1998). Discovery also has a central role in Kirzner's theory of the market process (Kirzner 1992, 1997) and in the first section of the paper we discuss his view of discovery in the market. There the central characteristic of discovery is that it reduces ignorance. In the following section we discuss ignorance and situations in which ignorance can be expected to exist, in particular with reference to emerging markets. In the subsequent sections we discuss how discovery is related to two kinds of firm activities, search activities and routine activities. We also present some cases (Andersson 2000; Bagelius 1996; Bergergård 1999) illustrating discoveries in connection with market entry into and expansion in emerging markets. We conclude the paper by introducing improvisation as a possible way to manage discovery.

IGNORANCE AND DISCOVERY

Kirzner (1992) argues that discovery drives change in the market. This is also closely related to March's thoughts (1991) about exploring new fields. Exploration involves things like search and discovery. However, these two concepts differ in terms of what one knows, and can know, at a specific moment of time; what one will know, and can know, at later moments of time. There is a type of knowledge, which is unknowable for the firm. Kirzner means that there is a fundamental difference between unknown (sheer) ignorance and known ignorance. In the case of unknown or sheer ignorance, the firm does not know that it does not know, at a specific moment of time (Kirzner 1997), until the moment the firm realizes that it has discovered something previously unknown. This is necessarily accompanied by surprise. Discovery occurs in processes characterized by unpredictable and unexpected events.

The discovery process is a wide-open road on which any firm might embark, but the activities performed during this process are dependent on whether the firm recognizes the existence of sheer ignorance and expects that it will face discoveries during the journey. Kirzner (1992) argues that discovery is a consequence of the firm's alertness, that is, firms may be more or less able to make discoveries. Barney (1986), on the other hand, claims that discoveries can only be described as luck, whereas Hayek (1980) sees the discovery as a consequence of accidents. Simply put, discoveries are impossible to avoid.

DISCOVERY AND MARKET TURBULENCE

Although practically all market processes are associated with ignorance among the market participants, sheer ignorance is probably most common in turbulent markets. Emerging markets are often viewed as turbulent. Consider, for example, the emerging markets in the transition economies (Czaban and Whitley 2000; Dana 2002; McCarthy 2000; Peng 2000). In this kind of market, firms often have to face situations that are impossible to plan and to predict beforehand (Hadjikhani and Johanson 1996). They are unknowable or as Tsoukas (1996, 22) put it: "Firms are faced with *radical uncertainty*: they do not know, they cannot know, what they need to know." Thus, discovering the unknown is an important element in the process of entering a turbulent market. And discovering the unknown is an important part of gaining market knowledge. For firms facing turbulence: "Nobody knows in advance what the knowledge is or needs to be" (Tsoukas 1996). Instead, the expectation makes up the frame for what one can imagine to be achievable in the future and thereby for what is worth searching for.

As an illustration of the problems associated with market turbulence consider the developments in Russia. The first aspect of the institutional changes was that the plan and the plan authorities were dismantled and that prices were liberalized. Pricing determined by market forces had profound effects both on cost and on revenues for firms. It also caused hyperinflation in Russia in the beginning of the 1990s. The planned economy provided neither incentives for firms willing to compete nor to cooperate, that is, interact more closely with their business partners (Mattsson 1993). At very short notice, the firms were given the possibility to reconsider their set of exchange partners, as well as the way and the place to do business. This freedom meant that dissolved business relationships were a widespread outcome of the change of market governance (Gurkov 1996; Johanson 2001). For instance, a lot of Russian firms lost their old networks in the other former Soviet republics after 1992 (Davis 1996). Two other effects of the new way of doing business were: weakened relationships as firms were letting each other down, and a shift back to barter trade (Aukutsionek 1998; Commander 2002; Gurkov 1996; Poser 1998). Golden et al. (1995) show that the uncertainty increased not only directly, owing to the institutional changes, but also indirectly, since the institutional changes led to demand changes, product obsolescence, growing competition, and the appearance of new products and technologies. Peng and Heath (1996) argue that transition economies are characterized by high transaction costs due to opportunism, lack of a property-rights-based legal framework, lack of a stable political structure and lack of strategic-factor markets.

The liberalization of foreign trade resulted in more foreign firms operating in the Russian market and in a more complex structure with greater competition, as foreign firms tended to change customers as an effect of the institutional changes during the early years of the transition (Salmi and Möller 1994). The foreign firms' market became more complex and unpredictable. Moreover, the institutional development affected the entry mode chosen by the foreign firms. It is likely that entrants adjusted their entry mode to the level of market turbulence (Meyer 2001), which is partly a consequence of an unsatisfactory institutional framework (Dyker 2001). However, once foreign firms had entered the Russian market, conflicts between Russian firms and foreign firms—for instance in joint ventures (Fey and Beamish 2000)—seemed to be commonplace, which increased the perceived market turbulence.

Turbulence is partly a consequence of the institutional changes, since they lead to reconsideration of the ends at the microeconomic level, and a reallocation of the means controlled and used in the economy. Moreover, turbulence is especially linked to the institutional changes in a market where the changes are frequent, unpredictable, and protracted over several years. Since both ends and means, owing to the institutional changes, are given new meanings, they also force the firm to repeatedly question its perception of the market. But turbulence is also a result of changed behavior. Firms interpret the institutional changes in different ways, and they also form their expectations differently. Consequently, it is likely that the behavior of the firms, as a result of the institutional changes, will be heterogeneous and unpredictable and also change over time; since some firms react quickly, sometimes almost instantly, while others do not change their behavior until much later. The turbulence that characterizes the Russian market since the perestroika period makes strategic planning difficult, since the institutional changes and the Russian firms' changed behavior challenge foreign firms' knowledge about the market. Firms entering the market have only limited knowledge about the market and one cannot understand the market turbulence by learning about the institutional changes. The institutional changes are only one aspect of the market turbulence. There seems to be a lead-time between an institutional change and its effect in the market, since the firm has to perceive, interpret, and relate the behavior of the firms in the market and the institutional change.

More or less similar developments can be seen in practically all the transition economies. But there are great differences between them due to history, culture, and political conditions (Dana 2002). And although market development can be characterized as turbulent, the specific changes are never the same, and hence are unpredictable for firms entering those markets.

SEARCH ACTIVITIES AND DISCOVERY

Search is an activity that follows a situation where the firm knows that it does not know, what it does not know, at a specific moment of time. Thus, search occurs in situations characterized by known ignorance. Finding this type of knowledge implies searching for something, which the firm is able to define. Search is when the actor knows both the ends and the means, but the actor does not simultaneously control them and has to search for one or the other. Since they are identified, the actor knows what he is searching for, which makes experience from past activities and expectation as to what could happen and what is desirable to happen crucial (Hayek 1980). Penrose (1959, 77) views search in the following way: "If we can assume businessmen believe there is more to know about the resources they are working with than they do know at any given time, and that more knowledge would be likely to improve the efficiency and profitability of their firm, then unknown and unused productive services immediately become of considerable importance, not only because the belief that they exist acts as an incentive to acquire knowledge, but also because they shape the scope and direction of the search for knowledge."

In turbulent markets, search often has a tendency to be interrupted by discoveries. This happens because sometimes, or perhaps most of the time, events, which are largely out of the control of the firm, take place. This happens also in stable markets, but it is likely that it is more common in turbulent markets and especially for firms that have limited experience operating in this market. When the firm begins to search for something it may make a discovery, that is, find ends or means, which it did not know previously or did not search for. Consequently, the discovery as a result of search can be identified in two cases.

It happens in the first place when the firm searches for counterparts in order to establish business. The firm decides the entry mode, the assumed counterparts, the products that are to be bought and sold, the strategy, the objectives, and so on. When doing this, knowledge from previous markets and expectations of the new market are essential, and provide the frame for the firm's search.

In the second place, discoveries are not uncommon when the firm is already expanding its business. A firm, which is already committed to the market and which has knowledge about the market, will continue to increase sales, cut costs, and search for new business counterparts, and while doing this, it will make two additional types of discoveries.

The first of these two of additional discoveries concerns the search for new combinations of the resources via the already existing business—selling parts and components, joint marketing promotion, and the like—with specific firms. However, during this process the firm will discover other combinations than those that initiated the search. Such combinations make the business exploitation more efficient, which, in turn, increases the degree of internationalization. The second discovery takes place when the firm searches for new ways of doing business with its counterparts; it may, through these counterparts, find new potential counterparts. Both these types of discoveries start from the search, and will be more common in turbulent markets since the conditions are so volatile and the knowledge so imperfectly spread. The market turbulence causes a revision of their expectations: while their search starts from knowledge that has become obsolete—at least partly—they make new and unpredictable discoveries.

ROUTINE ACTIVITIES AND DISCOVERY

Changes are sometimes not planned or desired. They are unintentionally or unconsciously combined in space and time. The internationalization process model (Johanson and Vahlne 1977) implies that the firm does not learn more about anything, but more about something special, about which it already has knowledge (cf. Cohen and Levinthal 1990). Learning by doing is the expression most suitable both for describing this process and for the result of this process. Doing—that is, using the resources—precedes learning. It happens when the firm runs the daily operations in various types of routine activities. Discovery is viewed as an important feature when firms develop new products (von Hippel and Tyre 1995). Learning by doing or by using implies that both the problem and the solution are discovered (von Hippel and Tyre 1995). Both the problem and the solution are discovered when running the daily operations, and it is not uncommon that the problems are vague and ill-structured, and that the solutions are unknown and uncertain.

Discoveries made through the performance of routine activities cannot be viewed as the result of a purposeful, intentional process in the sense that the firm searches in a specific way to achieve expected results. Thus, discovery is not the *primary aim* of performance of routines, but, depending on market conditions, discovery may be the result. Hence, if market conditions are turbulent, activities will be performed in an ever-changing and unpredictable environment where new opportunities and problems are discovered. Similarly, but not as importantly, heterogeneous market conditions can be expected to lead to discovery (cf. Johanson and Vahlne 1977). We can also expect that entry into foreign markets of great psychic distance will be accompanied by discoveries even in the case of running daily operations.

A problem with discoveries in connection with routine activities is that there will be strong psychological and organizational pressure to keep to the routine, and thereby suppress the perception of the discovery. Thus, it is likely that when discoveries are made by an organization performing routine activities they will be late and big, requiring revolutionary changes in activity patterns.

DISCOVERY AND MARKET KNOWLEDGE

When an entering firm makes discoveries, it is a process that starts in ignorance, and through various activities, gains knowledge that was unknown before the activities began. Thereby discoveries can produce knowledge, provided that they are recognized as such. Discoveries can result in both experiential knowledge and objective knowledge. Barney (1986) argues that the knowledge acquired through market analysis was never critical and did not give the firm any advantages; although he admitted that sometimes firms could stumble onto some information that did give them a knowledge advantage. That knowledge can be both objective and experiential in character; thus, knowledge that is acquired through performance of activities has an element of experiential knowledge and an element of objective knowledge. Based on this line of argumentation, a firm's ability to interpret and absorb the discovery becomes crucial.

Discoveries have so far not been viewed as an important cause of change during the internationalization of the firm. Discoveries often shatter expectations, because they do not fit in with the discovering firm's current business practices, or are perceived as having a negative impact on the firm's operations. Consequently, there are two types of discovery: the dysfunctional and the functional. The functional has a positive impact on the firm's entry and tends to increase the firm's willingness to commit more resources to the market, whereas the dysfunctional discovery increases the perceived uncertainty and thus has a negative impact on the firm's entry. We expect that the turbulence in transition economies, such as, for instance, irregular and inconsistent changes of legislation, corruption, bureaucracy, and organizations or firms that are closed down, make dysfunctional discoveries common. The firm can therefore, for various reasons, ignore or neglect discoveries. Usually, this happens because the discovery is perceived as having no value for the discoverer. However, one can also assume that the discovering firm does not understand the discovery—it may not even be able to recognize it.

Combining these two types of discoveries and types of knowledge, we believe that the functional discoveries and experiential knowledge is critical, because it is rich in terms of knowledge, moreover, it is difficult to replicate, since it is a result of specific activities. This combination of activities and knowledge is extremely difficult to predict beforehand and is, owing to its element of experiential knowledge, almost impossible to communicate to others. Objective knowledge as a result of functional discoveries also has a positive impact on the market entry, but it is more accessible to other firms, such as, for instance, competitors.

Acquisition of knowledge through participation in the market can be viewed as an adjustment and revision of expectation due to new experience (Kirzner 1973). Thus some discoveries might thereby be input in the search process. Since discoveries are not intended, it is likely that many discoveries are not turned into new ways of exchanging or using resources. This type of process is initiated by a discovery, which interrupts the continuity and stability.

THREE CASE STUDIES

Hörnell in the Chinese Market

Hörnell International AB develops and manufactures personal protective equipment for a welder's face, head, and lungs. The technology builds on autodarkening welding filters. The firm was founded in 1980 as a one-man company but grew and had, at the time of entry, 200 employees in 12 countries. Hörnell's turnover in 1998 was around 240 million Swedish kronor, of which around 90 percent were sold in foreign markets. Hörnell's products consist of a helmet with autodarkening welding filters and various types of respiratory protection equipment. Hörnell markets the products under the brands Speedglas and Adflo, and they exist in several different designs in order to satisfy the users' needs. Hörnell has representation in 58 countries. In seven countries: the United States, Germany, Great Britain, Italy, France, Poland and Brazil, Hörnell has subsidiaries. In other markets they are represented through offices or local agents or distributors. The biggest markets are in North America and Europe. The production facilities are located in Gagnef, Sweden and Twinsburg, Ohio.

Hörnell has been operating in East Asia since 1985, when they began their business in the Japanese market. Between 1985 and 1995, Hörnell established different contacts in Taiwan, South Korea, Thailand, The Philippines, Hong Kong, Indonesia, Malaysia and Singapore. The attempts to establish the firm in East Asia meant that representatives from Hörnell made repeated trips to Asia and, as a consequence, the firm began to think about establishing a permanent business in China. Hörnell started operations in the Chinese market in 1990 when it entered the Hong Kong market, but at that time the British Crown Colony Hong Kong was not an integrated part of China. When Hörnell, in 1995, began its operations in the mainland Chinese market, Hörnell had no agents or distributors, besides Hong Kong. In 1994, Hörnell found by coincidence a booklet about a Chinese firm called Autocontrol while participating in a trade exhibition in Germany. Autocontrol produced a product similar to Speedglas. Hörnell decided to establish contact with Autocontrol, and through cooperation with it, enter the Chinese market. After that, Hörnell began to search for information about Autocontrol, which resulted in an address for the firm in the city of Wuhan, which Hörnell thought was a small town in the countryside, but later appeared to be a big city. Autocontrol was interested in cooperation and the two firms began to discuss various types of cooperation and in the end they decided to form a joint venture. The Chinese partner claimed that it annually produced a considerable volume of Speedglas, a big share of which was exported.

When the initial contact with Autocontrol was established, Hörnell realized that it did not know very much about its future partner and thought an analysis of Autocontrol was needed. Since Hörnell's experience with the Chinese market was limited, it tried to find an external actor with experience in China in order to make a reliable analysis. Hörnell commissioned a Finnish consulting company, Netpoint, to conduct the analysis. Netpoint had been active in China since 1990. Hörnell was satisfied with the report and Netpoint's work and some kind of trust in Netpoint emerged. So, at the same time as Hörnell was discussing a joint venture with Autocontrol, it ran a joint project together with Netpoint with the aim of developing distribution channels for Speedglas in the Chinese market. The result was that Hörnell together with Netpoint took part in an exhibition in Shanghai for distributors of protective equipment for welders in June 1995, and they established contacts with about 200 to 300 firms that expressed interest in Speedglas.

After around six months, Hörnell became suspicious and began to question the cooperation with Autocontrol. The partner had difficulties in verifying the sales figures indicated for protective equipment with autodarkening welding filters. It became obvious that the figures were fictitious. Moreover, the potential partner could not make a substantial contribution to the joint venture. At this point of time, Hörnell sold around 100 Speedglas products in China, and 200 to 300 in Hong Kong. A big share of the volume sold in Hong Kong was exported to China, but Hörnell had no idea about how the distribution from Hong Kong to China functioned or who the actors were.

In August 1998, Hörnell was at a crossroads: either it should commit itself more to the Chinese market, or completely exit the market. The issue was discussed intensively by the top-management at Hörnell, but in the end it decided to continue the efforts to establish the firm in the Chinese market, however, Hörnell perceived that more resources had to be committed in order to achieve success. Hörnell terminated the cooperation agreement with Autocontrol and all plans for a joint venture were cancelled. At the same, Hörnell engaged a new manager for the Asian markets and increased the frequency of its visits from Sweden to China. In the beginning of 1999, Hörnell decided to hire the consultant at Netpoint to work for Hörnell on full time basis.

Jacobson & Widmark (J&W) Entering the Saudi-Arabian Market

J&W is a development-oriented consulting corporation that pursues operations through six interacting business areas: J&W Architecture & Design, J&W Construction Design, J&W Energy and Environment, J&W Management, J&W Civil Engineering, and J&W Systems. J&W has a staff of 2,000 and is represented nationwide; the corporation is part of the U.K.'s WSP Group plc, one of the largest consulting corporations in Europe, with a total staff of 5,000. Apart from the U.K. and Sweden, WSP is active in the U.S., Africa, and Asia. In 1998, the turnover was 825 Million Swedish kronor. J&W offers consulting services to private and public customers both in Sweden and abroad. The services cover all areas of construction, as well as architecture. Since J&W's international operations were various long-term and short-term projects, the top management has decided not to have as many subsidiaries abroad. J&W had offices in Estonia, Germany, Norway, and Poland. It has been difficult for J&W to compete in western market economies, since these countries have their own consultancy companies. J&W therefore decided to turn its international operations toward international aid and development projects, and to oil-exporting countries. In these cases, cooperation between both various domestic and foreign firms were common and J&W often learned about new projects through their ongoing operations. Saudi Arabia is a good example of a non-European market where J&W is operating.

In the 1970s, when J&W acquired a consultancy company called Hagconsult, it learned that Saudi Arabia, for military and defense reasons, planned to construct storage for oil underground. Hagconsult had, during the 1960s and the 1970s, designed for Sweden storage for oil in underground rock in order to make Sweden less dependent on imported oil in case of war or international tension. The underground storage had been constructed all over Sweden. J&W therefore tried to establish contact with the Saudi Arabian minister of oil, Sheik Yamani, and he agreed to receive a delegation from J&W. The planning process started at that time. Yamani knew that Sweden had built underground storage of the same type as Saudi Arabia planned to build. Consequently, Yamani reasoned that J&W would have the technological competence needed for the Saudi project. The project was called SSSP, which stands for Saudi Strategic Storage Program and it was a so-called turn-key-project and included, besides the construction of storage for oil underground, the construction of the buyer's head office in Riyadh, and also other offices, dwellings, workshops, roads, bridges, and construction for telephone and radio communication.

The contacts between J&W and the Saudi Arabian Ministry of Defense were maintained, and in the beginning of the 1980s, when the plans became more concrete, J&W was given the opportunity to prequalify for the project. The project, initially planned for completion in seven years, is still continuing in its eleventh year. The SSSP-project is the biggest of all of J&W's projects worldwide, amounting to one billion Swedish kronor, which is a little bit more than J&W's annual turnover. Since the project was so large, the biggest construction project in the world actually, the Swedish government and its Prime Minster Olof Palme committed themselves to the project. In the beginning, J&W and Swedish construction company ABV worked in parallel, but independent of each other. ABV attended to the construction, while J&W was the consultant for the construction. The manager of international operations at J&W had formerly worked for ABV and still had a good relationship with a lot of people there. This was a main reason why these two firms made an initial agreement, and after that, a joint offer on the project.

ABV had already been operating in Saudi Arabia, so when the firms made a joint offer they chose the already existing name ABV Rock Group for the new joint venture. After some time, the construction company Skanska joined the group. Skanska contributed excavating expertise and Swedish firms could thereby offer the buyer a complete solution. When the parties negotiated the contract everything went according to plan, until the Bofors case in India occured, and a bribery scandal came to light; ABV and Skanska were both concerned about being connected with the scandal—both projects were huge and related to defense. They did not dare to remain owners of the firm, and ABV Rock Group was sold to a group of Saudi Arabian businessmen. The head of this Saudi group had previously worked as a purchasing manager in, and was known for his love of, Sweden. ABV and Skanska continued to remain active in the project as suppliers to ABV Rock Group. The Saudi Arabian buyer wanted J&W as a participant in the contract, but J&W did not dare, but J&W did make an offer with fixed prices to ABV Rock Group.

In 1986, a representative from J&W met Sheik Yamani in London and made an inquiry about starting the project. At that time, no formal agreement had been made. J&W's top management viewed the project as so important, that it decided to tie both capital and human resources to the project. In 1987, J&W sent a group of 20 engineers to Saudi Arabia to begin a pre-feasibility study. During the same period, ABV Rock Group had four employees working in Saudi Arabia. In 1988, the buyer and ABV Rock Group signed the contract. J&W was included in the contract as the main supplier of consulting service and, therefore, an agreement with fixed prices was made with ABV Rock Group. In July of that same year, J&W began to make a personal agreement with the employees and soon the project was launched.

J&W and ABV Rock Group renegotiated the contract in 1989. The result of these negotiations was that J&W gave up its work based on the fixed prices and instead offered its services within ABV Rock Group's organization. From that moment on J&W was paid per hour. The personnel were still employed by J&W, who paid the salaries. In 1990, J&W had around 50 people employed in Saudi Arabia. In January 1991, the war between Iraq and Kuwait in the Persian Gulf region broke out, which, of course, had an impact on Saudi Arabia, but the SSSP project continued during the whole war, although under strain. Wives and children were evacuated and four employees, who did not feel well due to the war and Iraq's bombing of Riyadh, went back to Sweden. After the war, the number of employees grew and, by 1993, 107 employees were involved in the project. Initially, the contract between J&W and ABV Rock Group was valid until 1995, but since so much work remained undone by the middle of the 1990s, the contract was continued.

Sacco Entering the Russian Market

Sacco had been trading with the Soviet Union over 25 years and had representation offices in Moscow, Estonia, Kazakhstan, and Turkmenistan. Sacco traded mainly in oil products and different types of raw material, but had also established several joint ventures, which produced products of a quality competitive enough to be exported. Swedish suppliers of sawing equipment and felling equipment had initiated the joint venture projects. During 1987, Sacco discussed several industrial projects with Minlesprom, the Ministry of Forestry in the Soviet Union. At that time, Sacco had already made a number of investments in Soviet saw mills. Sacco had also participated in projects aimed at creating refined wood products in Russia, such as planing mills and factories for the production of stools, veneer, and particle board. Through its web of contacts, Sacco could procure machines and equipment of high quality from Swedish producers for the Soviet Union.

In 1990, Sacco began discussions with Minlesprom about how it could increase the efficiency of the logging in Archangelsk. Sacco and the Deputy Minister Sankin decided to investigate the conditions for logging in a district called Pechora; however, the parties came to the conclusion that the local infrastructure did not permit an increase of the efficiency of the felling. Min-lesprom, shortly after, invited Sacco to Archangels in order to evaluate the conditions for forestry in other parts of the region. The region was rich in saw mills and paper and pulp mills so, the region could offer favorable con-ditions for an expansion, but the regional wood-processing conglomerates had difficulty supplying timber to their sawmills and paper and pulp mills. The leading organizations in the logging industry were the regional forestry ad-ministration and the wood processing firm, Severoles, and the research and development firm, SevNIIP.

During 1991, several delegations from Severoles paid visits to various sup-pliers of felling machines and other kinds of equipment for forestry and wood processing in Sweden, including Söderhamns Verkstäder, Bruuns, Saab Au-topuls, and Kockums Industri. In parallel, Sacco sent Swedish specialists to Archangels in order to conduct an assessment of the conditions for efficient forestry in that region. During a meeting in Archangels in 1991, Sacco and Severoles signed a contract, which gave Sacco the concession to fell 300,000 cubic meters in 1992–93. A joint venture, Archlog, was founded, where Sacco had 50 percent of the shares and three Russian organizations shared the re-maining 50 percent. Archlog made an agreement with a sawmill called Krasny Oktyabr in December 1991. It would process the timber that Archlog sup-plied. Severoles would coordinate the Russian organizations' payment of eq-uity to Archlog while Sacco would contribute machines and equipment.

In January 1992, Sacco bought machines and equipment from Swedish pro-ducers and provided transportation of them to the felling area, together with ten instructors and operators. They would work in Russia for four weeks and then have a break for one week in Sweden before they returned to Archan-gelsk. Sacco also partly financed the training of 200 to 300 Russians. The operations began immediately. However, in January 1992, when the instruc-tors and operators, after logging for only five days, showed up for work one day, policemen and soldiers met them. They stopped the felling. The regional forestry administration had changed its mind and claimed that there initially was an intention to only fell trees with a diameter of 28 cm, but it did not come out during the negotiations, nor was it in the written agreement. In January 1992, Severoles offered Sacco another forest. The demand for timber was urgent, since Severoles had several sawmills and paper and pulp mills, but owing to the lack of timber, they could not run them at full capacity. The parties came to an agreement on quality, price per cubic meter, and on the infrastructure in the new area.

A new joint venture, Irbis, was founded in February 1992. Sacco, Severoles, and Ust-Pokshensky Lespromkhoz became the owners. Sacco rather quickly understood that the Russian counterparts transferred their part of the equity. Moreover, Sacco realized that the receiver of the timber, Ust-Pokshensky Lespromkhoz, reported volumes other than those Sacco thought it had de-livered. Sacco strove to accurately notify the receiver about the dimensions, diameter, and length of the timber so that no misunderstandings could happen. Sacco's trust in Ust-Pokshensky Lespromkhoz decreased dramatically and Sacco thought that there were no conditions left to continue the cooperation. In addition, the Russians had promised an efficient transportation system, but it did not work out at all. At that time, around 29,600 cubic meters of timber had been felled, when Sacco terminated the cooperation with the other owners of Irbis. This happened just after the *coup d'état*, when Russia had became an independent state. There was an atmosphere of political and social tension in Archangelsk. As a consequence Sacco loaded their machines and equipment on railway trains for transport to Estonia. Sacco had hired guards to protect the equipment all the way to Estonia. It was the result of a lesson they had learned when the equipment was transported to Archangelsk and large amounts had been stolen on the way from Sweden to Archangelsk. The second reason why Sacco could send the equipment away was that the Russian top management had left the region for some kind of party for the employees. They did not know what was going on until it was too late. A few days later, in August 1992, the machines and equipment arrived at Sacco's representation office in Tallinn.

DISCUSSION

In the three cases, we found that the firms performed both routine activities and search activities and that they resulted in two basically different types of discovery (see Table 11.1). One type occurs as a consequence of the frequently radical changes in the wider environment of the firm. Instances of such discoveries are the war, in the case of J&W, or the *coup d'état* in Russia in the Sacco case. This type of discovery can often be traced back to political or institutional changes in the emerging markets, while in other markets; it may more frequently be the result of technological changes.

The second type of discovery is related more to the close environment of the firm. Typically such discoveries can be related to specific actors, acting in unexpected ways. Here we can also distinguish two kinds of discovery. One occurs due to the actions by other actors who approach the focal firm, for instance by offering something, which might be interesting or valuable. Such discoveries may be the outcome of actions by firms or persons who were completely unknown to the focal firm. The other kind is when the firm for some reason learns that a counterpart, with whom they are doing business, is unreliable or otherwise not useful as a business partner. Evidently the two basic types may be intertwined in the sense that environmental changes expose the close market context to the firm in a way that a discovery is created.

IMPROVISATION AND DISCOVERY IN EMERGING MARKETS

Recently, improvisation has been discussed as a form of activity that may have strong beneficial consequences in many situations (Moorman and Miner

Table 11.1
The Firms and Types of Activity and Discovery

	Hörnell	J&W	Sacco
Types of activity	The case began with routine activities, which were interrupted by discovery. Hörnell was, after that, searching for infor-mation about Auto-control.	J&W was regularly searching for business opportunities in Middle East. Although it made some negative discoveries, it continued to search.	Sacco was search for business opportunities in the Soviet market and tried to follow an established strategy. Once a joint venture was established, Sacco strived to perform routine activities.
Types of discovery	The discoveries made during the entry process were related to firms and individuals. These discoveries caused both opportunities and difficulties.	The discoveries were results of changes in a wider environment. Bribery scandals and wars had influenced J&W's operations in the Saudi-Arabian market.	The discoveries in this case are related both to a closer and wider environment. The first type was a result of the regional forestry administration and Ust-Pokshensky Lespromkhoz while the coup d'état represented the second type.
Outcome of the discovery	The entry began after the first discovery. The second meant a change of distributor and an increased market commitment.	The discoveries were backlashes, but did not force J&W to decrease its market commitment.	The three discoveries forced Sacco to finally leave the project and transfer the resources to the Estonian market.

1998; Preston 1991; Weick 1987). Typically, improvisation is seen as a way of coping with environmental problems. Weick (1993) states that improvisation occurs where strategic planning and action are closely integrated. In an effort to operationalize improvisation, Moorman and Miner (1998) describe organizational improvisation as "the degree to which the composition and execution of action converge in time." An important outcome of organizational improvisation is problem solving, in particular, handling of unanticipated opportunities, by which we mean, discovery. It has also been reported to speed up action (Eisenhardt and Tabrizi 1995). Another important outcome, according to Moorman and Miner, is learning.

Discovery does not always take place completely at random. The intended result of improvisation is discovery, but the very essence of this type of activity is that the firm does not, in advance, know what it will discover. When a firm begins to improvise it aims to achieve some kind of change and discovers unknown ends or means that can make the entry easier or quicker. To reach discoveries through improvisation can be viewed as a trial and error process.

Firms can also learn to improvise (Chelariu, Johnston, and Young 2002). First, a firm, which has gained a lot of experience, will realize that it has to expect discoveries during the market process because that is an essential element in any market economy, but it is even more common in the turbulent emerging markets. Thus, the extent to which the firm has experience from similar turbulent markets, for instance from countries in Asia and Latin America, will affect the firm's willingness to initiate improvisation during the market entry. If the firm has such experience, it is likely that it will try to recycle the experience from those markets, and search in the same way for similar business opportunities as those that gave a positive outcome in the previous markets.

Second, if firms with experience from similar markets enter a new emerging market, it is likely that they have fewer difficulties handling discoveries than firms used to operating in stable markets. Based on their experience in turbulent markets, they have probably developed organizational routines that are adapted to the unpredictable. These routines can involve a deliberate slack or excess of resources within the organization. Moreover, the routines might also imply decentralized authority and freedom to act in the market, which improves the firm's adaptability, since it can react to discoveries more quickly and easily, both those perceived as dysfunctional and negative and those viewed as functional and positive for the firm. This view can also been seen in Hayek's discussion (1945, 524–25) about the economic problem: "[The] economic problems arise always and only in a consequence of change. . . . [As] the economic problem of society is mainly one of rapid adaptation to changes in the particular circumstances of time and place, it would seem to follow that the ultimate decisions must be left to the people who are familiar with these circumstances, who know directly of the relevant changes and of the resources immediately available to meet them."

Third, managers involved in the entry into emerging markets, both those who run operations in the market and those in the headquarters supporting the activities, are critical to the firm's ability to adapt to discoveries. If a firm has been doing business in a turbulent market the chances are better that the headquarters accepts that matters may not go exactly according to plan. Moreover, it seems that such firms are better at identifying people who have the capacity and capability to deal with turbulence. To hire people who can operate in a turbulent and uncertain market, and to give them freedom to act and react to those markets, are important steps for a firm in the entry process. Overall, these factors tend to make improvisation a successful way of coping with turbulent markets.

REFERENCES

Andersson, M. 2000. "Hörnell International: en marknadsetablering i Kina (Hörnell International: A Market Entry into China)." Bachelor's thesis, Department of Business Studies, Uppsala University.

Aukutsionek, S. 1998. "Industrial Barter in Russia." *Communist Economies and Economic Transformation* 10 (2): 179–88.

Bagelius, N. 1996. *Fallstudie: United Loggers Tallinn och Sacco i Archangelsk, Ryssland (Case study: United Loggers Tallinn and Sacco in Archangel, Russia).* Stockholm: Marknadstekniskt Centrum.

Barkema, H. G., J. H. J. Bell., and J. M. Pennings. 1996. "Foreign Entry, Cultural Barriers, and Learning." *Strategic Management Journal* 17: 151–65.

Barney, J. B. 1986. "Strategic Factor Markets: Expectations, Luck and Business Strategy." *Management Science* 17 (1): 99–120.

Bergergård P., K., Lindgren, and G. Silasson. 1999. "Bland konsulter och kungliga riyaler: Jacobson & Widmarks etablering på den saudiska marknaden (Among Consultants and Royal Riyals: Jacobson & Widmark's entry into the Saudi Arabian Market)." Master's thesis, Department of Business Studies, Uppsala University.

Blomstermo, A., and D. D. Sharma, eds. 2002. *Learning in the Internationalization Process.* London: Edward Elgars.

Chelariu, C., W. J. Johnston, and L. Young. 2002. "Learning to Improvise, Improvising to Learn. A Process of Responding to Complex Environments." *Journal of Business Research* 55: 141–47.

Cohen, W. M., and D. A. Levinthal. 1990. "Absorptive Capacity: A New Perspective on Learning and Innovation." *Administrative Science Quarterly* 35: 128–52.

Commander, S., I. Dolinskaya, and C. Mumssen. 2002. "Determinants of Barter in Russia: An Empirical Analysis." *Journal of Development Economics.* Forthcoming.

Czaban, L., and R. Whitley. 2000. "Incremental Organizational Change in a Transforming Society: Managing Turbulence in Hungary in the 1990s." *Journal of Management Studies* 37 (3): 371–93.

Davis, J. H., J. D. Patterson, and I. Grazin. 1996. "The Collapse and Reemergence of Networks within and between Republics of the Former Soviet Union." *International Business Review* 5 (1): 1–21.

Dyker, D. A. 2001. "Technology Exchange and the Foreign Business Sector in Russia." *Research Policy* 30: 851–68.

Eisenhardt, K. M., and B. N.Tabrizi. 1995. "Accelerating Adaptive Processes: Product Innovation in the Global Computer Industry." *Administrative Science Quarterly* 40: 84–110.

Epple, D., L. Argote, and R. Devadas. 1991. "Organization Learning Curves: A Method of Investigating Intra-plant Transfer of Knowledge Acquired through Learning by Doing." *Organization Science* 2: 58–70.

Erramilli, M. K. 1991. "The Experience Factor in Foreign Market Entry Behavior of Service Firms." *Journal of International Business Studies* 22: 479–502.

Fey, C. F., and P. W. Beamish. 2000. "Joint Venture Conflict: The Case of Russian International Joint Ventures." *International Business Review* 9: 139–62.

Golden, P. A., P. M. Doney, D. M. Johnson, and J. R. Smith. 1995. "The Dynamics of a Marketing Orientation in Transition Economics: A Study of Russian Firms." *Journal of International Marketing* 3 (2): 24–49.

Gurkov, I. 1996. "Changes of Control and Business Reengineering in Russian Privatized Companies." *The International Executive* 38 (3): 359–88.

Hayek, F. A. 1945. "The Use of Knowledge in Society." *American Economic Review* 35 (4): 519–30.

———. 1980. "Economics and Knowledge." In *Individualism and Economic Order.* London: Routledge and Kegan Paul.

Huber, G. P. 1991. "Organizational Learning: The Contributing Processes and Literature." *Organization Science* 2 (1): 88–114.

Johanson, J., and J.-E. Vahlne. 1977. "The Internationalization Process of Firm—A Model of Knowledge Development and Increasing Foreign Market Commitments." *Journal of International Business Studies* 8 (Spring/Summer): 23–32.

Johanson, M. 2001. "Searching the Known, Discovering the Unknown: The Russian Transition from Plan to Market as Network Change Processes." Doctoral dissertation, Department of Business Studies, Uppsala University.

Kirzner I. M. 1973. *Competition and Entrepreneurship.* Chicago and London: The University of Chicago Press.

———. 1992. *The Meaning of Market Process: Essays in the Development of Modern Austrian Economics.* London: Routledge.

———. 1997. "Entrepreneurial Discovery and the Competitive Market Process: An Austrian Approach." *Journal of Economic Literature* 35 (March): 60–85.

Levitt, B., and J. G. March.1988. "Organizational Learning." *Annual Review of Sociology* 14: 319–40.

Luo, Y. 1999. "Time-Based Experience and International Expansion: The Case of an Emerging Economy." *Journal of Management Studies* 36: 505–34.

March, J. G. 1991. "Exploration and Exploitation in Organizational Learning." *Organization Science* 2: 71–87.

Mattsson, L.-G. 1999. "How Can the Network View of Markets Inform Us about the Transformation Process toward a Market Economy?" In *Institutions and Post-Socialist Transition*, edited by R. Kosonen and A. Salmi, 122–38. Helsinki: Helsinki School of Economics and Business Administration.

McCarthy, D. J., S. Puffer, and A. I. Naumov. 2000. "Russia's Retreat to Statization and the Implication for Business." *Journal of World Business* 35 (3): 256–74.

Meyer, K. E. 2001. "Institutions, Transaction Costs, and Entry Mode Choice in Eastern Europe." *Journal of International Business Studies* 32 (2): 357–67.

Moorman, C., and A. Miner. 1998. "Organizational Improvisation and Organizational Memory." *Academy of Management Review* 23: 98–723.

Peng, M. 1999. *Business Strategies in Transition Economies.* Thousands Oaks, Calif.: Sage Publications.

Peng, M. W., and P. S. Heath. 1996. "The Growth of the Firm in Planned Economies in Transition: Institutions, Organizations, and Strategic Choice." *Academy of Management Review* 21 (2): 492–528.

Penrose, E.T. 1959. *The Theory of the Growth of the Firm.* Oxford: Basil Blackwell.

Poser, J. 1998. "Monetary Disruptions and the Emergence of Barter in FSU Economies." *Communist Economies and Economic Transformation* 10 (2): 157–77.

Preston, A. 1991. Improvising Order. In *Organization Analysis and Development*, edited by I. L. Mangham. New York: Wiley.

Salmi, A., and K. Möller. 1994. "Business Strategy during Dramatic Environmental Change: A Network Approach for Analysing Firm-Level Adaptation to the

Soviet Economic Reform." In *The Economics of Change in East and Central Europe—Its Impact on International Business*, edited by P. J. Buckley, and P. N. Ghauri. San Diego, Calif.: Academic Press.

Tsoukas, H. 1996. "The Firm as a Distributed Knowledge System: A Constructionist Approach." *Strategic Management Journal* 17 (Winter Special Issue): 11–25.

von Hippel, E., and M. J. Tyre. 1995. "How Learning by Doing is Done: Problem Identification in Novel Process Equipment." *Research Policy* 24: 1–12.

Weick, K. E. 1987. "Substitutes for Strategy." In *The Competitive Challenge: Strategies for Industrial Innovation and Renewal*, edited by D. J. Teece. New York: Harper and Row. Weick, K.E. 1993. "Organizational Redesign as Improvisation." In *Organizational Change and Redesign*, edited by G. P. Huber, and W. H. Glick. Cary, N.C.: Oxford University Press.

Yu, C. J. 1991. "The Experience Effect and Foreign Direct Investment." *Weltwirtschaftliches Archiv* 126: 341–63.

PART III

Prospects for Global Firms

CHAPTER 12

Strategies of Multinationals in Contemporary China

Peter Enderwick

INTRODUCTION

The continuing integration of a number of "transitional" or "emergent" countries into the world economy has provided immense opportunities and challenges for multinational enterprises (MNEs). In recent years transitional economies have consistently attracted a large share of international investment. For example, in 2000 eight emerging economies attracted over 70 percent of all inward FDI into developing economies (UNCTAD 2001). Their attractions include significant and often rapidly growing markets, low costs, underutilized resources, and opportunities for diversification. Of particular interest to MNEs are the so-called big emerging markets, which include China and India.

While emerging economies offer tremendous market opportunities, they also provide considerable challenges. In most emerging economies uncertainty levels are very high. This results from macroeconomic imbalances and instabilities, high rates of political change, social unrest, unpredictable policy shifts, underdeveloped institutional infrastructure, and high levels of inefficiency and corruption. Furthermore, many of the Asian emerging economies, including China, operate on the basis of relationships, which substitute for the lack of institutional infrastructure. This can place overseas firms at a considerable disadvantage when competing with well-connected local firms.

China is widely perceived to be the most attractive of all the emerging economies. It is the largest, fastest growing, and most globally integrated of the emerging economies (Child and Tse 2001). In 2000 China accounted for 28 percent of all inward investment in Asia, or 17 percent of all investment in developing countries (UNCTAD 2001). A large part of the attraction of China has been its very high growth rates. From 1990 to 1995, output growth in China averaged 12 percent per annum. While this slowed to an average of 8.3 percent in the period 1995–2000, these are, by any measure, exceptionally high rates. By 1993 China was the third largest economy in the world after the United States and Japan (Child and Lu 1996).

While future growth rates may not be as high, they are still likely to attract foreign investment. The World Bank estimates that China will experience average annual rates of around 6.6 percent in the years 2000–2020, slowing to perhaps 5.5 percent after this. The slowdown is attributable to the growing difficulty of mobilizing resources, the aging population, and diminishing returns from structural change. Growth rates will vary between sectors, with the highest rates in the service sector. For China, however, high growth rates are a necessity. To prevent rising unemployment, China must generate an additional 10 million new jobs each year, and that implies an annual growth rate of around 8 percent (Lingle 2000). China has also become more integrated into the world economy. Total trade as a percentage of GNP was less than 10 percent when reform began in 1978. By 1998 it had reached 42 percent and China was already the ninth largest trading economy in the world, with a 3.4 percent share of world trade (Chan 1999).

China has followed a unique transitional path. Unlike Eastern Europe, which sought to duplicate the structures of western-style market systems, China has experimented with reform in order to improve performance. A result of this has been a gradual and inconsistent reform path (Jefferson and Rawski 1994). Furthermore, reform has always been guided by the need to balance efficiency gains and social pressures. China continues to manifest high rates of state involvement in economic affairs, which creates high levels of uncertainty for foreign investors.

However, the transitional developments are bringing radical changes to the Chinese business environment. Deregulation and the attraction of foreign firms has greatly increased levels of competition within many industries. As expected, the dismantling of protective barriers has led to a decline in the dispersion of profitability across industry sectors (Naughton 1994). High levels of competition are likely to persist in the future as military industries convert to consumer products, internal trade barriers are removed, and China's membership in the WTO spurs the reduction of import barriers.

Increased competition has been in part the result of the changing structure of Chinese industry. The non-state sector has grown dramatically and now accounts for nearly 75 percent of industrial output. Almost all the job creation since 1993 has been in the private sector. Furthermore, the pressures to reform inefficient and loss-making state-owned enterprises (SOEs) are now considerable. Despite its shrinking share of output, the state-owned sector still absorbs 60 percent of all investment resources. This makes it difficult for small and high-technology firms to attract funds necessary for development.

In the long term Chinese industry will need to move beyond its current focus on low-cost production and upgrade technological capability. This will necessitate the importation of foreign technology and managerial and organizational skills. It is possible that internationally competitive Chinese firms could emerge in industries such as computers and telecommunications components.

The aim of this chapter is to provide an analysis of likely changes in MNE strategies within China in the foreseeable future. The discussion is based upon the belief that the primary influences on MNE strategy will result from the interplay of two sets of forces: those experienced at the global level, and those experienced within China. A shared manifestation of the global economy and an emerging country such as China is that both are subject to high rates of change and turbulence. Indeed, the sheer size and growing integration of the Chinese economy means that there is likely to be a powerful interplay between these two groups of forces. To facilitate the discussion, this chapter is divided into five principal sections. The following section sets out some of the key recent developments in the global economy and their implications for MNE strategy. Section three provides a detailed discussion of emerging opportunities and likely challenges for foreign firms within China. Section four integrates the discussion at these two levels, the global and the national, to assess future MNE strategy options within the Chinese market. The final section offers concluding comments.

GLOBAL DEVELOPMENTS AND THEIR IMPLICATIONS FOR MNE STRATEGIES

This section examines some of the key trends in the global economy in recent years. The global economy is characterized by rapid and complex change; indeed, change is a pervasive characteristic of the modern world. For this reason there are many significant trends and developments. The present discussion focuses on four trends that are thought to be of major significance for MNE strategy: the favorable business environment in recent years, the increasing importance of knowledge as a factor of production, the new geostrategic alliances, and the changing nature of the development process.

Favorable International Business Environment

The global economy has grown rapidly in the past three decades. Broadly, this period has coincided with increased liberalization and deregulation, rapid rates of technological change, and growing international exchange through trade and foreign investment. This has clearly benefited an economy such as China's, which began the process of reintegration into the world economy in late 1978.

This period has also seen a powerful economy driving world economic growth. For much of the 1970s and 1980s, Japan provided the driving force. As Japan entered a decade-long recession in the late 1980s, the United States emerged as the new engine of growth. While Japan offset slow growth in a restructuring U.S. economy during the 1980s, growth of the U.S. economy sustained a flat Japanese economy for much of the 1990s. Over this period, the other Triad bloc, the European Union, has achieved only modest growth rates. The onset of the Asian Financial Crisis in 1997 saw a worsening of the economic situation in this part of the world. However, the first simultaneous downturn since the late 1970s occurred only in the last quarter of 2000 and into 2001. Prospects were further damaged by the terrorist attacks in September 2001. The biggest threat to developing countries lies in weaker demand for their exports and declines in private capital flows. While FDI flows declined by nearly half in 2001, they appear to be recovering. China has maintained its relative attractiveness and is again the largest developing country recipient of FDI (UNCTAD 2002).

Recent years have seen a strong shift toward liberalization, deregulation, and the emergence of a closely integrated global economy. The extent of liberalization is apparent, for example, from the loosening of restrictions on FDI. Between 1991 and 2000, a total of 1,185 regulatory changes were introduced in national FDI regimes, of which 95 percent were in the direction of creating a more favorable environment for foreign investors (UNCTAD 2001). The strategies of MNEs have resulted in an increasingly globally integrated world economy. For example, during the period 1996–99 the annual average growth rate of the world economy was 0.6 percent, and that of world trade was 1.9 percent. This compares with growth rates of FDI inflows (40.8 percent), sales of foreign affiliates (10.5 percent), and intra-firm exports (11.0 percent). The result is an increasingly integrated global economy, primarily linked through deep integration driven by the expansion of MNEs (UNCTAD 1993).

GROWING IMPORTANCE OF KNOWLEDGE

The majority of advanced economies have now moved to the point where knowledge has become the primary resource. A knowledge-based economy can be defined as one in which the generation and exploitation of knowledge has become the dominant determinant of the wealth creation process. Such economies do not simply focus on the creation of knowledge, nor are they characterized merely by the existence of knowledge-intensive industries; rather, knowledge is increasingly applied to all sectors and stages of value-creation.

Knowledge is becoming increasingly important to all economies because of fundamental changes in economic and technological conditions. First, information and communications technology make it easier to create, capture, and exploit most forms of knowledge. Second, the pace of scientific and technological advance has accelerated. This is the result of the more systematic search for innovation by both governments and corporations, the growing corporatization of innovation, and the development of more effective organizational forms such as alliances in the creation, exploitation, and protection of knowledge. Third, global competition has increased reliance on knowledge advantages while simultaneously facilitating the transfer and diffusion of technological and organizational capability through trade, foreign investment, and the freer movement of people and ideas.

While knowledge has become critical for economic success, knowledge advantages are increasingly concentrated in the hands of MNEs. This is because such organizations enjoy considerable advantages in the creation, commercialization, and protection of knowledge (Dunning 1993). Furthermore, the considerable experience of large MNEs means that they are well placed to benefit from the unique characteristics of knowledge. These characteristics include the ability to manage the uncertainty that accompanies the innovation process, skills in acquiring and managing both codified and tacit knowledge, and experience in exploiting the increasing returns characteristic of many knowledge activities.

Increasing returns create complex challenges for the successful exploitation of knowledge assets. These include market instability (where demand and supply are no longer independent), unpredictability, the possible predominance of a technically inferior product, the ability to lock consumers into future markets through easier incremental learning, pricing issues where there are huge up-front (e.g., R&D) costs relative to unit production costs, network effects through the system compatibility of products and services, and the continuation of excess profits. Companies such as Microsoft, Intel, Sony, and eBay have demonstrated their competence in successfully exploiting such characteristics.

Developing countries such as China recognize that over time they will need to increase their technology and knowledge management skills. Indeed, this challenge is likely to increase in future years. This is a result of the accelerating pace of change, which will demand constant learning; the growing complexity of innovation as the current knowledge era is characterized by the simultaneous domination of both IT and biotechnology; the growing returns to "softer" forms of knowledge, such as organizational and marketing skills; and the increasing power of consumers in a knowledge-based society.

For these reasons, developing countries must acquire the necessary skills from leading MNEs. Failure to do so will be costly. Knowledge differences are likely to emerge as the primary source of economic divide. From the time of the Industrial Revolution, when knowledge was increasingly applied, productivity growth rates have accelerated. Since 1880, productivity in the advanced countries has increased some 50 fold. An alternative way to see the danger is to recognize that at the time of the Industrial Revolution income levels in the least and the most advanced economies were similar. By 1950 there was an eightfold difference (Sheehan 1999). By 1995 this gap had widened to 37 times (World Bank 2001).

NEW GEO-STRATEGIC ALLIANCES

The terrorist attacks of September 11, 2001, stimulated a radical shakeup in global geo-strategic alliances. During the Cold War era, alliances between countries were based primarily on military and ideological considerations that stemmed from a bilateral divide between East and West. For example, countries such as South Korea and the former West Germany were strategically supported by the United States as critical buffers between capitalism and communism. A number of countries enjoyed substantial economic and political benefits as a direct result of their locations. This changed in 1989 with the collapse of the Soviet Union. Subsequently, military commitments have been reduced, and the former locational advantage has disappeared. What has replaced it is a new so-called Global Era in which nations compete principally on economic grounds. This has elevated the importance of international competitiveness to a primary national objective. The consequent shift from a bilateral to a triad world has favored economies within, and contiguous to, the dominant economic centers of North America, the European Union, and Japan. Thus, certain economies within Central and Latin America, Eastern Europe, and parts of Southeast Asia have benefited from economic spillovers. At the same time, more peripheral regions, including much of Africa, the Middle East, and South Asia, have been marginalized within the global economy.

The terrorist attacks on the United States created a new set of strategic relations that have important implications for development. The creation of an alliance to combat world terrorism has brought together a disparate group of nations, including China, Russia, Iran, and Pakistan, a number of which struggled economically during the past decade. Their involvement is likely to have two principal economic impacts. First, to ensure their continuing commitment to the alliance, and in some cases to facilitate internal stability, these countries have been offered a number of economic benefits, including loans, the write-off of debt, and trading concessions. This has the effect of shifting the development stimulus from locational proximity to strategic importance. Second, there is a growing connection between the coalition and the promotion of free trade. The recent Doha trade round saw a new assertiveness and commitment from nations such as Pakistan, Malaysia, and Indonesia to support further trade liberalization, whereas a few years earlier they may have opposed this. Their new strategic importance has given them greater confidence in the area of trade and economic reform. Again, this will have important implications for future economic development.

Changing Nature of the Development Process

Economic development continues to be an important issue. More than one billion people still live in a state of abject poverty. The process of globalization has highlighted the growing dependency of any developing nation on the world economy, and at the same time has heightened economic inequalities between nations. While the fundamental economic development process remains the same (the generation and efficient use of capital and labor, the application of technology, and the creation of appropriate skills and institutional infrastructure), the context for development has changed significantly in recent years (UNCTAD 1999). The key change is that the resources necessary for development are no longer the preserve of governments; instead, they are now primarily found within MNE networks.

There are three main points concerning resources and their relationships to emerging economies. First, as discussed above, knowledge capital has become a key resource in the development process. The knowledge necessary for development is broad; it is not simply technical knowledge, but includes managerial and organizational know-how. Much of this knowledge is tacit and resides primarily within MNE networks. Second, competition to attract the necessary resources has increased dramatically. More economies seek such investment as they recognize that the basis for successful development has changed. It is increasingly difficult for an economy to compete solely through the advantage of low cost. To be competitive, an economy must display a range of tacit capabilities, including innovation, response flexibility, and market knowledge.

Third, the development process increasingly takes the form of successful interaction between the competitive advantages possessed by MNEs (termed firm specific assets, or FSAs) and elements of comparative advantage (country specific assets, or CSAs). This has encouraged MNEs to shift their strategies from relatively independent subsidiaries to more specialized and integrated production systems that often service complex global networks. At the same time, MNEs have become more selective in their choices of location. Between 1985 and 2000 the number of countries receiving sizeable amounts of FDI increased significantly, but the share of the largest 10 developing host countries remained stable at 77 percent of all FDI into developing countries (UNCTAD 2001). Multinational enterprises are also utilizing a wider range of organizational formats, including cooperative and network structures. To maximize the developmental impact of such investments, host country governments have eschewed restrictive and directive measures in favor of policies that focus on creating an attractive and productive investment environment.

CHANGES WITHIN CHINA AND THEIR IMPLICATIONS FOR MNE STRATEGIES

The second group of forces likely to impact MNE strategy are those within China. In an economy in transition, change is pervasive. This creates both opportunities and threats. Four key forces are summarized in Table 12.1. This table suggests that the most important changes are likely to result from the reform process, the influence of foreign firms investing in China, the management of internal and external relations, and the growth of high-technology industry.

Reform of the Chinese Economy

The opening up of the Chinese economy since 1978 has involved a long-term transition from a planned economy to a market economy (Boisot and Child 1996). However, China is not following a detailed blueprint for reform. Rather, reforms stem from the government's desire to improve economic performance (Jefferson and Rawski 1994). For this reason, reform has been uneven and has created considerable uncertainty for foreign firms.

Reform has substantially altered the structure of industry. Before the reforms, China's state owned enterprises (SOEs) accounted for three-quarters of industrial output; by 1998 this share was down to 28 percent. While the state sector's share of total output has declined, its poor performance places considerable strain on the economy. The most troubled state-owned industries include armaments, non-ferrous metals, coal, and textiles. Multinational enterprises are not active in these sectors and would not offer a viable vehicle for upgrading performance.

The growing private sector is characterized by a wide variety of ownership forms. Collectively owned and managed township and village enterprises now account for approximately 38 percent of output, foreign investors 15 percent, and private firms 17 percent (Child and Tse 2001). The private sector has been the fastest growing in China in recent years, and since the year 2000 private enterprise has been granted treatment equal to that of the state sector.

The changing industry structure is mirrored in other reforms. Today, approximately 95 percent of consumer goods are distributed through markets. In recent years there have been a number of institutional innovations to build futures markets and stock markets and to reform labor markets. The legal infrastructure has developed with significant new legislation favoring business and international investment. Further reform of the banking sector is also an imperative. China's four largest state-owned banks dominate lending, accounting for 60 percent of overall lending. Their lending is concentrated within SOEs and, as a result, they carry significant levels of nonperforming loans, perhaps as high as 40 percent of total lending. To date, China has chosen to reform the financial sector through re-capitalization rather than through privatization or foreign ownership. Nonperforming loans have been transferred to asset management companies. This approach may change after China's entry into the WTO; banking and financial services are among the most attractive opportunities for foreign firms (Perkins and Shaw 2000).

Reform must extend beyond the economic and financial sectors. Political

Table 12.1
Internal Changes and Their Implications for Business Strategy

Manifestation of Change	Implications for Business Strategy
Reform Process	
Uneven/idiosyncratic nature	High levels of risk and uncertainty
Increased competition	Falling returns, convergence of returns
	Loss of industry imperfections
Changing ownership forms/structures	Increased organizational choice
Differential industry reform rates	Differential opportunities
Broader reform (political, social)	Need for environmental assessment/opportunity to influence change process
New generation of leadership	Monitor policy changes, increased rationality
Social costs of economic reform	Risk, liability of foreignness
Unique reform path	Importance of learning, inability to arbitrage experience
Influence of Foreign Firms	
Continued acceptance of FDI	Rising expectations of contribution. Growing importance of soft technologies
Continuing importance of guanxi	Value of local partners/connections. First-mover advantages
Growing importance of Chinese market	Impact of China on regional/global success
Performance gap indigenous/foreign firms	Successful spillover requires a credible gap
Importance of intellectual property	Affects transfer process, organizational form
Timing of entry	First- versus late-mover advantages
Higher transaction costs	Preference for hierarchical structures, assets of local partners, network organizations
Internal and External Relations	
Uneven internal development	Differential costs/opportunities
	Directive policy
Increased external assertiveness to distract from internal problems	Considerable increase in risk
Continuing openness, adherence to rule-based international system	Ambiguous impact on uncertainty. Problem of managing within a dual system
Continuing integration in world economy	Extensive global division of labor
Continuing growth increases essential imports	Balance of payments concerns. Extortions to export
Importance of China as a regional leader	Extension of Triad strategies
	Integration of Asian regional strategy
Low probability of a crisis	Series of minor corrections
Management of relationships	Problems of corruption
Decentralization of control	Building/managing relationships at local level
Growth of High-Tech Industry	
Substantial growth of high-tech sector	New opportunities. Importance of technology transfer. IP issues. Emergence of strong local competitors
Reform process means continuing funding problems for high-tech SMEs	Contribution of FDI

reform is necessary to ensure effective economic reform. Political reform will help to prevent corruption, a significant problem in China. It is also needed to foster the creativity, risk taking, and entrepreneurship indispensable for a high-technology, knowledge-based economy. Without political reform, decreasing returns to further economic reform are likely. The challenge of achieving SOE reform highlights this problem.

Policy reform is also likely to occur. China's attempt to model its industrial policy on those of Japan and South Korea (in particular its attempt to nurture internationally competitive enterprises) appears to have failed. In all targeted industries, including aerospace, electrical power equipment, steel, mining, petrochemicals, and automobiles, Chinese firms appear to be farther than ever behind their international rivals (Nolan 2002).

Economic reform has generated more than just uncertainty for multinational enterprises. As the term "transition" suggests, the process is gradual and ongoing. This situation has created a dualistic economy, within which state-owned and private-sector activities coexist. This has a number of adverse effects for business. First, it has created opportunities for rent-seeking behavior, particularly by the state-owned sector. Second, interactions between the two parts of the economy distort values, incentives, and resource allocation. Third, dualism is mirrored in growing income inequality. Large gaps have appeared between state-owned and private firms as well as between the largely marketized coastal regions and less-developed inland provinces. Fourth, differential rates of reform between sectors create both opportunities and distortions. Marketization is most advanced in the case of physical goods and capital markets; it is far less developed in the case of business services. This limits the effectiveness of the market mechanism and encourages "gray" markets.

In the long term, reform will simply not be sufficient to sustain growth in China. To date, the principal sources of growth have resulted from the accumulation and redeployment of existing resources; productivity growth has been modest. In the future, productivity improvements will constitute the primary source of growth. To secure a high-technology, high-productivity future, China will need to move beyond a simple "catch-up" model. The absence of large, internationally competitive industrial enterprises may be less of a problem than current Chinese policy makers believe if the successful organization of the future is smaller, flatter, and more adaptable. However, as suggested above, such businesses flourish in a culture of political freedom and democracy. At the same time, as China struggles to manage the transition from a rural to an industrialized society, it must adapt to the immense challenges of globalization. This will require a range of responses, including greater openness, liberal information and communications policies, devolution of authority, and massive investments in human capital and technology.

The Influence of Foreign-Owned Firms

China has attracted a considerable amount of foreign direct investment. By the end of 2001, 400 of the Fortune 500 companies had invested in over 2,000 projects in China (Gelb 2000). Foreign investors have had a significant impact on the development of the Chinese economy. They have added considerably to industrial capacity and competition. They have also been at the forefront of developing domestic markets through the introduction of consumer goods and branding. Foreign firms seem set to play a key role in the development of knowledge-based industries within China (Sheehan 1999). A lack of understanding of the particular characteristics of such industries means that Chinese policy makers might be wise to follow a liberal policy and to allow foreign investors to initiate the early development of such industries. Foreign firms may perform a similar function in high-technology industries. China still places heavy reliance on its labor cost advantages. Over time, however, it will be necessary to stimulate more technology-intensive industries. R&D intensity in manufacturing in the leading OECD nations was some seven times higher than that of China in the mid 1990s (Sheehan 1999). Foreign investors, through both their domination of high-technology industries and the technology transfer process, are likely to play a major role in this technological upgrading. More generally, a significant foreign-owned sector, particularly one comprising most of the Fortune 500, will assist China in adjusting to the forces of globalization.

The impact of foreign firms on the Chinese economy has not been uniform. Clearly, the most significant managerial changes have occurred in sectors populated by foreign investors, as opposed to the state-owned sector. In heavy industry, the impact has been very modest. In lighter and import-substituting industries, such as car manufacturing, machinery, and pharmaceuticals, spillovers are considerable (Luo and Tan 1997). In electronics, the impact appears to be positive, although the spillover effect on productivity from a foreign presence is smaller than that associated with investment in human capital or increased scale (Lui et al. 2001). Similarly, ownership structure influences the extent of technology and managerial transfer (Tsang 2001). Joint ventures, widely used in China, have long been associated with higher rates of spillover (Child and Yan 2001).

Following China's acceptance into the WTO, the influence of foreign firms is likely to increase. Foreign firms may be expected to take a long-term view of the Chinese market and make a greater resource commitment to operations. They are more likely to include China in global supply and production chains. The obligations of WTO membership mean that Chinese policy makers will no longer be able to coerce foreign investors to meet their development needs. Industries previously considered closed to foreign investment because of their national importance will have to be opened. Similarly, foreign investors will enjoy greater choice in the selection of operating forms. This will affect relations with host governments, among other things (Sanyal and Guvenli 2000). Foreign investors will also benefit from a strengthening of laws, regulations, and institutional infrastructure.

This does not mean that linkages with local firms will decline. Judging by the experience of more developed Confucian societies, such as Hong Kong or South Korea, modernization does not eliminate heavy reliance on relationships (guanxi) and networks. Carver (1996) argues that this reflects the nature of such societies and the continuing importance of social obligations as opposed to legal stipulations. Furthermore, the growth of firms within a relationship-based culture appears to favor network type structures (Khanna and Palepu 1997; Peng and Heath 1996). This, in turn, creates barriers to new entrants, encouraging them to form partnerships with local firms (Lovett, Simmonds, and Kali 1999).

The timing of entry also influences the effects of foreign investors. Within China there are significant advantages of early entry (Luo and Peng 1998), particularly when a broad conception of such advantages is recognized (Arnold and Quelch 1998). Furthermore, the timing of entry appears to influence subsequent development, certainly in the case of pharmaceutical companies entering China (Van Den Bulcke, Zhang, and Li 1999). Entry timing is also linked to learning within the Chinese market. Financial and market performance both benefit from experience (Luo and Peng 1999). These relationships have important implications for the development of MNE strategy.

THE MANAGEMENT OF INTERNAL AND EXTERNAL RELATIONS

MNE strategy within China will depend, at least in part, on the perceived level of risk and uncertainty within the market. There are a number of sources of uncertainty, both internal and external. Internally, the process of transition has generated considerable tensions. A major contention is the emergence of significant income gaps, between the rural and urban sectors and between different provinces. Since 1987 urban income growth in China has significantly outpaced that of rural residents, and average rural income is now only about 35 percent of urban incomes. This trend shows no signs of changing; in fact, in the year 2000 the wealthiest urban residents enjoyed income growth more than five times that of the poorest rural groups (*Business Week* 2002).

Furthermore, much of China's recent modernization has been concentrated within the southern coastal cities and provinces. These areas have enjoyed high rates of income growth. More recently, the inland provinces of Guangxi, Hubei, Hebei, Anhue, Tianjin, Liaoning, Jiangxi, and Henan have started to enjoy some of the growth effects. However, the northwestern provinces have yet to experience any real discernible effects. The income of the most prosperous regions may be as much as five times that of the least prosperous by

2010. These gaps, coupled with rising unemployment as SOEs shed workers in an attempt to restructure, have triggered social protests (*Business Week* 2002). Foreign investors should be aware that the official response to these protests is likely to add to uncertainty. First, policies may signal a slowdown in the reform process. This has already occurred in the steel industry in Liaoning. Second, there could be a backlash against foreign influences, including foreign firms who may be seen as principal beneficiaries of the reform process.

A second source of internal uncertainty will result from the leadership succession process currently underway in China. As a group, the so-called fourth generation of leaders appears to be more technically competent, less ideologically rigid, and more commercially oriented than the previous generation. They appear committed to maintaining political and economic policies that have made China a far more predictable environment than under the leadership of Mao (1949–76) (Sutter 1999). Risk may arise from their limited understanding of the West and from the considerable internal challenges that they face. While they may continue the development of civil society and the growing institutionalization of Chinese society, there may be limits imposed on democracy. Perhaps the worst case scenario for foreign business would be if external aggression was used to distract attention from internal problems.

Third, investors should not expect the reform process to be particularly smooth. While China may not experience a financial crisis like the one that struck other parts of Asia in 1997, there are widespread difficulties in the financial sector that could result in further problems similar to the 1998 bankruptcy of the Guandong International Trust and Investment Company (GITIC). Such shocks are perhaps more accurately regarded as growing pains of reform and development than as signs of impending doom.

Externally, the picture is more complex. While China continues to deepen its economic and political integration with the rest of the world, there are marked instabilities in the evolution of that relationship. The strategy of neighboring states in the ASEAN group is to increase China's stake in both economic prosperity and regional security in the hope that this will bring external moderation. However, the turbulent nature of China's external relations—claims on large areas of the South China Seas, Tiananmen Square, the U.S. spy plane incident, the bombing of the Chinese embassy in Belgrade, and recent participation in the anti-terrorism coalition—all make prediction very difficult.

GROWTH OF HIGH-TECHNOLOGY INDUSTRY

As indicated earlier, it is likely that China's future competitiveness will depend not simply on advantages based on low cost labor, but also on the development of a high-technology sector. This sector will be populated by private firms, many of which are likely to be foreign-owned.

China's attempt to focus resources on the creation of high-technology sectors has not been that successful. Under the 863 program initiated in March 1986, over 5 billion yuan has been invested in advanced research programs. A further 15 billion will be made available over the next five years. Despite this, China's major high-technology firms are still a long way from the leading edge (Zhao, Qi, and Enderwick 2002). Well-known companies, such as Legend and Stone in the computing industry and Huawei in telecommunications equipment, have undergone restructuring to become more viable competitors. However, when compared with their global competitors, China's leading businesses, particularly within the high-technology sector, are at a huge competitive disadvantage (Nolan 2001).

Limited domestic resources and strongly competing demands for such resources mean that foreign firms are likely to play a major role in the development of high-technology industries within China. The motivations for technology transfer to China have shifted subtly as firms gain more experience and as China becomes a more important market to them. Simon (1997) reports evidence that the prime motive for technology transfer by foreign firms has changed from facilitating market access to ensuring a better alignment between Chinese and regional or global operations. In addition, the "softer" forms of technology, including management and organizational know-how, have become an increasingly important part of the technology package. While this means that MNEs are less likely to face problems of intellectual property protection, Chinese recipients are often reluctant to pay for these intangible forms of technology. Research suggests that the most effective vehicles for transferring technology to China are the largest, most diverse transnationals (Child and Yan 2001). Over time, technology spillovers may be expected to increase as MNEs enjoy a wider choice of operating modes, intellectual property rights become more firmly established, and Chinese operations become more closely integrated within MNE strategies. Inevitably, foreign firms will play a critical role in the technological upgrading of China.

IMPLICATIONS FOR MNE STRATEGIES

The preceding discussion has suggested that the future strategies of MNEs within China will be significantly influenced by a combination of external and internal factors. External factors—the increasingly liberal global business environment, the growing importance of knowledge, the new geo-strategic structure of the world economy, and the primary role that MNEs now play in the development process—will affect MNE strategies in a wide range of locations. The internal factors, those particular to China—the reform process, the expected contribution of foreign investment, the unique tensions experienced by China, and the desire to upgrade competitive advantage—will have a significant impact on strategy choice within China. This section examines the implications of these factors in more detail.

AREAS OF OPPORTUNITY FOR MNEs

The growth and transition of the Chinese economy has had a differential impact on industry sectors, creating many attractive opportunities for foreign investors. Perhaps the greatest opportunities exist in the service sector. The service sector is the most dynamic in the majority of developed and emerging economies, and China is unlikely to be an exception. The contribution of services to GNP in China is far lower than is normally seen in transition economies. China's membership in the WTO will undoubtedly spur growth and investment in services. Much of this will come from the multinational service firms that dominate business and professional services. As China becomes an increasingly important market, MNEs will reorganize their strategic focus to incorporate this. At the present time many firms operate a dual strategy within the Asian region, often establishing a presence to service the two key areas: Japan and other Asian markets. In the future, China may become a third key area in this region.

New market segments create specific opportunities. One segment is the older age group. Estimates suggest that by 2010 the proportion of the Chinese population over the age of 65 will reach 10 percent, and perhaps 15 percent by 2030. While similar trends are evident in developed economies, the aging process is particularly significant within China as a result of the one-child policy introduced early in the reform process. The over-65 segment offers tremendous opportunities. Similar attractions include the markets for environmental and energy products, infrastructure development, retailing (Chan et al. 1997), and personal financial services (Chrobocinski, Kempler, and Shavers 1997). More generally, there are huge opportunities for multinational enterprises to contribute to institutional infrastructure within China as the economy develops the business support and market intermediation services essential to an advanced economy (Child and Tse 2001).

Upgrading of the Chinese Economy

For much of the transition since 1978 the Chinese authorities have attempted to harness the resources of MNEs to contribute to development goals. Policies to date have focused on restrictive and coercive conditions. In the future, as China seeks to upgrade its sources of competitive advantage, it will need to tap into the skills and resources of MNEs. This will involve a relaxation of restrictive conditions, greater operational flexibility for MNEs, and the creation of conditions conducive to industrial upgrading. While evidence suggests that foreign firms have had a modest positive impact on labor productivity (Lui et al. 2001), the most promising opportunities for the future are likely to be found in high-technology and knowledge-based industries. China's economy is still primarily based on cost advantages and investment in research and development remains modest (Sheehan 1999).

There are a number of challenges in this area. One relates to appropriate policies with regard to e-commerce and the Internet. The difficulty of predicting the future course of e-commerce and the considerable externalities that arise suggest that the most appropriate policy would be one of minimal government involvement. However, this is unlikely to appeal to the Chinese authorities, who monitor and censor the Internet for political reasons. Second, the successful spillover of skills and knowledge from foreign to local firms assumes that the existing performance gap can be closed. However, there is growing evidence that in high-technology industries the gap may be insurmountable (Nolan 2001). If this is the case, foreign and local firms will increasingly be seen as competitors and not collaborators. In turn, this could create resentment toward foreign firms and raise the level of uncertainty that they face.

Externally, a significant foreign sector will assist China in integrating into an increasingly global world economy. While China struggles to manage the transition from a rural to an industrialized economy and the tensions that this transition will bring, its economy also faces the challenge of globalization. The experience, resources, and reach of MNEs will be invaluable in providing links to a rapidly evolving global economy.

Strategy in Competitive Markets

MNE strategies will have to adjust as markets in China become both more competitive and more significant. The opportunities to exploit market imperfections or to extract high returns from structural barriers are quickly disappearing. Competitiveness will increasingly depend upon the successful exploitation of firm-specific advantages. For many MNEs this has always been the chief source of competitive strength and has been used to overcome the challenges of operating in a difficult and unfamiliar market.

At the same time, rapid growth has increased the importance of the Chinese market for MNE operations. The rapid rise in per capita incomes has created a sizeable middle class with considerable discretionary income. In turn, this has stimulated MNEs to undertake several stages of investment within China. First stage investors focused on using cheap labor to produce relatively simple, labor-intensive products for export to more developed economies. The development of the domestic Chinese market encouraged a second stage of more market-oriented investment. There is now evidence of a third generation of investment, which recognizes the future importance of China and encourages the integration of Chinese operations into broader regional or global strategies. These strategies reflect the growing interdependence of country-specific and firm-specific assets and the increased likelihood of mandated products within China (Van Den Bulcke, Zhang, and Li 1999).

Spatial changes in the Chinese economy may also affect strategy. As the income and cost gap between the coastal and northern provinces grows, there may be incentives for firms to consider relocation. Given the low level of development in the northwest provinces, it will be some time before these areas become attractive. In the medium term there may be a preference for the small pockets of growth that have emerged, such as Shaanxi's Guan Zhong corridor. Wider spatial development also has important implications for the management of business-government relations within MNEs. As the Chinese authorities seek to encourage development in the inland regions, they may be prepared to increasingly devolve responsibility to local authorities who are better informed about conditions and opportunities. In return, the central authorities may settle for a share of revenue or a tax on activities. In such a case, a strategy of building coalitions with local governments and partner firms becomes increasingly attractive (Peng 2000).

China's importance within the Asia Pacific region seems likely to increase significantly in the future. This reflects the Chinese government's preference for a multipolar world where China's increased economic power counterbalances the United States and Japan. In this case, MNEs may be able to strengthen their standing within the Chinese economy by increasing commitment and independence in their Chinese operations. This could also be advantageous as further development within China provides opportunities for increased specialization. For example, Hong Kong is currently regarded as China's key financial center. In the future, if the mainland government maintains exchange controls but encourages financial market deepening and sophistication, Shanghai may emerge as the primary domestic financial center within China even as Hong Kong remains the key international financial center. Increased specialization within the MNE financial function may be expected. Similar trends may emerge within the R&D, marketing, and supply chain management functions.

Uncertainty and Learning

MNE strategy within China will also have to contend with high levels of operational and strategic uncertainty. The nature of China's transition is unique (Child and Tse 2001). Despite the growing globalization of the world economy, all transitional economies are not converging along similar lines. China retains a high degree of state intervention and appears to be following an uncertain course. Economic reform is tempered by the need to maintain social stability (*Business Week* 2002). For MNEs this means a high level of uncertainty. Uncertainty is greater when the development path is not clearly delineated or where policy changes are unpredictable. While investors see greater certainty in the incremental development of institutional structures and legal procedures, this does not obviate the need for local knowledge, relationships, and partnerships. While commercial uncertainty may be reduced over time, the potential risks that could arise from growing social tensions or radical departures in external policy should not be underestimated.

The strategic response depends on beliefs about the future power structure of China. While the move to widespread reliance on market forces and increased democratization does not appear consistent with the continuing domination of the Chinese Communist Party, China's unique development path means that this combination cannot be completely discounted. If, however, China's increased international commitments mean the strengthening of rules-based economic management and the desire for more equitable development processes, considerable policy discretion may be devolved. This is likely to discourage high-cost irreversible investments or the creation of highly specific assets that may be subject to opportunistic action by a domestic government or partner.

Selection of the appropriate risk-sharing mechanisms in the form of partnerships and network relations will differ. While greater commercial predictability could reduce the need for access to lower level political processes, the demand for access to key decision makers could increase. At the same time, political influence will likely be greater within ministries with external mandates, such as the Ministry of Foreign Trade and Economic Competition, than in traditional planning organizations, such as the State Planning Commission. Local competitors, perhaps better able to anticipate emerging political risks, are likely to focus on building their competitive advantages, which are often based on distribution networks, political connections, and local market understanding (Dawar and Frost 1999). Appropriate partner selection may become more difficult as government withdraws traditional forms of protection and support; a growing number of weakened domestic firms may seek foreign partnerships (Child and Tse 2001).

On the other hand, opportunity exists where successful MNEs learn from their operations in China. They learn to manage high levels of risk, to adapt strategies for a relationship-based system, and to compensate for the underdevelopment of institutional infrastructure. The skills acquired in China may be applied to emerging markets within Eastern Europe, Latin America, or Asia (Luo and Peng 1999). This reinforces the case for involvement in the Chinese market, not simply for resource or market reasons, but also as a source of learning.

Entry and Development Strategy

A significant strategy issue within the Chinese market is the timing of entry. There are arguments for both early entry and delayed entry. The case for early entry is based on initial establishment of leading brands, attainment of critical mass and the formation of entry barriers, preemptive domination of distribution channels, the creation of strong government relations, and learning effects (Arnold and Quelch 1998; Luo and Peng 1998). Furthermore, it is expected that levels of competition will increase over time as these economies mature. Advocates of late entry emphasize the high-risk environment of most emerging economies, the lack of institutional infrastructure, and the problem of competitor aggregation, in which a range of potential competitors spoil the attractiveness of a market by entering at the same time. Even though the Chinese economy has been open for more than twenty years, the issue of entry timing remains topical as WTO membership will open up a range of new market opportunities in banking, insurance, distribution, Internet services, chemicals, and agribusiness (Perkins and Shaw 2000).

Empirical research suggests that there are substantial first-mover advantages in China, particularly in terms of sales growth and asset turnover (Isobe, Makino, and Montgomery 2000; Luo and Peng 1998; Van Den Bulcke, Zhang, and Li 1999). At the same time, early entrants incur higher levels of operational risk and low levels of profitability in the early stages of establishment. While early entry appears to pay off in the long term, in the interim investors will need both patience and considerable resources to survive. An organization must align entry timing to strategic objectives. Early entry is favored when the goal of an organization is to build up strong positions in local markets, but not when the organization is seeking short-term profitability or global risk diversification.

The nature of the Chinese market favors early entry. Clearly, China's long-term market development potential is unrivalled. Furthermore, because the major source of uncertainty in China is political in nature, large politically influential investors who can afford a series of preemptive investments and the high costs of operating in the initial stages are likely to enjoy considerable advantages. There is also evidence of strong learning effects within China as early investors have now moved into second- and third-stage investments that focus less on experimentation and more on market dominance and deterring entry by other foreign competitors (Van Den Bulcke, Zhang, and Li 1999).

Market development strategy is also significantly influenced by the characteristics of a relationship-based emerging economy. Problems of measurement and enforcement in economies with incomplete price systems mean that transactions costs are likely to be high. This would suggest a preference for hierarchical governance arrangements and the need to avoid opportunistic behavior (Hoskisson et al. 2000). Local competitors are also likely to have developed in ways that reflect prevailing market conditions. Peng and Heath (1996) suggest that internal growth or external acquisition is difficult in economies lacking strong property rights and stable political systems. As a result, there is a preference for network type structures, often based around unrelated diversification (Khanna and Palepu 1997).

For multinational investors, local potential partners are likely to have strong capabilities in relationship-based management as well as the ability to succeed where markets are far from complete. There is evidence that the resources and skills sought by developed and emerging market firms are highly complementary (Hitt et al. 2000). Liberalization of ownership and governance structures in China will enable foreign investors to increasingly base partner selection decisions on rational considerations, including strategic intention, risk management, and transactions costs (Child and Tse 2001).

CONCLUSIONS

This chapter has examined the implications for MNE strategies within the emerging market of China in an atmosphere of rapid change in the world economy. The key external changes identified were the favorable business environment of recent years, the increasing importance of knowledge as a resource, the emerging geo-strategic alliances, and the changing nature of the development process. All of these changes have important implications for MNE strategy. Within China, strategic considerations will be impacted by the ongoing nature of the reform process, changing expectations of foreign investors, high levels of uncertainty resulting from internal and external pressures, and the need to upgrade the competitive foundation of the Chinese economy. In combination, these forces will significantly impact future strategies of MNEs and suggest a number of important conclusions.

First, while China has become more important to international business, international businesses have also become more important to China. MNEs are key providers of the resources necessary for development; similarly, they are at the forefront in the creation of knowledge-based activities. In the future, as China moves beyond cost-based advantages and into high-technology products and services, upgrading will depend increasingly on foreign investors. This has important implications for government policy in terms of attracting FDI and maximizing its developmental benefits. The development of high-technology products will also influence how MNE strategies evolve. The discussion in this chapter suggests that MNEs will enjoy higher levels of operating choice and flexibility, that China will become an increasingly important market for their operations, and that successful competitors will integrate firm-specific advantages with the considerable and changing country-specific assets offered by China.

Second, expectations of the role and impact of MNEs are changing. In the early stages of transition, foreign investors brought capital, technology, and management skills to an economy sorely lacking in such resources. In many cases their initial investments were limited and experimental. Over time, as China has deepened its institutional and market development and its commitment to international regulations and organizations, the role of MNEs has changed. Increasingly, MNE investors will be expected to contribute to market development, particularly in business services, to facilitate China's growing integration with the world economy, to assist in adjustment of the dynamic forces of globalization, and to contribute to the upgrading of China's technological base. MNEs are uniquely well-placed to fulfill such expectations. However, these goals must be balanced with the growing demands of a rapidly emerging domestic economy and significantly higher levels of competition.

There is evidence that many early investors have now moved beyond initial investments to second- and third-generation strategies that increasingly incorporate Chinese operations into regional and global strategy.

Third, these strategic shifts are occurring in a context of continuing high levels of risk. While transition appears to have lowered commercial risk, considerable uncertainty stems from the tensions of reform and the precarious nature of China's external relations. Despite this, China will continue to attract a very high proportion of all investment into emerging economies. For MNEs, the overwhelming attractions of the Chinese market means finding ways to deal with such uncertainties.

Finally, it is important to recognize that while MNEs will play an important role in the development of the Chinese economy, the reality is complex. While MNEs in China have undoubtedly assisted competitive upgrading, their overall strategies have actually widened the gap between China and the world's leading enterprises. As Nolan (2001) recognizes, the world's leading firms have driven a revolution in business strategy, commonly summarized in the concept of globalization. As suggested above, China's transition has focused on the shift from rural to urban society; there remain huge challenges in adjusting to the demands of a global, knowledge-based world.

REFERENCES

Arnold, D. T., and J. A. Quelch. 1998. "New Strategies in Emerging Markets." *Sloan Management Review* 40 (1): 7–20.

Boisot, M., and J. Child. 1996. "From Fiefs to Clans and Network Capitalism: Explaining China's Emerging Economic Order." *Administrative Science Quarterly* 41: 600–28.

Business Week. 2002. "China's Angry Workers." *Business Week*, 8 April, 20–24.

Carver, A. 1996. "Open and Secret Regulations in China and Their Implication for Foreign Investment." In *Management Issues in China Vol. 2: International Enterprises*, edited by J. Child and Y. Lu. London and New York: Routledge.

Chan, T. M. H. 1999. "Economic Implications of China's Accession to the WTO." Unpublished paper, Hong Kong Polytechnic University.

Chan, W. K., J. Perez, A. Perkins, and M. Shu. 1997. "China's Retail Markets Are Evolving More Quickly than Companies Anticipate." *McKinsey Quarterly* 2: 206–11.

Child, J., and Y. Lu, eds. 1996. *Management Issues in China Vol. 2: International Enterprises*. London and New York: Routledge.

Child, J., and K. Tse. 2001. "China's Transition and Its Implications for International Business." *Journal of International Business Studies* 32 (1): 5–21.

Child, J., and Y. Yan. 2001. "National and Transnational Effects in International Business: Indications from Sino-Foreign Joint Ventures." *Management International Review* 41 (1): 53–75.

Chrobocinski, P., L. S. Kempler, and T. B. Shavers. 1997. "Emerging Markets for Personal Financial Services." *McKinsey Quarterly* 2: 201–5.

Dawar, N., and T. Frost. 1999. "Competing with Giants: Survival Strategies for Local

Companies Doing Business in Emerging Markets." *Harvard Business Review* 77 (2): 119–29.

Dunning, J. H. 1993. *Multinational Enterprises and the Global Economy*. Harlow: Addison-Wesley.

Gelb, C. 2000. "Foreign Investors Wise Up." *China Business Review*. November/December 2000.

Hitt, M., M. T. Dacin, E. Levitas, J. L. Arregle, and A. Borza. 2000. "Partner Selection in Emerging and Developed Market Contexts: Resource-Based and Organisational Learning Perspectives." *Academy of Management Review* 43 (3): 449–67.

Hoskisson, R., L. Eden, C. M. Lau, and M. Wright. 2000. "Strategy in Emerging Economies." *Academy of Management Journal* 43 (3): 249–67.

Isobe, T., S. Makino, and D. B. Montgomery. 2000. "Resource Commitment, Entry Timing, and Market Performance of Foreign Direct Investments in Emerging Economies: The Case of Japanese International Joint Ventures in China." *Academy of Management Journal* 43 (3): 468–84.

Jefferson, G. H, and T. G. Rawski. 1994. "Enterprise Reform in Chinese Industry." *Journal of Economic Perspectives* 8 (2): 47–70.

Khanna, T., and K. Palepu. 1997. "Why Focused Strategies May Be Wrong for Emerging Markets." *Harvard Business Review* 75 (4): 41–51.

Lingle, C. 2000. "China's Future Still Uncertain." *Taipei Times*, 31 December.

Lovett, S., L. C. Simmonds, and R. Kali. 1999. "Guanxi versus the Market: Ethics and Efficiency." *Journal of International Business Studies* 30 (2): 231–48.

Lui, X., D. Parker, K. Vaidya, and Y. Wei. 2001. "The Impact of Foreign Direct Investment on Labour Productivity in the Chinese Electronics Industry." *International Business Review* 10 (4): 421–40.

Luo, Y., and M. Peng. 1998. "First Mover Advantages in Investing in Transitional Economies." *Thunderbird International Business Review* 40 (2): 141–63.

———. 1999. "Learning to Compete in a Transition Economy: Experience, Environment and Performance." *Journal of International Business Studies* 30 (2): 269–96.

Luo, Y., and J. J. Tan. 1997. "How Much Does Industry Structure Impact Foreign Direct Investment in China?" *International Business Review* 6 (4): 337–59.

Naughton, B. 1994. *Growing Out of the Plan*. New York: Cambridge University Press.

Nolan, P. 2001. *China and the Global Economy*. Basingstoke: Palgrave.

———. 2002. "China and the Global Business Revolution." *Cambridge Journal of Economics* 26 (1): 119–37.

Peng, M. 2000. "Controlling the Foreign Agent: How Governments Deal with Multinationals in a Transition Economy." *Management International Review* 40 (2): 141–65.

Peng, M., and P. S. Heath. 1996. "The Growth of the Firm in Planned Economies in Transition: Institutions, Organisations and Strategic Choice." *Academy of Management Review* 21 (2): 492–528.

Perkins, A., and S. M. Shaw. 2000. "What the WTO Really Means for China." *McKinsey Quarterly* no 2: 128–31.

Sanyal, R. N., and T. Guvenli. 2000. "Relations Between Multinational Firms and Host Governments: The Experience of American-Owned Firms in China." *International Business Review* 9 (1): 119–34.

Sheehan, P. 1999. "The Global Knowledge Economy: Challenges for China's Development." CSES Working Paper No. 15 (December), Victoria University of Technology, Melbourne.

Simon, D. F. 1997. *Technology Transfer Practices of MNEs in China*. San Francisco: Anderson Consulting.

Sutter, R. 1999. *Introduction and Key Findings in China's Future: Implications for US Interests* (September) Washington, D.C.: CIA.

Tsang, E. 2001. "Managerial Learning in Foreign-Invested Enterprises of China." *Management International Review* 41 (1): 29–51.

UNCTAD. 1993. *World Investment Report 1993: Transnational Corporations and Integrated International Production*. New York and Geneva.

———. 1999. *World Investment Report 1999: Foreign Direct Investment and the Challenge for Development*. New York and Geneva.

———. 2001. *World Investment Report 2001: Promoting Linkages*. New York and Geneva.

——— 2002. *FDI Downturn in 2001 Touches Almost All Regions*. Unpublished paper.

Van Den Bulcke, D., H. Zhang, and X. Li. 1999. "Interaction Between the Business Environment and the Corporate Strategic Positioning of Firms in the Pharmaceutical Industry: A Study of the Entry and Expansion Path of MNEs in China." *Management International Review* 39 (4): 353–77.

World Bank. 2001. *World Development Report 2000/2001: Attacking Poverty*. Oxford, U.K.: Oxford University Press.

Zhao, Y., M. Qi, and P. Enderwick. 2002. "Upgrading China's Competitive Advantage: The Case of Zhongguancun Science and Technology Park." In *Chinese Economic Transition and Marketing Strategy*, edited by I. Alon. Greenwich, Conn.: Quorum Press.

CHAPTER 13

Rethinking MNE-Emerging Market Relationships: Some Insights from East Asia

Mo Yamin and Pervez N. Ghauri

INTRODUCTION

It is generally agreed that over the past two decades or so, multinational enterprises (MNEs) have had the upper hand in less developed countries (LDCs) (Buckley and Ghauri 1999; Dunning and Narula 1999; Ghauri and Buckley 2002; Jenkins 1999; Narula and Dunning 2000). Over this period, the general trend has been for a steady change in the policy stance of LDCs away from control, structuring, and regulation of MNEs and toward the liberalization and facilitation of MNE operations in their economies. Governments were persuaded that the adoption of liberal and pro-MNE policies was generally beneficial to their economies. In any case, their bargaining power was generally weakening due partly to changes in the international policy environment, such as pressure from the World Trade Organization (WTO) toward increasing liberalization of world trade and investment, and partly to changes in MNE strategies toward greater cross-border integration and increasing emphasis on efficiency seeking investments.

Over the last several years, however, there has been a noticeable shift in the intellectual climate with respect to the appropriate policy stance in regard to LDCs vis-à-vis MNEs. This shift can be characterized as a retreat from at least the extreme forms of liberalization with their advocacy of a minimal state and is linked to a more general disenchantment with globalization and the emergence of a movement for a global civil society (Buckley and Ghauri 1999; Stiglitz 2002). In the specific context of LDCs, many scholars now reject the view that the economically valid or legitimate scope for government intervention is limited to establishing macroeconomic stability. The assumption that market forces, once liberated from government controls, can automatically generate economic development is increasingly questioned. This questioning has gained ground as liberalization failed to deliver the expected economic performance in most emerging economies and, even more dramatically perhaps, in a number of transitional economies (notably the Russian Federation) that implemented liberalization/marketization policies most enthusiastically (Stiglitz 2002).

Narula and Dunning (2000, 115) capture the emerging consensus succinctly when they observe that "On its own, liberalisation—as with excessive protectionism—is insufficient as a driver of growth." Also needed is a set of measures and policies that creates supporting institutions and stimulates a developmental orientation in market forces (Lall and Teubal 1998; Narula and Dunning 2000; Ocampo 2002; Perez-Aleman 2000; Stiglitz 2002; Yamin 1998).

This paper considers one particular manifestation of this change—the advocacy of a more active industrial policy, particularly in shaping MNE activities in emerging economies, than had hitherto seemed advisable. Our aim is to contribute to the critical perspectives on international business and the MNE (Forsgren 2002; Ghauri and Buckley 2002; Havila, Forsgren, and Hakansson 2002) and more specifically to highlight the changing views relating to the positive role that policy intervention can have in maximizing the developmental impact of the MNE. This paper explains that the change in the intellectual climate hinges specifically on two issues: first on a growing realization and emerging consensus that East Asian industrialization was a governed process (Wade 1990) and was not market led, and second on the stark contrast between rapid industrialization in East Asia and near economic stagnation in the bulk of LDCs where government had followed a liberalization approach.

THE DEBATE ON EAST ASIAN INDUSTRIALIZATION

Although the debate on the appropriate roles of national governments in economic development has a long history (see, e.g., Dunning 1997a), the current debate centers on opposing interpretations of the experience of East Asian tigers. These few countries are unique among LDCs in enjoying sustained and high rates of economic growth in the postwar period. For example, Korea had a lower gross domestic product (GDP) per capita than Ghana in 1960, but by 1990 its per capita GDP was seven times larger than Ghana's (World Bank 1999, 12). Until the early 1990s the impressive performance of East Asian tigers was trumpeted as being *the* model of a market-driven economic system based on free trade and an open door policy toward foreign direct investment (FDI) (Lall 1997). This interpretation was strongly promoted by the World Bank in particular and became one of the pillars of the so-called Washington Consensus. So strong was the belief that the superior performance of East Asia was a victory for the fundamental and universal truth of free market economics that those who challenged the consensus were dismissed as cranks (Gore 2000, 790).

The most detailed case for the Washington Consensus view on East Asian industrialization was elaborated in a study, appropriately titled *The East Asian Miracle*, by the World Bank (1993). This study articulated an accumulation explanation of East Asia's performance (Lall and Teubal 1998, 1369). Accumulation theories stress the role of physical and human capital investment, while assimilation theories stress the centrality of learning in identifying, adapting, and operating imported technologies. The accumulation view sees a limited role for government. The government's role is to concentrate on ensuring a stable macroeconomic environment and remove obstacles to the operations of factor and goods markets both domestically and internationally. The World Bank attributed East Asia's growth performance to the correctness of macroeconomic fundamentals, which permitted sustained high rates of saving and investment, including investment in education and export promotion. Government intervention beyond sound macroeconomics is seen as harmful.

The World Bank study devoted relatively little space to FDI policies—only 2 out of 360 pages (World Bank 1993, 301–3). It stressed East Asia's openness to foreign technologies but viewed this as just one facet of its openness to trade and investment. It did not comment in detail on specific policies, for example, in Taiwan and Korea, that tended to regulate MNE operations. However it specifically rejected the relevance of industrial policy (including those specifically targeting MNEs) that would promote certain industries or subsidize learning in technologically complex industries. It argued that industrial policies pursued in East Asia had been largely ineffective: industrial policies targeted to promote the development of specific knowledge and capital-intensive industries were not generally successful and imposed significant costs on the economy (World Bank 1993, 308–9). It viewed such policies as unnecessary, arguing that, as long as macroeconomic conditions are right for growth, industrial learning takes place automatically and rapidly with investment, particularly if growth is export oriented:

What then has contributed to [East Asia's] apparently superior performance in adopting and mastering international best-practice technologies? We argue that the combination of competitive discipline and well functioning factor markets with a pro-export orientation—the export push strategy—employed by these economies was responsible for their superior productivity performance. (World Bank 1993, 261)

However, this interpretation was in fact strongly challenged and there is now general agreement that strong government intervention was a key aspect of the East Asian economic experience. In particular, the World Bank's dismissal of industrial policy as a key explanation for East Asia's performance has been severely criticized by a growing number of commentators. Scholars have argued that the World Bank did not appreciate the degree to which macro-economic policies in East Asia were deeply anchored in micro-institutions that exhibit pervasive state intervention (Amsden 1989, 1994, 2001; Hobday 1995; Lall 1994, 1997, 1998; Lall and Teubal 1998; Wade 1990). These critics and others focusing more on the Latin American experience (see Perez-Aleman [2000] for a recent example) are of the view that the World Bank study ignores a crucial issue in economic development—the link between technological learning and industrialization. Physical investment alone does not ensure the development of capabilities needed to put the economy on a dynamic growth path. In other words, learning by doing, albeit important, is not on its own sufficient for economic development. Technological development plays as vital a role in the industrial success of developing countries as it does in developed countries. Even if developing countries are not on the frontier of innovation, they need to develop new skills, knowledge, institutions, and organizational capabilities to master the technologies they import and to grow efficiently. In fact, even in developed economies a significant proportion of the innovations involve large elements in imitation of technology already developed in other countries. There is often no clear-cut distinction between innovation and imitation. As Bell and Pavitt (1997) have stressed, "the argument that importing foreign technology and creating it locally are alternative means of generating technical change does not reflect the experience of developed countries" (Bell and Pavitt 1997, 97).

The critics of the World Bank argue that it did not pay sufficient attention to factors that specifically affect technological development. In particular, the World Bank study ignored the large number of empirical studies of technological change both in developed and developing countries showing (for review, see Bell and Pavitt 1997) that technological learning is an evolutionary and incremental process always beset, to varying degrees, by market failure in that it is subject to significant risk, uncertainty, and externalities. These characteristics imply that, especially in the context of developing countries, technological learning processes cannot be left to market forces alone.

This line of thinking has created coherent and convincing accounts of the East Asian experience. Thus East Asian governments adopted a whole range of not only functional policies (i.e., policies that promote all economic activities, such as investment in education and the infrastructure) but also selective policies that promoted particular dynamic activities and industries. The basis of such selectivity has been the degree of difficulty of the learning and knowledge acquisition process and reflects the premise that market forces would provide insufficient support for such activities. Reliance on market forces tends to encourage development along the existing structure of comparative advantage (typically promoting labor intensive activities). In East Asia, particularly in Korea, government policies used a set measure to encourage firms to gain skills and knowledge beyond that immediately available within their own economies and thus helped to create a new, more advanced structure of competitive advantage. As Wade (1990) has argued, the East Asian experience is one where market forces are *not* ignored but were extensively governed to generate economic development.

Policies toward multinational companies in East Asia were firmly set within this broader strategic vision of the governed development process. East Asian governments in the original tiger economies—the first-tier Newly Industrialized Countries (NICs) (except Hong Kong)—followed strategies toward MNEs actively geared to stimulate technology and knowledge diffusion to the local economy (see Table 13.1).

The experience of mainland China, which has enjoyed a similar sustained rapid growth, is also worthy of mention in the present context. In mainland China, the government has followed a two-pronged policy with regard to multinational enterprises. According to a recent United Nations Conference on Trade and Development (UNCTAD) study (Gabriele 2001), the vast majority of FDI has been low-tech and carried out by expatriate Chinese and firms from the East Asian region. This was encouraged mainly to generate employment in traditional, labor intensive sectors of light manufacturing rather than for its capacity to generate technological spillover or learning. On the other hand, the government has focused efforts on upgrading China's science and technology institutions and strongly promoting local research and

Table 13.1
East Asian Policies toward Multinational Companies

	FDI Strategy	Raising Local Content	Raising Technological Effort
Hong Kong	None, leave to market forces	None	None
Singapore	Aggressive targeting and screening of MNCs	Promoting sub-contracting for SMEs	MNCs targeted to increase R&D
Taiwan	Screening FDI, entry discouraged where local firms strong. Local technological diffusion pushed.	Pressure for raising local content, technology diffusion and local subcontracting	Intense support for local R&D and upgrading of SMEs. Government targeted and orchestrated high-tech development
Korea	FDI kept out unless necessary for technology access or exports, joint ventures and licensing encouraged	Stringent local content rules, creating support industries, protection of local suppliers and subcontracting promotion	Ambitious plans for R&D in advanced industry, heavy investment in technology infrastructure. Targeting of strategic technologies

Source: Based on Lall and Teubal (1998): 1377.

development (R&D) in order to raise local technological capability and enhance its own bargaining power in the case of the (much smaller) FDI flows by firms from more advanced countries.

MNEs, LDCs, AND THE INTERNATIONAL DIVISION OF LABOR

Since the early 1980s most developing countries, with the exception of the Asian tigers, were persuaded to follow liberal trade and foreign investment policies to a significant degree. As Table 13.2 shows, over the last decade, many less developed countries adopted very permissive policies toward MNEs.

At the same time, as Table 13.3 suggests, although there has been a very large influx of MNEs into LDCs, these have typically resulted in extremely shallow levels and types of investment. The sharp disparity between the share of LDCs in inward FDI stocks/flows and their share of the number of foreign affiliates is indeed telling. Some disparity would of course be expected, as investment in less developed countries would tend to be more labor intensive and absorb lower amounts of FDI. However, the magnitude of the disparity is also due to a change in the structure of MNE activity in many LDCs away from a focus on local markets and toward their incorporation in the rationalized internal production networks that they control.

This pattern fits well into Dunning's analysis of how globalization and greater mobility of firm-specific assets have influenced the pattern of MNE activities in LDCs (Dunning and Narula 1999; Narula and Dunning 2000).

Table 13.2
The Dominance of Pro-FDI Policies in Emerging and Developing Countries,
1991–2000

	1991	1992	1993	1994	1995	1996	1997	1998	1999	2000
Number of countries that introduced changes in their investment regimes	35	43	57	49	64	65	76	60	63	69
Number of regulatory changes	82	79	102	110	112	114	151	145	140	150
Of which:										
More favorable to FDI	80	79	101	108	106	98	135	136	131	147
Less favorable to FDI	2	0	1	2	6	16	16	9	9	3

Source: UNCTAD (2001): 6.

Table 13.3
Share of LDCs in FDI Stocks, FDI Flow, and Number of Affiliates in 1999 (Percentages)

	Stock of FDI	FDI Flow	Foreign Affiliates
Developed Economies	67.7	73.5	13.7
Developing Economies	30.1	24.0	51.5
Central and Eastern Europe	2.2	2.5	34.8

Source: UNCTAD (2000) and Ietto-Gillies (2001).

Most underdeveloped countries can at best attract asset-exploiting investment, while the vast majority of asset-augmenting investment will be highly concentrated in the developed triad economies. Asset-exploiting FDI takes place when a company's primary purpose is to generate economic rents through the use of firm-specific assets. Asset-augmenting FDI is motivated to gain new technological and other strategic assets and is mainly attracted to a relatively small number of regional clusters within the Organisation for Economic Cooperation and Development (OECD) countries, as these locations provide an ample supply of the required complementary resources such as high-level specialized skills, a sophisticated infrastructure, and advanced research centers and universities (Dunning 1997b). In the context of less developed countries, asset-exploiting FDI comprises the transfer of relatively low technology and low value activities to be combined with the main location-bound advantages of these countries—primarily cheap labor. In fact, the production of standardized manufacturing products is now increasingly organized through elaborate international production networks controlled by large multinational companies. This is a main reason for the rapid expansion of trade in manufacturing and it also helps to explain why manufacturing trade expansion has not produced the expected gains for LDCs. Thus, according to a recent *Trade and Development Report,*

International production networks promote a new pattern of trade in that goods travel across several locations before reaching final consumers, and the total value of trade recorded exceeds the value added by a considerable margin. Consequently, trade in such products can grow without a commensurate increase in their final consumption as production networks are extended across space. (UNCTAD 2002, 64)

As we have already noted, this has generated only shallow investments in LDCs, sometimes through the takeover and subsequent hallowing of domestic enterprises and with relatively little linkages with local suppliers (UNCTAD 2001).

Almost 30 years ago, Hymer (1972) provided an analysis of the impact of MNEs on the structure of the world economy in terms of two basic laws of development, namely the Law of Uneven Economic Development and the Law of Increasing Firm Size. It suggested that while North Atlantic MNEs would dominate, a geographical division of labor and dependence relationship, with one side being superior and the other being subordinate, would emerge. This situation would lead to tensions and conflicts and to further uneven development.

Using the Chandler-Redlich (1961) scheme, Hymer (1972) suggested that MNEs would spread their day-to-day, manufacturing activities all over the globe, thus diffusing industrialization to developing countries and creating new centers of production. The other activities, coordination and communication, would stay closer to the head offices, which would be completely centralized. As a result, the best highly skilled and highly paid manpower would concentrate in the major cities of the U.S. and Europe, while lower-level skills and manpower would remain in other parts and cities of the world. Most new products would be developed in the major cities and, once accepted there, would travel to other countries. MNEs would thus be greatly interested in the markets of these less-developed countries. This system would automatically force developing countries not to develop skilled manpower above a certain level, as there would be no market for their skills. The local governments would not even be able to invest in their own infrastructure, communication, education, and health to achieve growth, as they would not be able to finance these investments. They would not be able to tax MNEs to acquire finance, due to the ability of these corporations to manipulate transfer prices or to move to low-tax countries, whereas the home countries of these MNEs would be able to tax these corporations as a whole, as well as through their highly paid manpower.

It is remarkable that Hymer's (1972) projections appear to be strongly validated: the uneven development he predicated is indeed upon us and is fully reflected in the broad structure of the world economy and particularly in the global configuration of MNEs. His radical analysis of 30 years ago is now incorporated into the mainstream. We have already seen that mainstream analysis of multinational firms (e.g., Dunning 1997b) sees increasing divergence between a concentration of high value–added activities in advanced regions/ clusters within advanced countries, while low value–added, assembly operations are increasingly footloose and dispersed to cheap labor locations. Robert Wade (2001), in trying to explain how globalization may have created greater international inequality, suggests the following as one of the deep causes:

Perhaps it is through the tendency for knowledge intensive and high value added activities to cluster spatially, even though technology is available to close great distances. Think of Silicon Valley, a dense concentration of the very companies that are driving the world's communication revolution. But also think of the clustering of the higher value added activities of the multinational corporations in their home countries within the OECD world, despite high congestion costs, while they may outsource the lower value added activities in less developed countries. (Wade 2001, 17)

With liberalization, multinational companies have increasingly become the arbiter of the evolving pattern of international trade and capital movements. This pattern incorporated many LDCs in the global networks of trade and investment controlled by MNEs, and consequently both trade and foreign investment inflow have increased significantly. However, the promised land of high rates of economic growth is increasingly regarded as a mirage (Amsden and Van der Hoeven 1996; Ocampo 2002; UNCTAD 2002).

THE END OF THE WASHINGTON CONSENSUS?

As already noted, the Washington Consensus was sold to LDCs as a policy approach that had produced impressive performances in East Asia. The contrast between the successes of East Asia (misleadingly portrayed as free market economies) and the failures of import substituting policies of the 1960s and 70s meant that most developing countries were keen to embrace liberal policies, hoping to emulate the growth performance of East Asia. The intellectual environment is becoming less favorable for the Washington Consensus, not only due to the reinterpretation of East Asia's experience of industrialization, but also due to broader but still related developments. While the mantra of the Washington Consensus has been a dual emphasis on the liberalization of capital flows and macroeconomic stability, the Asian crisis revealed a contradiction between macroeconomic stability on the one hand and cross-border movement of short-term capital (hot money) on the other (see, e.g., Stiglitz 2000, 2002; Wade 1998). In fact, a prominent feature of the globalized world economy is the increase in the frequency and depth of international financial crises (Stiglitz 2000, 1075).

Interestingly, the current pressures for policy change again stem from the stark contrast between the experience of the East Asian tigers and the bulk of developing countries where liberal trade and investment policies have brought little growth or development of technological capabilities. However this is now based on a new realization: East Asian economies were far from being model implementers of the Washington Consensus. As Stiglitz (2002) has recently observed, a major achievement of East Asian tigers was to successfully resist international pressures to abandon industrial policies. In fact, these governments took industrial policy to be one of their central responsibilities and Stiglitz (2002, 26) pointedly observes that "It is crucial that the successful development we have seen in East Asia be achieved elsewhere."

However, criticism of the World Bank's analysis should not be taken as a justification for indiscriminate and wholesale government intervention in the economy. Such indiscriminate intervention, including indiscriminate promotion of all industrial exporting would be counterproductive precisely because it would not discriminate in favor of *selected* activities promising high rates of technological and industrial learning. Gup and Num (1999) for example, argue that in Thailand the government's heavy push of export activities helped to create a glut in many markets such as the steel market because other governments were promoting their exports at the same time. Gup and Nam (1999) consider that such policies were at least in part responsible for the financial crisis of 1997. In another study (Nam and Gup 1999), they put similar arguments forward in relation to heavy intervention in financial markets.

The emerging consensus relating to the lessons of the East Asian experience is thus a two-track policy approach and may be more promising. The two-track policy would retain the broadly open economy orientation while employing industrial policy to direct and shape investment activity, including those by the multinational companies in the direction of promoting industrial deepening and technological learning. According to the International Bank for Reconstruction and Development (1997), the role the governments play should be matched with the capabilities that they have, as shown in Table 13.4.

It is important to note that even the World Bank now appears to accept the important and broadly positive role that state intervention played in fostering technological learning in East Asian economies. As noted already, in its 1993 study, it dismissed the relevance of selective intervention and explained the miracle exclusively in terms of the adoption of market-friendly policies. However in the 1999 *World Development Report*, it had clearly revised its original assessment. Thus with respect to the Korean experience we read:

Some researchers argue that what is behind the emergence of this Asian "tiger" is a strong, interventionist state—a state that deliberately and abundantly granted tariff protection and subsidies, manipulated interest and exchange rates, managed investment, and controlled industry using both carrots and sticks. Relative prices were deliberately set "wrong" to generate and reap the benefits of evolving comparative advantage, instead of letting them adjust to the "right" levels by the free play of market forces. Korea's leaders judged that getting prices right would lead to short-run efficiency but long-run economic anemia.

Korea's development strategy has been mainly one of pragmatic trial and error, based on a twofold commitment: to the growth of exports and to the nurturing of selected infant industries through protection . . . these and other technology investments in the 1970s enabled Korea's firms to move up the technology chain, closing the knowledge gap. (World Bank 1999, 32)

We also observe a similar reassessment of the role of MNEs in economic development by UNCTAD, although this organization was not as firmly attached to the Washington Consensus as the World Bank. A comparison of

Table 13.4
Reinvigorating Functions of State

	Addressing market failure			Improving equity
	Providing pure public goods:			Protecting the poor:
Minimal Functions	Defense, Law and order, Property rights, Macroeconomic management, Public health			Antipoverty programs Disaster relief
Intermediate Functions	Addressing Externalities	Regulating Monopoly	Overcoming Imperfect Information	Providing Social insurance
	Basic education	Utility regulation	Insurance (health, life)	Redistributive pensions
	Environmental protection	Antitrust policy	Financial regulation Consumer protection	Family allowances Unemployment insurance Environmental protection
Activist Functions	Coordinating private activity: Fostering Markets Cluster Initiatives			Redistribution: Asset Redistribution

Source: Based on IBRD (1997): 27.

the analyses in *World Investment Report 1992* was optimistically titled *Transnational Corporations as Engines of Development*. *World Investment Report 1999*, entitled *Foreign Direct Investment and the Challenge of Development*, reveals a significant reduction in optimism in relation to the developmental impact of multinational firms between the two reports. The latter report puts much greater emphasis on needed policies to raise the quality of investments and formulates a strong and detailed infant industry case for the protection of domestic enterprises vis-à-vis multinational enterprises (UNCTAD 1999, 36–44). The following observation is particularly interesting and encapsulates perhaps the central dilemma for policy makers:

There are risks that the presence of TNCs [Transnational Corporations] inhibits technological development in a host economy. TNCs are highly efficient in transferring the results of innovation performed in developed economies, but less so in transferring *the innovation process itself.* . . . This may be acceptable for a while in the case of countries at low levels of industrial development, but can soon become a constraint on capability building as countries need to develop autonomous innovative capabilities. (UNCTAD 1999, 44, emphasis added)

The most recent publication of UNCTAD (2002) is even more critical of the liberal approach to international economic policy and presents a distinctly gloomy analysis of the consequences for LDCs from the current modality of participation in the global trade and investment system.

Mainstream scholars in international business also reject as simplistic policy prescriptions that limit the role of government to encouraging liberalization and ensuring macroeconomic stability (Dunning 1997b; Dunning and Narula 1999; Ghauri and Buckley 2002; Narula and Dunning 2000). In a number of recent contributions, Dunning has stressed that precisely because globalization has increased the mobility and flexibility of multinational enterprises, it is particularly important for governments to promote the creation and upgrading of created assets that would enhance their location-bound advantages:

It is the responsibility of national administration to ensure the availability quality and effectiveness of location bound societal assets, which firms need to use jointly with their core advantages to produce goods and services. At one time, these assets mainly consisted of transport facilities and public utilities. Today they embrace all forms of educational and telecommunication infra-structure necessary to foster an efficient and modern innovation-led economy. (Dunning 1997b, 117–8)

In the particular context of LDC policy toward MNEs, Dunning and Narula (1999, 484) note that the role of governments has a broader scope, going beyond created assets of a general type to providing and upgrading created assets at an industry specific level (and also at specific locations within the country) including the creation of institutions to support the acquisition and creation of knowledge and wealth-creating assets. In the absence of these supporting policies and institution, it is unlikely that countries can benefit greatly from FDI inflows.

CONCLUDING REMARKS

In this paper we have focused on the change in the intellectual climate. Whether and to what degree it translates to pressure for a policy change is difficult to predict, although it is clear that policy change will not usually come about without strong academic and intellectual advocacy. However, we already observe a certain pressure toward policy notably among the second tier tigers. In a study of technological capabilities in emerging economies in Asia, Lall (1998) found that the second tier tigers, which had mostly relied heavily on FDI, had failed to develop a significant technological base of their own. South East Asian economies in particular have participated in the international economy largely as subcontractors and have experienced little technological spillover from the export sector to the rest of the economy (Wade 1998, 1537). Not surprisingly, as Lall (1998, 317) observes, these economies are now "conscious of the constraint of this strategy" (that is, heavy reliance on FDI) adding that they are "making efforts to upgrade from essentially low-level assembly to more value added manufacturing with deeper local roots." Lall utilizes a distinction between know-how and know-why to explain the nature of upgrading faced by these economies. Know-how refers to skills and operational knowledge relating to an existing production system that may be transferred by MNEs to less developed countries. Know-why represents a more advanced level of learning, generated by more risky research and experimentation that can result in core capabilities for the organization. Multinational activities are more likely to promote local know-how rather than know-why. The latter requires a more significant embeddedness of MNEs in the local economies with resources committed to developing local content and technological activities. A recent study by UNCTAD (2001) has shown that existing linkages within LDCs are rather shallow with MNEs using local companies only as second or third tier suppliers.

REFERENCES

Amsden, A. 1989. *Asia's Next Giant: South Korea and Late Industrialisation.* Oxford: Oxford University Press.

———. 1994. "Why Isn't the Whole World Experimenting with the East Asian Model to Develop? Review of the East Asian Miracle." *World Development* 22 (3): 627–34.

———. 2001. *The Rise of "The Rest": Challenges to the West from Late Industrializing Economies.* Oxford: Oxford University Press.

Amsden, A., and R. Van der Hoeven. 1996. "Manufacturing Output, Employment, and Real Wages in the 1980s: Labour's Loss until the Century's End." *Journal of Development Studies* 32 (4): 506–23.

Bell, M., and K. Pavitt. 1997. "Technological Accumulation and Industrial Growth: Contrasts between Developed and Developing Countries." In *Technology Globalisation and Economic Performance*, edited by D. Archibugi and J. Michie, 83–137. Cambridge: Cambridge University Press.

Buckley, P., and P. Ghauri, eds. 1999. *The Global Challenge for Multinational Enterprises: Managing Increasing Interdependence.* Amsterdam: Pergamon Press.

Chandler, A. D., and F. Redlich. 1961. "Recent Developments in American Business Administration and Their Conceptualization." *Business History Review* 35 (1): 1–27.

Dunning, J. 1997a. "Governments and Macro-Organization of Economic Activity: A Historical and Spatial Perspective." In *Governments, Globalization, and International Business*, edited by J. Dunning, 31–72. Oxford: Oxford University Press.

———. 1997b. "A Business Analytic Approach to Governments and Globalization." In *Governments, Globalization, and International Business*, edited by J. Dunning, 114–31. Oxford: Oxford University Press.

Dunning, J., and R. Narula. 1999. "Developing Countries Versus Multinationals in a Globalizing World: The Dangers of Falling Behind." In *The Global Challenge for Multinational Enterprises: Managing Increasing Interdependence*, edited by P. Buckley and P. Ghauri, 467–88. Amsterdam: Pergamon Press.

Forsgren, M. 2002. "Are Multinational Firms Good or Bad?" In *Critical Perspectives on Internationalization*, edited by V. Havila, M. Forsgren, and H. Hakansson, 29–58. Amsterdam: Pergamon Press.

Gabriele, A. 2001. "Science and Technology Policies, Industrial Reform, and Technological Progress in China: Can Socialist Property Rights Be Compatible with Technological Catching-Up?" United Nations Conference on Trade And Development (UNCTAD) Discussion Paper no. 155. Geneva: United Nations.

Ghauri, P., and P. Buckley. 2002. "Globalization and the End of Competition: A Critical Review of Rent-Seeking Multinational." In *Critical Perspectives on Internationalization*, edited by V. Havila, M. Forsgren, and H. Hakansson, 7–28. Amsterdam: Pergamon Press.

Gore, C. 2000. "The Rise and Fall of the Washington Consensus as a Paradigm for Developing Countries." *World Development* 28 (5): 789–804.

Gup, B. E., and D. Nam. 1999. "Thailand: A Tale of Sustained Growth and Then Collapse." In *International Banking Crisis: Large-Scale Failures, Massive Government Interventions*, edited by B. E. Gup, 57–68. Westport, Conn.: Quorum Books.

Havila, V., M. Forsgren, and H. Hakansson, eds. 2002. *Critical Perspectives on Internationalization*. Amsterdam: Pergamon Press.

Hobday, M. 1995. *Innovation in East Asia: The Challenge to Japan*. Cheltenham: Edward Elgar.

Hymer, S. 1972. "The Multinational Corporation and the Law of Uneven Development." In *Economics and World Order from the 1970s to the 1990s*, edited by J. N. Bhagwati, 113–40. London: Macmillan.

Ietto-Gillies, G. 2001. *Transnational Corporations: Fragmentation amidst Integration*. London: Routledge.

International Bank for Reconstruction and Development (IBRD). 1997. *The State in a Changing World: World Development Report, 1997.* Washington, D.C.: IBRD, iii.

Jenkins, R. 1999. "The Changing Relationship between Emerging Markets and Multinational Enterprises." *The Global Challenge for Multinational Enterprises: Managing Increasing Interdependence*, edited by P. Buckley and P. Ghauri, 489–508. Amsterdam: Pergamon Press.

Lall, S. 1994. "The East Asian Miracle: Does the Bell Toll for Industrial Strategy?" *World Development* 22 (4): 645–54.

———. 1997. "East Asia." In *Governments, Globalization, and International Business*, edited by J. Dunning, 406–30. Oxford: Oxford University Press.

———. 1998. "Technological Capabilities in Emerging Asia." *Oxford Development Studies* 26 (2): 213–45.

Lall, S., and M. Teubal. 1998. "'Market Stimulating' Technology Policies in Developing Countries: A Framework with Examples from East Asia." *World Development* 26 (8): 1369–85.

Nam, D., and B. E. Gup. 1999. "The Economic Crisis in South Korea." In *International Banking Crisis: Large-Scale Failures, Massive Government Interventions*, edited by B. E. Gup, 107–24. Westport, Conn.: Quorum Books.

Narula, R., and J. Dunning. 2000. "Industrial Development, Globalization, and Multinational Enterprises: New Realities for Developing Countries." *Oxford Development Studies* 28 (2): 141–66.

Ocampo, J. 2002. "Rethinking the Development Agenda." *Cambridge Journal of Economics* 26: 393–407.

Perez-Aleman, P. 2000. "Learning, Adjustment, and Economic Development: Transforming Firms, the State, and Associations in Chile." *World Development* 28 (1): 41–55.

Stiglitz, J. 2000. "Capital Market Liberalisation, Economic Growth, and Instability." *World Development* 28 (6): 1075–86.

———. 2002. *Globalization and Its Discontent.* London: Allen Lane.

United Nations Conference on Trade and Development (UNCTAD). 1992. *World Investment Report 1992: Transnational Corporations as Engines of Development.* Geneva: United Nations.

———. 1999. *World Investment Report 1999: Foreign Direct Investment and the Challenge of Development.* Geneva: United Nations.

———. 2000. *World Investment Report: Cross-Border Mergers and Acquisitions and Development.* Geneva: United Nations.

———. 2001. *World Investment Report 2001: Promoting Linkages.* Geneva: United Nations.

———. 2002. *Trade and Development Report 2002.* Geneva: United Nations.

Wade, R. 1990. *Governing the Market: Economic Theory and the Role of Government in East Asian Industrialization.* Princeton: Princeton University Press.

———. 1998. "The Asian Debt-and-Development Crisis of 1997: Causes and Consequences." *World Development* 26 (8): 1535–53.

———. 2001. "Is Globalization Making World Income Distribution More Equal?" LSE Development Studies Institute, Working Paper no. 01–01.

World Bank. 1993. *The East Asian Miracle: Economic Growth and Public Policy: A World Bank Policy Research Report.* Oxford: Oxford University Press.

———. 1999. *World Development Report 1998/9: Knowledge for Development.* Oxford: Oxford University Press.

Yamin, M. 1998. "The Dual Risks of Market Exchange and the Transition Process." In *Privatization, Enterprise Development, and Economic Reform: Experiences of Developing and Transitional Economies,* edited by P. Cook, C. Kirkpatrick, and F. Nixson, 19–32. Cheltenham: Edward Elgar.

CHAPTER 14

Institutions and Market Reforms: A Logical Guide for MNE Investments

Ram Mudambi and Pietro Navarra

INTRODUCTION

Emerging market economies have been the focus of increasing interest for multinational enterprises (MNEs) over the past decade. This interest has been fueled by market liberalization that has granted MNEs considerably expanded flexibility in their operations and allowed them to operate in many sectors from which they were formerly barred (Soutello-Alves 2001). Traditionally, MNEs were interested in emerging economies as markets for goods produced elsewhere, but increasingly they are being viewed as low-cost locations for platform manufacture reexport and remote service delivery (Hooke 2001). The nature and drivers of market liberalization and reform in emerging market economies is therefore of considerable interest to the managers of MNEs and to scholars studying these firms.

In this chapter we begin with the premise—well established in the economic regulation and public choice literature—that special interests will seek to use the government to obtain economic advantage at the expense of the general population—the phenomenon known as rent-seeking behavior. We apply the tools of economic theory to study the comparative politics of rent seeking in the context of economic reform. This investigation builds on some of our earlier work (Mudambi and Navarra 1999) and follows the path suggested by Persson and Tabellini (1999). Several scholars have recently undertaken projects to study the political determinants of economic policy changes. Alesina and Drazen (1991) suggest interpreting the timing of stabilization policies and in particular their postponement as a war of attrition. In this context, the expected time of stabilization is a function of characteristics of the economy including parameters meant to capture the degree of political polarization. In another important contribution, Fernandez and Rodrik (1991) construct a theoretical model in which politicians are seen as those resisting the implementation of economic reform because of uncertainty over the distribution of gains and losses associated with the reform process itself. They use trade liberalization as an example to argue that there can be a bias toward the status quo in those cases in which the individual gainers or losers from the reform cannot be identified beforehand.

Our interest in this study is the political economy of economic policy reform in recently emerging market countries. Several bases have been used to describe economic policy choice and performance in such economics. These include international circumstances, cultural context or heritage, characteristics of the state of bureaucracy, organization of interest groups, and the nature of the electoral and party systems. However, we limit our analysis to the following broad question: what are the effects of legislative and electoral institutions on the level and pace of the economic policy reform in emerging market countries? By economic reform we refer to market liberalization in general. Our contention is that differing electoral and legislative institutions can affect the pace of reform through their creation of differing levels of rent-seeking opportunities.

The chapter is structured as follows. We discuss and specify our theoretical hypotheses, then we describe the data used in the empirical analysis, present the econometric model, and comment on the results of the empirical investigation. Next we discuss the implications of our findings, and finally, we offer some concluding remarks.

THEORY: THREE DETERMINANTS OF RENT-SEEKING OPPORTUNITIES

Starting from the vote-maximizing, or majority-maximizing model of representative behavior, we assume that in order to affect policy outcomes special interests must be able to affect election outcomes, i.e., the probability of a candidate winning. The extent to which rent seeking can take place is a direct function of the ability of interest groups to affect electoral outcomes and legislative response to the resulting incentives. Those institutional arrangements that reduce the threshold level of political support required to elect or displace a representative will result in an increased level of the rent-seeking opportunities being provided. The three principal differences in electoral institutions addressed here are proportional and plurality representation rules, the size of the electoral district, and parliamentary and presidential regimes. For purposes of exposition, three subsections develop the theoretical impact of each.

Two electoral institutions, the number of seats (which is greatly influenced by whether the electoral system is governed by plurality or proportionality), and the number of districts are measures of district magnitude. As the number of seats increases or the number of districts increase, district magnitude declines. District magnitude has been the primary focus of the study of electoral districts in the political science literature (for a detailed survey, see Taagepera and Shugart 1989). However, the relationship between district magnitudes and policy outcomes has yet to be addressed. Larger district magnitudes give representatives greater autonomy from local or particularistic interest and the need to cultivate support by means of redistributive programs, rent transfers (Weingast, Shepsle, and Johnsen 1981). Our expectation is that district magnitude and the creation of rent-seeking opportunities by legislators are inversely related.

The Role of Electoral Systems: Proportionality versus Plurality in Electoral Systems

The focus here is between two general classes of electoral systems, proportional representation (PR) and plurality representation (PL). The distinction between PR and PL electoral systems represents the difference between single-seat and multi-seat districts. In single-seat districts only one representative is elected to represent the entire electorate. In a multi-seat district, voters elect two or more representatives, reducing the effective size of the district. Consequently, in PR electoral systems the district magnitude is greater the larger the number of elected representatives per district, *ceteris paribus*.

Single-seat and multi-seat districts present different electoral incentives. In the single-seat district, which will predominate under the PL system, a representative will campaign on more general issues that affect a larger proportion of voters. In other words, candidates in single-seat districts will move toward the center of the policy space as to do otherwise would mean surrendering the majority policy position and reducing the probability of election. In multi-seat districts, under the PR system, the candidate may select a policy position that benefits a minority interest group in the district's population. Indeed in PR systems a candidate may be elected by appealing to a particularistic segment of the electorate sufficient in size to win one of the seats awarded in the multi-member district (Hinich and Ordeshook 1970; Navarra and Lignana 1997). Since PR systems create incentives for politicians to satisfy the demands of the particularistic interest group that elected them, in PR systems policies that favor rent-seeking interest will be more likely to be supported by a majority of legislators. Obviously, this policy fragmentation results in PR systems being less likely to pass general interest economic reforms.

There is a large literature that concludes that the behavior of legislators is motivated by their constituencies' particularistic objectives. For example, legislators intervene in the budgetary process to increase or defend particular programs that yield net benefits to their districts (Cain, Ferejohn, and Fiorina

1987; Fiorina 1977; Mayhew 1974). Marshall and Weingast (1988) employ an industrial organization model of legislatures to demonstrate how committees develop as a method to allow legislators to benefit from the gains to logrolling. In their model, legislators bid for committee memberships that have influence over the programs that most benefit their own constituents. This results in committees dominated by preference outliers, increasing the demand for government favors. The more specialized or particularistic the constituency the more polarized the policy stance of their representative. Thus, electoral systems should affect the types of policies selected and their durability.

A simple model may be used to demonstrate how the influence of particularistic interest groups increases as the effective size of interest groups declines. It is assumed that candidates are interested in generating a sufficient number of votes for election, or maximizing the probability of election. In the model the probability of election is positively related to the magnitude and allocation of rents to constituents, which benefits particularistic interest, and the level of economic reform undertaken, which benefits the general population. It is assumed that while the elected representative captures all the political support resulting from the provision of constituent services, reform generates benefits to the entire population regardless of whom individuals supported in the election. The number of seats in the electoral district is denoted by N, which takes a value equal to or greater than one. The representative's resource constraint is written as

$$T = RS \tag{14.1}$$

where RS is the effort allocated to providing particularistic constituent services or rent-seeking opportunities and GP is the effort allocated to general interest policies. Since it is assumed that the representative's objective function is to maximize the probability of election, the probability of election is given by

$$p = p \ [RS,GP/N] \ = \ p[T\text{-}GP,GP/N] \ p_1>0, \ p_2 >0, \ p_{11}<0, \ p_{22}<0 \tag{14.2}$$

Both RS and GP are positively related to the probability of re-election. However, the representative captures only $(1/N)^{th}$ of benefits of time allocated to general interest policies, since these function as nonrival public goods that benefit supporters and nonsupporters alike.

Maximizing the reelection probability function with respect to the choice variable, GP, results in

$$p_2/p_1 \ = \ N^* \tag{14.3}$$

Since both RS and GP are inputs into the probability of election function, as N increases, the marginal contribution of GP to the probability of election must rise and that of *RS* must fall. This means that an increase in the number of seats contested in a given electoral district will result in a reallocation of time away from the formulation of general interest policies to the generation of rent-seeking opportunities for particular groups of constituents. (This can be shown more formally by totally differentiating [3].)

Increasing the number of seats in a multi-seat district increases the incentive to support particularistic policies. Elected representatives in districts with a larger number of seats will, *ceteris paribus*, allocate a greater proportion of effort to the particularistic interest of constituents. This implies that PL systems with single-seat districts ($N = 1$) are less responsive to the rent-seeking demands of particularistic interest than PR systems with multi-seat districts.

The Number of Electoral Districts

Since most countries organize political representation on a geographical basis, election winners are determined by both the quantity of votes cast for each party and the spatial distribution of votes. The interaction of the number of votes and their geographical distribution determines the distribution of political power between political parties, voter groups, and geographical areas. The general rule is that larger district magnitudes result in a greater divergence of constituent interests.

As with increasing the number of seats in a given sized district, as district size declines polarization of party support increases, yielding increasingly homogeneous voter preferences. Larger districts will have a greater diversity of party support and a broader array of voter preferences. Smaller polarized districts will demand more particularistic legislation from elected representatives. As with multi-seat districts, smaller districts increase the incentives for elected representatives to support particularistic policies benefiting the narrow constituent interest. In both cases, particularistic electoral rules spawn particularistic politics (Cowhey and McCubbins 1995; Kernell 1991; Ramseyer and Rosenbluth 1993).

Presidential versus Parliamentary Systems

A fundamental difference between parliamentary and presidential election systems is that legislators select prime ministers while presidents are directly elected. As a consequence, in a presidential system with direct elections the chief executive will be more responsive to the general electorate, while in parliamentary systems where the prime minister is selected by the legislature, the chief executive will be more responsive to the demands of legislative representatives. Thus, in presidential regimes executive survival does not depend on support from a majority of representatives in the legislature. This reduces the incentives for the president to use policy legislation to maintain a stable coalition in the legislature. However, stable coalitions are crucial to the government's continuation in parliamentary systems. Coalition stability depends upon the behavior of elected representatives in the legislature. As discussed above, there is a large literature that concludes that legislators' behavior is driven by the particularistic interest of their constituencies. Persson and Tabellini (1999) have analyzed the effect of both the presidential-parliamentary and the pluralistic-proportional electoral systems on government size. They find that presidential regimes and pluralistic election rules result in smaller government.

Our expectation is that directly elected presidents are more resistant to special interest demands for government intervention and are therefore more likely to support policies that benefit the general population over particularistic interest. Thus, presidential systems will have a lower incidence of rent-seeking opportunities. Conversely, parliamentary regimes are expected to have elected representatives who are motivated to create and consolidate government-created rents for constituents and will resist economic reforms that threaten to dismantle the rent-generating apparatus.

DATA, ESTIMATION, AND RESULTS

Developed above were the theoretical relationships between three electoral institutions and the creation of rent-seeking opportunities. We turn now to the empirical testing of the hypothesized relationships.

We start with the basic contention, well accepted in the literature, that rent-seeking opportunities are created by imposing restrictions on markets (Kreuger 1974, 1992; Tullock 1967). Thus, the lower the level of restrictions on markets, and consequently, the higher the level of economic freedom, the lower the level of rent-seeking opportunities. Thus, our dependent variable, the magnitude of rent-seeking opportunities, is a measure of economic freedom taken from Gwartney, Lawson, and Block (GLB) (1995). This index has 17 components divided across 4 categories: money and inflation, taxation, government regulation, and international exchange. Complete details regarding the construction of the index are provided in Appendix A.

We examine both the level of this index of freedom of the economy's markets as well as the amount of reform, measured as the change in this index over a period of time. The economic freedom measure is for 1995 and the economic reform is for the period 1990–95. The data are for 29 countries in economic transition. The institutional and demographic variables were gathered from the CIA's *World Fact Book* (1998) and the World Bank's *Development Report* (1996). Summary statistics relating to the data set are presented in Table 14.1. The list of all countries in the data set is provided in Appendix B.

Two equations were estimated, one with the level of economic freedom as the dependent variable and one with the change in economic freedom as the dependent variable. The two estimation equations are

Table 14.1
Summary Statistics*

Variable	Mean	S.D.	Minimum	Maximum
REF	5.0448	1.3721	1.9	7.1
CREF	22.9655	34.4834	-39.0	114.0
PL	0.1034	0.3099	0.0	1.0
PRES	0.5172	0.5085	0.0	1.0
NDIST	53.7309	72.5326	1.0000	299.0000
LITER (%)	88.6379	9.3744	66.7	99.0
EASTEUR	0.1724	0.3844	0.0	1.0
LATIN	0.4827	0.5085	0.0	1.0
MILSP (%)	2.5072	1.7393	0.9	8.0
YRSIND (years)	105.2759	75.4992	6.0	189.0

* The data are for 29 emerging market economies (see Appendix B).

$$REF = f (POLINST, DEM) \qquad (14.4)$$

$$CREF = f (POLINST, DEM) \qquad (14.5)$$

where REF is the level of economic freedom in 1995 and the inverse of the level of rent-seeking opportunities. CREF is the change in the level of economic freedom from 1990 through 1995 and is the inverse of the change in the level of rent-seeking opportunities over this period. CREF can be viewed as a measure of reform (or deterioration) over this period. POLINST is the vector of measures of political institutions. The three measures we are interested in are the system of electoral rules (PR vs. PL), the number of electoral districts, and the organization of the executive (presidential vs. parliamentary). DEM is the vector of demographic control variables. The complete details of all variables used in the estimation are provided in Appendix B.

Equations (4) and (5) are estimated with OLS. However, the countries in the sample substantially differ in size, ranging from Malta to Brazil, and there is strong evidence of heteroskedasticity. Consequently, White's heteroskedasticity-consistent variance-covariance was used to estimate standard errors. This procedure solves the problem, since the Breusch-Pagan test is now passed in all cases.

In estimating equation (4), the regressand is REF, the level of economic freedom or the inverse of the level of rent-seeking opportunities. However, we encounter a problem in that we find that the dummy variable for a plurality electoral system (PL) is highly correlated with the dummy variable for a presidential system of government (PRES). Hence when we use both of them as regressors, we expect that one or both of them will appear insignificant due to inflated standard errors. We designate the model that includes both PL and PRES as Model 1. The model that includes PL but excludes PRES is designated Model 2. The model that includes PRES but excludes PL is designated to be Model 3. The estimates of all three models are presented in Table 14.2.

We carry out a number of specification tests to choose from among the three models. While all three models fit the data relatively well, all the specification tests point to Model 2, the inclusion of PL and the exclusion of PRES, as the appropriate specification. Model 2 provides the best fit to the

Table 14.2
Estimating the Level of Reform in 1995: Heteroskedasticity-corrected OLS Estimates[1]

Regressand: REF

Regressor	MODEL 1 Coefficient ('t' stat.)	MODEL 2 Coefficient ('t' stat.)	MODEL 3 Coefficient ('t' stat.)
Constant	-3.675 (1.79)*	-4.333 (2.53)**	-5.794 (2.31)**
PL	2.937 (6.35)***	2.465 (6.37)***	-
PRES	-0.895 (1.25)	-	1.989 (3.31)***
NDIST	-0.0059 (2.99)***	-0.0048 (2.56)**	0.0011 (0.30)
LITER	0.111 (4.58)***	0.119 (5.82)***	0.139 (4.63)***
EASTEUR	-2.653 (4.47)***	-2.820 (5.40)***	-3.671 (5.24)***
LATIN	1.902 (2.90)***	1.011 (3.23)***	-1.020 (1.69)
MILSP	-0.0112 (2.84)***	-0.0112 (2.84)***	-0.0133 (2.51)**
YRSIND	-0.0084 (2.40)**	-0.0087 (2.73)***	-0.0111 (3.02)***
DIAGNOSTICS			
Adjusted R^2	0.6597	0.6682	0.5212
F stat; (d.f.)	7.79***; (8,20)	9.06***; (7,21)	5.35***; (7, 21)
Log-likelihood	-29.3045	-29.6456	-34.9637
Restricted log-likelihood	-49.8136	-49.8136	-49.8136
Sum of Squared Errors	12.8124	13.1174	18.9292
Exclusion Restriction: F(1,20)	-	0.4761 (p=0.498)	9.5482 (p=0.006)
Akaike Information Criterion	2.6420	2.596	2.963
Breusch-Pagan Test: χ^2; d.f.; ('p' value)	6.0045; (8); (0.6467)	4.4726; (7); (0.7240)	9.9741; (7); (0.1900)

Notes: [1]'t' statistics are computed using White's heteroskedasticity consistent variance-covariance matrix.
* = coefficient significant at the 10% level.
** = coefficient significant at the 5% level.
*** = coefficient significant at the 1% level.

data in terms of adjusted R^2 as well as the F statistic. The Akaike Information Criterion, a more stringent degrees-of-freedom test, also points to Model 2 as the best specification. Finally, we test the exclusion restrictions. We find that the exclusion of PRES from Model 1 cannot be rejected (the resulting F statistic has a probability value of over 49 percent). However, the exclusion of PL from Model 1 is conclusively rejected (the resulting F statistic has a probability value of less that 1 percent). Excluding PRES from Model 1 and including PL yields Model 2, our preferred specification. Thus, while PRES appears positive and highly significant in Model 3, in our data set we are unable to disentangle its effects from those of PL.

We will discuss the results of Model 2 in detail. We begin by noting that our estimates are extremely good, both in terms of fit and in terms of statistical significance. The adjusted R^2 exceeds 66 percent and virtually all our regressors are found to be extremely statistically significant. We find that PL is positive and highly significant. Thus, a plurality electoral system creates a lower level of rent-seeking opportunities than a proportional system, as measured by a higher associated level of economic freedom, namely, reliance on markets. Second, the number of electoral districts (NDIST) is significant and negative. A larger number of electoral districts, *ceteris paribus*, reduce economic freedom and increase rent-seeking opportunities.

Turning to the demographic control variables, we find that they are all statistically significant at the 1 percent level in Model 2. First, increased literacy is associated with increased economic freedom and a reduced level of rent-seeking opportunities provided by the government. A better-educated electorate is more knowledgeable about the actual intent and consequences of special interest legislation and therefore more resistant to it. This result lends additional support to the positive externality argument for subsidizing education. Second, the negative sign on the dummy variable for Eastern Europe is evidence of the early stages of transition from a directed economy. Indeed, the high level of government market intervention is a remnant of the former dominance of rent-seeking interests. Third, the positive sign on the Latin American dummy variable indicates that these countries have relatively lower levels of rent-seeking opportunities. Fourth, the military's share of gross domestic product (GDP) is associated with significantly lower levels of economic freedom and higher rent-seeking opportunities. This may be evidence that military budgets are viewed as targets for rent seeking. Finally, increasing the years of independence, as a measure of the time rent-seeking interests have had to influence government to create opportunities, reduces the level of economic freedom. This supports the contention that regardless of the other institutional arrangements, a stable set of special interest groups will be able to influence the government to bring about creeping market intervention. Thus, the longer such special interests are undisturbed, the higher the associated level of rent-seeking opportunities.

In estimating equation (5), where the regressand is CREF or the change in the level of economic freedom over the 1990–95 period, we encounter the same specification problem with regard to the regressors PL and PRES. As above, we set up three models—one including both PL and PRES, designated Model 4; one including PL, but excluding PRES, designated Model 5; and one excluding PL, but including PRES, designated Model 6. Carrying out a similar set of specification tests, we select Model 5, which includes PL and excludes PRES. Again, while PRES is significant and positive in Model 6, its effects cannot be disentangled from those of PL. All these results are presented in Table 14.3.

The estimation of Model 5 explains just over 35 percent of the variation in the dependent variable. The inferior performance of Model 5 relative to Model 2 may be due to the fact that the independent variables are measured as levels rather than changes. However, in an absolute sense the fit is still very good and the F-statistic remains statistically significant.

For the variables of interest, the coefficient of the plurality system dummy, PL, is significantly positive while that of the number of electoral districts is significantly negative. Thus, plurality systems exhibit greater resistance to special interest manipulation than proportional systems in the area of reform as well. Further, the number of electoral districts is positively related to the success of special interest groups in blocking reform and maintaining rent-seeking opportunities.

Turning to the demographic variables, we find that literacy remains significant, but only at the 10 percent level, while the Eastern European dummy now is positive and significant at the 5 percent level. This suggests that while Eastern European countries are starting from a lower base level of economic freedom, they are making relatively more rapid progress in reducing rent-seeking opportunities. Military spending as a percentage of GDP remains negative and highly significant, suggesting that larger military establishments increase resistance to economic reform. Neither the Latin American dummy nor the period of independence appears to have a significant effect on the pace of reform.

DISCUSSION

We are interested in analyzing the important reality of the rising consequences of alternative legislative and electoral institutions on economic policy outcomes in terms of the opportunities for rent seeking. In this paper we applied economic theory and its methodological tools to study some of these effects. In particular, we analyzed the impact of alternative legislative and electoral institutions on both the level and the pace of change of rent-seeking opportunities (interpreted to be inversely related to market liberalization) in emerging market countries. We discovered that a plurality system of representation and a smaller number of large electoral districts are both elements that favor the process of market liberalization in transition economies, and

Table 14.3
Estimating the Change in the Level of Reform 1990–1995:
Heteroskedasticity-corrected OLS Estimates[1]

Regressand: CREF

Regressor	MODEL 4 Coefficient ('t' stat.)	MODEL 5 Coefficient ('t' stat.)	MODEL 6 Coefficient ('t' stat.)
Constant	-85.563 (1.51)	-88.603 (1.88)*	-118.519 (2.06)*
PL	45.659 (3.05)***	43.480 (5.78)***	-
PRES	-4.136 (0.21)	-	40.713 (3.96)***
NDIST	-0.299 (4.45)***	-0.294 (4.47)***	-0.190 (2.43)**
LITER	1.226 (1.63)	1.262 (1.95)*	1.662 (2.20)**
EASTEUR	40.751 (2.06)*	39.981 (2.26)**	24.928 (1.30)
LATIN	-0.054 (0.002)	-4.171 (0.29)	-45.493 (2.48)**
MILSP	-0.358 (2.94)***	-0.358 (2.93)***	-0.325 (2.46)**
YRSIND	-0.019 (0.15)	-0.021 (0.17)	-0.063 (0.51)
DIAGNOSTICS			
Adjusted R^2	0.3214	0.3534	0.2945
F stat; (d.f.)	2.66**; (8,20)	3.19**; (7,21)	2.67**; (7,21)
Log-likelihood	-132.8137	-132.8195	-134.0849
Restricted log-likelihood	-143.3143	-143.3143	-143.3143
Sum of Squared Errors	16138.8	16145.3	27617.6
Exclusion Restriction: F(1,20)	-	0.0080 (p=0.929)	14.2251 (p=0.001)
Akaike Information Criterion	9.780	9.712	9.799
Breusch-Pagan Test: χ^2; (d.f.); ('p' value)	6.4327; (8); (0.5989)	6.2712; (7); (0.5085)	4.4442; (7); (0.7274)

Notes: [1]'t' statistics are computed using White's heteroskedasticity consistent variance-covariance matrix.
* = coefficient significant at the 10% level.
** = coefficient significant at the 5% level.
*** = coefficient significant at the 1% level.

thus reduce rent-seeking opportunities. On the other hand, a proportional system of representation and a greater number of small electoral districts hinder economic reform.

Our results are in line with the predictions of theory outlined in section 2. Therefore they can be interpreted as the results of the different political incentives produced by alternative political institutions. Some legislative and electoral institutions generate greater incentives to implement particularistic policies to the detriment of the general interests of voters. Legislators confronted with such institutions are expected to hamper the path to economic reform. Efforts to free markets represent a reduction in politicians' ability to use the state to carve out divisible benefits for important constituents. When elected representatives are given incentives to serve particularistic interests, market liberalization directly threatens the viability of electoral strategies that are based on serving these interests.

The empirical analysis was carried out for both the level and the pace of economic reform. Examining Tables 14.2 and 14.3, we note that the two variables that refer to electoral institutions (PL vs. PR and the number of electoral districts) maintain the expected sign and statistical impact on the market liberalization process. The difference in legislative institutions under observation (presidential vs. parliamentary regimes) cannot be disentangled from the electoral system measure in our data set. However, specification tests indicate that the electoral system (PL vs. PR) dominates the legislative regime in terms of its effects on the level and pace of reform. This suggests that election rules and the districting mechanism play a more important role than the organization of the executive in the dynamics of economic reforms.

This paper would be incomplete if we did not discuss our choice of the economic freedom index proposed by GLB (1995). We are aware of the large literature related to the measurement of freedom from Banks and Textor (1963) and Gastil (1972) to more recent works published by De Haan and Siermann (1995, 1998). This literature has focused on the relationship between economic liberty and economic growth, and has been dominated by a debate over two main related difficulties: the lack of a clear definition of economic freedom and of a unique methodology to measure it.[1] An analysis of this issue goes beyond the limited objectives of this paper. Therefore, we limit ourselves to very briefly explaining why we selected the GLB index. As opposed to most of the earlier and contemporary efforts, GLB aims at specifically measuring *economic* freedom, separating it from political and social freedom. This is not to say that the latter are of less or more importance, but just that we have to be careful in understanding the conceptualizations that can be made about different schemes of values and use those that are most appropriate. In this paper we are concerned with market liberalization processes and therefore pay more attention to the elements of economic liberty rather than political and social liberty.

CONCLUDING REMARKS

The empirical results support the theoretical predictions. Plurality electoral systems are more resistant to the political demands of rent seeking as compared to proportional systems. Fewer electoral districts reduce the incentives of elected representatives to create rent-seeking opportunities. However, the regime type, presidential or parliamentary, emerges as less important than the electoral system. This inquiry is seen as the first step in understanding the position of importance electoral systems play in determining the effectiveness of special interest group demands.

We have two recommendations for future research. First, a more complete modeling of electoral institutions with an emphasis on voting rules would significantly expand our understanding of the relationship between electoral rules and the effectiveness of particularistic interest in creating rent-seeking opportunities. Second, testing the implication of electoral institutions with an expanded set of countries will determine if the empirical results reported here may be generalized or are unique to countries with emerging economies.

Our empirical results support the argument that the Eastern European countries are moving toward a new equilibrium position with lower levels of market intervention (and associated rent seeking) as evidenced by the positive sign on a dummy variable for Eastern European countries in our estimation of reform. This is good news as it demonstrates the possibility of reversing rent gains and fostering the economic growth that results from reliance on the more efficient market mechanisms to coordinate economic activity. Our results reemphasize the importance of high levels of literacy in maintaining the control of the citizenry over elected representatives. Finally, we suggest that military establishments have both direct costs in terms of explicit expenditures as well as indirect costs as targets of efficiency reducing rent seeking.

The results we report in this paper provide some general guidelines for managers planning investments in emerging market economies. Generally, MNEs prefer a more liberal, market-focused economy. Therefore, institutions that favor market-oriented reforms should be positive factors in their location decisions. In this context, some well known positive factors like the level of literacy functions in multiple positive roles—both as an indicator of higher local demand and skills and as an indicator of the persistence of market reforms. Military institutions and long-standing local vested interests will typically be inimical to MNE goals.

ACKNOWLEDGMENTS

This chapter represents a modified and rewritten topic, an earlier version of which appeared in *Public Choice*, vol. 112 (1): 185–202. The authors wish to thank Sebastiano Bavetta and Bernard Grofman for stimulating earlier discussions of the topic. The present chapter has benefited from the comments of one of the anonymous reviewers. The usual disclaimer applies.

Appendix A
Composition of the Index of Economic Freedom

The index of economic freedom is based on the economic freedom survey conducted by Gwartney, Lawson, and Block (1995). The index has 17 components divided across four categories: money and inflation, taxation, government operations and regulations, and international exchange. Component weighting is a major challenge in constructing such indices. They construct three different indices following different component weightings. One weights each component equally. A second is based upon expert surveys of which components are most important, generally speaking. A third weights components according to the judgment of country experts regarding the importance of the different components. We used the average of the three different indices in this paper.

1. Money and Inflation (protection of money as a store of value and medium of exchange):
   a. Average annual growth rate of the money supply during the last five years minus the potential growth rate of real GDP
   b. Standard deviation of the annual inflation rate during the last five years
   c. Freedom of citizens to own a foreign currency bank account domestically
   d. Freedom of citizens to maintain a bank account abroad
2. Government Operations and Regulations (freedom to decide what is produced and consumed):
   a. Government general consumption expenditures as % of GDP
   b. The role and presence of government-operated enterprises
   c. Price controls—the extent that businesses are free to set their own prices
   d. Freedom of private businesses and cooperatives to compete in markets
   e. Equality of citizens under the law and access of citizens to a nondiscriminatory judiciary
   f. Freedom from government regulations and policies that cause negative real interest rates
3. Takings and Discriminatory Taxation (freedom to keep what you earn):
   a. Transfers and subsidies as % of GDP
   b. Top marginal tax rate (and income threshold at which it applies)
   c. The use of conscripts to obtain military personnel
4. Restraints on International Exchange (freedom of exchange with foreigners):
   a. Taxes on international trade as % of exports plus imports
   b. Difference between the official exchange rate and the black market rate
   c. Actual size of trade sector compared to the expected size
   d. Restrictions on the freedom of citizens to engage in capital transactions with foreigners

Appendix B
Variables Used in the Estimates and Their Sources

Variable	DEFINITION AND SOURCE
REF	level of economic reform—1995 (Gwartney, Lawson, and Block 1995)
CREF	change in economic reform—1990—95 (Gwartney, Lawson, and Block 1995)
PL	dummy, 1 if PL, 0 if PR (Grofman and Reynolds 2000)
PRES	dummy, 1 if presidential system, 0 if parliamentary system (Grofman and Reynolds 2000)
NDIST	number of electoral districts per million registered voters (CIA *World Factbook* 1998)
LITER	literacy rate—% of population over age 15 who can read and write (CIA *World Factbook* 1998)
EASTEUR	dummy, 1 if East European country, 0 otherwise
LATIN	dummy, 1 if Latin American country, 0 otherwise
LILSP	1995 military spending as a percentage of GDP (CIA *World Factbook* 1998)
YRSIND	years of independence (CIA *World Factbook* 1998). Year of independence set as 1989 for East European countries

The countries in the data set are Argentina, Bolivia, Botswana, Brazil, Chile, Colombia, Costa Rica, the Czech Republic, Dominican Republic, Ecuador, Greece, Hungary, Iran, Jordan, Malaysia, Malta, Mexico, Panama, Paraguay, Peru, Poland, Romania, Slovakia, South Korea, Syria, Tunisia, Turkey, Uruguay, and Venezuela.

NOTE

1. Papers by De Haan and Siermann (1995) and Scully and Slottje (1991) provide useful surveys of the literature on democracy and economic growth.

REFERENCES

Alesina, A., and A. Drazen. 1991. "Why Are Stabilizations Delayed?" *American Economic Review* 81 (5): 1170–88.

Banks, A., and R. Textor. 1963. *A Cross-Polity Survey.* Cambridge, Mass.: M.I.T. Press.

Cain, B., J. Ferejohn, and M. Fiorina. 1987. *The Personal Vote: Constituency Service and Electoral Interdependence.* Cambridge: Cambridge University Press.

Carey, J., and M. Shugart. 1995. "Incentives to Cultivate a Personal Vote: A Rank Ordering of Electoral Formulas." *Electoral Studies* 14: 231–48.

Central Intelligence Agency. 1998. *World Fact Book.* Washington, D.C.: Central Intelligence Agency.

Cowhey, P., and M. McCubbins. 1995. *Structure and Policy in Japan and the United States.* New York: Cambridge University Press.

Crisp, B. 1997. "Electoral Rules and Government Spending Patterns in Latin America: Institutional Determinants of Rational Behavior." Paper presented at the annual meeting of the American Political Science Association, August 1997, Washington, D.C.

De Haan, J., and C.L.J. Siermann. 1995. "New Evidence on the Relationship between Democracy and Economic Growth." *Public Choice* 86: 175–95.

———. 1998. "Further Evidence on the Relationship between Economic Freedom and Economic Growth." *Public Choice* 95: 363–80.

Eaton, K. 1998. *The Politics of Tax Reform: Economic Policy Making in Presidential Democracy.* Ph.D. diss., Yale University.

Fernandez, R., and D. Rodrik. 1991. "Resistance to Reform: Status Quo Bias in the Presence of Individual-Specific Uncertainty." *American Economic Review* 81: 1146–55.

Fiorina, M. 1977. *Congress: Keystone of the Washington Establishment.* New Haven, Conn.: Yale University Press.

Gastil, R. D. 1972. *Freedom in the World: Political Rights and Civil Liberties.* Westport, Conn.: Greenwood Press.

Grofman, B., and A. Reynolds. 2000. "Electoral Systems and the Art of Constitutional Engineering: An Inventory of Main Findings." In *Rules and Reason: Perspectives on Constitutional Political Economy*, edited by R. Mudambi, P. Navarra, and G. Sobbrio. New York: Cambridge University Press.

Gudgin, G., and P. J. Taylor. 1979. *Seats, Votes, and the Spatial Organization of Elections.* London: Pion.

Gwartney, J., R. Lawson, and W. Block. 1995. *Economic Freedom of the World.* Toronto: The Fraser Institute.

Haggard, S., and R. Kaufman. 1995. *The Political Economy of Democratic Transition.* Princeton, N.J.: Princeton University Press.

Hausmann, R. 1998. *Latin America after a Decade of Reforms.* Washington, D.C.: Inter-American Development Bank.

Hinich, M. J., and P. C. Ordeshook. 1970. "Plurality Maximization vs. Vote Maximization: A Spatial Analysis with Variable Participation." *American Political Science Review* 64: 772–91.

Hooke, J. C. 2001. *Emerging Markets: A Practical Guide for Corporations, Lenders, and Investors.* New York: John Wiley and Sons.

Huntington, S. P. 1968. *Political Order in Changing Societies.* New Haven, Conn.: Yale University Press.

Johnston, R. J., and D. J. Rossiter. 1982. "Constituency Building, Political Representation, and Electoral Bias in Urban England." In *Geography and the Urban Environment: Volume 5*, edited by D. T. Herbert and R. J. Johnston. Chichester, England: Wiley.

Kernell, S. 1991. *Parallel Politics: Economic Policy-Making in Japan and the United States.* Washington, D.C.: The Brookings Institution.

Kreuger, A. O. 1974. "The Political Economy of the Rent-Seeking Society." *American Economic Review* 64: 291–303.

———. 1992. *Economic Policy Reform in Developing Countries.* Cambridge, Mass.: Blackwell.

Marshall, W., and B. Weingast. 1988. "The Industrial Organization of Congress; or Why Legislators, Like Firms, Are Not Organized as Markets." *Journal of Political Economy* 96 (1): 132–63.

Mayhew, D. 1974. *Congress: The Electoral Connection.* New Haven, Conn.: Yale University Press.

Mezey, M. 1985. "Third World Legislatures." In *The Handbook of Legislative Research.* Cambridge: Harvard University Press.

Mudambi, R., and P. Navarra. 1999. "A Complete Model of Strategic Alliances in the Context of Electoral Reform." *Discussion Papers in Economics and Management,* no. 411, University of Reading, U.K.

Navarra, P., and D. Lignana. 1997. "The Strategic Behavior of the Italian Left in a Risk-Sharing Framework." *Public Choice* 93: 131–48.

Persson, T., and G. Tabellini. 1999. "The Size and Scope of Government: Comparative Politics with Rational Politicians." *European Economic Review* 43: 699–735.

Ramseyer, M., and F. Rosenbluth. 1993. *Japan Political Marketplace.* Cambridge: Harvard University Press.

Scully, G. W., and D. J. Slottje. 1991. "Ranking Economic Liberty across Countries." *Public Choice* 69: 121–52.

Shugart, M., and J. Carey. 1992. *Presidents and Assemblies.* New York: Cambridge University Press.

Soutello-Alves, L. E. 2001. "A View from the South." *OECD Observer,* 3 May.

Taagepera, R., and M. Shugart. 1989. *Seats and Votes: The Effects and Determinants of Electoral Systems.* New Haven, Conn.: Yale University Press.

Taylor, P. J., and G. Gudgin. 1976. "The Statistical Basis of Decision Making in Electoral Districting." *Environment and Planning* 8: 43–58.

Tullock, G. 1967. "The Welfare Costs of Tariffs, Monopolies, and Theft." *Western Economic Journal* 5: 224–32.

Waterbury, J. 1992. "The Heart of the Matter? Public Enterprise and the Adjustment Process." In *The Politics of Economic Adjustments,* edited by S. Haggard and R. Kaufman. Princeton, N.J.: Princeton University Press.

Weingast, B. R., K. A. Shepsle, and C. Johnsen. 1981. "The Political Economy of Benefits and Costs: A Neo-classical Approach to Distributive Politics." *Journal of Political Economy* 89 (4): 642–64.

World Bank. 1996. *Development Report.* Washington, D.C.: World Bank.

CHAPTER 15

On Economic Liberalization in India

Rose M. Prasad

INTRODUCTION

The purpose of this essay is to offer an external observer's impressions—based on occasional observations of changes in the marketplace, especially in the cities in southern India, 1991–2001—and to compare these impressions to selected published literature, raise some relevant questions, and discuss them in light of market liberalization. The paper makes no claims to either a field or a longitudinal study. The narrative is set in the 1990s in the context of southern India. The impressions are related to market liberalization in India. The bases of the impressions are the author's observations of scores of retail shops and a few department stores whose shelves are full of packaged goods bearing local, national, and international brand names. The retail shops in the Indian cities of Bangalore and Coimbatore are ubiquitous. The same is probably true in many other towns and cities in India. Formal visits included ones to a few larger industrial firms, and several smaller enterprises engaged in a gamut of secondary and tertiary industries—producing clocks, gold jewelry, knitting needles, motorcycle frames, news printing, silk brocades, and watches. There has been a noticeable change[1] in India in the wake of the liberalization of economic activities.

SIGNIFICANCE

When personal observations are juxtaposed with the research data as reported in the literature of the 1990s, there arises an inarguable premise: Economic and market liberalization have had positive benefits. To put it simply, economic liberalization, by definition, is a change in economic and industrial policies by a government in a country or region. Changes are twofold: One is legislative action for either the removal or reduction of restrictions on banking, currency transactions, financial markets, and imports. The other is privatization of public sector enterprises[2] that have historically played a vital role in many developing and developed countries in building up the physical and institutional infrastructure of a geographic region. The Shannon Area, in the Republic of Ireland, in the 1970s is a sterling example of the success of the public sector in an English-speaking nation. The Republic of Ireland has been a member of the European Community since 1973, and is now a member of the European Union (EU) with the euro as the national currency. We make no claims to either a field or a longitudinal study, or any grounding on the transaction cost economics.

Our focus is on emerging India in the 1990s. One ponders the need for public enterprises in the British era in the first place.[3] That public sector industrial enterprises are inefficient is often treated as an equivalent to the post-1989 argument that governmental bodies need undertake no planning. A recent empirical study (Saez and Yang 2001) makes a compelling argument for the role of the state in economic planning in the twenty-first century in two of the world's most populous and low-income nations—China and India. These two nations are not only low-income countries, but poverty in both envelops more than 51 percent of the total population compared with about 15 percent in the Latin American countries. Of course, the ruling parties in both China and India have long recognized the enormity of their demographic problems.

The central postulate of economic liberalization, as demonstrated recently by Pitlik (2002), is that when property rights are secured, and when there is freedom for individuals to engage in economic transactions (buy and sell goods or services), there will be a solid foundation for economic prosperity for the entire country. This tenet is generally accepted by almost all nations. Over the past two decades, India has been slowly, but gradually, privatizing its public enterprises, and liberalizing its earlier tight grip on the vast economy. Liberalization efforts tend to make the country context more conducive to foreign direct investment (FDI). The pace in India accelerated in the 1990s, the post–Berlin Wall era. Inward direct foreign investment (DFI) in both China and India significantly increased during the 1990s. The impact on the host country is rather difficult to measure. A recent study (Chakraborty and Basu 2001) that employs a structural co-integration model—with a vector correction mechanism—indicates that, in India, the causality is from gross domestic product (GDP) to DFI, that (import) trade liberalization has had some positive short-run impact on the flow of inward direct foreign investment, and that DFI tends to be labor displacing. Liberalization is a complex process. As Reed (2002) sums it up, "The reform process seems to have escalated to a new height." The momentum to privatize the previous government sector industrial enterprises on the one hand, and to liberalize the economy on the other, in India, is perhaps also due to the technology-driven competition that has spurred international production and trade worldwide.

Liberalization of trade and investment rules by governments has been occurring in national economies of the world for many years. Were one to mark off the 1970s on a time line, the first stage can be said to have begun with the year 1972 ending the regime of fixed currency exchange rates. The advent of the second stage can be placed around a few momentous months during 1989–90 that, after the breakup of the U.S.S.R., ushered in the process of market liberalization and privatization in the Eastern European countries. The world is experiencing a spate of deregulation. Commenting on the end of the era of planned economies, as in Russia and its ex-satellite countries, Danis and Parkhe (2002) aptly note, "Similar comprehensive system transformations are occurring in a number of Asian countries as well, including China and Vietnam."

HOW POSITIVE HAS BEEN THE IMPACT?

For the purpose of this chapter on India, this paper assumes that the positive benefits are a given, and that the democratic institutional framework, a sine qua non for liberalization policies to produce long-term benefits, exists. As most readers are aware, since its independence in 1947, India has been the most populous democratic nation. The positive benefits are gauged in so many ways that it is hard to fathom the net benefits and to identify their recipients. To delve a little deeper, a range of questions can be raised. In our view, the two questions that seem important are seldom analytically elucidated for the generalists. We attempt to briefly discuss the questions with the aid of some published data. The questions raised are not necessarily dissected or answered in a scientific sense. There are other data that shed light on the questions. But, for the narrative in the chapter, the data we have reproduced suffice.

The two questions are (1) Are the impressions conveyed in this chapter in consonance with the conclusions of researchers and scholars? and (2) Assuming a link between increases in a country's foreign exchange reserves and its speed of market liberalization, how did some of the non-oil exporting emerging nations augment their foreign reserves? These questions are apparently so intertwined that unraveling them could be a daunting task for empirical researchers. It is the hope that this chapter, with many limitations, will shed some light on issues of main concern for emerging markets, in particular, India. At present, there are 25 such markets. Nearly 10, constituting the old second world will, by 2004, be admitted to the European Union (EU). Let us turn to scholarly views, about how India is still considered by many to be a third-world country.

VIEWS OF SOME RESEARCHERS AND SCHOLARS

Indian historians—with a nationalistic fervor and specializing in the British colonial era—generally conceptualized "deindustrialization and the drain of wealth as an exclusively Indian problem, isolated from general international developments," according to Gupta (2002). When interpreted in a broader context, as Roy (2000) lucidly does, it stands to reason that the growth in (international) trade[4] in the nineteenth century introduced greater degrees of commercialization and rising per capita income.

Economic historians O'Rourke and Williamson (1999) demonstrate that, in the nineteenth century, reduction in transportation costs was the most important variable explaining the internationalization of trade in the Atlantic economy. In the middle of the nineteenth century, such events as the repeal of the Corn Laws, the Irish famine and emigration, and the laying of ocean cables that linked the world's financial centers—London, New York, Paris, Tokyo—all had significant impact on the decline of transportation costs. "European capital, freed from war time finance, was starting to look for promising returns in distant New Orleans, Chicago, Bombay," write O'Rourke and Williams. Extending beyond Bombay, trade expanded further east to Canton,[5] for there is ample evidence to suggest that European mercantile groups had been multinational investors especially in the coastal regions of southeast China. Since then, international trade and international direct investment grew at a fast clip as the vast amount of international business literature indicates. Different countries have been deregulating different domestic sectors. In the United States, service sectors such as trucking, air transportation, and banking were deregulated just a couple of decades ago. India as a newly independent nation has been deregulating the financial services industries since the mid-seventies. The liberalization trend, as Dunning and Narula (1996) put it, is a product of many major developments in the world in addition to the rapid advances in information and communication technologies, and the renaissance of market economy. The financial environment in India, during 1975–2000 as Mathew (2000) notes, has undergone discernible changes in freeing the restrictions on matters of financial transactions. One such change is the internationalization of the capital market, which ushered in gradual reforms introduced in the 1980s.

Any significant change in policy is likely to bring about some change in structure. As capital markets are opened up to foreign investors, in some degree, the relationships among the agencies of the public and the private sector undergo changes. As Aggarwal (1997) observes, there has been a complex relationship among policy changes, market conditions, and internalization advantages for multinational corporations. Since 1991, India has been implementing economic reforms to liberalize and globalize its economy, writes Dutt (1997). Timberg (1998) notes that India's actual and potential roles in the world economy have changed significantly, improving its commercial and political relationships with the United States. Based on statistical measures and econometric analysis, Fujita (1994) infers that the liberalization policies in India improved productivity, which led to increased exports of manufactured products. Murillo (1998) points out that market liberalization in India has brought notable benefits to final consumers in the form of abundant durable household products. Examining cross-sectional data, Pravin and Mitra (1998) find strong evidence of increased competition and moderate evidence in the growth of productivity. The production of industrial products is often achieved with the help of foreign technology within constraints. "Due to India's inward looking philosophy complete with protective measures," writes Bowonder (1998), Indian firms did not have wide access to foreign industrial technology. That might be the case. However, others, who measured the performance of firms during 1991–98 (Katrak 2002) suggest that the growth performance of enterprises that made products based on their own in-house research and design (R&D) efforts compared favorably with the growth rates of other enterprises that heavily relied on foreign technology. In other words, while some did not seek technology from abroad, they either imitated or copied sophisticated industrial technologies. Copying books is probably easier than copying a bridge across the river.

A COMPENDIUM OF PROGRESS

The topic of how changes from a planned economy toward a market economy come about in a subset of emerging countries, including China, India, and Vietnam, is captured in a scholarly compendium edited by Padma Desai (1999). One insight that surfaces, from the anthology prefaced by Desai's detailed 94-page introduction, is that some countries are slower than others in liberalizing their economies, underlying reasons aside. In summing up, Desai (1999) concludes the research findings on a dozen countries, said to be in economic transition, in these words: "Speedy reforms appear to promote both higher growth and faster inflation control, but they also seem to create a short-run trade-off via an adverse effect on employment. Thus, speedy reforms are not necessarily superior to less ambitious gradualist reforms." In the totality of a larger number of countries than the 12 economies in transition that are more and less industrialized, the rate at which national governments have been relaxing one type of restriction on trade or investment can be gleaned from the Fraser Index.

ON THE SPEED OF MARKET REFORMS

Among the measures of estimates of the speed of liberalization at the international level, the Fraser Index of Economic Freedom is said to be the most comprehensive. This index includes numerous measures of the structural changes in the regulations of a number of countries spanning a longer time

frame. From the viewpoint of a nontechnical discussion, the indices can provide a comparative perspective of how far different countries have come along
the path toward Adam Smith's market maxim—laissez-faire, or minimum governmental interference, in economic activities and transactions. For a contrast,
for 1976–95, six countries with vast institutional differences are cited from
Pitlik (2002) and included in Table 15.1.

The Fraser Index—an econometrically derived index of some 83 variables,
for more than 100 countries, spanning a time frame of 10 or more years—
indicates the rate at which a country is liberalizing its economy and its product
markets. The indices for all of the six countries, shown in Table 15.1, are
positive. Argentina and Chile in Latin America speeded up the process. The
two European Union members—Republic of Ireland and Norway—with their
large private sector basis cruised along. Then there is Zambia (at = +0.2),
the slowest among the six. Its recent history is replete with civil strife, internal
political conflicts, and deteriorating terms of trade.[6] Even so, its Fraser index
is positive. Finally, there is India, (with an index of +1.4), which in the 1990s
became more liberalized than it was in the post-independence decades of the
1950s and 1960s. According to Standard and Poor's credit ratings of the developing countries, India maintained a respectable BBB- rating, albeit in October 2002, it was slightly downgraded to BB+. But its foreign exchange
reserves, at the time of this writing, looked healthy at about $60 billion, which
suggests the second query: How did a few nations build up their foreign

Table 15.1
Fraser Index (1976–1995) for Selected Six Countries

Country	Fraser Index*
Argentina	+4.7
Chile	+4.5
India	+1.4
Ireland	+2.4
Norway	+2.4
Zambia	+0.2

Note: * An estimate of the speed of liberalization or market reforms.
Source: Pitlik (2002: 76).

reserves? The standard explanation that some countries export more than they import is a necessary, but not sufficient in modern times.

FOREIGN EXCHANGE RESERVES

Among the six countries listed in Table 15.1, the currencies of Argentina, Chile, India, and Zambia have been weaker currencies, known earlier as soft currencies, meaning the international demand for these currencies is soft or not as robust as that of harder currencies such as the pound, dollar, or yen. Suppose a soft currency country somehow[7] begins to augment its foreign exchange reserves. It implies then, but does not prove, that something positive is transpiring within the country as it has been in the case of India, as well as China. In other words, the recent foreign exchange reserves of a few immensely large countries—referred to as the big emerging markets—would suggest that net exports of goods and services, and their peoples' emigration, have been favorable to the home countries in terms of additions to the foreign reserves held[8] in convertible foreign currencies.

Table 15.2 contains two columns; one is a set of reliable numerical data[9] for 11 selected developing countries of which 4 also appeared in the first table. The second column merely represents a subjective evaluation of their speed[10] of market liberalization, abbreviated as MLP. The intent here is not to draw any associative impact between the two, but simply to inject an insight.

There is a plethora of economic literature on the subcontinent of India in regard to the government policies decided in New Delhi. At the national level of many countries, the impact of economic liberalization has become so significant a subject matter that there is now an abundance of empirical literature on, for example, entire countries (Toulon 2002), industrial sectors (Fujita 1994), and service sectors such as oligopolistic industries like banking and telecommunications in India (Bhattacharya 1997; Dornisch 2002; Siddharthan and Pandit 1998). The findings of many of these research studies lead to a key converging point, namely, that the impact of liberalization is uneven. This is not to assert that market freedom has negative benefits. It is to subscribe to the notion that, as Buckley and Casson (1993) put it, in many cases the market is not the best coordinating mechanism. We would add that in emerging nations, it may not be the best mechanism in some significant sectors of the economy, but perhaps it is also a complex mechanism as it was in the eighteenth and early nineteenth century United States.

In the case of India, both the largest democracy in demographic terms (1.01 + billion people compared with China's 1.27 + billion, and 0.285 billion in the United States), and one of the most ancient civilizations, traceable to 4500 b.c., the struggle for national independence in the twentieth century climaxed less than 60 years ago, in 1947. During the past two decades or so, market liberalization came to India, gradually and in stages. The theme has been incremental.

Table 15.2
Foreign Exchange Reserves and Liberalization in 11 Emerging Nations

Emerging Nations	Foreign (Exchange) Reserves*				Market Liberalization Pace [MLP]	
	May 2000	July 2001	July 2002	Aug. 2002	MLP	
ASIA						
China	160	180	246	258	S→M	
India	36	40	58	59.5	S→M	
Malaysia	33.5	25.6	33	33	M	
Thailand	31.5	31.4	37	37.7	M	
AMERICAS						
Argentina	24.5	20	9	9.2	R	
Brazil	37	35.5	39	37.6	M→R	
Chile	14	14.4	15	14.9	R	
OTHER						
Egypt	14	13	12.5	13.0	M	
Turkey	23	19.5	24.5	25.1	M	
Poland	24.5	26.9	27	28.2	M→R	
Russia	13.4	29.9	40	41.9	M→R	

Notes: *Foreign reserves = Foreign exchange reserves, for purposes of the article.
**MLP Paces: S = Slow, M = Moderate, R = Rapid (Author's subjective ratings).
Sources: The Economist, July 8, 2000; August 17, p. 76; Sept. 14, p. 98; and October 19, 2002, p. 96.

The diverse regions and peoples in India, not dissimilar to the subcontinent of modern China, are not unique. But in order to comprehend the extent, the speed, or the setbacks of economic liberalization, one has to factor in the diversity of peoples and regions. One could describe the changes introduced as gradual, or incremental, rather than *impromptu.* It has been a transition. Kedia, Dibrell, and Harveston (1998) have advanced a framework to comprehend the transition in India. Included are the levels and degrees of liberalization. There is an effort, in this model, to analytically deconstruct laissez-faire in the specific context of modern India.

Slow and Steady

As noted earlier, liberalization measures relate mostly to relaxing rules regarding the private sector, and privatization plans pertain to reducing the state-owned industrial enterprises. In tandem, these two measures, at least in theory, make a country's economy more open, more FDI-friendly, and more transparent than before. Subsequently, when new measures generate concrete results, the direction of the results make a country eligible to be considered by the international financial community as an emerging nation. There are 25 such countries (see Appendix) Unfortunately, for theory and policy prescriptions, corruption surfaces as a facet in most of these countries.

Seen from the current (July–October 2002) perspective, the portents for those countries that introduced economic liberalization in large and sudden doses do not bode well. Argentina,[11] more so than Zambia perhaps, has become a basket case while India's situation, but for its border-conflict-linked political problems, does not look too ominous. With current foreign exchange reserves of $60 billion, a fairly stable U.S.$-rupee exchange rate (hovering between 45 to 55 rupees per U.S. dollar), and the recent strides in its information and biotechnology sectors, it would be less than objective to characterize India's recent progress as lagging. That there are millions of poor people, in India, China, or elsewhere, is recognized by all. But only a few can easily recognize billions of people or dollars as in the reported net worth of Bill Gates. While exponents of an American-style free market highlight the market potential with such phrases as the globe's poor constituting a hugely untapped market awaiting multinationals, the question of who could spearhead that process, which electronic commercial tools to use, and how to formulate corporate capital expenditure algorithms are parts of a broader, complex, global question. That question, it would seem to us, is one of alleviating global poverty. That is too profound a question and is beyond the scope of this chapter.

This chapter is concerned with arguing the author's firsthand impressions. The aspired goal of liberalization is clear enough. Its accomplishment is something else, due in large part to the power of the figurative gold.

The goal of privatization or market liberalization, simply put, is to make market transactions adhere to Adam Smith's market maxim—laissez-faire. The price system, advocated long ago by classical economists, however, does not operate under all conditions in the same country, or in all countries at the same level of industrialization, for a variety of reasons—economic or non-economic. The economic concepts of imperfect markets and market failure have many of the same underlying reasons. Theories of market price and of market hierarchy diverged since the 1940s. The influence of Coase-

Williamson transaction cost economics is widespread in the economics of international business.[12] To paraphrase Buckley and Casson (1993), the emphasis on markets is likely to be further weakened once nonmarket mechanisms[13] are expressed in economic terms. While agrarian markets always prevailed, spread of free-market notion has a relatively short history. The notion of market in the twentieth century is much more complex and confounding, and how to juxtapose market freedom and government regulation in a prudent way remains a paradox. Some of the contemporary economists are less familiar with history, while others, particularly in Europe, relate history to economics cogently. Views differ if Austrian economist von Hayek in the 1940s was an exception in his *Road to Serfdom.* That economists will discover, say Buckley and Casson (1993), that in many cases the market is not the best coordinating mechanism. Why not, one might ask.

In a historic sense, disruptions of the market mechanism have not been uncommon. Yet, the success of Western European societies and Japan, with varying yet high degrees of market freedom, has time and again proven to be a better system benefiting more of the people than the ownership and control of means of production by national or provincial governments. The fall of the Berlin Wall in 1989 underscored the importance of Smith's ideas in the late twentieth century. In short, during the first half of the 1990s, the Western industrialized nations showcased privatization, and the developing countries launched market liberalization, including making their economies conducive to foreign direct investment albeit at different speeds, and in varying forms such as is evident in the case of capital controls. Thus, there is the constant need to review and examine the measurable results of privatization and/or deregulation, not to abandon its avowed goal but to enhance the efficacy of the market mechanism which, by definition, is not perfect.

Necessary Conditions

One of the expected goals of liberalization is to make a country context as conducive to foreign direct investment[14] as possible. Setting aside international joint business ventures, increased FDI, that is, capital inflows from abroad, could be both good and bad, seen from the perspective of independent local, or domestic firms—firms whose equity control is in the hands of nationals rather than foreigners. There is also another cardinal condition, often not amplified, under which FDI is theoretically considered good. Simply stated as an axiom, if a local, or domestic, company is a producer of intermediate goods, it is not as bad off as a maker of final products, for the latter has to contend with foreign or foreign-branded substitutes. To put it another way, companies that seek foreign markets would have some distinct resource advantage—financial or technological—and hence locally owned firms are better off in some form of collaboration with the powerful rather than competing head-on. In this regard, the observation of Das (1996) that scores of Indian companies are repositioning their organization and business in order to remain competitive is noteworthy. One such company with which the author is acquainted, is a domestic joint venture named Titan Industries Limited, India's own watchmaker.

Titan is a joint venture between the Tata Group and Tamilnadu Industrial Development Corporation (TIDCO). The company annually produces more than six million watches; about 10 percent of this output is exported to the Middle East and Europe. It can be considered one of the most progressive domestic companies in India. Its Computer-Aided-Design/Computer-Aided-Manufacturing (CAD/CAM) center, along with a research and development laboratory, introduced four hundred models into the market in 2001. In recent years, due to the intensive competitive nature of the global watch industry, it has emerged as a nationally branded maker of gold jewelry. Just as in the earlier decade when its watchmaking technology was transferred from Switzerland, its jewelry business is in concert with the Swiss gold maker, Pecinox. Although Titan is a large company, a profitable affiliate member of the Tata Group, it is not immune from the vagaries of competitive threats in the global economy, or in the current liberalized business environment in India.

Similar is the challenge to the tens of thousands of small and medium-sized privately held, and often family-controlled, companies in industrial towns dotted all over India. One of the industrial cities is Coimbatore. For more than a century, the city has been the one of the country's major centers of the textile (garment) industry—knitting in particular—and light engineering. How managers think and express their sentiments of liberalized market regulations has been a matter of research interest. Exploratory field studies (Palaniswami and Prasad 2002) shed some empirical light.

The positive benefits of market liberalization—including financial and trade liberalization—may be ephemeral for no other reason than managers, as decision makers in their respective firms, may shelve their plans, or postpone new investments in the face of new uncertainties, due to internal or external factors. For managers, especially of the small and medium-sized industrial firms, their estimates of the future revenue streams of their firms are of utmost importance. Thus, the question of how managers see positive benefits remains an important research question.

In India, many of the millions of firms engaged in a wide variety of industries ranging from pottery making to textiles, from biscuits to biotechnology, from stoneware to software, are small and medium-sized enterprises. Of note is that a number of them employ both labor-intensive and capital-intensive state-of-the-art technologies.[15] Driven by the necessary export orientation, one could surmise that their business goal is not merely to earn profits in local currency, but in the form, if not of gold, of U.S. dollars, the euro, British pound, or the Japanese yen. These and other hard currencies constitute the national reserves of a country, in short, the net worth on a current year basis.

A continuous rate of accumulation also suggests that, given the nature of global competition, such large countries as China and India have realized the comparative advantages in international trade.

SUMMARY

The intent of the narrative was to offer a commentary on India's liberalization from a foreign perspective, and to make a case for a moderate pace of liberalization. The commentary included many opinions of the author, and for illustrative purposes, some secondary data. Broadly speaking, economic liberalization is intended to free firms or industries from restrictive limits imposed by the central government and also to embark upon the sale of public sector undertakings. In most countries, in the 1990s, public sector enterprises were being unbundled. Whether or not there is a complete divorce from the central government of those industries that are deemed to be essential to the moral and economic foundations of a country has been under debate for over a century under the rubric of national security.

Assuming that, as O'Rourke and Williamson (1999) have demonstrated, falling shipping costs in the nineteenth century spurred enormous growth in international trade in the Atlantic region, the twentieth century witnessed further progress, and many other subsequent events and forces. The abolition of the gold standard was fairly recent, only 28 years ago. The fall of the Berlin Wall was still more recent, 15 years ago. Many of the emerging markets have existed for more than 4,000 years, India and China, in particular. The fall of the Berlin Wall in 1989 underscored the importance, in the late twentieth century, of Adam Smith's ideas.

In short, during the first half of the 1990s, Western industrialized nations showcased privatization. The developing country launched market liberalization, albeit at different speeds, and in varying forms such as is evident in the case of financial capital controls. Thus, there is a constant need to review and examine the measurable results of privatization and deregulation, not to abandon or revert to the old measures, but to enhance the efficacy of the market mechanism. In many country contexts the market may not yet be the best coordinating mechanism. As Arrow (2000) recommends, more capital-intensive industries should be gradually liberalized while the government retains the power to restructure legal and financial institutions. Meaningful and desired changes in such societies are likely to come slowly. In today's global economy, liberating the financial environment comes to the fore. One such change is the opening up of capital markets. This change represents a major change, a strategic change. Any such policy change implies structural change. FDI-friendly rules inevitably herald intense competition for product markets.

In addition, outcomes would differ at the macroeconomic and microeconomic levels. At the industry level, production for export in countries has emerged as the main mission (Fujita 1994) that can be achieved with the enhancement of the in-house technological competencies of firms (Katrak 2002). At the aggregate level, in the market place, one can observe an ample supply and availability of consumer durable products (Murillo 1998). Yet, the overall productivity has been moderate (Pravin and Mitra 1998); FDI tends to be labor displacing (Chakraborty and Basu 2001). The role of the state in economic planning is not to be construed as over and done with, but is to be redefined. To emphasize that the new role is crucial in India (Saez and Yang 2001), the most populous low-income democratic nation in the world, is not to argue against privatization of the public sector. Rather it is tantamount to restate that whichever activity a country believes to be critical or strategic to its security, that country, through a democratic process, is likely to directly participate and retain its control; the nation does not have to be a poor or underdeveloped country.

CONCLUSION

So the overall effect of liberalization in India has been positive. While other essays in this volume cover statistical measures, it is pointed out here that India's foreign reserves during 2000 and 2002 have gone up, from $36 billion to $59 billion. Even so, other factors that enter into the credit ratings of nations are not favorable at this time. Standard and Poor's degraded India from 8.3 to 6.6 (on a 12-point scale). Is the B-level rating to be the verdict that reforms in India have been too slow and therefore potential growth is limited? To the contrary, with teeming millions, India and China have been dubbed as the big emerging nations. Just observing the products of Japanese joint ventures in India, and the eagerness of American companies to locate factory or office space in Bangalore would dispel concerns about the slow speed of economic reforms. Reforms in India could only be slow, but they appear to be progressing slowly and on a selective basis. What the present essay attempted to do was to focus on two related issues and evoke a general discussion. The issues were framed in terms of one, scholars' views about liberalization in India in the 1990s, and two, benefits from liberalization as measured by India's mounting foreign reserves.

A conclusion that can be drawn from the narrative of this chapter is that accelerated gradual liberalization in India is more likely to have long-term benefits than sudden drastic and impromptu changes that may award benefits in the short run. This statement is consistent with the argument of Arrow (2000) and the inference of Desai (1999), who synthesized research on 12 countries. Speedy reforms are not necessarily superior to less ambitious grad-ualist reforms. An immanent inference of my narrative is that accelerated gradual liberalization of the markets, not unlike a systematic savings plan on the part of an individual, is more likely to have a higher long-term payoff than sudden and drastic policy alterations that may, in the short run, bestow positive benefits on many but not on most of the poor people in today's global economy.

ACKNOWLEDGMENTS

The author owes a debt of gratitude to the editors of the book for their guidance, and to M. Dinks, M. J. Jones, B. Korplu, A. Pant, S. Srinivas, and A. Sutherland, for their generous research help in the course of preparing the manuscript. Errors and omissions are of author's alone.

Appendix
Relative Status of 23 Emerging Countries, December 2002

Country	GDP (%)	Δ Country's Currency per $ Dec '02	'01	Short-term interest rate	Foreign Reserves ($b, rounded)
Argentina	-13.6*	3.51	1.00	6.20	10
Brazil	2.4	3.53	2.53	21.90	34
Chile	1.8	696	664	2.76	15
China	8.1	8.28	8.28	n.a.	263
Colombia	1.9	2.82	2.30	7.72	11
Czech Republic	1.5	30.4	35.4	2.58	23
Egypt	4.9**	4.62	4.54	6.10	13
Hungary	3.4	30.4	35.4	8.40	10
India	6.0	48.1	47.8	5.43	65
Indonesia	3.9	8,900	10,150	13.72	29
Israel	-0.8	4.67	4.27	6.14	24
Malaysia	5.6	3.80	3.80	3.10	33
Mexico	1.8	10.2	9.1	6.98	46
Peru	4.5	3.54	3.44	3.61	10
Philippines	3.8	53.7	51.6	7.13	13
Poland	0.8	3.89	3.97	7.00	29
Russia	4.3	31.9	30.3	21.00	43
Singapore	3.9	1.75	1.84	0.81	80
South Africa	3.1	9.00	12.20	6.14	6
South Korea	5.8	1202	1287	4.96	80
Taiwan	4.8	34.80	34.71	1.80	200
Turkey***	7.9	16.21	14.45	42.00	26
Venezuela	- 5.5	1255	752	31.30	8

Notes: *Not meaningful for comparisons.

**GDP change is for 2001.

***Turkey's currency rate is written as 1,621,950 for Dec. 2002, and likewise for Dec. 2001. Restated as 16.21 and 14.45.

Source: The Economist, December 21, 2002, p. 146.

NOTES

1. Professor Lawrence Jenicke, Central Michigan University conveyed to the author the following contrasts from his visit to India in 1990 and in 1994: In 1990, in a visit to the construction site of a DuPont plant, the foundation trenches were dug by hand with pitch-shovels and material was carried away by women with baskets on their heads. In 1994, on other construction sites there was the presence of Japanese bulldozers; backhoes were used in both building and road construction. There was the use of German laser optical measuring instruments to check rotary compressor machined dimensions in a plant in Coimbatore. In terms of consumer goods, even the tiny music stores carried both Western and Indian music in CDs of varying quality.

2. For a perspective, see Arun and Nixson (2000).

3. In simple classical terms, the presence of land and labor alone, in the absence of capital and organization, do not make a viable system. In contemporary terms, land, labor, and capital might be represented, respectively, by physical endowments of a country, the skills of its populace, and embodied technology in primary, secondary, and tertiary industries—real capital. Yet organization, (administration or management) as it is at present, remained a critical factor. The public enterprises in many developing countries probably filled the void in order to make the then system durable. Introduced in nineteenth-century British India, the public sector enterprises were either initiated or influenced by the British administrative mode. Even though economic efficiency—measured as a unit cost of a defined good—may not have been the major organizational goal, many such enterprises in the past had as their goals the production of goods for domestic consumption or for international trade. Over time, these enterprises grew into huge unmanageable bureaucracies resulting in diminished returns to scale. Administrative inefficiencies could not be contained or corrected, for they had become endemic. An undeclared war on administrative and operational inefficiencies, one feels, could never be waged or won in India.

4. Trade, by Polyani's apt definition, "is a method of acquiring goods not available on the spot. It is something external to the group; the point [of trade] is acquiring and carrying goods from a distance" (Pearson 1977). Both the Silk Road and the sea routes were the main avenues in the past centuries for Europeans as well as Arab merchants to bring in silver, woolen textiles, opium, or explosives, and to take back ivory, porcelain, silk, tea, and spices from Asia. In the seventeenth and the eighteenth century mercantilism was the dominant guiding principle in Europe; in China, the rulers of the Qing dynasty followed the Confucian tenets with a healthy dose of disdain for trade though Han Chinese merchants in the southeast coastal areas were well versed in international trade.

Modern India, however, was guided and administered by the British. The British managing agency system was well entrenched within the country, and international trade was probably influenced by these enterprises headquartered in the largest cities in India. Thus, the nineteenth century trade benefits in India, seen from a social historical perspective, may not have directly accrued to the common people in India but to the Indian agents and their British principals. Yet, historical data show a causal link as noted by Roy (2000)—circumlocutory though it probably was—between per capita income and a rise in the volume of trade. The end of British rule in 1947 opened up a set of opportunities and serious threats to India as the most densely populated democratic nation in the then slowly expanding global economy. Probably the oil crisis of 1975 was a milestone for the non-oil exporting economy.

5. See Jonathan Spence. 1999. *The Search for Modern China*. New York: Norton.

6. For an assessment of privatization in Zambia, see, for example, Craig (2000). Also, the following summary table illustrates the declining exchange value of Zambia's soft currency, the kwacha. The decline, in 1996–2002, was steep: it was four-fold (2002 index: 422), and the implications are fairly obvious in terms of rising domestic prices and declining interest on the part of international portfolio investors.

Year	Kwacha per $	Index (1996 = 100)
1996	1207.9	100
1997	1314.5	108
1998	1862.1	154
1999	2388.0	197
2000	3110.9	257
2001	4024.5	333
2002	5100.0	422

7. Such as hard currency remittances from overseas nationals or expatriates.

8. According to the IMF-guided national income accounting standard, foreign currency reserves include, in the main, securities, deposits with the Bureau of International Settlements, IMF, commercial bank deposits, IMF reserves, SDRs, and gold. Foreign reserves thus represent a portfolio of assets held in convertible, preferably hard, currencies. That China and India are accumulating foreign reserves at a fast clip is known, but how such countries as these ought to budget those reserves productively is less known.

9. Sources include national statistics offices, central banks, Thomson Financial database, J.P. Morgan Chase, and the International Monetary Fund.

10. For theoretical insights, see Arrow (2000).

11. See "Doubts in the Barricade." *The Economist.* 28 September 2001, 63–65.

12. The study of transaction—not production—costs economics notably associated with Oliver E. Williamson. As in the case of international business organizations (MNEs), there are variants of the 1963 expositions of Oliver E. Williamson. Papers by Peter Buckley or Jean-Francois Hennart are illustrative.

13. The full quote includes what they label as cultural manipulation, which we are reading as cultural trends that have less to do with money and more to do with values or beliefs.

14. In regard to some thoughts on enriching the mainstream FDI theory, see Oxelheim, Randoy, and Stonehill (2001).

15. The following example is illustrative of a number of firms in many regions of India. ELGI is the corporate name of a medium-sized metallurgical firm that has been owned and managed by a family in Coimbatore, an industrial center in the state of Tamil Nadu (previously, the province of Madras under British rule). A simplistic conceptualization of this enterprise would include the following salient features of the firm as a multi-plant operation with its core competency in engineering and metallurgy, and its technology, as can be expected, as labor-intensive. The average annual employment has hovered around 1,200 during the late 1990s. During the late 1970s and early 1980s, ELGI participated in the Indo-German technical collaboration programs. Subsequently, several of the engineering graduates were sent to Germany for

advanced technical training. To make a long story short, in the making of screw compressors, the firm utilizes German state-of-the-art equipment and technical knowledge producing products that have met international standards (ISO 9000). The products of the firm are marketed in India as well as abroad, particularly in the Middle East and in Africa. The managers realize that, while global marketing and servicing opportunities abound, there are rival producers elsewhere as in China. And despite market liberalization, skilled labor costs and transportation costs remain significant constraints. In short, within ELGI one smaller unit is fashioned after a German firm, and to this limited extent, the firm can be construed as having been internationalized. Is this development unique to India? One does not surmise so.

REFERENCES

Aggarwal, Aradhna. 1997. "Liberalization, Internationalization Advantages, and Foreign Direct Investment: The Indian Experience in the 1980s." *Transnational Corporations* 6 (3): 33–54.

Arrow, Kenneth. 2000. "Economic Transition, Speed, and Scope." *Journal of Institutional and Theoretical Economics* 156 (1): 9–18.

Arun, T. G., and F. I. Nixon. 2000. "The Disinvestment of Public Enterprises: The Indian Experience." *Oxford Development Studies* 28 (1): 19–32.

Bernstein, Peter J. 2000. *The Power of Gold.* New York: Norton.

Bhagwathi, Jagdish. 2000. "No Magic Bullet" Review of *The Mystery of Capital: Why Capitalism Succeeds in the West and Fails Elsewhere,* by H. Desoto. *New Leader* 83 (5): 36–7.

Bhattacharya, A., et al. 1997. "The Impact of Liberalization on the Productive Efficiency of Indian Commercial Banks." *European Journal of Operations Research* 98 (3): 332–45.

Birnbaum, J. 2002. "The Return of the Big Government." *Fortune,* 16 September: 112.

Bowonder, B. 1998. "Industrialization and Economic Growth of India: Interactions of Indigenous and Foreign Technology." *International Journal of Technology Management* 15 (6,7): 622–45.

Buckley, Peter J., and Mark Casson. 1993. "Economics as an Imperialist Social Science." In *International Business,* by P. Buckley. London: Macmillan. First published in *Human Relations* 46 (9): 1035–51.

Chakraborty, Chandana, and Parantap Basu. 2001. "Foreign Direct Investment and Growth in India: A Co-integration Approach." *Applied Economics* 34 (3): 1061–73.

Chand, Satish, and Kunal Sne. 2002. "Trade Liberalization and Productivity Growth: Evidence from Indian Manufacturing." *Review of Development Economics* 6 (1): 120–32.

Craig, John. 2000. "Evaluating Privatization in Zambia: A Tale of Two Processes." *Review of African Political Economy* 85: 357–66.

Danis, Wade M., and Arvind Parkhe. 2002. "Hungarian-Western Partnerships: A Grounded Theoretical Model of Integration Process and Outcomes." *Journal of International Business Studies* 33 (3): 423–55.

Das, Ranjan. 1996. "Deregulation and Liberalization in India: The Managerial Response." *Journal of General Management* 21 (2): 48–58.

Desai, Padma, ed. 1999. *Going Global: Transition from Plan to Market in the World Economy*. Cambridge, Mass.: M.I.T. Press.

Dornisch, David. 2002. "Competitive Dynamics in Polish Telecommunications, 1990–2000." *Communication Abstracts* 25 (1): 3–14.

Dunning, John H., and Rajneesh Narula, eds. 1996. *Foreign Direct Investments and Governments: Catalysts for Economic Restructuring*. London: Routledge.

Dutt, Amitava K. 1997. "Uncertain Success: The Political Economy of Indian Economic Reform." *Journal of International Affairs*, vol. 51 (summer): 57–83.

Fujita, Natsuki. 1994. "Liberalization Policies and Productivity in India." *The Developing Economies*, 32 (4): 509–24.

Gupta, Bishnupriya. 2002. Review of *The Economic History of India*, by Tirthankar Roy. *The Economic History Review* 55 (1): 212–3.

Katrak, Homi. 2002. "Does Economic Liberalization Endanger Indigenous Technological Developments. An Analysis of the Indian Experience." *Research Policy* 31 (1): 19–30.

Kedia, B. L., C. C. Dibrell, and P. D. Harveston. 1998. "Enhancing India's Competition through the Process of Privatization and Economic Liberalization." In *Managing Economic Liberalization in South Asia*, edited by C. Jayachandra et al., 61–9. New Delhi: Macmillan India Limited.

Madsen, Tage K. 1998. "Executing Insights: Managerial Judgments of Export Performance." *Journal of International Marketing* 6 (3): 82–93.

Mathew, P. A. 2000. "Econometric Evidence of the Internationalization of Indian Capital Market." *Finance India* 14 (1): 143–64.

Morck, Randall, and Bernard Yeung. 2002. "The Puzzle of Harmonious Stock Prices." *World Economics* 3 (3): 105–19.

Murillo, L. 1998. "Market Liberalization, Alliances, and Technology Transfer: India and Its High Technology Sector." In *Managing Economic Liberalization in South Asia*, edited by C. Jayachandra et al., 81–7. New Delhi: Macmillan India Limited.

Murphy, C. 2002. "The Hunt for Globalization that Works." *Fortune*, 28 October: 163–76.

O'Rourke, Kevin H., and Jeffrey G. Williamson. 1999. *Globalization and History*. Cambridge, Mass.: M.I.T. Press.

Oxelheim, Lars, Trond Randoy, and Arthur Stonehill. 2001. "On the Treatment of Finance-Specific Factors within the OLI Paradigm." *International Business Review* 10 (4): 381–98.

Palaniswami, Shanthakumar, and S. Benjamin Prasad. 2002. "Management Perceptions of Market Liberalization." *International Journal of Value Based Management* 15 (3): 237–48.

Pearson, Harry W., ed. 1977. *The Livelihood of Man—Karl Polyani*. New York: Academic Press.

Pitlik, Hans. 2002. "The Path of Liberalization and Economic Growth." *Kyklos* 55 (1): 57–80.

Pravin, Krishna, and D. Mitra. 1998. "Trade Liberalization, Market Discipline, and Productivity Growth: New Evidence from India." *Journal of Development Economics* 56 (2): 447–62.

Reed, Ananya M. 2002. "Corporate Governance Reforms in India." *Journal of Business Ethics* 37 (3): 249–68.

Roy, Tirthankar. 2000. *The Economic History of India.* New Delhi: Oxford University Press.

Saez, Lawrence, and Joy Yang. 2001. "The Deregulation of State-Owned Enterprises in India and China." *Comparative Economic Studies* 43 (3): 69–97.

Siddharthan, N. S., and B. L. Pandit. 1998. "Liberalization and Investment: Behavior of MNEs and Large Corporate Firms in India." *International Business Review* 7 (5): 535–48.

Timberg, Thomas A. 1998. "The Impact of Indian Economic Liberalization on U.S.-India Relations." *SAIS Review* 18 (1): 123–36.

Toulan, Omar N. 2002. "The Impact of Market Liberalization on Vertical Scope: The Case of Argentina." *Strategic Management Journal* 23 (6): 551–60.

PART IV

Looking toward 2010

CHAPTER 16

A Look Ahead: Multinational Enterprises and Emerging Markets

Pervez N. Ghauri

In this volume of invited research papers, the authors have tried, from different perspectives, to capture the changing sensitive relationships between multinational firms and emerging markets. There has been a profound change in this relationship discernible especially since the decade of the 1990s. After enjoying a long period of high level cooperation and harmony, this relationship is on the verge of a collapse, and appears to be moving towards a long term conflict of corporate goals and national interests resulting in such constraints as would hamper the progress of the global economy. In a way, this situation mirrors the type of relationship that prevailed in the post–World War II period (1950–70), as recounted by several authors (Boddewyn 1992; Buckley and Ghauri 1999; Ghauri and Buckley 2002).

One major development, after the 1970s, was the emergence of Asia's newly industrializing countries (NICs), in particular the Asian Tigers, posing new competition to multinationals originating from the Western nations. These new dynamics led to protectionist policies and a sense of "loss of competitiveness" (Buckley and Ghauri 1999) to the Western economies. Since 1989, the value of liberalization of centrally planned economies brought a number of countries into a new subset of countries—those classified as emerging markets. The emergence of China as an important player in the international economic scene has also changed the balance of power in this relationship.

While the earlier important changes were in the economic realm, the significant changes of the last decade have been triggered by incidents in the geopolitical scene. The tragic events of September 11, 2001, and the protectionist and unilateral policies of the United States of America and a few other governments have had a profound impact on international trade, and international investment policies of multinational enterprises (MNEs) and host countries.

The actors involved in managing this delicate relationship are governments—home and host—and MNEs. MNEs are considered "islands of conscious power"; their boundaries of power and their activities are defined by the equilibrium point at which the cost of using the market (transactions) falls below the cost of internal organization (Buckley and Casson 1976). In short, internalization becomes the guiding tenet. The governments on the other hand, are trying to deregulate their economies at a pace consistent with the best long-term interests of their population. In other words, they believe pure market mechanism would not enable them to achieve their goals (Ghauri and Buckley 2002). This situation is particularly prevalent in the Emerging Markets, as the free market maxim and its outcome have not been satisfactory for them. Such a divergence of goals inevitably leads to a conflict between MNEs and the governments in emerging markets. It is also clear that while markets are not perfect, as Buckley (1996) puts it: "governments are seeking to appropriate rents in a world of imperfect markets. Yet, governments are as much actors as the multinational enterprises in the globalized economy of the 21st century."

The flow of foreign direct investment (FDI) had been for years predominantly from the Western countries to emerging countries, due, among other factors, to a lack of competition in the local markets. Japan became a notable exception as a direct investor in the early 1980s. More recently, however, firms and economies from a number of emerging markets have proven to be equally competitive and expect to be treated as equal partners to MNE/emerging market relationship. As a result, the question that was relevant several decades ago that—"is FDI good for a country?"—is relevant again. As Caves put it: does a MNE's presence in a country mean more capital formation or productivity growth than would occur otherwise? (Caves 1996). Moreover, other than capital formation and productivity growth, the implication of MNEs for a nation's security and political independence has become more important. Emerging markets are also concerned about income distribution and the ability of different regimes to remain in power (Wells 1998). These are not new issues but have reemerged as important concerns. There is little doubt that tensions between MNEs and some emerging country governments have gained momentum in recent years. These feelings have been further enhanced thanks to changes in the political scene and stance.

The current (post-2001) political shift toward the right, in most emerging markets has led to substantial changes in the internal domestic policies of these governments. However, a number of changes in the international environment have politically weakened the position of the host governments, forcing them into a defensive posture. It has thus resulted in the weakening of the bargaining power of host governments in emerging markets vis-à-vis MNEs. We surmise it will lead to an increase in the tensions over the activities of MNEs. This will also lead to an increasing desire to control the activities of MNEs both by the host as well as the home governments, leading toward a more antagonistic relationship as was the case in the era of the 1970s (Jenkins 1999). Given this possibility, there are likely to be in academic writings, various models and paradigms touting the virtues of the MNEs, and critical of the domestic policies of emerging nations reluctant to participate in the global economy.

In the context of international business, the important changes in recent years have been the globalization of business and world trade, evolution of cooperation as a competitive tool (e.g., alliances, mergers, and acquisitions), and the nonconfrontational behavior of governments towards MNEs. Corporate governance, in a pragmatic sense, would be a domestic topic, contrary to current expressions in the broad field of international management. These changes have had a profound impact on the strategies of MNEs, and important implications for policy decisions of governments, particularly from emerging markets. Firms have realized that for survival in the globalized economy, they have to be present in emerging markets as effective and responsive organizational, and operating units in the major emerging markets such as China, India, and Brazil. The governments of these countries are becoming less convinced of the benefits of MNE activities, suspicious of their strategic intent, and wary of their impact on local industries and cultures. In our opinion, the protectionist strategies induced by changes in the above mentioned political environments have created great anxiety and will create some hurdles for the globalization of business for the next few years. This could however, subside, once companies and firms realize that in achieving their long term goals—growth and profits for firms, and for the governments and populations of the emerging market countries, benefits and higher standards of living— that they are actors who would need to seek quick resolutions to the tide of issues that have emerged during the past 36 months.

Moreover, as Landes (1998) pointed out: leadership among nations, economic or political, is a mantle that passes from country to country over time. The last thousand years have seen this mantle change hands from China to the Italian City State, to Portugal and Spain, to the Low Countries, to Britain and then to the United States. Who knows who is next in the succession?

REFERENCES

Boddewyn, J. J. 1992. "Political Behavior Research." in *New Directions in International Business*, edited by P. J. Buckley. Cheltenham, U.K.: Edward Elger

Buckley, P. J. 1996. "Government Policy Responses to Strategic Rent-Seeking Transnational Corporations." *Transitional Corporations* 5 (2): 1–17.

Buckley, P. J., and P. N. Ghauri, eds. 1999. *The Global Challenge for Multinational Enterprises*, Oxford, U.K.: Pergamon.

Caves, Richard E. 1996. *Multinational Enterprise and Economic Analysis.* 2nd Edition, Cambridge, U.K.: University Press.

Ghauri, P. N., and Buckley, P. J. 2002. "Globalization and the End of Competition: A Critical Review of Rent-Seeking Multinationals." in *Critical Perspectives on Internationalization*, edited by V. Havila, M. Forsgren, and H. Hakansson. Oxford: Pergamon.

Jenkins, R. 1999. "The Changing Relationship Between Emerging Markets and Multinationals Enterprises." in *The Global Challenge for Multinational Enterprises*, edited by P. J. Buckley and P. N. Ghauri. Oxford: Pergamon.

Landes, David S. 1998. *The Wealth and Poverty of Nations.* New York: W.W. Norton.

Wells, Louis T. 1998. "Multinationals and the Developing Countries." *Journal of International Business Studies* 29 (1) First Quarter: 101–14.

Selected Bibliography

(Not a general bibliography, but the listing is limited to the books cited in Table 0.1.)

Behrman, Jack N. *National Interests and the Multinational Enterprise; Tensions among the NorSelth Atlantic countries.* Englewood Cliffs, N.J.: Prentice-Hall, 1970.

Brooke, Michael Z., and H. Lee Remmers. *The Strategy of Multinational Enterprise: Organization and Finance.* New York: American Elsevier Publishing, 1970.

Buckley, Peter J., and Mark Casson. *The Future of Multinational Enterprise.* New York: Holmes and Meier, 1976.

Caves, Richard E. *Multinational Enterprise and Economic Analysis.* New York: Cambridge University Press, 1982.

Hays, Richard D., Christopher M. Korth, and Manucher Roudiani. *International Business: An Introduction to the World of the Multinational Firm.* Englewood Cliffs, N.J.: Prentice-Hall, 1972.

Heenan, David A., and Howard V. Perlmutter. *Multinational Organization Development.* Reading, Mass.: Addison-Wesley Publishing, 1979.

Hornell, Erik, and Jan-Erik Vahlne. *Multinationals: The Swedish Case.* London: Croom Helm, 1986.

Jackson, Richard A. *The Multinational Corporation and Social Policy; Special Reference to General Motors in South Africa.* New York: Praeger, 1974.

Kann, Robert A. *The Multinational Empire: Nationalism and National Reform in the Habsburg Monarchy, 1848–1918.* New York: Octagon Books, [c.1950] 1964.

Kindleberger, Charles P. *The International Corporation: A Symposium.* Cambridge, Mass.: M.I.T. Press, 1970.

Kolde, Endel J. *International Business Enterprise.* Englewood Cliffs, N.J.: Prentice-Hall, 1972.

Negandhi, Anant R., and S. Benjamin Prasad. *The Frightening Angels: A Study of U.S. Multinationals in Developing Nations.* Kent, Ohio: Kent State University Press, 1975.

Neufeld, Edward P. *A Global Corporation: A History of the International Development of Massey Ferguson Limited.* Toronto: University of Toronto Press, 1969.

Ogram, Ernest W. *The Emerging Pattern of the Multinational Corporation.* Atlanta: Bureau of Business and Economic Research, School of Business Administration, Georgia State College, 1965.

Penrose, Edith T. *The Large International Firm in Developing Countries; The International Petroleum Industry.* Cambridge, Mass.: M.I.T. Press, 1969.

Phatak. Arvind V. *Managing Multinational Corporations.* New York: Praeger, 1974.

Robock, Stephan H., and Kenneth Simmonds. *International Business and Multinational Enterprise.* Homewood, Ill.: Irwin, 1973.

Rolfe, Sidney E., and Walter Damm. *The Multinational Corporation in the World Economy: Direct Investment Perspective.* New York: Praeger, 1970.

Rugman, Alan M. *Inside Multinationals: The Economics of Internal Markets.* New York: Columbia University Press, 1981.

Steiner, George A., and Warren M. Cannon. *Multinational Corporate Planning.* New York: MacMillan, 1966.

Stopford, John M., and Louis T. Wells. *Managing the Multinational Enterprise: Organization of the Firm and Ownership of Subsidiaries.* London: Longman, 1972.

Turner, Louis. *Invisible Empires: Multinational Companies and the Modern World.* London: Hamish Hamilton, 1970.

Vaupel, James W., and Joan P. Curhan. *The Making of the Multinational Enterprise: A sourcebook of Tables Based on a Study of 187 Major U.S. Manufacturing Companies.* Boston: Division of Research, Harvard Business School, 1973.

Wilkins, Mira. *The Emergence of Multinational Enterprise: American Business Abroad from the Colonial Era to 1914.* Cambridge, Mass.: Harvard University Press, 1970.

Index

About the Editors and Contributors

S. BENJAMIN PRASAD (Ph.D. in Management and Organization) University of Wisconsin (Madison), has been on the faculties of the University of Minnesota, the University of Nevada, Ohio University (Athens), and Central Michigan University. His visiting faculty appointments include the Graduate School of Business, University of Minnesota (Minneapolis); the MARA Institute of Technology (Malaysia); Kuwait University (Safat, Kuwait); the University of Groningen (The Netherlands); and King's College (Vancouver, BC, Canada). He has also been a visiting researcher/scholar at the Institute of Management Development (Belo Horizonte, Brazil), the University College-Dublin (Ireland), the Universidad Auto Noma de Guadalajara (Mexico), and the Center for Cross-Cultural Management at Sophia University, Tokyo (Japan). His articles have appeared in the *Academy of Management Journal, Business and Economic History, Columbia Journal of World Business, Journal of International Business Studies, Management International Review, Management Science, Technovation,* and others. He edited the *Advances in International Comparative Management* research series, 1989–96. He is a director at York Research Center, New Jersey.

PERVEZ N. GHAURI received his Ph.D. from Uppsala University (Sweden). His previous faculty and administrative positions include Dean for Research, Faculty of Management and Organization, the University of Groningen, The Netherlands; Academic Advisor for Curricular Development, Open University in Milton-Keynes (U.K.); Copenhagen International Management Institute (Denmark); Provost, Oslo Business School (Norway); and Visiting Professor, University of Lahore (Pakistan). His European visiting faculty positions include Maastricht University (The Netherlands); IECS, Strasbourg (France); Henreich Heine University, Düsseldorf (Germany); Copenhagen Business School (Denmark); and during 2000–2001, he was a visiting professor of international business at the Broad School, Michigan State University, Lansing. He is the founding editor of *International Business Review*. His books include *Doing Business in Emerging Markets: Entry and Negotiation Strategies* (2002) and *International Business Negotiation* (1996). He is Professor of International Business at the Manchester School of Management, University of Manchester Institute of Science and Technology (UMIST), United Kingdom.

S. TAMER CAVUSGIL is the Endowed Chair Professor of Global Marketing at the Eli Broad School, Michigan State University.

KWONG CHAN is a doctoral candidate at the Eli Broad School, Michigan State University.

ALVARO CUERVO-CAZURRA is an Assistant Professor at the Carlson School of Management, University of Minnesota.

PETER ENDERWICK is Professor in the Department of Marketing and International Management, University of Waikato, New Zealand.

W. HARVEY HEGARTY is Professor of Administrative Behavior at the Kelley Business School, Indiana University.

DANIEL C. INDRO is Associate Professor of Finance at Penn State University-Great Valley.

JAN JOHANSON is a Professor in the Department of Business Studies, Uppsala University, Sweden.

MARTIN JOHANSON is a faculty member in the Department of Business Studies at Uppsala University.

DESTAN KANDEMIR is a doctoral candidate at the Eli Broad School, Michigan State University.

DAEKWAN KIM is Assistant Professor at Florida State University.

THOMAS C. LAWTON is a faculty member in the School of Management, Imperial College, University of London.

HAIYANG LI is in the Department of Management at Texas A&M University.

JI LI is a faculty member in the Department of Management at Hong Kong Baptist University.

ANDRÉS LÓPEZ is a Professor at the School of Economics, University of Buenos Aires, Argentina.

STEVEN M. McGUIRE teaches at the School of Management, University of Bath, United Kingdom.

STEWART R. MILLER is a faculty member at McCombs School of Business,University of Texas-Austin.

MARCELA MIOZZO is a faculty member at UMIST, United Kingdom.

RAM MUDAMBI is Associate Professor of Strategic Management at the Fox School of Business, Temple University.

PIETRO NAVARRA is Director of the Ph.D. program in Economics at the University of Messina, Italy.

ROSE M. PRASAD is Professor of Finance at Central Michigan University.

HEIKE PROFF is a faculty member in the Department of International Management at Mannheim University, Germany.

MALIKA RICHARDS is Assistant Professor of Management, Penn State University-Berks, Philadelphia.

C. ANNIQUE UN is an Assistant Professor at the Johnson Graduate School of Management, Cornell University.

MO YAMIN is Associate Professor of International Businessat UMIST, United Kingdom.

YAN ZHANG is a faculty member at the Jones Graduate School, Rice University, Houston.